The Transformation
of the
Roman World
AD 400–900

Edited by Leslie Webster
and Michelle Brown

Published by British Museum Press
for the Trustees of the British Museum
in association with the
British Library

The overall 'Transformation of the Roman World'
programme is a European Science Foundation
Research Project, in which the exhibitions and
this book are supported by the European Union

Published in 1997 by British Museum Press
A division of The British Museum Company
46 Bloomsbury Street, London WC1B 3QQ

A catalogue record for this book is available
from the British Library

ISBN 0 7141 0585 6

Designed by James Shurmer

Typeset by Rowland Phototypesetting

Printed in Great Britain by Butler & Tanner

Contents

Illustration acknowledgements

ABBREVIATIONS

AAA   =   The Ancient Art and Architecture Collection
BL   =   The British Library
BM   =   Trustees of the British Museum
CL   =   The Conway Library, Courtauld Institute of Art
JT   =   Jim Thorne, illustrator

Black and white illustrations

Essays

AAA: 8; Bibliothèque nationale, Paris: 18, 19; BL: 31, 47; BM: 2, 7, 17, 29, 48; CL: 5, 6, 13, 41, 42, 43, 44, 46 (photo H. McGuire), 52; Deutsches Archäologisches Institut, Madrid: 10; Deutsches Archäologisches Institut, Rome: 9, 14; Philip Dixon: 51; Fototeca Archivi Alinari, Florence: 4, 49; Gnecchi collection, Gabinetto Numismatico, Museo Nazionale Romano delle Terme, Rome: 3; JT: 1, 22, 23, 27, 30; Musée Carnavalet, Paris: 37; Musée de Louvre, Department des Antiquities, Paris. Photo: M. Chuzeville: 12; Musée du Petit Palais, Paris. Photo: Bulloz: 25; Museo civico christiano, Brescia. Photo: Fotostudio Rapuzzi, Archivo fotografico Brescia: 50; Museo del Duomo, Monza. Photo: © Parroccia di San Giovanni Battista: 16; The Photograph Collections, Dumbarton Oaks Centre for Byzantine Studies, Washington, D.C.: 45; Real Academia de la Historia, Madrid. Photo of replica courtesy of Römisch Germanisch Zentralmuseum, Mainz: 11; Sitten, Hohes Domkapitel, Schatzkammer St. Valeria, Sion, Switzerland. Photo: Abegg-Stiftung, Riggisberg, Switzerland: 15; Service Photographique des Archives nationales, Paris: 28; The Trustees of the National Museums of Scotland, 1997: 21; The Board of Trustees of the Victoria and Albert Museum: 53; David Wright: 54.

Catalogues

The photographs for the catalogue sections of the volume were provided by the institutions themselves, with individual credits as follows:
ATA, Stockholm: 92, 93; M. Biddle and B. Kjølbye-Biddle: 99; BL: 105; BM: 95, 96, 97, 98, 101, 102, 103, 104; P. J. Bomhof: 78; Crown copyright, illustrations by Ian G. Scott: 100; Frisian Museum, Leeuwarden: 82; JT: 77 (after Pohl), 88b; Museum of Byzantine Culture, Thessaloniki: 55, 56, 57, 58, 59, 60, 61, 62, 63, 64; Rheinisches Bildarchiv, Bonn: 65; Rheinisches Bildarchiv, Cologne: 66, 67; Rijksmuseum van Oudheden/Rijksmuseum Het Konninklijk Penningkabinet, Leiden: 79, 80, 81, 83, 84; Römisch-Germanisches Museum, Cologne: 73; S. Siegers: 71, 72; H. Wagner: 69; Statens Historiska Museum, Stockholm: 87; 89, 90, 91; University of Trondheim, Videnskasmuseet: 88a.

Colour plates

AAA: 9 (photo B. Norman), 26, 36 (photo R. Sheridan), 27 (photo R. F. Hoddinot); Bibliothèque nationale, Paris: 32; Bibliothèque nationale, Cabinet des medailles, Paris: 24; BL: 61, 63, 68; BM: 6, 19, 28, 31, 35, 60, 62, 67; Bodleian Library, Oxford: 1; Cahiers d'Archéologie Subaquatique, Fréjus: 21; Cambridge University Library: 69; Carthage Museum, Tunisia: 5; M. Carrieri: 45; Crown copyright, reproduced by permission of Historic Scotland: 65; Dean and Chapter, Durham Cathedral Library: 64; Drents Museum, Assen. Photo H. Brandsen: 14; Fries Museum, Leeuwarden: 52; Sonia Halliday Photographs: 23; Magyar Nemzeti Múzeum, Budapest. Photo A. Dabasi: 3, 7, 11; The Master and Fellows of Corpus Christi College, Cambridge: 30; Musée des Beaux Arts et d'Archéologie de Troyes. Cliché des Musées des Troyes. Photo J-M. Protte: 12; Musée National du Moyen Age, Thermes de Cluny, Paris. Photo © RMN - Jean Schormans: 8; Musée Saint-Raymond, Toulouse. Photo F. Liege: 16; Museo dell'Alto Medioevo, Rome: 2; Museo Arqueológico Nacional, Madrid: 18; Museum Het Rondeel Rhenen: 50; Museum of Byzantine Culture, Thessaloniki: 29; Dr Uwe Muss, after Graham-Campbell, *The Viking World* (London 1980): 22; National Museums of Scotland: 66; Nationalmuseet, Copenhagen: 13; Österreichische Nationalbibliothek, Vienna: 34; Procuratoria di San Marco. Photo M. Carrieri: 25; Public Library, Leiden: 33; Rheinisches Bildarchiv, Cologne: 47; Rijksmuseum Het Koninklijk Penningkabinet, Leiden: 17; Rijksmuseum van Oudheden/Rijksmuseum Het Konninklijk Penningkabinet, Leiden: 48, 49, 51, 53, 54, 55, 56; Römermuseum, Augst. Photo D. Widmer, Basel: 15; Römisch-Germanisches Museum, Cologne: 46; S. Siegers: 44; Statens Historiska Museum, Stockholm: 57, 58, 59; Stichting Schatkamer Sint Servaas, Maastricht, photograph courtesy of Abegg-Stiftung, Riggisberg, Switzerland. Photo Chr. von Viràg: 20; Uppsala Universitetsbibliotek, Uppsala: 10; The Walters Art Gallery, Baltimore: 4.

Editor's acknowledgements

This book has been a challenge in almost every respect; sufficient to say that any errors resulting from a complicated text and a precipitous schedule are ours alone. Our desire is rather to thank those who have made this particular transformation possible, and frequently enjoyable. First, the contributing authors, who in their individual ways have made this a very exciting book to assemble; we are especially grateful to our museum colleagues, who have been conspicuously conscientious in meeting deadlines and providing so many of the splendid illustrations which enliven these pages. For their support of the exhibition project from its outset, and much wise advice, Leslie Webster would like to thank Max Sparreboom and Vuokko Lepistö-Kirsälä of the European Science Foundation, and the three academic co-ordinators of the overall 'Transformation of the Roman World' programme, Javier Arce, Evangelos Chrysos and Ian Wood. This volume could not, however, have been achieved without the heroic contributions of two people in particular: Noël Adams, whose academic, organisational and editorial input has helped us through several dark hours, and Carolyn Jones, our editor at the British Museum Press, who willingly suspended disbelief at all crucial moments. Our book designer James Shurmer has also worked wonders. There are many others who have contributed to the book and the exhibitions which underpin it whom space does not permit us to acknowledge individually here; we know who they are, and thank them for their unstinting support.

Foreword

The period of transition between the world of late antiquity and the Middle Ages has – at least since Gibbon wrote *The Decline and Fall of the Roman Empire* – traditionally been seen as one of chaos and obscurity, the 'Dark Ages'. Yet modern scholarship is increasingly revealing how profoundly dynamic and influential were the cultural and intellectual shifts which mark the period. Far from initiating an age of barbarism, the various successor states saw themselves as part of a Roman continuum, and readily exploited the institutions and intellectual traditions of late antiquity, adapting and reinventing them to suit their own changing circumstances and cultural traditions.

Some of the fruits of recent work are presented in this book, and in the five exhibitions which accompany it. These have grown from a 1993–1997 international research programme of the European Science Foundation, 'Transformation of the Roman World AD 400–900', in which scholars from all over Europe have collaborated, through working parties, on a variety of themes central to the period. This book is the first of a series of publications to emerge from this programme, and, appropriately, aims to present the work of the project to a wider public. Such, too, is the purpose of the five linked exhibitions which will take place at different European venues in 1997, and which are catalogued in this volume.

The book, in every sense, represents a European endeavour. Europe's national identities and its cultural and intellectual heritage are central themes for this period, where so much of European political and cultural tradition has its origins; the European Science Foundation research project which gave rise to it has been a wholly European co-operative project, reflected in the authorship of the essays and catalogues in this volume; and we have been very fortunate also in receiving financial support for the exhibition series from the European Union.

Many people, too numerous to list here, have been involved in the making of this book and in the exhibitions associated with it. The editors, Michelle Brown, and Leslie Webster who also coordinated the exhibition programme, have expressed their individual thanks elsewhere in this volume; but we should like to take this opportunity of thanking all those who have helped to bring this into being: the authors, the curators and other museum and library staff, the editors and designers, the institutions which have sponsored the work, and those who in many different ways helped to inspire it.

This has been a new direction for the British Museum and British Library, who have collaborated both in the production of the book, and in the exhibition which forms the British contribution to the project. Such a book and such a series of linked exhibitions have not, we think, been attempted before; we are very proud to be associated with this innovative and exciting project.

Dr Robert Anderson, Director, British Museum

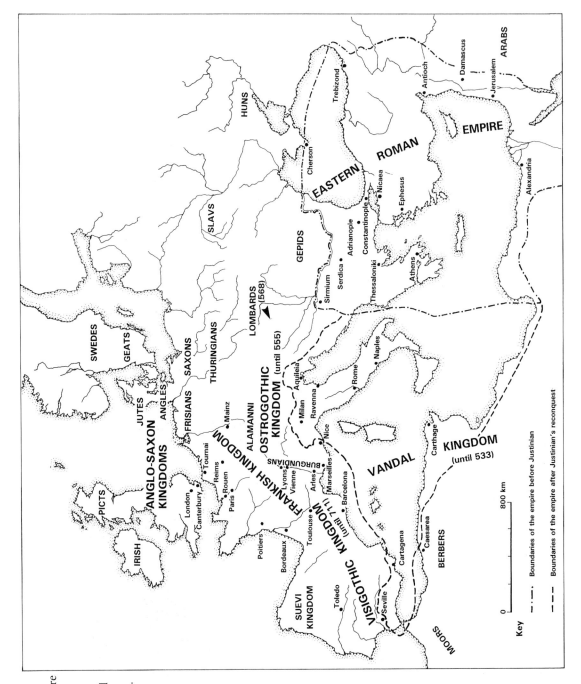

Fig. I
The eastern
Roman empire
and the
barbarian
kingdoms in
the sixth and
seventh
centuries AD.

SWEDES

GEATS

JUTES

ANGLES

IRISH

PICTS

ANGLO-SAXON
KINGDOMS

London
Canterbury
Reims
Rouen
Paris
Tournai

FRISIANS

SAXONS

THURINGIANS

Mainz

ALAMANNI

FRANKISH KINGDOM

BURGUNDIANS

Lyons
Vienne
Poitiers
Bordeaux
Toulouse
Arles
Marseilles
Nice

SUEVI
KINGDOM

VISIGOTHIC KINGDOM
(until 711)

Toledo
Seville
Barcelona
Cartagena

MOORS

Caesarea

BERBERS

Carthage

VANDAL KINGDOM
(until 533)

OSTROGOTHIC
KINGDOM
(until 555)

Aquileia
Milan
Ravenna
Rome
Naples

LOMBARDS
(568)

SLAVS

HUNS

GEPIDS

Sirmium

Serdica

Adrianople

Thessaloniki

Athens

EASTERN ROMAN EMPIRE

Cherson

Trebizond

Constantinople
Nicaea
Ephesus

Antioch
Damascus
Jerusalem

ARABS

Alexandria

800 km

0

Key

—·—·—   Boundaries of the empire before Justinian

— — —   Boundaries of the empire after Justinian's reconquest

The empire in east and west

Evangelos Chrysos

In the fourth century AD the lands and peoples of much of Europe were either included as integral parts of or attached to the Roman empire (the only polity of the time distinguishable by its structure and organisation), or at least oriented towards it. Several divisions of the imperial power occurred in this period. A significant partition occurred after the death of Emperor Theodosius I in 395, when the administrative authority and the military command was divided for about seventy years between east and west, with an emperor as the head of each part (*pars Orientis* and *pars Occidentis*) residing in two capitals, Constantinople, the 'New Rome' in the east and Milan, later Ravenna, in the west. Rivalries and animosity often dominated the relationship of the two courts. However, the *imperium*, the constitutional and legitimising power of the Roman state, as inherited from classical Rome, remained undivided because it was believed to be indivisible. One important expression of this real unity of the two parts is the fact that the legislation of both emperors was automatically applicable, even if not always implemented, in both parts of the empire (fig. 1).

When Odovacer as head of a multi-ethnic army overthrew the boy emperor Romulus Augustus, the last emperor of the west, in AD 476, he argued that 'there is no need for a divided rule and that one, shared emperor was sufficient for both territories . . . and that Zeno [the incumbent emperor in Constantinople] should confer upon him the rank of patrician and entrust him with the government of Italy' (fig. 2). Seen from the experience of later developments and from a western point of view, this event was loaded with an historic significance unjustifiable by the historical facts. Zeno (474–91) had never recognised Romulus but remained faithful to the emperor Julius Nepos

(Right) Fig. 2 Obverse of silver half-*siliqua* of Odovacer (AD 476–93), struck in his own name at Ravenna in 477 by the Roman general who in 476 had deposed the last western emperor to rule from Italy.

(Far right) Fig. 3 Gold triple *solidus* of Theoderic (AD 471–526). Struck at Rome or Ravenna for donative purposes, this coin is unique for a barbarian king. Theoderic presents himself as a Roman caesar, with the grandiose inscriptions *King Theoderic, (our) pious ruler/king Theoderic, conqueror of the barbarians.*

(emperor in 474–5, died in 480), who had been overthrown by the forces that had brought Romulus to power and now lived in his Dalmatian residence in exile: this alone proves that the year 476 was indeed 'manufactured into a turning point' by later western interpreters distorting what had really happened. It is a matter of record, for instance, that the lamentation *Romanum imperium periit* ('the Roman empire disappeared'), which was to become the cliché interpretation for this episode, had originally mirrored merely the feelings of certain circles in Italy.

With the emperor's consent and encouragement, the Ostrogothic king Theoderic overthrew Odovacer and established himself as indisputable ruler over Italy in AD 493 (fig. 3). Although he asked for 'the imperial mantle and all the insignia of the palace' to be sent back, he left no doubt that he regarded himself merely as the emperor's viceroy in his kingdom, or, as a Syriac source would put it, his 'anticaesar'. Indeed, Theoderic never questioned that he was commissioned to exercise the royal power in Italy for the legitimate emperor. In his *History of the Gothic War* Procopius of Caesarea described correctly Theoderic's 'constitutional' role and his relationship to the imperial power:

Though he did not claim the right to assume either the garb or the name of emperor of the Romans, but was called *rex* to the end of his life (for thus the barbarians are accustomed to call their leaders), still, in governing his own subjects, he invested himself with all the qualities which appropriately belong to a legitimate emperor.

The Ostrogothic king's 'constitutional' status was exemplary for the position of many other barbarian rulers who lived on the soil of the former provinces of the Roman empire at this time. The emperors in Constantinople seem to have accepted this pattern of procedures; in addition, most of the barbarian rulers agreed to behave in the same way. Once the imperial army was unable to keep barbarian tribes outside their territory, the Romans regarded it as second best to have their rulers exercise their power in the name or on commission of the emperor at the Bosphorus. On the other hand, it came to be an acceptable or even politically desirable solution for some of the new leaders to acquire imperial approval and recognition of their own political arrangement at the insignificant cost of formally appearing as imperial appointees in their own land. Thus the Burgundian king Sigismund (516–23) had no difficulty assuring the emperor that 'our homeland is [part of] your world and my royal administration does not reduce your sovereignty in your provinces'. The distinction between 'royal administration' and 'imperial sovereignty', however theoretical it might be, presented itself as a very useful instrument in the hands of the Byzantine diplomats in their effort to accommodate the political needs of the tribes without harming the idea of the empire of eternal Rome.

A wide range of options was at the disposal of the imperial government in its engagement with the increasing need to confront the pressure at the frontiers. Some emperors were more ready than others to take the risk of a military response to this challenge by meeting the barbarian troops on the battlefield, and occasionally they grasped the chance of intervening forcefully in the internal affairs of the ruling families. At other times, however, it proved to be a less expensive, though very unpopular, measure to buy the peace instead of engaging in war. The elementary needs of the invading barbarians for peaceful and prosperous settlement were met by offering them arable lands and long-term financial aid, mainly in cash, on condition that, if requested, they should comply with imperial orders to provide military help (pl. 1). The imperial diplomats had to take great care that in the written agreement with the newcomers the allocated land was defined as imperial dominion offered to the barbarian possessors for a certain period of time and that the annual subsidies were declared either as salary to mercenaries or as indemnity to allies. In the ambiguous language of the time, both categories were labelled *foederati*, a name deriving from the generic term *foedus* in use for any agreement but especially applied in the characteristic peace conclusions of the time. The written sources seldom mention such negotiations and agreements, but from recent research it seems quite probable that diplomats constantly had reasons to be on missions, travelling with a large entourage and impressive gifts for serious negotiations or for ceremonial representations, and that the net of bilateral treaties was much thicker and tighter than it appears in the sources.

An additional set of tools was at the emperor's disposal to appease his neighbours in his own empire and indicate his benevolence towards them, marking at the same time the limits of their power. Thus honorary titles of high court officers, like *patricius* or *consul*, together with the officers' insignia and even the salary, were meant both to please the recipients and to place them in a certain position within the imperial order (pl. 2). By granting Roman dignities to barbarians the emperor recognised the ruler's authority over a group of people who had either entered or returned to the imperial orbit. Highly illustrative of this, if not clear in all its details, is Gregory of Tours' description of Clovis' parade at Tours in 508 after his victory over the Visigoths:

> He returned to Tours and offered many gifts to the basilica of St. Martin. In these circumstances, he received a letter of appointment concerning the consulate from Emperor Anastasius, and in St. Martin's basilica he donned a purple tunic and a *chlamys* and put a diadem on his head . . . and from that date on he was acclaimed like a consul or an Augustus.

Apparently, the ceremony as a whole represented imperial confirmation for Clovis' new, expanded kingdom and simultaneously his recognition of the imperial dominion, without hiding 'the king's practical independence as demonstrated by gestures actually bordering on usurpation'. This explains why the sources only seldom mention any dissatisfaction on the part of the recipients of such imperial gestures, and then only in order to express their disappointment at not having been favoured highly enough.

Of course, under no circumstances did the rulers of that time try to usurp the imperial titles *imperator* and *Augustus*, which were reserved exclusively for the emperors. In fact, through the whole period royal dignity was always second to imperial dignity. Two late examples should suffice. In AD 799 Alcuin declared in a letter to Charlemagne that 'three persons were the most exalted in the world, the *apostolica sublimitas* (of the pope), the *imperialis dignitas* (of the emperor) and the *regnalis dignitas*'. On the other hand, in an official document of Cœnwulf, king of Anglo-Saxon Mercia, dated 798, we find the term *imperator*. Whatever is implied by this title – a supremacy over the other kings in the region and/or an imitation of the Roman title – the mere use is indicative of its importance. In fact these rulers normally did not fail to apply the established ceremonial rhetoric of the Romans in their correspondence with the emperor and to express their respect by addressing him as their *pater*. It seems that at no time did the barbarian rulers aim at destroying the Roman empire: *eversio* (abolition) was never their goal. The most they intended or hoped for was to secure a prosperous settlement and favourable accommodation in the empire.

A famous tale, preserved in Orosius' *Histories Against the Pagans*, has it that Athaulf, the Visigothic king and successor to Alaric, at his wedding with the Roman princess Galla Placidia (fig. 4) at Narbonne in AD 414, a ceremony totally Roman – or, rather, Byzantine – in character:

declared that at first he had wanted to replace Romania with Gothia ... But he had realised that the Goths would never be able to abide by the laws, nor could the laws be forbidden – for without them a state is not a state – and therefore he decided to become the renewer of the empire instead of its transformer.

Regardless of the historicity of this story, it is astonishing how clearly people in the fifth century regarded the 'laws' as the most constitutive element of statehood: a perception of law prevails in many other documents too. Thus we can understand the promulgation of the law codes of the barbarian kings in our period, the so-called *leges barbarorum*, as cornerstones in the 'constitutional' development of the *gentes* (tribes) into *regna* (kingdoms), a transformation conceivable only within the empire's world of political ideas and structures. As Herwig Wolfram has pointed out, the formation of the barbarian *regna* took place in the environment of Roman political ideas and practices.

The change, *immutatio* in Orosius' text, was certainly not a political aim in the fifth or even the sixth century. However, later generations, without dismissing the advantages of the *imitatio imperii*, became more vulnerable to the temptation to attempt the *immutatio*, or at least to propagate it for internal ideological purposes, and increasingly in a Christian context, where the Church as the *res publica Christiana* was presented as a substitute for the *res publica Romana*. Thus in remote Visigothic Spain, where people experienced the Roman empire as an occupier and therefore as a foe, represented by the Byzantine administration in the southern provinces, Isidore of Seville at the

Fig. 4 The tomb of Galla Placidia, with the sarcophagi of Placidia and her brothers below mosaic vaults, Ravenna, Italy, AD 450.

beginning of the seventh century prayed for the decline of the distasteful Roman empire in favour of all nations comprising an Augustinian *civitas Dei*.

Furthermore, the leaders of the new kingdoms learnt from their acquaintance with the imperial administration that the only way to transform their peoples into political constituencies, their realms into states, was to acquire as many as possible of the characteristic elements of statehood belonging to a proper *res publica* or *politeia* of Mediterranean political culture. Thus the Germanic kings of the fifth, sixth and seventh centuries deployed a surprisingly elaborate ceremonial of substantially Byzantine origin in the context of the *imitatio imperii*. And the Visigothic kings, despite the Byzantine *reconquista* of the southern coastal provinces of Spain, or perhaps because of that, did not hesitate to imitate imperial forms of representation; especially King Leovigild who is known to have promoted the 'imperialisation' of his kingdom.

At the end of our period, the ninth century, Europe was dominated mainly by two Roman empires, the eastern Roman empire of the 'Greeks' and the western Roman empire of the Carolingians; Britain was under her Anglo-Saxon kings and Spain and the southern and eastern shores of the Mediterranean Sea had fallen to the Muslims.

Fig. 5 Charlemagne's Palatine Chapel (AD 798–c.815); west gallery of the octagon with the imperial throne: a conscious evocation of Roman tradition. Aachen, Germany.

The two empires were quite different in shape and function, but both were united in claiming the same Roman heritage and thus the same legitimacy. In the east, Constantinople claimed to rule over the civilised world as the New Rome, while Charlemagne and his court in the west made every effort to present his capital, Aachen, as the Second Rome (fig. 5). The rulers of both empires exercised their authority as perpetuators and heirs of the Roman emperors. During the initial phase following the coronation of Charlemagne in AD 800 (seen in the east as an act of usurpation of the imperial name) this unprecedented move was excused in terms of a *translatio imperii*, because the throne of the emperors was seen as vacant since Irene, a female, was holding it; apparently female rulership was still beyond most people's imagination. Later, presumably in accordance with the agreement of the two courts in 812, when Byzantine diplomats came to Aachen to address Charlemagne as *basileus* (king), the Carolingians refrained in their official documents from using the epithet 'Roman'. In contrast, or perhaps as part of the agreement, the Byzantines started using this epithet as a constant attribute to their emperor's title and name. However, the ultimate legitimation of both *imperia* sprang from their *romanitas*. Although most titles, insignia, costume and behaviour had developed quite apart from each other, both adjusted the symbols of statehood to resemble those of the Roman emperors. Their occasionally bitter antagonisms admittedly emerged from actual issues of political interest, but all their controversies were calculated and articulated on the one cardinal issue: that of their Roman legitimacy. Jealous rivalry was increasingly becoming the characteristic attitude of both empires to each other.

On the one hand, the Carolingian empire embraced the Church of Rome and appeared as her protector, denouncing at the same time the eastern Church as heretical, while the eastern empire supported the authority of the ecumenical patriarch of Constantinople and refused to recognise the universal authority of the pope for exactly the same reason. In sum, the imperial ideology at both imperial courts cultivated *romanitas* as the sacrosanct foundation of their being. Rome, not the city but its *genius* as a mobile mystical and mythical idea, functioned as the commonplace for the promotion of their political identity.

The city of Rome on the banks of the river Tiber had ceased to exercise any imperial power: since the third century AD, it no longer hosted the emperors for more than short visits. In the late eighth century a document was forged, known as the 'Donation of Constantine', claiming that the first Christian emperor, before moving to the east to found Constantinople as the New Rome, transferred to the bishop of Rome his authority over the west, his palace on the Lateran and his imperial insignia. This most influential forgery in history served as a successful tool in establishing the unique (semi-)political position and reputation of the pope as ultimate depository and guarantee of *romanitas* in the medieval world. Occasionally in the seventh century the popes would represent themselves to the emperor in Constantinople as having performed a special service, enlarging the empire by exercising spiritual authority over lands that

Fig. 6 Santa Maria Maggiore, the nave looking east towards the apse; an enduring image of Roman *imperium Christianum*. Rome, second quarter of the fifth century AD.

had never been part of the Roman world, such as Ireland. After the middle of the eighth century the Apostolic See rendered such services to the Carolingians. In this way the wandering idea of Rome was returning to the city of Rome in its ecclesiastical shape. The once capital of the *imperium Romanum* was becoming the centre of the *imperium Christianum* (fig. 6).

The kings and peoples outside the territories of the two empires pursued their own political interests, sometimes in contradiction to and less often in accordance with the imperial agendas. However, they all perceived themselves in comparison, in imitation or even in rivalry with the existence – and the *raison d'être* – of the two empires, in accordance with the medieval principle 'the king is emperor in his own realm' (*rex imperator in regno suo*).

Classical Hellenistic and Roman political culture had developed the image of the ideal ruler not in legal documents or treatises, but in purely rhetorical texts written mainly in the service of royal or imperial propaganda. In late antiquity eulogists of emperors used every opportunity provided by the imperial calendar to propagate the existing or expected virtues of the ruler of the day. As an essential element in this political tradition, the image of the ideal emperor was furnished with two cardinal virtues: (a) a concern for the security and consolidation of the empire; and (b) a correct and benevolent attitude towards its citizens. This image crossed the borders of the empire and acquired validity for every ruler in the wider Roman orbit.

Roman political rhetoric praised the emperor as 'lord of the whole world' and expected him to rule according to his universal majesty. Notwithstanding this fictitious and ceremonial claim and the imperial symbols at his disposal, like the globe depicted in the hands of the throned sovereign, the late antique and early Byzantine empire's policy was normally directed by the principle of a 'defensive imperialism' aiming not at expanding into new lands, but at preserving by all means the territories inherited from the past; nothing beyond that. As it happened, the imperial government was traditionally pragmatic enough to avoid dangerous adventures to regain lost territories. However, the discrepancy between the ideological claims on the one hand and the reasonable approach to the possibilities and the needs of the day on the other, created an ambiguity with occasionally disillusioning results. At times Byzantium was forced drastically to adjust its international relations. The emperor Constantine IV (668–85), above all, made a substantial shift by adopting a realistic policy towards neighbouring powers in officially recognising the Arab caliphate of Damascus, the Avars and their possessions of Roman territory in the north and the Longobards in Italy (pl. 3).

In addition to these two dominant strands of policy, the emperors had always to take into account a third dimension, the empire's legal obligations to the other states, as they were stipulated in the peace treaties. Accordingly three parameters influenced their policies: (a) the political reality provided by the current constellation of the military strength of the empire and its neighbours; (b) the traditional ideology of ecumenical claims, as demonstrated by rhetoric and the traditional symbols of statehood; and (c) the net of the existing international treaties, a notoriously interwoven complex of peace agreements concluded with the *gentes* and the *regna*, commonly with a terminal validity of thirty years. It was especially this third parameter which bound the sub-Roman world in east and west into a common orbit. Late Roman and early Byzantine governments defined this orbit traditionally as Roman. On the other hand, eulogists and scholars at the court of Charlemagne, who presented and justified his offensive wars against the Avars and Saxons as enterprises for the christianisation of central and eastern Europe, tended to describe it as *Europa*, praising the Frankish emperor as the lighthouse of Europe or even as the father of Europe! This was indeed a crucial moment in the 'making of Europe'.

Towards the empire's citizens, who from the sixth century onwards are referred to and treated rather as the emperor's subjects, the autocrat was expected to exercise *philanthropia*, a benevolent attitude, care for their needs and correct application of the law. It was especially his relationship to the law and its application that characterised the good ruler. A chain of sources starting in classical Greek political philosophy and crossing through all stages of medieval history – several of them written in our period

– present this relationship as the element which makes the difference between a good and a bad ruler. 'While the law is the emperor's way, the tyrant's disposition is law.' A monarch not respecting the law is considered a tyrant. For in an era of autocratic rulership, when the democratic procedures of the ancient republic were reduced to bare reminiscence, empty ceremonial gestures and meaningless words, it was crucial that the monarch respected the law and performed in accordance with it. The ruler had to be under, not above, the law. This essential maxim of Roman political culture was, of course, not always followed. But in theory it survived through the centuries as a golden rule and passed through the post-Roman and medieval international community of states into modern times. In this political tradition Isidore of Seville produced the etymology of the word *rex* from *recte faciens* (doing right) and defined kingship as lawful rulership. Otherwise the king was identified as a tyrant.

The political structure of the early Middle Ages as described here, with the empire in its elevated position in what modern scholarship eloquently but misleadingly has described as a 'family of nations and princes', had little impact on the social and private life of the people. On the contrary, people were much more affected by the mobility of individuals within the local societies and beyond them in the wider post-Roman orbit. Merchants, monks and pilgrims, exiles, missionaries and scholars moved freely from one part of the world to the other and joined groups of different origin and formation. Thus it should not surprise us to see easterners involved in everyday life in remote Mérida, in western Spain, western bishops travelling through the east to the Holy Land, or an impressive number of Greeks from different parts of the east elevated to the papal throne in Rome, and Theodore from Cilician Tarsus becoming Archbishop of Canterbury.

At the same time members of the higher social echelons mixed easily with their peers in different surroundings. In fact all known political leaders of the period in east and west had a good reason to share some feeling of affinity. Recent studies have shown how extensive and tight the nexus of affinity and kinship was, which included almost every single ruler of the period: emperors, kings, generals and occasionally bishops are to be found in one and the same 'family tree'. It is true that the system of dynastic intermarriages as a means of political affiliation is responsible for much of this spectacular phenomenon. However, it seems that not all these kinships can be explained as products of a system of dynastic loyalties. Social reasons and personal taste played their role too. In this context, it is very striking to note that all Byzantine emperors from Constantine the Great to the members of the Isaurian dynasty of the eighth century, and most of the kings of the successor states including the Bulgars and the Carolingians, have a seat in the common impressive 'family tree' of early medieval rulers.

However, in spite of all these relationships a new reality was emerging that no one could fail to recognise: the routes of communication between east and west were breaking down; and in the political as well as in religious and cultural spheres, estrangement increasingly overtook the former ties.

Otium et negotium: the great estates, 4th-7th century

Javier Arce

It is certainly no coincidence that it was towards the end of the fourth century AD that the treatise on agriculture (*Opus Agriculturae*) by Palladius Rutilius was published. Within this treatise all kinds of rules, advice and procedures are given, not only agricultural directives such as how to cultivate fields, but also precise information on construction techniques for the actual building of the villa, something Palladius significantly defines as a *praetorium*, that is to say the building materials, the floor and wall decorations and the different layouts and types of construction.

As was the case both with the publication of the *De Agricultura* by Cato in the second century BC, and that by Varro in the first, Palladius' treatise on agriculture corresponds to a historical moment in time when the tendency to live in the country rather than in town becomes more and more prevalent, leading to the emergence of the great estates. This was especially so among the large and middle level Roman landowners, both in Italy and in the provinces. This custom was not a new phenomenon: in fact it was never abandoned within the historical span of Roman society, where the ideal of *otium* (leisure) in contrast with *negotium* (business) represents a way of life, no matter how fictitious or abstract may have been these ideal categories of the Roman aristocracy. In late antiquity this tendency was even more accentuated. Not only was this a consequence of the power of this ideal; it was also the result of the accumulation of wealth and a form of economic exploitation. It was, as such, clearly a phenomenon closely related to the historical, political and military experiences of the empire.

This fact – confirmed in literary sources, in the correspondence of Q. Aurelius Symmachus (fig. 7), in the works of the poet Ausonius and in the letters of Sidonius Apollinaris – is also sufficiently supported by archaeological evidence. The use or the reuse of villas in late antiquity is a phenomenon largely proved by archaeological surveys throughout the empire. The building typology is varied. The size of the estates is not uniform; on the one hand, for example, we have the magnificent Sicilian villas (e.g. Piazza Armerina), and on the other we find functional rural establishments laid out for a very specific use (e.g. in Pannonia, Belgica and Germania). Alongside villas with very modest domestic sections, which allocate more space for rural work, cattle or storage, there exist others, notably those which emphasise almost exclusively the *pars urbana*, the owners' living quarters designed for entertainment, leisure or comfortable living. On his retirement, Diocletian had already chosen his villa at Split in Dalmatia to live out his remaining days. He converted it into a palace, with its own

(Left) Fig. 7 Ivory diptych probably commemorating the apotheosis of Q. Aurelius Symmachus after his death in AD 402. The letter writer was a member of one of the leading pagan families in Rome at the end of the fourth century.

(Right) Fig. 8 Main entrance, Palace of Diocletian, Split, Croatia, *c.*AD 300.

mausoleum included (fig. 8). IIis example was followed by a multitude of aristocrats and senators, as well as emperors and caesars. The latter owned the kinds of buildings that can be found on the Appian Way, such as Maxentius' villa, which included a hippodrome, a mausoleum and the house–palace complex, whereas various aristocrats and senators owned the whole of Piazza Armerina, Cercadillas (Cordova, Spain), Mountmaurin (Gaul) and Centcelles.

There was also, at the same time, an increasing trend towards realistic representations of rural estates, including all the enjoyment and activities that go on in them. It is not infrequent to see reproduced on the floors of the villas, even if they were lived in only sporadically by their owners, images of the dwelling itself, with its porticoes, fortifications, towers and fantastic perspectives. Within this framework, daily work and leisure activities go on: here can be seen either the *domina* (mistress) supervising housework, or the *dominus* (master) returning from the chase, or rural work carried out by the servants or the tenant farmers (fig. 9). This iconography recalls idealised Hellenistic landscape painting. African mosaics, or other earlier ones from Spain or Syria, are well-known examples. It does not matter whether these scenes offer images taken straight from daily life or whether they follow artistic stereotypes. What is essential is the *idea* that they transmit, the *image* they offer. In any event, the rural tradition, the labour of the land, had not changed much over the centuries. The observations, comments on techniques and general advice given by Palladius hardly differ

Fig. 9 Mosaic of Dominus Iulius depicting a fortified villa with scenes of country life; at the top and bottom, the *dominus* and *domina* receive gift and seasonal produce. Carthage, Tunisia, late fourth century.

from those given by his predecessors, Columela and Varro, three hundred years before.

The increasing importance of the villa in late antiquity has in the past been considered as an aspect of a historical phenomenon whose importance ranges far and wide: de-urbanisation, the abandonment of the towns, gradual as it was, but still the departure from the *civitas*. In other words it is connected with the decline of urban life and the loss of the essence of classical civilisation. However, this equation is not precise enough. The great landowners, who had become extremely wealthy, owned several villas, both in Italy and in the other provinces. These were often far from one another. As governors of one kind or another these functionaries had established strong family ties and broad networks of influence – which sometimes stretched back over a long period of time – in the provinces where their career paths had led them. They became landowners. A good exemplar is that of Melania (the Younger), a lady related to aristocratic families, who possessed land and estates in 'Spain, Campania, Sicily, Africa, Mauritania, Britain and other provinces', and eventually sold them to dedicate her wealth to charitable works.

Symmachus could say to his friend, the senator Marcianus, that 'wherever we go we lead a consular life' (*ubique vitam agimus consularem*) from one villa to another, without fear of being disturbed. Many such examples can be given. However, owning properties such as these did not necessarily mean abandoning city life, whether in the case of Symmachus or in those of many others. The poet Ausonius famously defined the villa as a city in the country (*urbs in rure*). *Urbs* because the type of comforts it offered made it possible to carry on different kinds of activities: handicraft production, rural work, storage, leisure, reading, the receiving of dignitaries, friends and magistrates – even up to the emperor himself, if he happened to be travelling in that area – baths, the cult of the gods and so on. Villa architecture combines all of these possibilities and functions, including, of course, security and self-defence (the villa is a *praetorium*). The poet at the court of Gratian also carefully describes how these residences were put to use: *transeo et alternis rure vel urbe fruor* ('I move from house to house so enjoying both the countryside and the city'). This situation had not changed from the time of Cicero or from that of the eccentric Trimalchio, the protagonist of Petronius' *Satyricon*. The very existence of these villas does not necessarily mean de-urbanisation, but

Fig. 10 Mosaic with nuptial inscription for Vitalis and his wife, Torre del Mar, Girona, Spain, fourth century.

23

rather shows a way of accumulating wealth and, more to the point, a means of economic exploitation.

Within the villa the epicentre of every action is the *dominus*. He may or may not live on his estates throughout the year. His name, however, is written on the mosaics that adorn the best rooms of the house. To mention but a few examples from Spain: Dulcitius is shown hunting in the mosaic at the villa of El Ramalete (Navarre); Fortunatus testifies to his presence in the villa of Fraga; Vitalis, in order to remind all those who belong to his estates as well as possible visitors, declares that so long as life remained in him there would be no problems relating to the estate: *salvo Vitale/felix Turissa* says the inscription in the mosaic of the Torre del Mar (Girona) (fig. 10). This is but a short and concise means of expressing the dependency of the tenants on the *dominus* and the running of the farm regime. It has a direct correlation with an identical formula used by the owners of the villa of Torres Novas in Portugal: 'So long as Cardilius and Avita dwell in this house (*Turris*) happiness will abound within'. Again, in the villa of Cuevas de Soria, in the central mosaic of the dining-room, we come upon an anagram of the Faventinii, which was probably also used as a brand, an indelible mark of ownership, whether on horses or on any other belongings; finally, in the bedroom of the owners of the villa of Carranque (Toledo), the landowner, Maternus, is encouraged to use the room for his own pleasure: *utere felix Materne hunc* [sic] *cubiculum*.

Even if the name of the *dominus* does not appear on the inscription, his own portrait may adorn the mosaics so that he is recognisable to each and every visitor. In the entrance portico of the villa at Piazza Armerina the scene is depicted of the arrival and ensuing welcome of the landlord by his dependants who carry torches, olive branches and laurel. In the villa of Malena (Saragossa), as if for a mythical wedding ceremony, the landlord on his betrothal has himself depicted together with his bride in the propitious presence of the gods Jupiter, Juno, Neptune, Hermes (Mercury) and Hercules.

The landlord is also portrayed during the adornment ceremony, dressed in his most precious garments. (Rank is closely associated with dress: the formal belt indicates an official position, and everybody must visibly show off his *insignia*.) In this self-representation it is not infrequent to find scenes in which the *dominus*, accompanied by the *domina*, portrays himself as assisted during this ceremony by helpers who are

(Left) Fig. 11
Silver gilt *missorium* of Theodosius I, issued to celebrate his *decennalia* in AD 388.

(Right) Fig. 12
Terracotta bowl with relief decoration of a victorious charioteer above palm branches; second half of the fourth century.

buckling his belt and putting on his footwear and tunic: this can also be seen in the tomb of Silistria (Bulgaria) and in the mausoleum of Centcelles (near Tarragona, a mausoleum wrongly attributed by some archaeologists to the emperor Constans).

As owner of vast tracts of land in which the fields are under cultivation, where wine and oil are produced in self-sufficient quantities, where there are other cottage industries such as glass, ceramic, brick and tiles, and where livestock are reared, the landlord may often go hunting, a favourite passion, indeed a knightly passion, a passion which puts him on an equal footing with the emperor and his court. Usually, however, the *dominus* is absent, and rarely visits his estates. In the maintenance and day-to-day running of the estate, in the management of the production and the harvest, it is the agents who take charge. It is they who pay the taxes, and with the surplus it is they who go to market or do the trading. The unusual and sporadic relationships between the owner and his workers are described at the end of the fourth century AD by Eutropius, a monk from Aquitaine, in his treatise *De Similitudine Carnis Pecati*.

The material culture that these villas had to offer goes hand in hand with the type of activities carried on within them: that is to say, the implements for reaping, the farm equipment, the tools used in carpentry and the various instruments necessary for the rearing of animals. Such materials have been found in the villa of Cocosa, near Mérida, and in the necropolis of Fuentespreadas (Zamóra). Luxury items are also frequently found, such as objects imported or received as presents or simply exotic products: the *missorium* of Theodosius (fig. 11), the situla of Bueña and large ceramic stamped plates (fig. 12).

Finds related to war are not common, although hunting knives, javelins, belt buckles and horse bits are frequently found. (For the absence of arms, see below.) Horses are yet another essential element in late antiquity. Considered prestigious animals both for racing and for games, they were indispensable to the aristocracy and, above all, to the army. They could cost, according to papyri and legal documents, up to 20–25 *solidi*, and were requisitioned on compulsory orders from both the local populace and from the provinces, who, of course, offered only their worst. Horses brought news fast, by way of the postal service. Admired throughout the ancient world, they were represented on mosaics alongside names drawn from mythology (fig. 13). In short, owning horses was equivalent to what Symmachus defined as 'leaving a consular life'. Some of the landlords of Spanish villas owned herds of horses that were pastured on their vast estates, as Symmachus knew. In many passages of his correspondence we find a desperate and urgent demand for them to be transported as quickly as possible for the games that his son, recently appointed praetor in Rome in AD 400, was organising. These landowners – Euphrasius, Flavianus, Sallustius, Pompeia and Aventius – kept their horses *in re sua* – in their villa – and hastened to satisfy any request from an influential friend.

All the names of the owners of villas in Spain that we know for some reason or other, from mosaic inscriptions or from literary references in texts, were most likely people of aristrocratic rank, but they did not form part of the senatorial aristocracy. They were landowners of extreme wealth, but somehow of secondary standing. (In contrast, members of the senatorial aristocracy preferred to acquire properties in Sicily, Africa and even Gaul.) They were, however, influential; it was they who shaped the panorama of late Roman society in the provinces (or more exactly in the *dioceses*); it was they who in October AD 409 met the first Suevi, Vandals and Alans coming from Aquitania in southern Gaul. These tribes came through the Pyrenean passes to settle in the peninsula, and by the late eighth century had become totally assimilated into that same Hispano-Roman society.

Villas offered desirable and necessary land to the barbarian tribes, who needed sustenance, corn and fields to cultivate. Sources point out that land was conceded to some of them, in that same year AD 409, as *premium victoriae*, a victory award – victory for the resistance that some of these owners ('wealthy nobles', as the historian Orosius calls Theodosius' relatives, Didimus and Verinianus) had put up against the usurper Constantine III. The war and the subsequent resistance was fought against the usurper who wanted to annexe the *diocesis* of Spain to his already secure territories in Britain and Gaul. Once again there recurs the dream of a Gallic empire that so many times had inspired the usurpers of the third and fourth centuries. Hoping to win the barbarians over to his cause, Gerontius, himself a usurper of power from his old lord Constantine III, allowed them to pass through, and settle in the peninsula.

Emperor Theodosius, himself Spanish according to Orosius, had properties in Spain

Fig. 13 Circus horses named *Amor* and *Dominator*, branded with stable marks and the name of the estate, *Sorothi*; part of a larger mosaic depicting a stud farm. Sousse, Tunisia, late second century.

which he exploited when he retired to his estate after the death of his father Flavius Theodosius. His descendants and relatives, Didimus, Verinianus, Lagodius and Theodosiolus, made their fortunes and increased their influence over their clientele by taking advantage of the fact that they were related to the imperial family (they were first cousins to the emperor Honorius). This practice was carried out to such an extent that they were able to put together, from their servants, serfs and farmers alone, a whole army – 'the rural army of the family of Theodosius' – able to face the organised and professional army of the usurper Constantine III at a place in Lusitania that has not yet been clearly identified – a battle that they almost won.

This episode is more than just an important historical fact: its subsequent significance for the dependent relationship between landlord/owner and his subjects is of great relevance. At a certain point in time, the dependant offers himself as defender and soldier in return for work and sustenance. This was definitely not a new phenomenon in the late Roman period. We have only to remember the revolt by Firmus in Africa, under the governorship of Valentinianus, who managed to save himself through his ability to recruit private troops.

The villas found by the barbarian tribes – in Spain the Suevi, the Vandals, the Alans and later the Visigoths; in Africa the Vandals; in Italy the Ostrogoths and the Longobards; in Pannonia the Avars – beside being excellent structures for the cultivation and exploitation of the surrounding natural resources, represented the quintessence of classical civilisation. These villas offered spaces for banquets, secret retiring rooms, guest rooms, porched patios, gardens, fountains, apsed reception halls, heating systems and *thermae* for bathing rituals – undressing and swimming in either cold, lukewarm or hot water. These villas were embellished with statues or sculptural groups portraying gods and mythological beings, had polychrome mosaics depicting scenes taken from Ovid's *Metamorphoses*, or from the *Iliad*, or from the most varied mythical legends, or else scenes from the grand circuses with horses or hunting images, paintings and stuccoes, cryptoporticoes, altars and inscriptions (fig. 14). As well as all of this, they contained elegant baroque furniture: lamps, candelabra, heaters and decorated beds. Within the villa could be found all the latest agricultural innovations, storage jars and granaries, oil presses, millstones to grind corn and ovens for a variety of needs. The pattern was the same, whether in Africa, Antioch, Gaul or Spain.

The main historical issue is to know how these barbarian tribes dealt with this impressive architectural and technological heritage. The answer varies according to area and context. First of all it must be stressed that many of these barbarians were already familiar with these villas and their way of life. But the question remains, were they prepared to adapt to them? Many of the people from the north preferred to continue with their former domestic way of life and their own social customs, as in Germania and Belgica. In some cases they preferred exploitation, even total destruction; in others they opted to take up residence.

Fig. 14 Late Roman mosaic with a charioteer identified as Eros, driving his *quadriga* before the starting gates (*carceres*) of the hippodrome. Dougga, Tunisia, late fourth century.

Three passages taken from the historian Procopius explain very well the different attitudes of the barbarians towards the villas, their owners and their lands. In the first passage, Procopius tells us that the Vandal king Genseric subjected all the owners of the villas in Libya to slavery, seizing their lands and their wealth. Then he goes on (*War Against the Vandals* I.5.11):

Concerning the rest of the Libyans, he robbed them of their estates, which were both very numerous and excellent, and distributed them among the nation of the Vandals. As a result, these lands have been called 'Vandal estates' even up to the present time. And it fell to the lot of those who had formerly possessed these lands to dwell in extreme poverty. But as much of the land that he did not deem worthy he allowed to remain in the hands of former owners, but assessed so large a sum to be paid in government taxes that nothing whatsoever remained to those who were able to retain their farms.

In another passage, however (I.17.8), we find the king of the Vandals living in a magnificent palace – a villa – a few kilometres outside the capital, Carthage, enjoying and cultivating the gardens and orchards. Finally, Procopius describes (II.6.9) how the Vandals made use of the Roman *thermae*, intent on celebrating splendid banquets

29

in their dining-rooms each and every day, adorned in rich and ostentatious ornaments of gold, dressing 'in true Persian style' (pl. 5), amusing themselves at theatres and hippodromes and, above all, devoting themselves to the art of the chase. He concludes: 'Most of them dwelt in parks, which were well supplied with water and trees, and they had great numbers of banquets and all manner of sexual pleasures were in great vogue amongst them.' There is no doubt that Procopius wanted to denigrate the Vandals' style of life as well as to show the necessity of the wars conducted by Justinian's generals; all the same, his texts do appear to be realistic where they concern the Vandals' manner of land-use and settlement in the recently conquered Roman provinces of North Africa.

The Vandals arrived in Africa as conquerors, but this was not the case in all the other provinces of the empire where the barbarians settled. In most cases they installed themselves as a result of treaties or agreements with the Romans. Where this was the case, patterns of behaviour were totally different. When the Romans distributed or alloted lands to the barbarians, was their settlement in the villas or on some of the estates included in these treaties? Likewise, how long did this form of exploitation of the villas last, and if they went through certain changes, of what kind were they? Finally, how great was the impact of the ever-expanding Christian faith that was moving into these rural areas and villas? However briefly, we must attempt to answer these questions.

We do not know for certain how the partition of Spanish lands proceeded, whether regarding the contingent that passed through the peninsula in AD 409 (the Suevi, the Vandals and the Alans), or that of the Visigoths at a later date, from 452 onwards. It is not even clear whether the system of *hospitalitas*[1] was applied in this case. This system implied a sharing *in tertias* of all the properties, i.e. a third of the properties passed on to the new tenant, and only a part of the total remaining went to the previous owner. That this old rule of Roman law could be applied in Spain with the barbarians in the fifth century is very debatable (and not only in relation to Spain but also to Italy and the other provinces). Did the barbarians keep for themselves a part of the villa, including its tenants, or did they settle down in uninhabited regions? Did the great *domini* concede only a portion of the estate, keeping the greater part for themselves? Initially, as in the case of Spain, this phenomenon did not affect the whole peninsula but only the northern part. We know for sure that part of the lands (i.e. the forests and other uncultivated areas), according to law, was assigned to common use and common exploitation. However, living as they did in basically urban surroundings, the question is whether it was the property that the new owners received, or rather the usufruct or revenue coming from it – as Walter Goffart has maintained in a controversial book.[2]

Archaeological evidence, namely that relating to the archaeological study of the villas and their cemeteries, seems to support Goffart's theory, at least as far as Spain is concerned. Archaeological remains and materials from the villa tombs and cemeteries do not show clear and consistent evidence of being in the possession of peoples who are not in the Roman, or rather the Hispano-Roman, tradition. Yet our knowledge of the number of barbarian tribes that came to the peninsula is highly relevant here. We estimate that the number of Visigoths was about one hundred to two hundred thousand out of a total of four or five million people (pl. 4). One factor in the interpretation of these materials is recorded documentation stating that the barbarian peoples had already been settling on Roman territory over a long period of time, and so had already been assimilated into it. Much of the material found in Spanish villas goes back to the period of the Visigoths (fifth–seventh century) although they cannot as such be named or listed as Visigoths. It therefore seems appropriate to speak, certainly in the majority of cases, of an archaeological continuity in the villas that lasts up until the seventh century.

On the other hand, archaeology clearly shows that these villas underwent various changes during this period (fifth–seventh century). In the first instance, many parts of the villas were transformed to accommodate small industries. There were kilns for glass and clay, and installations of agricultural equipment, where once had stood a portico, a dining-room or a thermal bath. Occasionally part of the villa was abandoned, and only some of the rooms and/or some of the thermal baths were preserved. What we cannot say with precision is who it was that brought about these changes.

Second, for various reasons, some of the villas were simply abandoned: it may have been through fear of being sacked, the depletion of the workforce or a desired move on the part of the owners; in time these areas became cemeteries or centres for the Christian cult. This phenomenon can be observed usually from the sixth century onwards, and in some cases from a later date: part of the villa of Baños de Valdearados (Soria) was utilised as a cemetery in the tenth century.

Some parts of the villa were perfectly suited for transformation and reutilisation as Christian basilicas. The great apsed halls with their front porticoes, hydraulic systems and the very magnificence of the buildings themselves allowed for both the crowd of believers as well as the ebb and flow of the liturgical rite. In Spain as well as Gaul and Britain many villas changed into Christian basilicas during the fifth and sixth centuries, resulting in the presence and proliferation of tombs and cemeteries around them. Another reason why the villa changed, at least in part, into a centre for the Christian cult, was undoubtedly the very beliefs held by its owners. With the progressive christianisation of the *domini* or *possessores*, a basilica or a centre for Christian worship was included in their villas or on their estates. It would seem, however, that at least for a period the two phenomena are independent of one another: a Christian owner may have retained his ideals of classical culture without transforming his dwelling place, although there is no doubt that the structural and architectural layout of the villa favoured this process.

Lastly, we must not forget that the Church, through private donations or concessions from kings, was slowly beginning to own very large properties and estates – the *Vitae Patrum Emeritensium* of the sixth century, among other texts, provide clear proof of this – properties that would later pass on to bishops. The *dominus* would in turn be replaced by a Christian bishop, while the specific characteristics of some of the villas provided the perfect architectural layout for conversion to monasteries.

One cannot speak of uniformity in the evolution of the villa in late antiquity, as far as their transformation, abandonment, destruction or reutilisation is concerned. No one model exists. Their evolutions are as varied as are the many different cases and regions to be considered. Even within the same regions, different variations exist.

The continuation of the lifestyle within the villa, with all that this implied, remained an aristocratic phenomenon. In Spain the last will and testament of King Alphonso III (AD 905) mentions among his possessions the villa Liño alongside his palaces, baths and the Church of S. Miguel (fig. 52). Magnates, aristocrats and kings refer to the villa as an alternative way of life, as a form of prestige and standing. This is, to a certain extent, a way of retaining the classical ideal, a form of interrupted continuity, as it were.

When the Arabs arrived in the peninsula in the eighth century they brought with them their vast experience, developed in Syria, Egypt and North Africa, of contact with Roman civilisation, and consequently with its types of dwellings and its architecture. Their palaces, like the one of Medina-al-Azahara in Cordova, are nothing more than a complex transposition of the great Roman villas. When they came into contact with the Roman villas of Spain they used them as quarries, taking away precious materials such as marble, as well as columns, capitals and models for geometrical or floral mosaics. The Arabs, however, brought with them a different concept of exploiting the land and a different concept of agriculture altogether. They brought a 'water culture' as well as the irrigation systems that the Romans had not fully developed. This partially represented the end of the Roman villa. Indeed, what is the Andalusian *cortijo* if not a form of land exploitation, including within it its peasants and its Roman villa?

NOTES

1 Codex Theodosius VII. 8.5.
2 Goffart 1980.

The barbarian successor states

Walter Pohl

The empire of Rome was firmly established by the singular and perfect coalition of its members. The subject nations, resigning the hope and even the wish of independence, embraced the character of Roman citizens ... But this union was purchased by the loss of national freedom and military spirit; and the servile provinces, destitute of life and motion, expected their safety from the mercenary troops and governors who were directed by the orders of a distant court.[1]

More than two hundred years ago, this is how Edward Gibbon characterised the inner contradictions that led to the 'Decline and Fall of the Roman Empire': a civilised state whose citizens have lost their ambition and military virtues and abandoned the values of public service under the influence of the Church becomes an easy prey for the raw strength and courage of the barbarians. Since Gibbon, scholars have proposed many more, and widely differing, explanations.[2] The debate about the relative weight of factors in the process that turned the Roman empire into a loose commonwealth of barbarian states, a Roman *res publica* without Roman rule (*imperium*), will certainly go on. However, some of Gibbon's points can be modified in the light of recent research.

Instead of a 'perfect coalition of its members', the Roman empire may also be seen, with Peter Brown, as a way 'in which 10 per cent of the population, who lived in the towns and have left their mark on the course of European civilization, fed themselves from the labours of the remaining 90 per cent who laboured the land'.[3] Among these elites 'national freedom', as Gibbon saw it, was hardly an issue. The empire had usually been careful to respect the symbols and sentiments of cities, regions, tribes and other groups, and thus provided space for the coexistence of various forms of organisation. Before asking why the *imperium Romanum* in its classical form did not last, one should think for a moment why, unlike most previous empires in the ancient world, it lasted so long; in a certain sense, it even outlasted its own 'barbarian successor states', as the contribution by Evangelos Chrysos in this volume suggests. One could go even further and claim that the barbarian kingdoms themselves were a Roman achievement, as Patrick Geary put it:

The Germanic world was perhaps the greatest and most enduring creation of Roman political and military genius. That this offspring came in time to replace its creator should not obscure the fact that it owed its very existence to Roman initiative, to the patient efforts of centuries of Roman emperors, generals, soldiers, landlords, slave traders, and simple merchants to mold the (to Roman eyes) chaos of barbarian reality into forms of political, social and economic activity which they could understand, and, perhaps, control.[4]

The extraordinary success of the Roman empire, therefore, was also due to its capacity to integrate various groups, even beyond its frontiers, more or less firmly into its social and cultural texture. It was a complex system of a 'classical' centre and a 'barbarian' periphery which was drawn into the dynamic of the Roman way of life. It is not surprising that many of the most beautiful and significant Roman objects ever found come from beyond the Roman frontier, for instance the Scandinavian bog finds of hundreds of Roman weapons, or the treasures from Traprain Law in Scotland, Hoby in Denmark, Hildesheim in Germany, Pietroasa and Szilágy-Somlyó in Romania, to mention just a few examples (pl. 7). The empire offered several ways to profit from the Roman system: by peaceful exchange, by military careers within the Roman army, but also by plundering Roman provinces. All these perspectives contributed to a change in the barbarian societies, strengthening the position of elites who knew how to deal with the Romans, and how to follow their model in establishing firmer dominion over their own people. Fighting for, or against, the Romans could both serve to attain extraordinary prestige – and the objects in which it could be expressed: gold and silver, silk and textiles, weapons and jewellery, wine and spices (fig. 15).

The Roman system was also flexible enough to offer further perspectives for the most ambitious of its barbarian neighbours. It was the Roman army that provided the opportunity for courageous barbarians to adapt to *romanitas* and gradually merge into the imperial elite. The regular pay and rations (*annona*) that the soldiers received, plus donatives and gifts of land to the veterans, made the army attractive for those who preferred a warlike existence.[5] Towards the end of the fourth century more than half of the Roman officers were of barbarian origin. The poet Pacatus, in a panegyric to the emperor Theodosius delivered in AD 388/9, extolled him: 'Attracted by your kindness, all the Scythian nations flocked to you in such great numbers that you seemed to have imposed a levy upon barbarians from which you exempted your subjects.'[6] The senatorial aristocracy, despite its enormous wealth and influence, had lost control of the armed forces, and the rift between a barbarised army and the civil authorities widened. Especially in the western empire, the access to power now required being at home in both worlds, and in the long run that gave barbarians who envied and imitated Roman ways a clear advantage over Romans who despised the barbarians and could not inspire lasting loyalty in the soldiers they paid. Romanised barbarians like the Vandal Stilicho (fig. 16), the Suevian Ricimer, the Burgundian Gundobad (pl. 6) or the Scirian Odovacer dominated the power games in the west throughout the fifth century. In 476 Odovacer closed the series of insignificant western emperors and continued to govern as king in the name of the emperor in the east, 'one of the most famous non-events in history', the 'non-end of the Roman empire'.[7]

This process of assimilation of barbarian warriors was made easier by the fact that the networks of power that controlled the empire allowed for forms of personal loyalty within the bureaucratic system, for ethnic or regional ties underneath the

Fig. 15 Imported Byzantine silk decorated with a pattern of nereids riding on leocamps used as a relic wrapping. Sion Cathedral, Switzerland, *c.*AD 600.

imperial superstructure. Late Roman generals, however barbarian or Roman in origin, used to keep their personal retinue of *buccellarii*, privileged private soldiers who were named after the better bread they ate. Units of the Roman army had often been organised according to ethnic or regional features, which inspired specific loyalties even though the members of the unit did not actually have to be of the same origin. What we would regard as imperial versus 'barbaric' forms of organisation were never clear opposites throughout Roman history. Roman as its ideology and content was, the empire did not bar members of regional elites, even from the periphery, from the access to central power, although barbarians could not become emperors themselves.

The empire had never relied on central bureaucracy alone for its survival; only recently has it become clear how much influence patronage systems and power networks had. Their rivalries had been a continual source of inner conflict, but the Roman system knew intricate mechanisms of dispute settlement and compromise between the powerful. From the end of the fourth century, however, the checks and balances the imperial administration had developed against these centrifugal tendencies failed in many parts of the empire. In a sense, the barbarian successor states were predominantly

35

Fig. 16
Ivory diptych
panel depicting the
Vandal general
Stilicho (*c.*AD
360–408),
magister militum of
the emperor
Theodosius, in
official attire,
*c.*400.

based on smaller-scale forms of social integration that the empire had managed to control for so long: regional and ethnic solidarity, personal loyalty and the collective access to power of new groups from the periphery of the empire. The emblem of this new form of organisation was kingship. Royal *tyrannis* had long been despised by the Roman republic and its imperial heirs as a barbaric form of rule. Now, from the year 400 onwards, barbarian kings spread their rule within the Roman system, gradually filling the widening spaces that late Roman society provided for successful military commanders, but giving them a new character and splendour.[8]

The first of these kings who aimed directly at the old heartland of the empire, Italy, although in vain, was the Visigoth Alaric. Visigoths, who had long lived as more or less peaceful neighbours of the empire, crossed the lower Danube in AD 376, together with numerous other groups, under Hunnic pressure. The emperor Valens had first rejoiced at the prospect of winning so many new soldiers, but his corrupt officials handled their integration so badly that they rebelled, killing the emperor and destroying his army at Adrianople in 378. By the treaty of 382, they were settled in a Roman province as a distinct group to replace the regular Roman troops that should have been stationed there. This solution that combined a long tradition of treaties with barbarians beyond the borders with administrative forms developed for garrisoning and provisioning the Roman army provided a model for many future settlements.[9]

Soon, the Visigothic army in the Roman Balkans raised a king of their own who strove to get a better deal in richer provinces: Alaric (fig. 17). In the course of his career, he became, by turns, the principal enemy and one of the highest officers of the Roman army, while his Gothic troops both ravaged and protected Italy. In AD 410, to step up the pressure, the Goths plundered Rome; although Alaric managed to spare the churches and avoid excessive brutalities, the symbolic effect was enormous. But still, no lasting agreement could be achieved, and it took some more years until, after Alaric's death, influential circles in Gaul arranged to settle the Visigoths around Toulouse (pl. 8). Soon, the Visigoths expanded to Spain where they prevailed against the Vandals. After the defeat by the Franks in 508, the residence was moved to Toledo. Through the pioneer work of the Gothic bishop Ulfila in the fourth century, who had translated the Bible into their language, the Goths had embraced the Arian form of Christianity, thereby setting a standard for most of the early barbarian kingdoms; only in 589 did they turn to the Catholic creed. Despite many crises, the Visigothic kings

Fig. 17 Obverse of gold *solidus* of the puppet emperor Priscus Attalus, appointed by Alaric during his occupation of Rome AD 409–410.

ruled Spain and a diminishing part of southern Gaul up to the Muslim invasion in 711, when the kingdom quickly collapsed.[10]

The contemporary historiographer Orosius had called Alaric 'a Christian and closer to a Roman', compared to many other barbarians; the Visigoths had already embraced *romanitas* to quite an extent. The Vandals, and their king Genseric, encountered much less favourable responses. The country around the Carpathians where they came from had been more remote from Roman influence, though not completely. On New Year's Eve AD 406, Vandals, Alans and others crossed the Rhine into Gaul, later moved on to Spain and finally crossed to North Africa in 429. Only in 442 did the western emperor recognise the new Vandal kingdom, not as a sovereign state, but as a legitimate power centre on Roman territory. The rich province of Africa, around Carthage, was the principal source of corn for Rome, and in the fourth century enough corn had been shipped from Africa to feed more than half a million Romans.[11] The Vandals soon adapted to the new luxurious life in the rich province; but they also took Arianism very seriously, and the drastic history of the persecutions by the Catholic Bishop Victor of Vita has fixed their disastrous image for posterity. The empire never abandoned the hope of recapturing Africa, and in 533–4 Justinian's general Belisarius destroyed the Vandal kingdom in a single campaign.[12]

Even shorter was the period of Ostrogothic rule in Italy; despite this, Theoderic's kingdom and its heroic end have always inspired considerable interest and admiration, from medieval epic to contemporary scholars (pl. 9).[13] For a few decades after AD 488–93, Theoderic's Italian kingdom seemed to achieve an admirable synthesis between Roman administration and *civilitas* on the one hand, and Gothic rule and military achievement on the other hand, based on treaties and cooperation with the Roman emperor in Constantinople. The magnificent buildings and mosaics in Theoderic's capital Ravenna, the sophisticated collection of official letters by his Roman advisor Cassiodorus, or the purple *Codex Argenteus* of the Gothic Bible are impressive traces of Theoderic's representation and practice of rulership (pl. 10). But the compromise between Roman senators and Gothic generals had been easier to construct after decades of unrest when the Ostrogoths came into power than to maintain after decades of peace that they had guaranteed, and Theoderic's troubled successors soon came under pressure from both sides. When Theoderic's daughter Amalasuntha was murdered by her cousin Theodahad in 535, the emperor Justinian took the opportunity to unleash his successful armies against the prosperous Ostrogothic kingdom. A war of almost twenty years ensued in which Roman armies, 'patched together from men from the greatest possible number of peoples', as Procopius wrote,[14] ravaged much of the infra-structure of the old heartland of the empire. In the end, Italy came back under Roman rule, which many of its inhabitants already regarded as Greek dominion.

It was not long before another barbarian people victoriously appeared in Italy: the Lombards or Longobards (AD 568). They had spent almost eighty years in the abandoned Roman provinces of Noricum and Pannonia (pl. 11), until their king Alboin had managed to accumulate a large coalition of different barbarian groups that were ready to follow him into Italy. Unlike Theoderic, the Longobards never managed to control the whole peninsula, and a peaceful agreement with the emperor in Constantinople could not be reached for a long time. Cooperation and integration between Longobards and Romans thus had to happen on a lower level, and its success and extent differed considerably from region to region. Even more than in the case of the Goths, the Church played an essential part as an institution that could represent the Roman majority of the population and achieve reliable agreements with the Longobard warriors. Both Rome and the late Roman capital, Ravenna, remained in the Byzantine sphere up to the eighth century, whereas the Longobard kings ruled from Pavia, and the powerful Longobard dukes of Spoleto and Beneventum controlled much of central and southern Italy – a fragmentation of the peninsula that was to survive into the nineteenth century.[15]

The power that finally ended the rule of Longobard kings in Italy in AD 774 was the most successful of all barbarian successor states: the Franks.[16] From a Roman perspective, Goths and Vandals (to an extent even Longobards) came from beyond the Danube, had been influenced by the nomadic culture of the eastern Steppes and thus predominantly fought on horseback. Their contemporaries did not call them Germans but Scythians or Gothic peoples. The Germans, on the other hand, lived roughly beyond the Rhine, fought on foot, and their organisation was much looser. In the course of the third century many of the tribes well known from the Germanic wars of Augustus, like the Cherusci or the Semnones, had disappeared, and new, broad tribal coalitions had formed beyond the Rhine frontier: the Franks in the north and the Alamanni in the south.[17] When the Gothic peoples, led by strong military kings, moved through the provinces of the empire in the fifth century, Franks and Alamanni were still governed by numerous local kings and leaders and only gradually expanded into the neighbouring Gallic and Raetian provinces.

It was only around AD 500 that one man came to control the whole mosaic of regional powers along the Rhine. This was the Frankish king Clovis, and his ascent to power went parallel with an overall confrontation with the Alamanni which established the lasting supremacy of the Franks. Clovis was ruthless enough to get rid of his Frankish rivals, clever enough to stage his conversion to Catholicism and style himself as an ally of the distant emperor at Constantinople, and finally strong enough to grab much of southern Gaul from the Visigoths. His successors, in spite of endless dynastic quarrels and bloodshed in the family so vividly depicted by Gregory of Tours, continued this successful expansive thrust (fig. 18). One of the victims was the short-lived Burgundian kingdom around Lyon and Geneva with its fascinating blend of carefully preserved *romanitas* and Burgundian mythical overtones, both of which would survive under Frankish rule. A little later, the fall of the Ostrogothic kingdom not only

CONDOLENS · SEDDOLODICEBAT SIFORTE POTUIS
SET ADHUCALIQUEM REPERIRE UTINTERFICERET
HIS ITATRANSACTIS APUD PARISIUS OBIIT ·
SEPULTUSQUE INBASILICAM SCORUM A
POSTULORUM · QUAMCUMCHRODECHILDAE RE
GINA IPSE CONSTRUXERAT · MIGRAUIT AUTEM
POST UOCLADINSE BELLUM ANNO QUINTO · FUE
RUNT QUE OMNES DIES REGNI EIUS XXX T RICINTA
A TRANSITUERGOSCI MARTINI USQUE ADTRANSI
TUM CHLODOUECHI REGIS QUIFUIT UNDECIMO
ANNO EPISCOPATUS LICINII TORONICIS ACERDO
TIS SUPPUTANTUR ANNI CENTUM DUODECIM
CHRODECHILDIS AUTEM REGINA POST MORTE
UIRI SUI TORONUS UENIT · IBIQUE ADBASILICA
BEATI MARTINI DESERUIENS CUM SUMMA PU
DICITIA · ATQUE BENIGNITATE INLOCO COM MO
RATA EST OMNIBUS DIEBUS UITAE SUAE RARO
PARISIUS UISITANS ·

EXPLICIT LIBER SECUNDUS

INCIPIUNT CAPITULA LIBER

made the highly romanised regions of south-eastern Gaul an easy prey for the Franks, it also gave them control of most of the Alpine passes, with easy access to the plains of northern Italy. In the middle of the sixth century, a Frankish king could claim that he would soon march on Constantinople to complete his exploits. For Byzantine authors, the Franks became the *Germanoi* par excellence because they now ruled over most of the other Germanic peoples; similarly, the Spanish 'Chronicle of 754' simply calls Charles Martel's army that defeated the Saracens at Poitiers *Europenses*, the Europeans (ch. 80).

The Merovingian dynasty that Clovis and his sons had established as a hegemonal force in western Europe enjoyed unrivalled prestige for about 250 years, although its power was usually fragmented between more than one king (fig. 19). In the orbit of Merovingian kingdoms – roughly, Austrasia in the east, Neustria in the west, Burgundy

(Left) Fig. 18 Gregory of Tours, early eighth century copy of the Ten Books of Histories. Paris, BN Lat. 17654 f.21v.

(Right) Fig. 19 Bronze throne of Dagobert, the last effective Merovingian king to hold power in both Austrasia and Neustria. Seventh century with later additions.

in the south, although the constellation frequently changed – peace and unanimity was the exception; but their plurality also guaranteed the basic unity of the Franks and helped to establish a balance between widely different regions and factions: 'Thus the civil wars, so decried by Gregory, actually held the kingdom together, because the struggles between members of the Merovingian family provided a focus around which other conflicts could cluster.'[18] The Frankish world comprised both highly romanised regions where the heirs of the Roman senatorial aristocracy continued to wield considerable power, and areas that had never been under Roman rule, like the subdued Thuringian kingdom east of the Rhine, or provinces in which Roman life had collapsed to a certain extent and where smaller barbarian peoples enjoyed a changing degree of autonomy, like Bavaria along the upper Danube or Frisia and northern Gaul.

Of course, this variety of regions was primarily held together by the military strength the Frankish elites could muster, but force alone would not have been enough. Many practices of Roman administration and jurisdiction were continued and modified; Latin was unrivalled as a language of state, and indeed continued to be for many centuries to come. Classical learning still enjoyed some respect; for instance, King Chilperic I (died AD 584) wrote poetry, hymns and masses, and the poet Venantius Fortunatus praised him: 'Warlike pursuits make you like your family, but your literary pursuits single you out as exceptional' (poem 9.1). Nevertheless, the civilian elites that had upheld ancient civilisation for a millennium were fading away. Since the fourth century many of the best men had chosen to serve the church of God instead of the state, with the obvious result that they often ended up doing both, but in the interest of the Church whose dignitaries they were. In the cities that still formed the backbone of the system in most of Gaul in spite of their general decline, the bishops who often came from the old regional elite found ample opportunities to dominate public life and assume responsibilities in many secular fields. Gregory, bishop of Tours towards the end of the sixth century, provides extensive evidence that episcopal power struggles could be as merciless and perfidious as those among the Frankish aristocracy.

Despite the occasional scenes of bloodshed in which Gregory's history indulges, there is little to suggest that the 'barbarian' state of the Franks was, as a system, more violent or unjust than the late Roman world at large. The Frankish warriors had become landowners within a late Roman system of property, and the status of agricultural labourers was hardly affected by this change. But something else changed fundamentally: the late Roman army, including its officers, had been maintained from tax revenues; indeed, it had been the principal beneficiary of the tax system. Although there is some debate as to when and how the change happened, the Franks basically had to use their own possessions to cover their military expenses, including that of their retinue. This does not mean that the tax system collapsed at once;[19] King Chilperic I, according to Gregory (5.28), did not only write religious poetry but also invented several new taxes, provoking riots and the burning of tax registers. But tax exemptions

were abundant, and the Frankish aristocracy must have felt entitled to keep for themselves what under the Roman system would have gone to the central authorities. In
the course of time, grants of land came to be seen as a reward for military or other
services to the king, and as a basis to maintain an appropriate number of soldiers or
to hold a certain office. Eventually, this process led to the medieval system of distribution
of wealth and power that is usually called feudalism. Its basic features were developed
in the conflict-ridden social laboratory of the Merovingians.

The first to take advantage of the potential created by this system were the Carolingians, who gradually usurped *de facto* power within the Merovingian system and finally
ousted the old dynasty in AD 751. As heirs of 'the Merovingian achievement',[20] they
fabricated a sombre picture of their predecessors that has misled even modern historiography, which was more impressed by the deeds of Charles Martel, Pippin III and
Charlemagne. In the second half of the eighth century the Frankish kingdom of the
Carolingians gained control of almost the whole western empire, as far as it was not
under Muslim rule (as North Africa and most of the Iberian peninsula). Charlemagne,
through his Frankish counts (*comites*), ruled Italy as the heir of the Ostrogoths and
Longobards; both flanks of the Pyrenees as heir of the Visigoths; Pannonia where
Huns, Longobards, Avars and others had built their kingdoms; directly governed
Alamannia and Bavaria; and, after the long struggle against the Saxons, he also
controlled larger areas beyond the old Roman border than any of his predecessors.
Thus, to a certain extent, the Frankish kingdom became *the* Roman successor state.
Although the renewed Roman empire of the Franks soon began to disintegrate, the
Frankish synthesis between Roman heritage and new modes of social integration
superseded many older forms and became the basis of the medieval world in large
parts of Europe.

Only one important Christian part of the old western empire did not pass directly
through the Carolingian mould: Britain.[21] As in some other peripheral parts of the
empire at different times – Dacia, the tithe-land between the Rhine and the Danube,
Noricum between the Danube and the eastern Alps – the Roman army was withdrawn
from the British provinces soon after AD 400. Unlike the other regions where that
happened, this did not lead to an immediate collapse of provincial life, but rather to
a slow process of erosion of *romanitas*, progressing from east to west. The leaders of
the Britons had encouraged Angles and Saxons to cross the North Sea and come to
Britain, according to the record, to serve as federates against the pressure from the
Picts. Soon, the newcomers began to establish their own power centres, plundering
and subduing large areas of the island. Without any threat or support from the empire,
and no competition from any large compact power, the Angles and Saxons in due
course organised themselves in regional kingdoms such as Wessex, East Anglia, Mercia
or Northumbria, mostly designated by geographical names. As the direct impact of
the Roman tradition seems to have been weaker than elsewhere, christianisation played

an extraordinary part in the development of medieval Britain. Irish missionaries and, from the time of Pope Gregory the Great, the Roman church competed for souls, and for the support of Anglo-Saxon kings and warriors. By the time Bede wrote his *Historia Ecclesiastica Gentis Anglorum* around 730, the Roman church had curbed Irish influence, established a highly creative Latin and monastic culture and shaped a political world of Christian kingdoms.

The Latin kingdoms that succeeded the Roman empire in the west, different as they were, had a lot in common. The new elites that had wrung power from the crumbling institutions of the empire were warriors; to a different degree, their tactics and their outlook had been formed in barbarian units of the Roman army. But the complex and disciplined organisation of the Roman army did not survive; the barbarian kings could not maintain paid officers and soldiers, and had to rely on the personal loyalty of free warriors and aristocrats with their retinue instead. Initially, the barbarian armies profited from Roman tax revenues which were regularly paid to their royal leader under treaties with the emperor. The success of these barbarian armies was due to the fact that they were cheaper to maintain than Roman armies. Barbarian kings did not have to pay their warriors as Roman soldiers were paid; often it was enough to guarantee supplies and provide a chance to win booty and prestige. A good ruler, as Isidore of Seville wrote about the Visigothic king Reccared, 'enriched many with gifts and elevated even more with honours' (*Historia Gothorum* 56).

Once they were settled, barbarian units were allotted tax or land shares;[22] in the course of time, the tax system declined or disappeared, and a warlike landed aristocracy appeared, supporting a personal retinue through the revenues from his own land. But the social hierarchy between these powerful men (*potentes*) and the rest of the barbarian army was much less marked than later in the Middle Ages; usually, simple warriors also had their own share of land, and contemporary sources do not normally offer any systematic distinction as to their respective status. Together, they were the free men, the *liberi*, *milites* or *exercitales*, on whom the barbarian monarchy rested.

Apart from these personal bonds of loyalty, shared experience and personal acquaintance, the barbarian kingdoms also relied on a number of other forms of integration they had inherited from the Roman provincial administration, directly or through the Church. They preserved the old language of power,[23] encouraged the growth of Christian discourse and stimulated the development of written narratives that gave meaning to the new communities.[24] Communication was still based to quite an extent on writing,[25] as a considerable body of letters demonstrates. Latin was the language of literacy, used for diplomacy and politics; if a Frankish king wrote to a Longobard or Visigothic ruler, the letter was not only written in Latin, but it also made ample use of the rhetoric appropriate for late Roman letters of state. For many offices or ranks, Latin titles continued to be in use: *dux*, *comes*, *centenarius*, *miles* etc. Law codes, juridical texts and charters were written down in Latin, although some in Britain are preserved in Old English. It has long been discussed whether the relatively numerous law codes from the barbarian kingdoms, for instance the Frankish *Lex Salica*, the Visigothic *Codex Euricianus*, the Longobard *Edictus Rothari* or the Bavarian *Lex Baiuvariorum*, reflect Germanic judicial traditions or rather continue the tradition of late Roman vulgar law (pl. 33). Roman models certainly were more influential than traditional scholarship assumed. But in the first place, the law codes were expressions of the barbarian Latin kingdoms that produced them, rather than of any hypothetical 'authentic' Germanic society (that had been under Roman influence since we first hear about it), or as a simple continuation of late Roman provincial jurisprudence. This is a basic clue to the study of these states: a clear distinction between Roman and Germanic origins, even where it might be arguable, would not help to understand a process in which there was a continuum of solutions to problems that were common to 'Romans' and 'barbarians', who were becoming harder and harder to distinguish. The states were both Roman and barbarian, and so, in a sense, were most of their leading members. Thus, when the Franks west of the Rhine, the Visigoths or the Longobards gradually abandoned their languages for Romance dialects, this change was not even highlighted by contemporary observers.

Certainly, if the king of one of the successor states looked for forms of representation, Latin language, late Roman and Christian art and architecture, Byzantine prestige objects and dress played an important part. We know that Byzantium, or barbarian rulers of Mediterranean countries, sent architects, ship-builders, musicians and other specialists to other countries where they were needed, even to Huns or Avars. Theoderic the Great sent a waterclock and a sundial constructed by the philosopher Boethius to Gundobad of Burgundy and wrote to him: 'Possess in your native country what you once saw in the city of Rome ... Through you, Burgundy lays aside its tribal way of life, and, in its regard for the wisdom of its king, it properly covets the achievements of the sages' (*Variae* 1.46). Diplomats who regularly came and went at Constantinople diffused the knowledge of the Byzantine court and its forms of representation, and they diffused the still unique prestige of the emperor. Precious objects that reflected the prestige of the owner circulated as gifts between the emperor and the kings, between the kings and their nobles, and on all levels of society. Grave goods and treasures demonstrate how highly Roman objects were valued, and over what distances precious things were exchanged (pl. 3). But they also show that the distinction between Byzantine imports, local production in Roman tradition and the work of barbarian artisans is rather blurred. The symbolic language these objects might have been part of is often hard to reconstruct.

The Mediterranean world was still perceived as a unity, although communication and exchange was gradually decreasing. Spanish chroniclers between the sixth and the eighth century took ample note of events in Byzantium and even Persia, and Paul the Deacon's late eighth-century *History of the Langobards* provided reliable information about Byzantine emperors, Frankish, Visigothic and even Anglo-Saxon kings. On the surface, the Roman empire had been replaced by a world of *gentes*, of independent peoples. Certainly, ethnic communities had been successful in wresting political power from the international elite that had governed the Roman world. But these 'ethnic' states cannot be compared to national states in the modern sense. Ethnicity was a factor of cohesion among its elites, but it seems to have mattered little to the majority of its inhabitants. Goths, Langobards and Franks were small minorities in their own kingdoms where they governed a rather mixed Romance-speaking population. But even these minorities were peoples in the making, incorporating numerous other barbarian groups who often preserved their traditions for a long time, among them Alans, Huns, Rugians and Suevi in the case of the Goths, Gepids, Suevi, Goths and Bulgars in the Langobard kingdom, Burgundians, Alans, Alamanni and many others under Frankish rule, and in Britain, Britons, Picts, Irish 'Scotti' plus a mix of continental Germans that only came to be known by the comprehensive name 'Anglo-Saxons' from the ninth century onwards. The archaeological evidence clearly shows that in most cases ethnic origins are hard to distinguish. In the fifth century the 'Danubian style' current in Attila's kingdom can be found from the Black Sea to Gaul (pl. 12), and in the sixth century the 'Merovingian row graves' stretched as far east as Transylvania.[26]

The ethnogenesis of early medieval peoples, therefore, was not a matter of blood, but of shared traditions and institutions; belief in common origins could give cohesion to rather heterogeneous communities. The early medieval kingdoms were, for a time, a successful form of making such ethnic communities the focus of states on the territory of the empire. These 'kingdoms of the empire'[27] were flexible enough to integrate late Roman and barbarian forms of life in a largely Roman framework. They were, however, not the only form in which the transition from late antiquity could be achieved. The Roman empire continued to rule large territories in the east, and the sudden expansion of the Islamic world in the seventh century created an alternative model of transforming the Hellenistic heritage. Both Byzantium and the caliphate were hierarchical societies in which, even more than in the west, religion was at the heart of the state. A completely different but in the long run very successful model was the expansion of the Slavs; early Slavic society presents a striking example of how a widespread aggregate of local and regional groups, initially without any central institutions or strong elites, can still form a loose ethnic community and leave its stamp on huge areas.[28] Kingship or similar types of rulership, warrior aristocracies and hierarchic societies, with all their specific forms of expression, developed only gradually among the early Slavs, and often under foreign influence. Nevertheless, before AD 600, Slavic communities had rapidly spread over almost all of eastern Europe, from the Baltic Sea to the Peloponnese, and they proved surprisingly stable in spite of repeated subjugation.

By comparison, the Latin successor states of the west proved rather vulnerable in times of crisis. The kingdoms of the Vandals, Visigoths and Longobards collapsed within months after one major military defeat. The Anglo-Saxon kingdoms suffered huge losses against the Vikings and finally succumbed to the Norman invasion in 1066. The Frankish kingdom fell into pieces shortly after Charlemagne's imperial heyday, and for a long time was unable to defend even its core areas against Viking or Magyar attacks. Thus, none of the successor states survived unchanged into the later Middle Ages, and none of the modern peoples of Europe can claim to be the direct heir of an early medieval *gens*. However, after complex ethnic processes, some of the names of peoples that witnessed the transformation of the Roman empire now designate European nations, even if modern France has little to do with the Franks, England with the Angles or Germany – in French called Allemagne – with the Alamanni. All the same, these names may remind us how much of Europe was invented in the successor states of the Roman empire.

NOTES

1 Gibbon, 1981, 625–6.

2 Demandt, 1984.

3 Brown, 1971.

4 Geary, 1988.

5 Jones, 1964, 607–86; Demandt, 1989, 255–71.

6 Pacatus, 32.

7 Cameron, 1993, 33; Wolfram, 1990, 263.

8 Wolfram, 1990.

9 Chrysos, 1972; Wolfram, 1988; Heather, 1991.

10 Claude, 1970; Collins,1983; Kazanski 1991; Ripoll and Velázquez, 1995.

11 Jones, 1964, 698.

12 Courtois, 1955.

13 Wolfram, 1988; Moorhead, 1992; monographs by Peter Heather and Patrick Amory are in print.

14 Procopius, *Goth.* 4.30.

15 Wickham, 1981; Jarnut, 1982; Harrison, 1993; a monograph by Walter Pohl is in preparation.

16 Geary, 1988; Lebecq, 1990; Wood, 1994.

17 Christlein, 1978.

18 Wood, 1994, 100.

19 Durliat, 1990; Wood, 1994, 62–6.

20 Wood, 1994, 322.

21 Campbell, 1982; Bassett, 1989; and elsewhere.

22 Goffart, 1980; Wolfram and Schwarcz, 1988.

23 McCormick, 1986.

24 Goffart, 1988; Scharer and Scheibelreiter, 1994.

25 Cf. McKitterick, 1990.

26 Wolfram and Schwarcz, 1980; Wolfram and Pohl, 1990.

27 Cf. Pohl, 1996.

28 Pohl, 1988.

Wealth and treasure in the West, 4th-7th century

Max Martin

Nowhere, not even in the most communicative of written documents, do we find a more vivid and colourful picture of the true wealth of the late antique and early Middle Ages than in the treasure of the period. From the fourth to the seventh centuries AD many collections of 'treasure', sometimes of substantial proportions, were buried in the ground or hidden in water in the territory of the declining western Roman empire and the barbarian states which succeeded it, as well as in the neighbouring and more remote regions of free Germania. They contained coins of precious metals or silver tableware and utensils or, in some cases, even gold jewellery. It is not uncommon for the finds to include a combination of these objects.

It goes without saying that in these hoards of precious metals – archaeological finds of the very first order – only those parts of bygone wealth which were mobile are to be found; substantial holdings of land or property, as well as certain other valuable possessions, can usually at best only be inferred from written sources,[1] as they leave no trace in the ground. It can be assumed that the owners of such riches, which imply aristocratic table manners, were prosperous landowners and high-ranking military and civilian officials.[2]

The most concrete information about the wealth of the period is thus handed down to us through treasure, yet this kind of source material is in fact more complex and inconsistent than any other. The regularity with which possessions of precious metal were buried in the ground depends both on the time and the place. The reasons for burying treasure, and the occasion of its successful and for us permanently unknowable recovery, depend on a multitude of factors, all of which demand close scrutiny.[3] Certainly a number of deposits of treasure have been thoroughly analysed to date in terms of their contents, and in many cases interpreted historically – one need only think in this context of coin deposits. With the exception of the northern Germanic region,[4] however, we entirely lack thorough and comprehensive studies of all the finds in larger geographical areas and across longer periods of time. These would enable us to make preliminary comparisons between wider areas and could thereby lead to significant cultural and historical discoveries.

Riches in the form of money, jewellery and other possessions made of precious metals and jewels were not normally buried in the ground; they passed from hand to hand either legally, as inheritance or gift, or illegally, through theft or robbery. Gold and silver jewellery, whether whole or incomplete, was also, like broken silverware, hardly

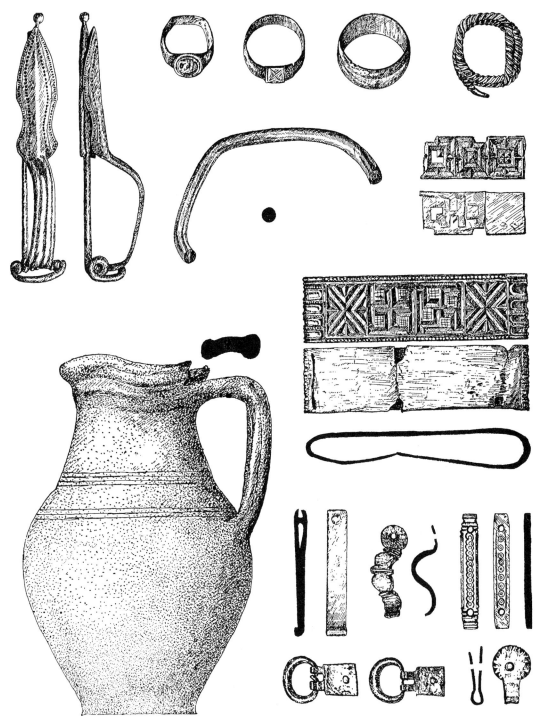

Fig. 20 Silver dress fittings, rings and military equipment, together with sixteen gold and some 500 silver coins (*t.p.*AD 408), buried in a pottery jug. Wiesbaden-Kastel, Germany. (After Schoppa 1962.)

ever thrown away. Rather, it was reworked or periodically recast into new shapes to conform to changes in taste.

There are only two exceptions to this rule, both of which have provided archaeological evidence of bygone wealth in the form of valuable possessions: the first is the custom of entrusting the high-ranking and wealthy dead with, amongst other things, valuable objects made of precious metals as grave goods on their journey into the beyond. In what follows, this expensive burial custom, which during the period in question was only really practised with some prodigality by populations of Germanic descent, will not be addressed.[5] Our treasures constitute the second exception – the deposits in the ground, or even in the water, of valuable objects made of precious metals.

Deposits of valuable objects – those which would retain their value – were made throughout the period for a number of different reasons.[6] Expensive objects could be consigned to the earth as votive offerings, i.e. for ritualistic or sacred purposes, for which water or marshland was often preferred. More common and widespread is the category of hidden treasure, whereby valuable possessions were concealed either under the ground or above it, for example in a wall or under the floor of a building, to safeguard them from danger. Hoards of treasure deposited above ground were undoubtedly more common than the few examples known to us would suggest. Understandably, they have almost all been lost.

Provided they were not votive offerings, all surviving deposits of precious metals constitute, to some extent, mishaps – a fact which should be accorded greater weight than it has been up until now. Normally, hidden treasure of this kind would be unearthed again, either by the owners or others, after the transient danger had receded. Their former owners were either affluent private individuals from the highest social strata or churches and monasteries. In the case of ritualistic deposits and votive hoards the former owners were likely to have been pagan sacrificial communities.

The following valuable possessions have repeatedly been found in secular hoards representing private or ecclesiastical wealth and prosperity: silver tableware and utensils, coins and medallions (*multipla*) as well as silver ingots, cut-up silver (so-called *Hacksilber*), jewellery and traditional clothing accessories made of precious metals and – in ecclesiastical finds – vessels, utensils and votive crosses. It is not uncommon for silverware and coins, or jewellery and coins, to be found hidden in the same hoard (fig. 20). Glass vessels on the other hand, which at the time were highly prized as precious drinking vessels, appear not to have been buried in the ground on account of their fragility.

Whenever possible valuable objects in a hoard of hidden treasure were buried in the ground intact and well protected, as they were to be used again. The hoards of cut-up silver – to be found only outside the boundaries of the former Roman empire – constitute an exception to this rule.

In the transitional period between late antiquity and the Middle Ages, the only people to sacrifice valuable objects by burying them in the earth or in water as sacred offerings were those in the Germanic regions outside the boundaries of the Roman empire. These objects sometimes included items captured in battle. Votive deposits containing exceptionally valuable gold and silver objects, together with notable offerings of weapons, have chiefly survived in Scandinavia; these include those found in the bogland site near Ejsbøl in southern Jutland (pl. 13) and, of course, other Danish and Swedish sacrificial sites.[7]

To the well-known hoards, including Broholm, there has recently been added a whole series of new precious metal deposits from the territory surrounding the seat of power near Gudme ('Home of the Gods') on Fyn and neighbouring districts.[8] Despite their differing dates, these deposits can be interpreted as hidden treasure rather than sacred offerings.

The hoards of scrap silver found only on territories populated by Germanic (and Celtic) peoples constitute a special group. They consist of deposits of cut-up or chopped silver vessels and utensils, often with Roman silver coinage, complete or broken silver ingots of Roman or native origin and, from time to time, also jewellery and the like. Deposits of this kind have been found above all in Denmark, Ireland and Scotland.[9] The peoples of these northern regions appear to have stopped using the original antique silver tableware; one is reminded of the famous story of the 'vase de Soissons' of AD 486, in which a Frankish warrior demanded of his king, Clovis (482–511), that an unbroken silver vessel be divided. As with coins and ingots, silver scrap was valued and traded by weight, which leads one to suppose that these deposits of precious metals were generally secular hidden treasure belonging to wealthy individuals or, in certain cases, to communities.

One of the most famous hoards of this kind is the treasure of Traprain Law in Scotland, which came to light in 1919 during excavations of a hill settlement close to the Firth of Forth, an estuary which flows into the North Sea.[10] Together with a quantity of scrap silver tableware, weighing in total over 20 kg and identified as the remains of around a hundred vessels, in some cases finely tooled, there were some pieces of clothing and four silver coins dating from before or around AD 400 (fig. 21).

Unlike the cut-up silver hoards, which can be identified as dating from the early fifth to the sixth century AD, and thus span a relatively long period, there is another series of precious metal hoards which were apparently laid down in a very short period during the first half of the fifth century (fig. 22).

In addition to this chronological concentration there is also a striking geographical one: first, there is the territory populated by Frankish tribes and situated close to the late antique border of the empire and its outlying districts, and, second, the border

Fig. 21 Cut-up silver bowl from the late Roman hoard at Traprain Law, Borders Scotland; fourth century.

regions to the west of the Lower and Middle Rhine. The contents of this distinctive group of deposits comprise gold and, less frequently, silver coins, as well as (on the right bank of the Rhine) gold jewellery with designs exclusive to the Germanic peoples, in particular neck rings, some of them tightly twisted together before burial, and, less commonly, arm rings. Both of the latter are as a rule decorated with a punched design typical of the first half of the fifth century (pl. 14).

In 1851 a hoard of gold was discovered near Velp (Gelderland, Netherlands), which, besides two finger rings, contained no less than seven neck rings, also made of gold. As early as 1715 a large number of gold coins (*solidi*) of the usurper Johannes (AD 423–5), came to light in the same district, as well as splendidly set medallions – three of the emperor Honorius and two of his sister Galla Placidia, the latter struck in 425 (pl. 17). These most recent objects from the latter hoard also allow us to date the Velp hoard of 1851, which stands out from related hoards thanks to its seven neck rings, just as the latter hoard is preeminent on account of its medallions. Remarkably, the large deposit of coins in Dortmund, Germany, found together with three gold neck rings, can also be dated to the beginning of the second quarter of the fifth century on the basis of a number of Frankish silver coins struck around 420–30, although

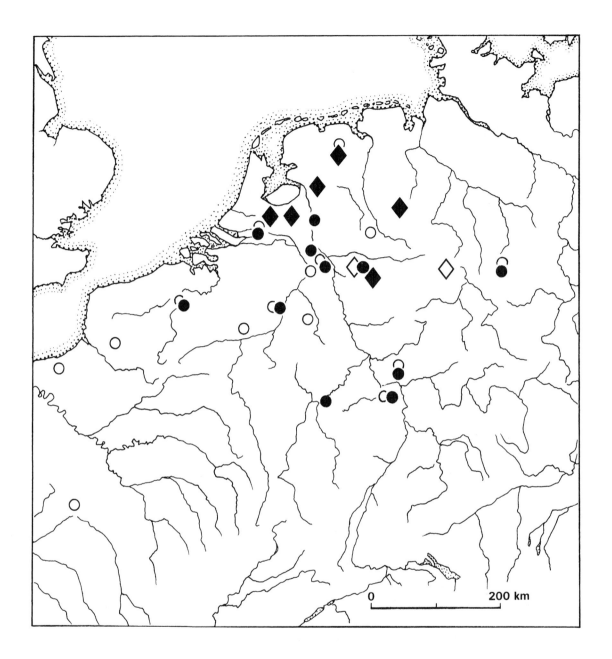

Fig. 22 The distribution of deposits of *solidi* and silver coins, with *t.p.* AD 393–406 ◯, with *t.p.* 407/8 or 11 ◆, and with *t.p.* 425 ●, together with the distribution of hoards from the first half of the fifth century, containing stamped or plain gold neck-rings ◇. (After Bloemers 1969, with additions.)

the series of 440 *solidi* found at the same site conclude with issues of Constantine III
(AD 407–11).

Certain commentators have attempted to see in the deposits from the right bank of
the Rhine evidence of internal conflicts amongst the Germanic peoples.[11] It is, however,
problematic to identify the hoards containing neck rings as votive offerings made –
only during the first half of the fifth century – by Frankish leaders in need of support
from the gods in the face of political instability, a permanent state of war and other
difficulties.[12] An interpretation of this kind is confounded by the fact that the deposits
all date from a very short time span. It is much more likely that they are hoards of
hidden treasure, given that arm bands were repeatedly buried together with the neck
bands, as were finger rings, coins and a fragment of a neck(?)-ring.

Even more conclusive is the fact that these deposits of neck-rings are located both
chronologically and geographically within a clearly defined zone of coin deposits,[13]
apparently dating from the same period (fig. 22). This zone of hoards extends in the
east to the collection of scrap silver and *solidi* found in Grossbodungen, in the west to
Schelde, and in the south to Trier and the area around Mainz and Wiesbaden. In Gaul
it does not extend beyond the Tournai–Mainz–Trier line, given that during this period
there are no deposits of precious metal coins to the south. Could it be that this striking
geographical concentration once corresponded to a chronological one?

Of the approximately seventeen series of coins which can be evaluated from these
deposits, five end around AD 393–4 and seven end with issues of 407 or 411; four
further deposits were laid down at the earliest in 425 or around 420–30. Two of these
deposits from the left bank of the Rhine, the neighbouring hoards of Menzelen (*terminus
post* [= *t.p.*] 411) and Xanten (*t.p.* 425), comprising over two hundred and a minimum
of four hundred *solidi* respectively, can be dated to the same historical context, irrespec-
tive of the difference of fourteen years between the dates of the most recent coins. This
may also apply to the majority of the other deposits, given that the importance of the
differing deposit dates should not be exaggerated in the light of the irregularities in
the supply of Roman currency, even in the case of coins struck in precious metals.
Given, for example, that the two hoards of neck rings and gold coins in Velp (*t.p.* 425),
the neck rings from Rhenen and the hoard of *solidi* from neighbouring Lienden (*t.p.* 407)
were excavated within 30 km of each other, it is hard to imagine that there could
have been a sequence of different catastrophes separated by only a few years. In the
light of these factors, and the high material value of the hoards, there is every reason
to believe that there is a single zone of precious metal deposits covering both groups.

If this zone of finds really dates from the beginning of the second quarter of the fifth
century, then it can be interpreted in a very different way than has been the case to
date. During this period, Aetius (died AD 454), the energetic commander of the western
Roman empire, succeeded in driving back the Franks in northern Gaul. Perhaps the
Germanic hoards represent Roman retaliatory measures in the northernmost border

regions of Gaul, those already occupied by the Franks, and preventative measures modelled on Valentinian I (365–75) in the form of attacks beyond the border of the empire amidst the chaos following the death of Honorius (423). As the 'last Roman', Aetius attempted during this period to prevent the Franks from gaining political control over northern Gaul, just as he took assertive action in 436 (this time successfully) against the Burgundian empire when it attempted to extend its sphere of influence further in the direction of Gaul.[14]

In Gaul – an important part of the Roman empire which had been swiftly and thoroughly romanised from the time of Caesar and Augustus – an enormous number of hoards of hidden treasure was buried in fear of the increasing campaigns of looting and pillage undertaken by both Germanic and native bands of robbers during the late third century. Apart from statuettes and other equipment from private, domestic shrines (*lararia*) they contain almost exclusively valuable objects of a secular nature. As well as numerous deposits of bronze coins, there are hoards of non-ferrous metal vessels and deposits of tools.[15] Deposits of gold and silver coins, as well as hoards of hidden treasure with fine silver tableware and equipment, are much rarer.[16]

Valuables continued to be buried after AD 300, but there are significant changes in the contents of the deposits. The wealthy middle stratum of the provincial population, which up until the fourth century had buried plainer treasure including bronze utensils, is less frequently represented in the hoards, suggesting that this section of society had become either decimated or impoverished. More modest deposits of bronze coins were buried until the mid-fourth century and later much more infrequently.

In the case of late antique and early medieval hoards of precious metals in Gaul,[17] current research has led to a remarkable discovery.

The famous silver treasure of Kaiseraugst on the Upper Rhine,[18] together with a few less opulent deposits of silverware and a considerable number of contemporaneous coin deposits,[19] mark out a clearly defined and short-lived zone of hoards (pl. 15). This phase coincides with the years in which Constantius II (AD 337–61), emperor of the eastern empire, attacked the usurper Magnentius (350–53) in his native Gaul with the help of Alamannic mercenaries, and finally succeeded in forcing him to surrender.

Curiously enough this zone of hoards, which can easily be explained in historical terms, is the last one known to us in Gaul dating from the long, turbulent period leading up to the end of the western Roman empire (AD 476). It is a well known tradition that the whole of Gaul became 'a single burning pyre' after the invasion and migration of the Vandals, Suevi and other Germanic peoples (406–7).[20] There are barely any archaeological traces of these dramatic events, about which we are informed through written documents; the only exceptions are a small number of deposits of bronze coins which may have been buried during this period.

The absence of a significant number of hoards of precious metals also characterises the reign of the Frankish founding king Clovis I (AD 482–511), although he was not able to bring either the other small Frankish kingdoms or the Toulouse-based kingdom of the Visigoths under his control without a struggle. The question is whether in Gaul, from c.350 into the sixth century, the indigenous, in some cases rich, senatorial families and the new Frankish upper social stratum had learnt their lesson from what had happened in the past and now secured their valuables in a different way. Were they able to keep the catastrophes at arm's length through payment or by some other means, if indeed these catastrophes really occurred?

From the period after AD 400 two small deposits of silver tableware from Toulouse and Monbadon near Bordeaux are known to us; they were discovered in the nineteenth century and thus, unfortunately, are insufficiently documented. These deposits can be attributed to the first half of the fifth century and may be associated with the events following the settling of Aquitaine by the Visigoths in 418. Moreover, three large silver dishes (*missoria*) from the Rhône valley also cannot be dated to the years, or indeed even the decades, around 400, but rather were buried separately in the course of the fifth and early sixth centuries.

Not until the early sixth century do we encounter once again further sporadic examples of gold coin deposits, first *solidi* and then, increasingly, *tremisses*, with the value of one third of a *solidus*.[21] In the coin deposit of Gourdon, south-west of Chalon-sur-Saône, two sacred vessels made of gold, a goblet and paten, were buried together with gold coins. Certain sixth-century hoards of coins, such as that at Gourdon, may well go back to the Frankish conquest of the kingdom of the Burgundians (AD 534), while others may have been buried during the course of internal Frankish conflicts.

There are also attested coin deposits from the seventh century, which consist almost entirely of *tremisses* (also known as *trientes*), normally so-called monetary strikings, which bear the name of the master of the mint (*monetarius*), and often also the name of the place for which he had struck the coin (pl. 16, fig. 23). Valuable objects are only buried with coins in a few exceptional cases.

It is notable that apart from these early medieval coin deposits there are barely any other contemporary hoards known to us in which silver tableware or jewellery in precious metals are buried. We know from written sources that in the Merovingian kingdom silver tableware was popular in the upper social stratum and in ecclesiastical circles. Moreover, gold jewellery is also known from the graves of wealthy women. Secular hoards of hidden treasure containing anything other than precious metal coins are, however, a rarity between AD 500 and 700, in Gaul as elsewhere.

During the third century, Roman Britain, unlike Gaul, had not thus far had to suffer Germanic invasions. During the fourth century plain vessels of non-ferrous metals or pewter were still being deposited. The notion that these late antique hoards – some more valuable than others – could perhaps be interpreted as ritual deposits has quite rightly been brought into question.[22]

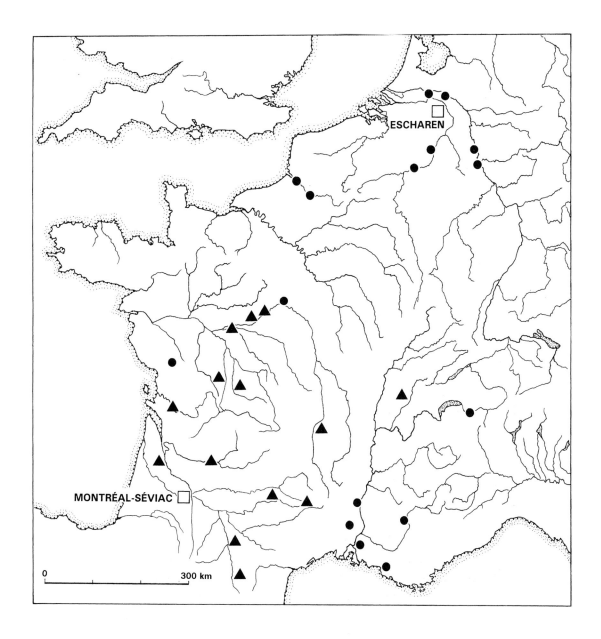

Fig. 23 Distribution of places where the gold coins found in the coin hoards of Montréal-Séviac ▲ and Escharen ● were struck. (After Toulouse and Lafaurie 1959/60.)

An ever increasing number of remarkably rich finds exists from the later period of Roman Britain. These contain silver vessels and utensils of high quality, gold jewellery or large quantities of gold or silver coins; it is not uncommon that two or three of these categories are found in one and the same hoard. In some deposits a further category of valuable objects has also been discovered – unworked silver in the form of ingots, either stamped or unstamped (fig. 24).

One of the earliest hoards with late antique silverware, from Water Newton, north-west of Cambridge,[23] is the only one in Britain whose contents – vessels and metal votive offerings with inscriptions and christograms – can be interpreted as being hidden treasure belonging to a Christian community. Indeed the Water Newton hoard is the oldest such deposit in the entire western Roman empire. All the other hoards of silver tableware, including the famous collection from Mildenhall, and many other valuable individual pieces which may well represent remains of hoards which once consisted of several parts, could have been buried by aristocratic families of the late antique empire.[24]

We also encounter extreme wealth in the treasure found in 1993 in Hoxne in Suffolk (pls. 31, 60).[25] Consisting of 19 exquisite pieces of gold jewellery, 98 spoons and other silver utensils and containers for use at table, together with 565 *solidi* and over 14,000 silver coins, it may well have been the most valuable possession of a noble family, to which we must mentally add the silverware which was not found with the other pieces but which, presumably, was buried at a different location.

According to the evidence provided by the unusually large number of contemporaneous coin deposits,[26] the majority of these rich finds appear to have been buried during the first half of the fifth century. Both the late hoards of silver and the most recent coin deposits are, to an unusual extent, clustered in one area, that of East Anglia and neighbouring regions. The question must therefore be asked whether these deposits do not in fact, for the most part, represent a zone of treasures for which there may be an historical explanation. It should be borne in mind that the findings here are entirely different from those in Gaul, where, despite the almost complete absence of hoards, the upper social stratum is unlikely to have been very much poorer.

With the exception of isolated coin deposits from the seventh century,[27] hardly any hoards of hidden treasure have come down to us from post-Roman Britain until the practice is renewed during the Viking campaigns of the ninth century.

A large number of the coin deposits buried on the Iberian peninsula, chiefly around AD 400[28] and in the years that followed, reflect the restless times following the invasions and settlement by the Suevi, as well as the influence of the Vandals, who settled in southern Spain before moving over to North Africa. On the other hand, hardly any contemporaneous hoards have been found containing silver tableware or jewellery. It is well known that the large Madrid *missorium* of Theodosius, made in the year 388, was found in one of these rare silver hoards, together with two bowls since lost (fig. 11).

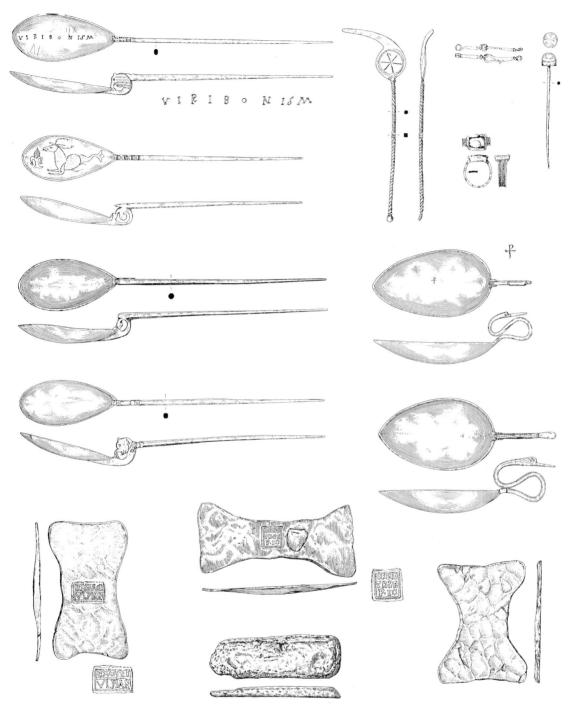

Fig. 24 Six (out of twelve) spoons, four ingots, toilet equipment and hair-pins in silver, together with a finger-ring and chain clasp in gold from the Canterbury, England, hoard; about AD 400. (After Johns and Potter 1985).

In the settlement of La Alcudia near Elche, a number of valuable pieces of jewellery were buried around 400, together with three gold coins and a small gold ingot.[29]

Only two kinds of hoard can be dated to the Visigothic period of the late fifth to seventh centuries. There are, first, a few coin hoards,[30] the deposition dates of which do not suggest any clear chronological correlation, with the exception of two or three which may have been hidden in the wake of the Arab invasions and conquests after AD 711.

The second, and smaller, group consists of three finds of hidden treasure containing sacred objects.[31] The famous votive crowns of the Visigothic kings and a number of extremely valuable votive crosses originate from the richest of them, the hoard of Guarrazar near Toledo (pl. 18);[32] the other two hoards also contained gold votive crosses, but of a much simpler design. To date no secular hoards from the Visigothic period have been found in which, besides money, rich families may have buried precious metal objects such as silver tableware and jewellery to keep them out of harm's way.

In Italy very few hoards of hidden treasure were buried in the period before AD 400. On the other hand, there are a remarkably large number dating from the fifth to the end of the seventh centuries. The earliest deposits, which are again a function of the unstable times at the beginning of the fifth century, include the hoard of jewellery from the Piazza della Consolazione in Rome,[33] as well as the substantial hidden treasure consisting of valuable silver tableware discovered in 1797 at the foot of the Esquiline Hill, which included silver caskets for cosmetics and clothing as well as silver ornaments and elements from a state carriage (fig. 25).[34]

In Upper Italy, a number of early coin deposits were buried between AD 400 and 500 which often also contained pieces of jewellery. As well as Mediterranean gold jewellery consisting of necklaces, finger rings and earrings set with stones (of the kind customarily found in other deposits) a pair of bow brooches belonging to a traditional costume worn by Ostrogothic women has come down to us from the hoard of hidden treasure in Reggio Emilia, dating from the late fifth century. Together with a gold Germanic neck ring found in the small hoard of Carpignago near Pavia,[35] these brooches reveal that among those burying valuable objects in Upper Italy at the time there must have been a number of people of Germanic origin.

In the period after AD 500 secular deposits of hidden treasure are outnumbered, as on the Iberian peninsula, by hoards in which vessels and utensils with a sacred provenance and function were buried; these include patens, chalices, spoons and wine sieves.[36] In the treasure of Galognano, which was buried 2.5 km from the church, there are vessels which according to their inscriptions were donated by the faithful (fig. 26). These Italian 'church treasures' were also buried to protect them against looters, who may have included Alamannic or Longobardic warriors.

As regards secular hidden treasure in the period after AD 500, we know only of

Fig. 25 Silver *patera* with Venus and cupids, and Adonis with a hunting dog. Esquiline hoard, Rome, Italy, fourth century.

Fig. 26 Silver chalices, patens and spoons from the hoard at Galognano, near Poggibonsi, Italy; sixth century. After von Hessen *et al.*, 1977.

isolated hoards of vessels, utensils or jewellery, such as the one found at Isola Rizza near Verona,[37] and a large number of deposits of gold coins.[38]

We would be expecting too much of the archaeological discoveries that have come down to us if we were to attempt to draw definitive conclusions solely on the basis of these finds as to the wealth and status of the upper strata of society caught up in the upheavals of the antique world. For too long now, archaeology has tended to rely exclusively on concrete findings for its conclusions, and has too infrequently posed the follow-up questions: why have these discoveries rather than others come down to us? Which valuable objects, such as coins, may well have once existed but not come down to us due to a lack of deposits? When was this the case and for what reason? The category of hidden treasure, a particularly erratic and unevenly preserved group of finds, has not to date been sufficiently questioned in this way.

The fact that neither sacred nor ritual deposits of precious metal objects or scrap silver were commonly buried in the soil of the western provinces of the Roman empire, and the fact that this practice did not escalate, demonstrates, on the one hand, the endurance of antique ideas and, on the other, the assimilation of the recently settled Germanic peoples and communities. It is open to question, however, whether certain objects recovered from underwater sites in Burgundy, comprising helmets, weapons and bowls made of non-precious metals, were not in fact fluvial sacrifices.[39]

Accordingly, wealth is archaeologically manifested primarily in precious metal objects and coins buried by private individuals or churches to safeguard them against danger. A single deposit of precious metal may well be the consequence of an isolated, individual action, the motivation for which is unlikely ever to come to light. More meaningful in this context are geographical and chronological concentrations of deposits. The occasion behind a clearly defined zone of hoards of this kind is not likely to be a series of discrete individual actions, but rather processes of paramount importance, which in certain circumstances we can interpret historically with the help of written evidence.[40]

Objects of precious metal retain their value, and those placed in safekeeping to escape danger would, as mentioned above, wherever possible be retrieved. Each hoard which was not recovered, and which has therefore come down to us, thus represents a genuine misfortune for its former owner, a catastrophe which, in many cases, he may well not himself have survived.

The famous late Roman silver treasure of Kaiseraugst provides us with an instructive example. Given that there are no known chronological or geographical counterparts to this valuable hoard of silver, the most recent object of which dates from the year AD 350, the supposition that the deposit was the result of a decisive, isolated incident suggests itself. However, three more modest deposits of copper coins were buried in the same fortress at the same time, obviously in the face of the same extreme danger. As a result we are presented with a set of hoards which can be dated very precisely to the years 351 or 352 and which can be explained in terms of the historically verifiable Alamannic invasions of the period. Comparable deposits of copper coins and contemporaneous strata of devastation have also been found in other areas of northern Switzerland and the Alsace, which clearly implies that this is not simply a local zone of hoards, but also a regional one.

The example of Kaiseraugst also illustrates another point: despite protection as unassailable as humanly possible – in a secure fortress – an unusually valuable set of possessions was buried, which, together with the distinctly more modest coin hoards, was never to be recovered. This is surprising given that the eminent former owner of the silver tableware must undoubtedly have had much better opportunities open to him at the time to recover his riches and, indeed, to protect them in the first place. For this reason we may surmise that the fortress was stormed and burned down, and that there was an abrupt discontinuity in the composition of its predominantly military inhabitants.

A single, unrecovered hoard can to some extent be seen as evidence of a sporadic or local discontinuity of ownership. On the other hand, geographical and chronological concentrations of hoards do not simply amount to several sporadic discontinuities, but may instead represent a widespread, or indeed complete, discontinuity in the owners concerned, or even of the entire social stratum to which they belonged. It must always be borne in mind that an unknown number of hoards may have immediately been expropriated by new owners, with the result that there may well have been a considerably greater number of discontinuities than we are able to ascertain today. At any rate there could not have been fewer.

Moving from banal explanations to more complicated ones, it is possible to formulate the following hypotheses regarding precious metal treasure remaining in the ground against the wishes of its former owners. In general, it can be stated that the more valuable the hoard of precious metal objects, the richer and more powerful the former owner is likely to have been. The higher his social standing within the ruling social stratum, the more likely it is that he would have been able to protect himself against low or medium level danger; certainly he would have been better protected than men of humbler means. In addition, members of the influential upper social stratum would have had a considerable number of contacts at their disposal and been informed more swiftly of new developments than the rest of the population. Someone who possessed great wealth was thus able to protect himself both sooner and more thoroughly than others, and it is possible that he was consequently also less frequently forced to bury his possessions.

From what has been said above it is possible to conclude, conversely, that the richer the hoard, the greater and more all-embracing the danger which precipitated the deposit. In the case of a widespread zone of hoards, and thus a widespread danger, the following should be borne in mind. A wealthy upper stratum of society will not expose itself and its assets to extreme danger over a number of years, let alone decades, but rather will respond with recourse to its extensive connections and varied opportunities for self-defence. Thus even in the case of precious metal deposits constituting a true zone one should not think in terms of a period of years separating them, but rather at most a few months. It is highly unlikely in the case of a region with a number of precious metal deposits proven archaeologically to be roughly contemporary – spanning perhaps ten years – that the deposits were buried at a rate of, for example, one a year. If during a particular period a high social stratum in one geographical area was unable to recover a large number of valuable hoards, it should be assumed that a major discontinuity rapidly overtook this stratum, enveloping its closest members and servants. Causes could include either wars or a powerful social revolution, which can lead to a swift replacement of one upper stratum of society by another.

It is undoubtedly the case that an impressive number of late antique and early medieval deposits of precious metals has come down to us. They prove that the transformation of the Roman world which was taking place at the time certainly also led to far-reaching changes amongst the wealthy upper social stratum in the western Roman empire. It is remarkable, however, how unevenly spread the hoards are, both chronologically and geographically, despite the fact that we can assume that overall there are comparable conditions of preservation across the board. There is nothing in Gaul, for example, which corresponds to the striking zone of hoards in Britain, which itself needs to be dated more specifically within the early part of the fifth century. Just as in the late fourth century, so also the events of AD 406, when the Vandals and other peoples apparently descended on the whole of Gaul, did not lead to an increase in the number of precious metal deposits.

In the Mediterranean countries it was above all the first half of the fifth century which appears to have been dominated by vigorous upheavals amongst the ranks of both the old and new wealthy upper social stratum. The frequency of hoards suggests that these upheavals lasted longer in Italy than on the Iberian peninsula. On the Iberian peninsula itself, ecclesiastical possessions, such as those found at Guarrazar, may well have been hidden from the advancing Arabs. Strangely enough, however, there is an almost complete absence of corresponding private deposits of valuables, not only around AD 700 but also earlier. This is also the case in Italy. On the other hand, hoards of coins are represented, which leads to the conclusion that this category of hoard, indicating a willingness to bury money, should be evaluated differently from the hiding of valuable silver tableware or jewellery.

It is clearly not coincidental that from the point of view of hoard discoveries the most marked discontinuities and upheavals should have occurred in the northernmost frontier regions of the Roman empire, in Britain and in the Lower Rhineland. Possessions also passed from hand to hand in other areas in which the newly arrived Germanic upper social stratum had to contend – not always peacefully – with the native population. The amalgamation and integration of these new, Germanic upper social strata and the installation of their political rule was, however, not as violent or tumultuous as was the case in the eastern part of Britain.

In the case of the Visigoths in Aquitaine (from AD 418), the Burgundians on the Rhône (from 443) and the Ostrogoths in Italy (after 489–90) we encounter peoples comprising a fair number of individuals born within the frontiers of the Roman empire who were more completely assimilated than their parents. And finally it should be emphasised that – in Gaul especially – the new Germanic and older native upper social stratum had learnt their lesson from the first violent confrontations and that, consequently, during a second phase, the redistribution of wealth occurred through the payment of ransoms, the assignment of property and, in the end, through the levying of taxes; former looters had become partners.

NOTES

1 Claude, 1973.

2 Painter, 1993.

3 Reece, 1988.

4 Geisslinger, 1967.

5 See the contribution by Alain Dierkens and Patrick Périn in this volume.

6 Geisslinger, 1984.

7 Hagberg, 1984; Headeager, 1991.

8 Nielsen *et al.*, 1994.

9 Johns and Potter, 1983; Munksgaard, 1987.

10 Curle, 1923.

11 Bolin, 1929; Zadoks-Josephus Jitta, 1976.

12 Heidinga, 1990.

13 Van der Vin, 1988; Kent, 1994.

14 Ewig, 1988.

15 Künzl, 1993.

16 *Trésors d'orfèvrerie* (exh. cat., Paris).

17 Baratte, 1993.

18 Cahn and Kaufmann-Heinimann, 1984.

19 Wigg, 1991.

20 Whittaker, 1995.

21 Grierson and Blackburn, 1986.

22 Johns, 1994.

23 Painter, 1977.

24 Painter, 1993.

25 Johns and Bland, 1993.

26 Archer, 1979.

27 Grierson and Blackburn, 1986.

28 Bost *et al.*, 1992.

29 Ramos Fernandez, 1975.

30 Barral i Altet, 1978.

31 Hübener, 1975.

32 Caillet, 1985.

33 Ross, 1965, vol. 2.

34 Shelton, 1981.

35 Degani 1959; *Milano* (exh. cat., Milan).

36 Hauser, 1992.

37 Von Hessen, 1968.

38 Ercolani Cocchi, 1992; Gorini, 1992.

39 Pauli, 1983; Schulze, 1984.

40 Reece, 1988.

ACKNOWLEDGEMENT

The author would like to thank Martin Brady for translating this paper.

Plate 1 (*Right*)
Notitia Dignitatum, a
corpus of documents
belonging to a late
Roman imperial
official; f. 141 depicts
the insignia of the
Master of Offices,
responsible for the
imperial arms
factories (*fabricae*)
which supplied the
regular army and
the *foederati*; from a
fifteenth-century
copy of a lost
Carolingian
manuscript formerly
in Speier Cathedral.
Oxford, Bodleian
Library, MS Canon
Misc. 378, f. 141r.

Plate 2 (*Far right*)
Gold cross-bow
brooch of the type
issued to the highest-
ranking military and
civil officials. Such
insignia were also
worn by barbarians
within the imperial
system, such as the
Vandal, Stilicho, (fig.
16) and the Frankish
king, Childeric I
(d.481/2). Palatine
Hill, Rome; fifth
century.

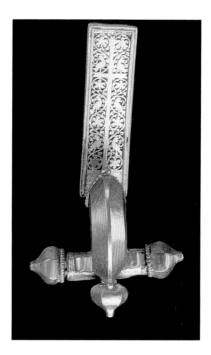

Plate 3 Byzantine-style jewellery from an Avaric woman's grave in the cemetery at Ozora (Kom Fejèr), Hungary, second half of the seventh century.

Plate 4 (*Opposite, above*)
Gilt-bronze and gold eagle brooches with
garnet and glass cloisonné and other
semi-precious stones; Tierra de Barros,
Badajoz, Spain. Visigothic, first quarter of
the sixth century.

Plate 5 (*Opposite, below*)
Gold, glass, mother-of-pearl and garnet
cloisonné brooches and buckle found with
eastern-style gold garment plaques; from a
Vandal woman's burial at Koudiat Zateur,
near Carthage, Tunisia; fifth century.

Plate 6 (*Below, left*)
Reverse of gold *solidus* of the Burgundian
king, Gundobad (*c.*AD 473–516). The
king's monogram is added to a Byzantine-
style reverse. (See also *Heirs of Rome*,
cat. 28.)

Plate 7 (*Right*)
Gold, onyx, glass and garnet cloisonné
fibula imitating a late Roman imperial
brooch. From Szilágy-Somlyó (Simleul-
Silvaniei) Romania; fourth century.

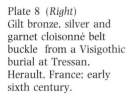

Plate 8 (*Right*)
Gilt bronze, silver and
garnet cloisonné belt
buckle from a Visigothic
burial at Tressan,
Herault, France; early
sixth century.

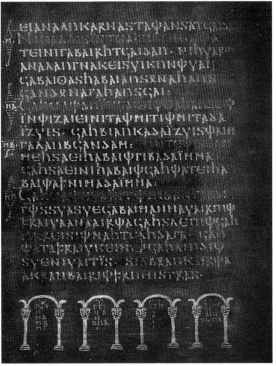

Plate 11 Pair of silver-gilt radiate brooches from a Longobard woman's grave. Grave 56, Szentendre, Hungary; mid-sixth century.

Plate 9 (*Above, left*) Mausoleum of Theodoric at Ravenna, Italy; begun AD 526.

Plate 10 (*Above, right*) The *Codex Argenteus*, f.97, a luxury edition of the bible in the Gothic language, written in silver on purple-dyed parchment, probably at Theoderic's command. Ravenna, early sixth century. Uppsala, University Library, UB DGI, f.97. (See *Heirs of Rome*, cat. 128.)

Plate 13 (*Right*) Three silver-gilt belt buckles from a votive hoard deposited in wetland at Ejsbol, Jutland, Denmark; fifth century.

Plate 12
Gold neck-ring,
arm-ring, and
finger-ring with
gold and garnet
cloisonné sword
fittings and buckles
in the 'Danubian'
style. Pouan, near
Troyes, France;
mid-fifth century.

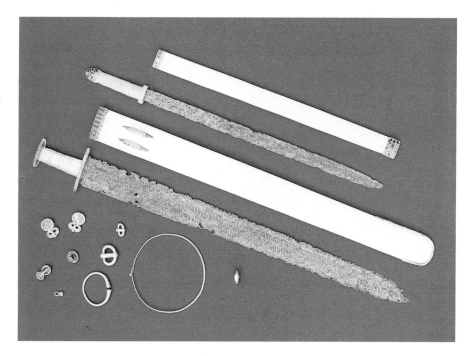

PLATES 14, 15

Plate 14 (*Opposite, above*)
Gold neck-rings and an arm ring found with 22 *solidi*, from a hoard at Beilen, Drenthe, Netherlands; *c.*AD 400.

Plate 15 (*Opposite, below*)
The so-called Ariadne dish, silver and niello, from the Kaiseraugst, Switzerland, silver hoard; deposited AD 350–1.

Plate 16 *Tremisses* with mint-names from around AD 600 and after, from the coin hoard of Montréal-Séviac, Gers, France.

Plate 17 Obverse and reverse of one of two gold medallions set with *multipla* of Galla Placidia from the first Velp hoard, Gelderland, Netherlands; *c.*AD 450.

Plate 18 (*Left*)
Votive crown with hanging cross and pendants, some of them forming the latinised name of the Visigothic king Recceswinth (r.653–672). The golden crown is also embellished with garnets, sapphires, pearls and other semi-precious stones. From the hoard of votive crowns and crosses found at Guarrazar near Toledo, Spain. This magnificent symbol of Christian kingship combines Germanic and Byzantine techniques and motifs in a powerfully transformational image.

Plate 19 (*Opposite, above*)
Purse-lid (originally of ivory or bone) with gold, garnet and glass cloisonné mounts, together with thirty-seven Merovingian gold coins, two billets and three blanks found within it. From the Mound I ship-burial at Sutton Hoo, Suffolk, England; first quarter of the seventh century.

Plate 20 (*Opposite, below*)
Imported Byzantine silk found in the twelfth-century shrine of St. Servatius at Tongeren, depicting the *dioscuroi*, the heavenly twins who were patrons of the hippodrome at Constantinople; eighth century.

PLATE 18

PLATES 21,22

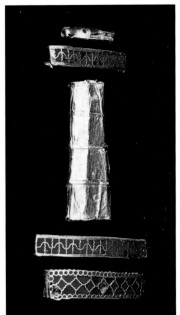

Plate 21 (*Opposite, above*)
Divers excavating amphorae from the 'Heliopolis I' shipwreck, Ile du Levant, Var, France. The amphorae, which carried wine, are of a type made in Tunisia during the fourth to fifth century.

Plate 22 (*Opposite, below*)
Aerial view of the Viking-age trading site at Hedeby (Haithabu), Germany, founded in the ninth century.

Plate 23 (*Above*)
Tintagel, Cornwall, view of the high-status Celtic site; sixth century. (See also *Heirs of Rome*, cat. 12.)

Plate 24 (*Above, right*)
Gold and garnet cloisonné sword fittings from the burial of Childeric I (d.481/2), Tournai, Belgium.

Plate 25 (*Right*)
Glass bucket with silver handle, wheel-cut with a Dionysiac scene. From the Treasury of San Marco, Venice, Italy; fourth century.

Plate 29 Dome mosaic, with the martyr St. Demetrios shown in secular dress between the prefect Leontios and Bishop Johannes; Hagios Demetrios, Thessaloniki, AD 629–43.

Plate 26 (*Opposite, above*) Mosaic showing the emperor Justinian, Archbishop Maximianus and members of the court; San Vitale, Ravenna, Italy; AD 546–7.

Plate 27 (*Opposite, below left*) Interior of Hagia Sophia, Istanbul; AD 532–7.

Plate 28 (*Opposite, below right*) Ivory diptych panel of an archangel; Constantinople, second quarter of the sixth century.

Plate 30
Folio with biblical scenes from the so-called Augustine Gospels, an Italian gospel book of the kind familiar to the first Roman missionaries to England, such as St. Augustine. The Gospels were at Canterbury until the Reformation. Italian, late sixth century. (Cambridge, Corpus Christi College, MS 286 f.125r.) (See *Heirs of Rome*, cat. 92.)

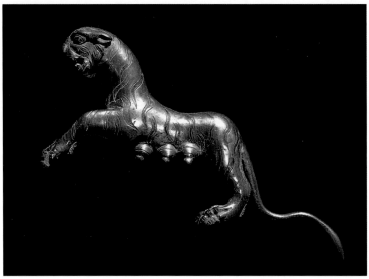

Plate 31
Silver gilt and niello tigress from the Hoxne hoard, Suffolk, England; early fifth century. A late antique leaping animal of this kind must have played a part in establishing the model for this form of the evangelist symbol (c.f. pl.32).

Plate 32 (*Above*)
The lion, symbol of St. Mark, from the Echternach Gospels; Anglo-Saxon (Northumbria), eighth century. (Paris, Bibliothèque Nationale, Ms lat. 9389, f. 75v.)

Plate 33 (*Above, right*)
Frontispiece from a Visigothic recension of the *Codex Theodosianus*, showing Theodosius II as a law-giver in the Mosaic tradition; the imperial image is modified by the horns traditionally given to Moses. The veiled hands of the officials holding the law code also recall images of the Scriptures held in veiled hands; eighth century. (Leiden, Public Library, BPL 114.)

Plate 34 (*Right*)
The Vienna Dioskurides; dedication miniature depicting the Byzantine princess Anicia Juliana between personifications of Magnanimity and Prudence; AD 512–13. (Vienna, Osterreichischen Nationalbibliothek, Cod. Vindob. Med. graec. 1 f. 6v.)

Plate 35 (*Left*)
The Franks Casket; general
view of this whale bone
box, showing the front
panel with parallel scenes
from the legend of Weland
the Smith and the
Adoration of the Magi.
Anglo-Saxon
(Northumbria); first half of
the eighth century. (*See
Heirs of Rome*, cat. 116.)

Plate 36 (*Below*)
Mosaic showing the
empress Theodora and her
court; San Vitale, Ravenna,
Italy; AD 546–47.

Routes of change: Production and distribution in the West (5th-8th century)

Stéphane Lebecq

It was the Belgian historian Henri Pirenne who first put forward an interpretation of the economic transformation of western Europe between late antiquity and the early medieval period. In his opinion, the late Roman economy, based on long-distance trade and linked by urban markets scattered throughout the empire, continued until the late seventh/early eighth century, by which time the Arab conquest had effectively disrupted all contact by the west with the Mediterranean world, resulting in a shift in economic focus from the south to the north, and compelling individual communities to fall back on their own resources. Since this model was defined earlier this century, in a series of articles which he subsequently developed into a book,[1] it has stimulated a great deal of research among medieval economic historians. An anthropological approach now prevails, by which historians attempt to produce a more rounded view of the economic and social realities of early medieval society, looking at its members as both producers and consumers in the context of their material culture, their environment and their social systems. Documentary sources, hitherto dismissed as being of limited value, have been re-examined, and found to be less anaemic than previously thought; advances in numismatic studies have substantially increased our knowledge; and above all the enormous contribution made by archaeology and its satellite sciences has transformed our view. Historians do not disagree with Pirenne's basic chronology, but looking at all the possible spatial and chronological variables, as they continue to study the principal production systems and the long-distance exchange mechanisms which formed the heart of his thesis, it is his estimation of the volume of trade and his explanations for it which need to be reassessed.

At first glance, one can indeed agree with Pirenne that the late antique economy continued well into the seventh century, and in particular that the Mediterranean remained until then the principal vector of exchange between east and west. The *Life of John of Cyprus*, known as John the Almoner, patriarch of Alexandria (AD 610–19), tells us in the section added by Leontios of Neapolis, shortly after the death of the saint, of a merchant ship loaded with 20,000 bushels of corn which sailed from Alexandria to the 'islands of Britain' (the 'Cassiterides' of the Greeks) in twenty days, and returned carrying gold and tin. The reader might dismiss the account as mere fable were it not for several sites in western Britain, such as the royal foundations at Garranes and Clogher in Ireland, the fortress of Dinas Powys in Wales or the high-status site at Tintagel in Cornwall (situated close to tin mines which supplied the raw material for bronzeworking over several centuries) (pl. 23), all sites where archaeologists have found a significant quantity of jars and amphorae from Tunisia, the Aegean and the eastern Mediterranean in levels dated to the fifth to seventh centuries. Elsewhere the same types of amphorae have been found at Carthage, Rome, Luni (very near the Carrara marble quarries), Marseille, and all along the coast of the Iberian peninsula, from Ampurias in Catalonia to Gijon in Asturias.

So according to the evidence, the ports of the western Mediterranean remained in contact with the east and with North Africa. It is also clear that the reconquest by Byzantium during the course of the sixth century of Ostrogothic Italy, of Vandal Africa and of part of Visigothic Spain reinforced the connections between them. Documentary sources such as the letters of Gregory the Great confirm the continuity of economic relations which, at the end of the sixth century, still united Rome to Sicily and to North Africa, where Carthage played an important pivotal role between the east and west Mediterranean. The other works of Gregory the Great, those of Cassiodorus, the Byzantine chronicles and saints' lives all suggest not only the coming and going of ships between the ports of southern Italy, but also between Ravenna and the nascent Commachio and Venice, and the great cities of the eastern Mediterranean like Constantinople and Alexandria. And if the *War Against the Vandals* by Procopius of Caesarea highlights the links which united Spain (for example Seville), to North Africa (for example Carthage), the law code drawn up a century later in AD 654 for King Recceswinth accorded special status to the *transmarinis negotiatoribus* who ensured overseas contacts for the Visigothic kingdom of Spain.

The celebrated *Histories* of Gregory of Tours, written towards the end of the sixth century, also give the impression that the port of Marseille remained the gateway to the Mediterranean. Ships came there from Spain, from Italy (Ostia), from Africa (Carthage again) and from the east (Constantinople). They were carrying jars containing wine, *garum* (a condiment made from fish) but chiefly olive oil. Archaeology has confirmed the information to be found in the *Histories* on all counts: not only in Marseille itself, where local workshops and warehouses persisted through the sixth century, and where quays inherited from the Romans were refurbished around AD 500, and again about 600, but also in the sea around the harbour, where underwater archaeology has revealed wrecks like the ship found at Saint Gervais, opposite Fos-sur-Mer, and La Palu, opposite the island of Port Cros (pl. 21). The first wreck, discovered in 1978, and dated to the beginning of the seventh century, yielded African amphorae containing pitch and corn. The second, excavated in 1993–4, and dated to the second half of the sixth century, had several amphorae of eastern origin, but its main cargo was amphorae from Africa filled with oil and *garum*.

As well as Gregory of Tours, seventh-century diplomatic sources reveal the sort of commercial activity which animated the port of Marseille and others along the coast

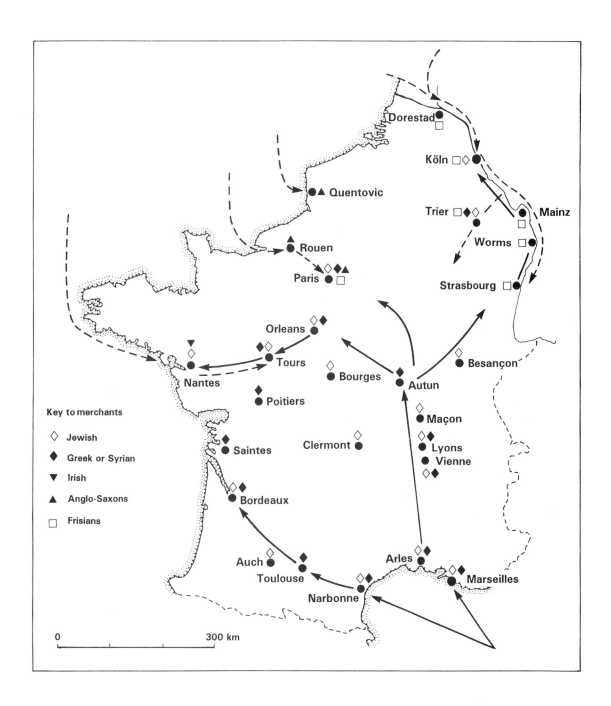

Fig. 27 Map showing recorded activity of foreign merchants in Gaul, fifth–ninth centuries.

Key to merchants

◇ Jewish
◆ Greek or Syrian
▼ Irish
▲ Anglo-Saxons
☐ Frisians

Dorestad
Köln
Trier
Mainz
Worms
Strasbourg
Quentovic
Rouen
Paris
Orleans
Tours
Nantes
Bourges
Autun
Besançon
Poitiers
Maçon
Clermont
Lyons
Vienne
Saintes
Bordeaux
Auch
Toulouse
Arles
Marseilles
Narbonne

0   300 km

of Mediterranean Gaul, such as Fos, Toulon and Narbonne. In this region, particularly at Marseille and Fos, important customs offices existed which kept the portion of goods deducted by the fiscal authorities in *cellaria fisci*. The ports were equally frequented by independent merchants, some of whom worked for traders dispersed over a vast hinterland (Gregory of Tours mentions a Jewish merchant of Paris who did business with a fellow-Jew from Marseille), as well as those sent from the great ecclesiastical institutions of the north, such as the monasteries of Corbie and Saint Denis, which sometimes obtained from the king the right to draw an income from the warehouses (fig. 21).

So we are afforded a glimpse of the coming and goings of ships, and of carts or mule convoys, going back up into Gaul and the other regions of the west, following internal trade routes, distributing not only such indispensable products as corn, wine, oil or even salt from the Mediterranean or the Atlantic, but also luxury items, the presence of which is revealed less by documentary sources than by archaeological finds and the contents of church treasuries. Among these we note first of all the gold coins (*solidi* and their smaller denominations, *semisses* and *trientes*, or *tremisses*, which are more widely distributed), whether of Byzantine origin or western copies of eastern coins. These remained virtually the only monetary unit in circulation in the west during the fourth to seventh centuries, making the Byzantine standard (the *byzantium* or besant), as Roberto Lopez has pointed out,[2] the equivalent of the modern dollar in the early Middle Ages. Spices, exotic fruits and essential oils, listed in customs' privileges given to certain churches, also come into this category, as does silk, which occasionally survives in high-status burials (pl. 20). We should also note the traffic in Egyptian papyrus which continued to be used by western chanceries until well into the seventh century (fig. 28), as well as the metal vessels of eastern Mediterranean origin which have been discovered at several sites including the ship-burial in Mound 1 at Sutton Hoo in Suffolk (fig. 29).

The example of Sutton Hoo should make us circumspect. Does the presence of the silver tableware found in the great ship-burial reflect mercantile activity? Surely not. Even the small group of gold coins found beneath the purse-lid (thirty-seven *tremisses* struck at thirty-seven different Gaulish mints, as well as three coin blanks and two miniature ingots) have all the characteristics of an artificial collection, perhaps, as Grierson suggests,[3] put together to pay the forty oarsmen or ferrymen of the soul of the dead man to another world (pl. 19). Over and above their funerary significance, the items accumulated in this obviously high-status burial should be interpreted in a political or diplomatic sense, rather than in an economic one. And it is not just the case of Sutton Hoo. So many coins of distant origin, or objects of all kinds found in burials, could not have been the result of trade, but represent all sorts of contact between the producer and the ultimate recipient: diplomatic gifts, presents given to celebrate kinship or marriage, or the reciprocal gift-exchange favoured by barbarian peoples.

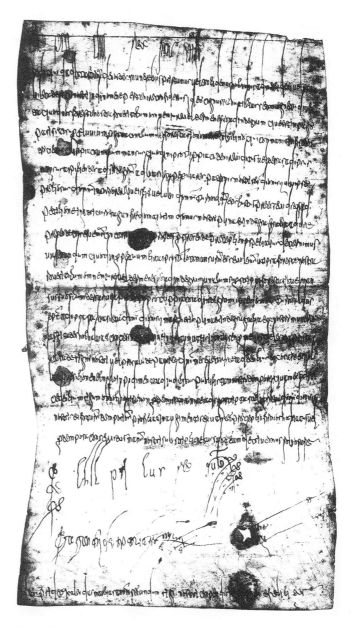

Fig. 28 Papyrus diploma of Chilperic II granting the forest of
Rouvray and forest rights at Saint-Ouen to the Abbey of
Saint-Denis at Paris, issued at Compiègne, 28 February AD 717.
Paris Archives Nationales, K4, no. 3 717.

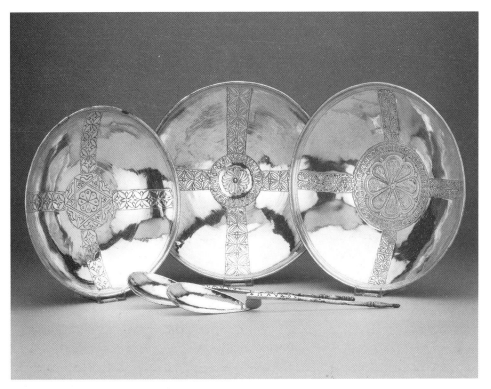

Fig. 29 Silver bowls from the set of ten, and a pair of silver spoons of eastern Mediterranean origin, from the early seventh-century Mound 1 ship burial at Sutton Hoo, Suffolk, England.

It is not even certain if, when they came into the empire, barbarian tribes were familiar with the practice of monetary exchange, as is shown by the number of scales and weights intended to weigh precious metal which have been found in Germanic contexts on its periphery, and in regions where barbarian presence was strongest, as detailed by Joachim Werner and Heiko Steuer.[4] The *wergilds* or compensation payments often found in barbarian law codes, such as the seventh-century *Lex Ribvaria* (the law code of the Rhineland Franks), state that whoever had to pay compensation for a murder could give a bullock instead of two gold *solidi*, a cow for one *solidus* and a horse for six *solidi*. A sword and its scabbard were judged to be worth eight *solidi*, a cuirass was valued at twelve *solidi*, a helmet at six and a shield and a spear at two, and so on. From this perspective, one can conclude that a major part of distribution of goods was based on barter, and that recourse to precious metals was only to make up the balance.

And exchange must have very often taken place within a limited network, for example that of a great estate. This is clearly the case with regard to properties owned by major religious institutions, the result of donations from various sources, where the complementary products from properties with different specialisations were brought together at the estate centre after the harvest. Then again, exchange must also have occurred within a network restricted to a very local horizon. It is thus tempting to interpret Grave 10 at Hérouvillette (Calvados), the so-called 'Smith's Grave', as that of a freeman (on account of a number of weapons found with him) who sold his services to members of his immediate community, as well as to neighbouring communities, since there were several coins in the grave as well as a pair of scales enabling him to weigh the metal. He was an especially well-equipped artisan, as he was buried with his tools, including hammers, knives, pincers, files and tweezers, together with crucibles and scrap metal.

The spatial distribution of products – metalwork, but above all pottery – made by craftsmen strongly suggests that most of them were distributed within a relatively small area, as we see with the hand-made pottery on the borders of Champagne and Picardy, in Flanders, in the Campine district, in Limbourg and in the western Rhineland. And while so-called 'Anglo-Saxon' pots have been found at such sites as Waben (Ponthieu), or in Flanders at Oudenberg, it is the archaeologists' view that they were not imported, but rather manufactured on site by Anglo-Saxon potters.

It is therefore likely that the supposed extensive Mediterranean trade which continued until the seventh century was nothing more than a secondary process, where a few merchants, principally of eastern origin, or certain sailors who were familiar with ancient routes, provided, at high cost, supplies for a number of old families claiming senatorial descent, barbarian parvenus eager to improve their social standing and churches anxious to celebrate divine worship in a sumptuous manner.

And what of the 'great trade of the North' which appears to have come into being in the seventh century, and to have contributed to the shift in the centre of gravity of the western economy to northern Europe in the centuries that followed? If most of the peoples of the west at the beginning of the seventh century still lived within the economic orbit of the Mediterranean, and expressed this dependence by the exclusive minting of gold *solidi* in the form of copies of Byzantine *solidi*, and above all of Byzantine *tremisses*, the maritime peoples of the north (Celts, Anglo-Saxons and Frisians) around AD 600 slowly and systematically began to exploit sea-routes which hitherto had only been used sporadically, thus opening up the possibility of long-distance trade (fig. 30). They restored several ports used by the Romans at the height of the empire, or more often used the immediate area nearby (as at Nantes, Rouen and London), but above all they developed new harbours such as that at Walcheren/Domburg in Zeeland, where a great many coins have been found not only from the Continent but also from England; or Ipswich in Suffolk, which has yielded substantial amounts of pottery from south-eastern England, northern Gaul and the Frisian Rhineland.

The impetus was thus provided for the proliferation of new trading ports, called

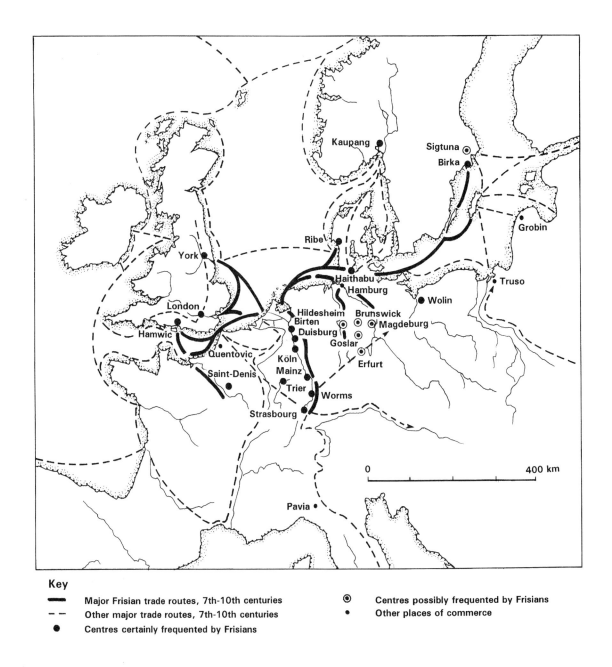

Fig. 30 Map showing Frisian trade in the west, seventh–tenth centuries A D.

vicus in Latin, a word which occurs in numerous toponyms such as *-wich, -wic, -wijk* or *-wig*, and which are generally known as *wics*. In England these included not only the suburbs of London and York, respectively rechristened Lundenwic and Eoforwic, but also Sandwich, Fordwich and above all Hamwih on the site of the future Southampton, where excavations have shown that occupation begins again at the end of the seventh century. In northern Gaul it was Quentovic, at the mouth of the Canche estuary, on the left bank of the river at the foot of the plateau of Montreuil-sur-Mer, which grew up during the course of the seventh century. Situated at the head of the Rhine delta, at the exact point where its waters divide into the river Lek westwards towards the British Isles, and into the Kromme Rijn and the Oude Rijn in a northerly direction towards Scandinavia, was Dorestad, which is mentioned in documentary sources from AD 690 to 695, although archaeological excavation and the numismatic evidence suggest it developed somewhat earlier in the seventh century. Finally, on the Jutland peninsula, there was Ribe, on the western coast, founded around 700, and Haithabu (or more accurately Sliasthorpe or Sliaswich), according to the first mention in the sources, on the Baltic coast, established around 750 (pl. 22). Both of these provided a base for the first contacts established between westerners and the Scandinavian world.

This spread of new trading places, of which only the most important have been highlighted, is very instructive. Most of them were totally empirical in origin, due to the initiative of maritime communities, which, no doubt encouraged by the stabilisation of society along the North Sea littoral after centuries of migration and piracy, from then on threw themselves into trading activity. Eventually they maintained particularly sheltered harbours along sandy coasts, generally situated at the mouths of estuaries or on the shores of sounds, where their clinker-built boats with their broad, flat keel-planks could be easily beached, giving protection to what must initially have been modest trading posts, sometimes used only on a seasonal basis. It is in such a context that we should view the apparently Anglo-Saxon origin of Quentovic, which began as a simple base on the Continent for traders from the British Isles, the exclusively Frisian origin of Dorestad (the first development of which owed nothing whatsoever to the Franks) and the impetus given to the first establishment of the southern settlement of Sliaswich/Haithabu by Frisians and/or Anglo-Saxons. If certain *wics*, such as Hamwih and Ribe, which grew up under the control of Anglo-Saxon and Danish kings, appear to have been planned from the outset, suggesting that they were publicly organised, and possibly royal foundations, it is certain that those wielding power in the hinterland, notably the kings, quickly took an interest in the development of those sites which had come into existence outside their jurisdiction, for example in carrying out the effective re-establishment of Dorestad in AD 675 and Sliaswich/Haithabu at the beginning of the ninth century. In each case they imposed their authority by means of an agent known as a *gerefa, praepositus, procurator* or *prefectus*, who was, according to the sources, responsible for keeping order, for the lucrative collection of customs duty – estimated at 10 per cent of the value of goods at sites like Quentovic and Dorestad – for deciding disputes between merchants and possibly controlling the minting of coins.

But the contact between the maritime peoples of the north and the continental hinterland was not limited to the ports along the North Sea coast. From around AD 700, perhaps even earlier, there is evidence for Anglo-Saxons, chiefly from Wessex, sailing up the Seine and regularly frequenting the fairs which, since their foundation by the Frankish king Dagobert in 634–5, the monks of Saint Denis organised each year on 9 October, the feast day of their patron saint, to sell their wine from the previous year's grape-harvest. At the same time Frisians, sailing up the Rhine and the Moselle, established colonies in numerous cities, sometimes within the city walls, sometimes in the protective shadow of the great suburban churches, in order to stock up on weapons, pottery, wine, corn, rare stones such as Eifel lava, suitable for making millstones, or wood, which their country, a vast maritime plain formed of recent alluvial deposits, decidedly lacked. Such settlements grew up at Cologne, in the shadow of the Church of St. Géréon; at Trier by the Church of St. Maximin; at Mainz (where they occupied the *optimum partem civitatis* – the 'best part of the town'); at Worms (where they appear to have monopolised the export of wine); and finally at Strasbourg, where the poet Ermoldus Nigellus reproached them towards 826 with having secured a dominant position, and emptying Alsace of all its raw materials.

One of the essential facts of European numismatic history is that the Anglo-Saxons and the Frisians, who began to mint their first coins around AD 600 (imitations of the gold *tremisses* struck in Gaul), were responsible around 670–80 for the spread of small silver coins with their barbarous designs which historians continue to describe incorrectly as *sceattas*, although they were in fact prototypes of pennies or medieval deniers. Confirming the difficulties the west had in renewing its gold reserves, and above all far better adapted for use in exchanges of which the value had diminished over the centuries, this coinage was such a success that it soon became widespread and was even copied in the south; it led to the rejuvenation of almost the whole of the west in the second half of the eighth century, and resulted in the exclusive use of silver coin. From the advent of the Carolingians, when it had already come to an end, and for the five centuries that followed, no gold coin was minted in the Frankish kingdom. And soon the silver denier, as witnessed both by the rents recorded in the polyptychs, and above all by numerous coin finds, had infiltrated everywhere, even to the farthest corners of the country.

It seems that the northern maritime peoples who had previously used the markets of the south turned their attention more and more towards those of the north, acting as purveyors of raw materials and potential buyers of estate surpluses, which a certain increase in agricultural production had made more substantial. So the great landowners of northern Gaul and Rhineland Germany sought to establish themselves at sea, a distinct possibility in the stimulating environment provided by the *wics*. The example of Quentovic and of the lower Canche valley is particularly illuminating: not only did the nearby abbeys of Centula/St. Riquier, St. Bertin and St. Vaast wish to acquire property in the *wic* itself, or in its immediate area, but monasteries further away, such as Ferrières-en-Gâtinais and Fontenelle/Saint-Wandrille (which could, after all, take advantage of its own harbour in the lower Seine valley), acquired churches there. Why were these great Neustrian institutions so eager to secure a foothold on the banks of the Canche? It is the polyptych of Saint-Germain-des-Prés which provides the answer. This great Parisian establishment, which possessed a *villa supra mare* at Quillebeuf on the Seine estuary, but which had no property at Quentovic itself, demanded from its men at Villemeult in the Beauce, and at Combs-La Ville in the Brie region, periodical transport to the *wic* on the Canche; doubtless the exemption from tolls (which the monastery had been granted by Charlemagne in AD 779) meant that these monks could sell part of their estate surplus there, and find an import market capable of providing them with a return cargo which, after all, might be anything from raw materials such as the minerals from Britain which are mentioned here and there in texts, to the religious books which the Anglo-Saxon *scriptoria* were producing in large quantities.

In such a way one can consider that the first burgeoning of a north European

Fig. 31 Anglo-Saxon toll charter of King Aethelbald of Mercia, AD 733/4, granting toll due on one ship at London to the bishop and church of St. Andrew at Rochester; copy and confirmation of 844/5. BL, Cotton Charter xvii.I (see also pp. 231–2).

merchant-based economy during the seventh to ninth centuries, which made itself felt even in the countryside, resulted, at least in part, from the combination of two factors: first, the dynamism of the interior, fuelled by the return of agricultural growth since the third century, supported by a powerful aristocracy and given impetus by the peace during the Carolingian period; and second, the dynamism of the maritime milieu which assured it not only the perspective of unhoped-for expansion, soon to extend to the Baltic world and Scandinavia, but also the possibility of financial remuneration in silver coinage which was much better adapted to the volume and the value of trade. In the end, it is not only silver that replaces gold as a method of payment, with greater economic efficiency, but also parchment which replaces papyrus as writing material (fig. 31), wax which replaces olive oil as a means of lighting, and so on until walrus ivory replaces elephant ivory in artists' workshops.

As Pirenne saw it, the western centre of gravity therefore shifted from the south towards the north, and the role previously performed by the Mediterranean was taken over by the North Sea which, over the course of several centuries, became the principal intermediary for long-distance exchange and, by opening up commerce with the Baltic, paved the way for communicating with the east by new routes. Was this phenomenon caused by the Arab conquest? Apparently not. Mediterranean trade had started to falter several centuries previously, and the repeated outbreaks of plague which devastated the west at the end of the sixth and in the seventh century, and which certainly affected the southern regions of Europe through its repeated outbursts more deeply than those in the north, perhaps succeeded in disrupting it further. That was the precise moment when, after centuries of instability, the seafaring peoples of the north came to life commercially and began to penetrate the markets of Europe, above all those throughout south-eastern Britain, and in Neustria, Austrasia and Germany. It is indisputable that these new markets were won by the beginnings of economic growth achieved by kings careful to maintain peace and public order, by a dynamic aristocracy and by a flourishing peasantry.

NOTES

1 Pirenne, 1939.
2 Lopez, 1951, II, 209–34.
3 Grierson, 1979
4 Werner, 1954; Steuer 1987, 405–527.

ACKNOWLEDGEMENT

The author would like to thank Cathy Haith who translated this paper.

Death and burial in Gaul and Germania, 4th-8th century

Alain Dierkens and Patrick Périn

Among the most revealing changes in mentality that occurred between late antiquity and the early Middle Ages, those in attitudes towards death (specifically, in burial rites and the organisation of cemeteries) are perhaps the best known. A brief comparison of two 'normal' graves – one at the beginning of the Roman empire, the other dating to the eighth century – will be sufficient to indicate the extent of the change. The typical grave of the early empire is a cremation, situated in an *extra muros* cemetery, or in any case outside the settlement, with the ashes of the deceased accompanied by various grave goods. The medieval grave, on the other hand, is an inhumation in which the dead person is buried naked in a shroud, normally with an east–west orientation, with no grave goods; the medieval cemetery grew up around the church, itself more often than not built in the centre of the village, or *intra muros*.

The development sketched out here is inevitably somewhat distorted, for the situation was not uniform throughout the Roman empire, and in the kingdoms which succeeded it; the intermediate stages varied considerably in their nature and chronology according to whether the cemeteries were in the town or in the countryside, in the eastern Mediterranean or in the western part of the empire. In this short contribution to a book that covers an immense enterprise, taking into account the whole of the Roman empire as well as areas beyond the Rhine–Danube *limes*, it is not possible to outline anything but general trends. We have therefore deliberately chosen to concentrate our attention on Gaul and Germania, that is to say the area between the Alps, the Pyrenees and the Rhine.

In order to understand the development of burial rites between the fourth and eighth centuries, it is necessary to take into account both Roman traditions and the contributions of others, notably those of the Germanic peoples, whilst simultaneously bearing in mind the religious factor, especially Christianity after it became the state religion under Theodosius. The christianisation of the Roman empire and of the Germanic kingdoms played a major role in this evolution, but is insufficient on its own to explain all the nuances and shifts in emphasis, since the abandonment of cremation for inhumation in the later empire affected pagans as much as Christians. Moreover, the reasons for the presence of abundant grave goods in certain burials are often social and not religious.

When we consider the question of graves and cemeteries of late antiquity and the early Middle Ages, we cannot escape the fact that there are certain limits to the knowledge to be gained from archaeology. The first concerns the possibility even of dating graves, which – unless of course we know the identity of the dead person – relies upon objects or other evidence (such as paintings or inscriptions) associated with the burial. Absolute dating, for example by dendrochronology or the less precise method of radiocarbon dating, is rarely possible, and we have to be content, more often than not, with good approximations. Dating methods, particularly typological studies, have been considerably refined since the pioneering work of such scholars as Werner,[1] and Böhner,[2] using matrices, or, more recently, computer analysis. Nonetheless, a margin of error still remains, which should make us cautious. The problem is particularly acute when we are confronted with graves completely devoid of grave goods, and therefore, apart from some exceptions, not susceptible to dating. The absence of grave goods may be a reflection of wealth or social status, but may also represent philosophical or religious beliefs that emphasised the immateriality of the soul or made a distinction between the status of the deceased in the afterlife from that here on earth. The historian is thus frequently incapable of dating the abandonment of a burial ground for a cemetery developing around a church; similarly the hundreds of unfurnished graves found in cemeteries belonging to parish churches could date to any period between the eighth and eighteenth centuries.

Another problem stems from the variability of the archaeological record. It is easy to understand that cemeteries located outside a village or town centre are more likely to have survived – apart from those destroyed by road-building, railway construction or housing developments – than those in major residential areas. Many of the latter had to be abandoned to comply with public health measures at the end of the eighteenth and beginning of the nineteenth centuries, and the sites have subsequently been redeveloped. Similarly, the excavation of *extra muros* burial grounds is generally more extensive than that undertaken on urban sites, where cemeteries often only come to light during the course of building works, and are perforce fragmentary. Thus the very nature of the archaeological record favours our understanding of rural or peripheral cemeteries rather than urban, central ones. This contrast is further amplified by the fact that the richest archaeological finds (and those of most interest to museums or private collectors) tend to occur in outlying cemeteries – in this case for reasons of chronology and fashion. In addition, many cemeteries belonging to parish churches – where space is at a premium – have been disturbed by later burials, or have been partially destroyed by the enlargement or refurbishment of the church.

A third difficulty is the interpretation of religious faith or attitudes from information provided by archaeological excavation. How far is it possible to extrapolate beliefs from material remains? The natural desire of archaeologists to explain everything only too often leads them to favour one or other religious or cultural hypothesis, and to view every problem in terms of paganism or Christianity. However, on many issues that seem nowadays to be essential, the Church held no original or exclusive views before the Middle Ages or even comparatively recent times; and often it did not interfere in the organisation of burials, considering this to be the province of the family or society in general, or a matter of tradition. Careful source analysis is essential here.

The final problem that we wish to draw attention to concerns the pooling of information gleaned from archaeological excavation, and approaches derived from other academic disciplines such as anthropology and the history of law, together with textual analysis. These provide a documentary corpus which, to all intents and purposes, may be deemed to be exhaustive, but continued reassessment constantly produces fresh insights. In addition, dialogue between specialists, all with their own methods of study, is far from simple.

We shall now consider the evolution of burial rites from late antiquity to the early Middle Ages in more detail. Archaeologists generally distinguish three characteristic features of burial rites, which some scholars take to indicate the passage from paganism to Christianity: the choice of inhumation as opposed to cremation; the east–west orientation of graves; and the abandonment of the practice of depositing grave goods. They also take into account the decoration and symbolism of objects placed in or on the grave. Much has been written on the relative value of such distinctions. It has been shown that there is no direct or certain correlation between a burial rite and the concept of an afterlife; the continued use of certain practices, independently of the meaning originally ascribed to them, has also been stressed, as has the importance of social factors in the organisation of burials and in the commemoration of the deceased. Nevertheless, in a number of archaeological publications, even very recent ones, there are still signs of simplistic deductions, or ones lacking the essential spirit of criticism; thus a brief review of the question would appear to be useful.

It was during the course of the third century that cremation in the Roman empire began to be progressively replaced by inhumation, whether directly in the ground or in sarcophagi (obviously a more costly solution and therefore confined to a wealthy elite). This development formed part of a general trend linked to the diffusion of eastern religions, including Christianity, and from philosophical beliefs of a neo-Platonic type; but equally it must have been influenced by the settlement within the empire of Germanic peoples (as *laeti* and *foederati*), who practised inhumation. It was not until the end of the eighth century, during the Carolingian conquest of Saxony, that cremation – classed as paganism and therefore considered to be a rejection of state religion – was explicitly condemned. Before that date Christian cremations of the first and second centuries are known, and St. Augustine defended the idea that Heaven is not closed to someone who might have been cremated. Nonetheless the Church affirmed more and more clearly the resurrection of the body at the Last Judgement, and normally a Christian was not cremated. In general terms, during late antiquity and the early Middle Ages, a cremation implies pagan beliefs on the part of the dead person, his family and/or those around him; but inhumation, the usual burial rite in this period, does not carry any specific religious implication.

Indeed, cremation is very rare within the limits of the Roman empire after the sixth century, and is often indicative of an incoming population, such as the Saxons; on the other hand, beyond the Rhine *limes* cremations are abundant until the Carolingian period.

With regard to east–west orientation (or rather west–east, with the head to the west looking towards the east), it is sufficient to note that, for the period under consideration, the Church did not impose any direction on graves. However, orientation could have been interpreted in the Christian sense, the more so since the parish church – itself necessarily or virtually always oriented – logically influenced the direction of graves dug around it. In the absence of religious legislation, other criteria – such as topographical features, or alignment with a 'founder's' grave – could have determined grave orientation. Without complementary elements, orientation is not a pertinent factor in the question of religion.

The presence – or absence – of grave goods is a very complex issue. Nowadays it is accepted that grave goods should be analysed in social terms, as they were used during burials to show the status of the deceased, recall their origins and perpetuate their memory. In addition, the wealth of a burial can reflect the opposition between a marginal or peripheral culture and a developed one; this acknowledged fact notably explains the sometimes exceptional richness of 'Germanic' graves dating to the second half of the fifth and beginning of the sixth centuries. The Church never condemned the deposition of grave goods, even if numerous churchmen sought to emphasise their vain and illusory character. It gave its support to laws that laid down severe penalties for grave robbing (implicit proof that the objects themselves were not condemned); and numerous richly furnished Christian graves are known, including some under churches (fig. 32). Furthermore, royal or episcopal funeral ceremonies are sufficient to indicate that, during the whole of the Middle Ages and the modern period, the Church tolerated and encouraged certain funerary deposits to which a symbolic value was then attached. In brief, the progressive disappearance of grave goods was a phenomenon of the period, linked to the diffusion of Christianity; but it was also associated with more pragmatic considerations, such as not removing precious metals or useful objects from circulation. However, a burial without grave goods is no more logically Christian than a richly furnished grave is indicative of pagan beliefs.

In this superficial overview, with its inevitable lacunae, we would have liked to have added some remarks on the interpretation of 'Christian' objects, or those bearing Christian motifs, which are occasionally found in graves; and to have considered other rarer practices, some of which (such as horse and dog burials, and barrows) have an ethnic or social explanation and others (such as the removal or substitution of skulls) that are not so easy to interpret. However, it seems preferable to arrange this

Fig. 32 Reconstruction of the princely boy's grave, Cologne Cathedral, Germany; early sixth century. (After Doppelfeld, 1960).

survey of cemeteries of the fourth to seventh century according to topographical criteria, distinguishing between town and countryside (although once more lack of space will create a somewhat distorted picture), then to examine various special cases and finally to emphasise the connections between cemeteries, settlements and cult-places.

We shall look first at funerary topography in an urban milieu. Although our knowledge of the topographical development of towns and their cemeteries during the Roman period is very variable, there remains a certain number of constants. Thus it appears that the destruction produced by the invasions of the third century, as well as the defensive measures that they inspired, led to quite a significant reduction in urban areas, which, during the period of the later empire, were effectively contained within walled defences. This explains why cemeteries of the fourth and fifth centuries do not necessarily occupy the same sites as earlier burial grounds, and were allowed to intrude upon certain parts of the urban fabric, dating to the early empire (first to third century), that appear to have been deserted, or deliberately razed for reasons of defence. The walled defences had not always strictly defined the effectively urbanised zone, since suburbs – particularly industrial areas – could have existed outside the walls; graves appear strung out along the approach roads to urban agglomerations, often over long distances and in varying concentrations, from the point where the urban area finishes (see fig. 65).

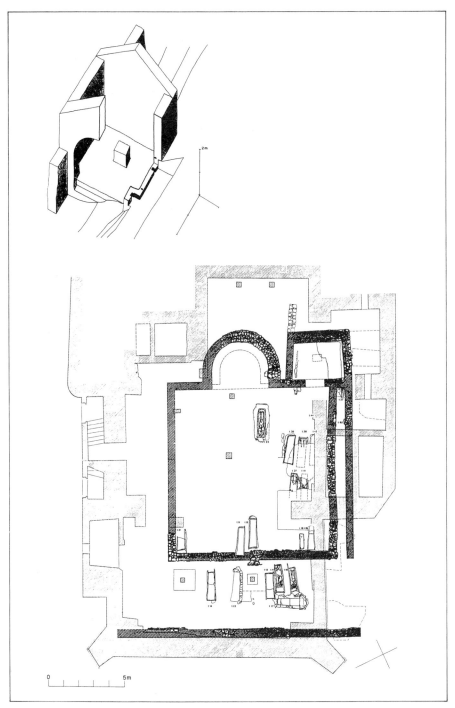

Fig. 33 The church of La Madeleine, Geneva: a) the primitive *memoria* (fifth century); b) plan of the first church with burials within and adjacent to the building (sixth century). (After Bonnet).

It was in these civil suburban cemeteries that members of the first Christian communities were buried; apart from rare exceptions, they did not have private burial grounds. As we have seen, in the absence of epitaphs or indisputably Christian symbols it is impossible to distinguish pagans from Christians by their burial customs. However, other archaeological evidence enables us to measure the progress of christianisation in the suburban cemeteries of the later empire. Indeed, it appears that 'privileged' burials were the object of particular veneration there. The official authorisation for adoption of the Christian faith is represented from the beginning of the fourth century by rather elaborate architecture, notably the construction of small buildings, among which historians like to distinguish the *martyrium*, which housed the graves of martyrs or those considered to be such; the *confessio*, when the saint has not actually undergone martyrdom; and the *memoria*, which contained relics of the dead person, but was not a grave (fig. 33). These elaborate tomb constructions, and their associated cults, led to the rapid multiplication of inhumation burials *ad sanctos*: given the belief in the efficacy of the intercession of saints, lying as close as possible to their graves or relics constituted a decided asset and a guarantee for the Day of Judgement. As a result, a certain number of these *loca sancta* were the origin of suburban churches which developed on the sites of late antique cemeteries. Apart from the graves that were genuinely *ad sanctos* and encircled these cult-places, and which were sometimes built up on several levels due to lack of space, the cemeteries retained their extensive aspect. However, very few examples of a *martyrium* or a *confessio* which later became a church have been subjected to archaeological investigation capable of isolating the successive stages of their architectural development: the exceptions are La Madeleine in Geneva (fig. 33), St. Denis in northern Paris, St. Servais in Maastricht, St. Germain at Auxerre, etc.

Fig. 34 Reconstruction of the episcopal complex, Cathedral of Saint-Pierre, Geneva, *c.*AD 500. (After Périn 1987.)

It was not in the *extra muros* funerary churches, which from the outset were dedicated to the cult of a saint, that the everyday liturgy and the celebration of the Eucharist took place, but in the *ecclesia* situated *intra muros*; such a church could, in the case of episcopal towns, take on the aspect of an imposing monumental complex, comprising several churches, (often a 'double cathedral'), a baptistry, the bishop's residence, the conventual buildings of the clergy attached to the bishopric and so on (fig. 34). As time went on, other churches would be built *intra muros* as necessary.

With regard to religious organisation, no significant modification can be observed after the deposition of the last emperor of the west in AD 476: the successor states kept Christianity as the state religion, and did not bring any significant or long-lasting changes to the nature of episcopal office. A certain number of suburban Merovingian churches were built over existing cemeteries that were still in use. A celebrated example is the basilica of the Saints-Apôtres in Paris, which became the church of St. Geneviève. It was based upon the church of the Holy Apostles that Emperor Constantine had built at Constantinople, and was constructed at the very beginning of the sixth century over the tomb of Geneviève (d. *c.*502) by King Clovis and his wife Clothilde to serve them as a dynastic mausoleum. Imitating the imperial model, this funerary basilica was built on the site of a cemetery known since the late empire; the multiplication of burials *ad sanctos* around the *confessio* of St. Geneviève probably ensured its survival and development (fig. 35).

Very often the suburban cemeteries in use at the beginning of the Merovingian period were not new foundations but continuations of former burial grounds, indicative, among other factors, of the continuity of urban life. Thus, in the town of Tournai on the right bank of the Scheldt, on the edge of the Roman cemetery that had grown up on an abandoned settlement site in the third century, King Childeric. (d. 481) was buried under a large tumulus accompanied by three horse burials. This exceptionally rich grave became the nucleus for later burials; a church was built on the site of the cemetery, but not before the end of the seventh century (pl. 24).

Elsewhere, often on the initiative of aristocratic families eager for church burial, oratories were built where there was no saint's grave to provide the focus for a church. Their main function was funerary and private, and their founders sought to endow them with the most prestigious relics possible. When setting up these cult-places *extra muros*, it was not necessary to take an existing cemetery into account. At Arlon, in the modern Belgian province of Luxembourg, the church of St. Martin was clearly built as a funerary church in the first half of the sixth century; it later became the local parish church. In Paris it was in an area which apparently had no funerary associations that King Childebert I founded, in AD 558, the church of St. Croix-et-St. Vincent (the modern

(*Right*) Fig. 35 Urban cemetery with burials *ad sanctos*, Saints-Apôtres (later St-Geneviève), Paris; sixth century. (After Lenoir 1867.)

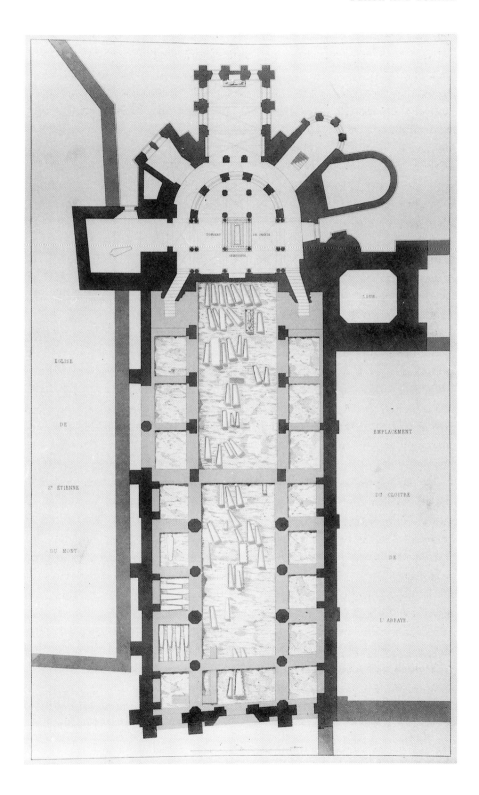

Fig. 36 Aerial view of the Gallo-Roman and Merovingian cemetery at Frénouville, Calvados, France, showing the different grave orientations reflecting the adoption of Frankish burial customs by the indigenous population. (After Pilet, 1980.)

St. Germain-des-Prés), the dedication of which is explained by prestigious relics brought back from Spain: a fragment of the True Cross and the tunic of St. Vincent. From the end of the sixth century the cult of St. Germain of Paris developed to such an extent that it completely overshadowed the church's original funerary function, which was to be a royal mausoleum similar to that at the Saints-Apôtres. A comparable example is St. Médard at Soissons, founded by King Clothair in about AD 560.

The suburban churches and the cemeteries founded at the end of the Roman period and the beginning of the early Middle Ages continued to exist for the most part until modern times; new buildings on the same site succeeded one other, whilst continual burials disturbed earlier cemeteries. Furthermore, the urban growth of the Middle Ages led to their inevitable integration within the walls of fortified towns, while the former *intra muros* churches, until then devoid of burials, received inhumations in their turn.

As with the towns, there are two categories of rural cemeteries of the early Middle Ages to be considered, divided according to whether they coincide or not with a late Roman cemetery.

A certain number of rural Merovingian cemeteries developed first of all on the sites of – or in the immediate proximity of – cemeteries in use during the fourth or fifth centuries; such a coincidence cannot be fortuitous, and is indicative of the permanence of the associated settlement, and, in many cases, of the stability of the population. The continuity of these cemeteries is, however, difficult to establish, for, as happened in the towns, the practice of clothed inhumations and the deposition of grave goods – still decidedly prevalent in the fourth century – shows a marked decrease in the following hundred years. Continuity is principally supported by the fact that late Roman burials are often respected by later ones (proof that they were still visible on the surface), and that they are sometimes included in the alignments of Merovingian tombs – as can be seen at Lavoye, Dieue-sur-Meuse or Nouvion-en-Ponthieu. However, such coincidences between late Roman and Merovingian cemeteries are comparatively rare.

On the other hand quite a few cases of cemetery juxtaposition are known. One can postulate that certain aristocratic Frankish, Burgundian or Visigothic families did not initially mix their graves with those of the indigenous population, but that they established their burials on the edge of existing cemeteries. These early inhumations later became the nuclei for quite large cemeteries, which led to the progressive abandonment of pre-existing sites, and sometimes to the imitation of the funerary customs of new masters. This phenomenon can be seen for example at Krefeld-Gellep, at Frénouville (Calvados) and at Mézières in the Ardennes (fig. 36).

Other rural cemeteries of the Merovingian period – most frequently between the Loire and the Rhine – do not appear to have succeeded earlier burial grounds, and must be considered new creations. Their earliest inhumations are usually later than the reign of Clovis, and therefore correspond to a period where it is no longer really possible to distinguish the ascendant Frankish population culturally and archaeologically from the Gallo-Roman rootstock: by this time the inhabitants of northern Gaul all saw themselves as Franci, and cannot be distinguished from one another by differences in dress fashions or burial rites. It is possible that these cemeteries without antecedents correspond to new settlements of the Merovingian period, and that they represent the reoccupation of land which had been abandoned, or less densely settled, after the unrest of the third century or the conquest of new areas. One can also postulate that a number of these villages, known to have existed from the Merovingian period by their cemeteries, actually pre-existed, since they rarely coincide with rustic Gallo-Roman villas, although they are seldom far away; they could have played a complementary role from the fourth or fifth century on the edge of large estates, and might have survived the decay of the villas by adapting better to the agrarian economy at the beginning of the early Middle Ages. In this case, we still need to explain why the continuity of village settlements did not involve continuity of burials.

These cemeteries are characterised by a predominant grave orientation, which can vary from one site to another and which has often been dictated by the direction of the slope on which the burials are situated; the juxtaposition of alignment thus tends to produce row-grave cemeteries that are fairly regular in plan. Obviously these cemeteries are near to the settlements to which they correspond, and the nearest slope, where there is one, has doubtless been chosen as the site in order to cement the relations between the living and the dead. Elsewhere certain foci, such as ruins of Roman villas or megalithic monuments, have equally played a part in determining the choice of site. The case of ruined villas has often been considered to be proof of topographical and historical discontinuity of settlement, but it should be viewed on the contrary as indicative of the permanence of these antique sites; some of these 'ruins' were in fact portions of buildings still standing or even restored, which then acquired a funerary and cultural importance. It is quite often the case that cemeteries on high ground close to a spring and with a sacred toponym indicate a later Christian adoption of the site, but not a determinant cult relationship between the springs and the cemetery.

The combined study of historical sources and archaeological evidence, carried out at village or parish level, enables us to propose several models of rural cemetery development during the early Middle Ages.

The most common situation was the abandonment of Merovingian cemeteries, which, as in the towns, were always situated on the edge of settlements. Generally these seem to have developed in the course of the eighth century and owe their existence to the foundation of village churches, the parochial status of which was definitively established in the middle of the eighth century. This quite rapidly resulted in the accretion of inhumation burials. This change was certainly not dramatic, and

several examples of high-status graves (in Normandy and in the Meuse valley) show that the latest burials in the peripheral cemeteries have the same characteristics as the first graves established around the church – definite proof that both cemeteries were in use for a certain period of time.

In any case, it cannot be inferred from this development of rural funerary topography that the peripheral cemeteries were those belonging to a 'pagan' population. On the one hand the process of Christianisation in the countryside, widely developed since the seventh century, still did not necessarily imply a relationship between the cemetery and the church. On the other hand, the burial rites that have been observed in these cemeteries are no different from those in the cities and small market towns during the same period, where they were indisputably the work of a Christian population.

It is important to examine the nature of this uniformity in burial customs in the towns and in the countryside. From the Merovingian period onwards, the suburban

(*Left*) Fig. 37 Stone sarcophagus from Paris, sixth century.

Fig. 38 Suburban cemetery; the priory of Saint-Martin, Niort, France; sixth century. (After Bosset.)

cemeteries became indissociable from the churches in and around which graves accumulated. In certain areas a number of these burials are in stone or plaster sarcophagi and only occasionally contain grave goods, and the practice of clothed inhumation is rare (fig. 37). The individuality of the grave is respected less and less, notably because of the increase in reburial. This suburban funerary model based upon Christian burial customs permeated rural society through certain staging-posts such as villages with an administrative function or notable religious centres (fig. 38).

These places saw the implantation of churches from the beginning of the Merovingian period, and thus the formation of cemeteries *ad sanctos*, where the funerary characteristics of the suburban cemeteries are found once more, because they naturally served as models. Good examples of this include Isle-Aumont (Aube, fig. 39), Quarré-des-Tombes (Yonne) and Civaux (Vienne). It is possible that cemeteries associated with these notable religious centres were held to be too important to be reserved exclusively for the local population, and naturally attracted Christian burials from neighbouring areas, at least until the creation of a network of parishes. It was perhaps these 'intermediate cemeteries' that contributed little by little to spreading 'Christian' modes of burial in the countryside.

In order to see the nuances of this development of rural Merovingian funerary topography, two possibilities should be envisaged. In the absence of systematic exca-

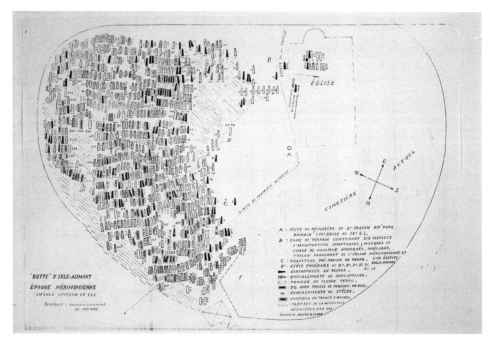

Fig. 39 Rural cemetery of surburban type, Merovingian period; 'Butte' d'Isle Aumont, Aube, France. (After Scapula.)

Fig. 40 View of the excavations in the funerary chapel of the Merovingian cemetery, Hordain, Nord, France; two Frankish-style warrior burials are accompanied by other Christian graves and, outside the chapel, the pagan cemetery. (After Périn 1987.)

vations, one cannot reject the potential existence of modest funerary structures of wood or stone, which may have had a religious function, and which were erected in cemeteries before being abandoned when new burial grounds were established around parish churches. Certainly this happened at Hordain (Nord, fig. 40), Chassey-les-Montbozon (Haute-Saône), Briord (Ain), Tavers (Loiret) and St.-Julien-en-Genevois (Haute-Savoie). On the other hand, it has often been noticed that, in areas where the deposition of grave goods was widely practised, there are few 'aristocratic' graves in rural cemeteries after the sixth or seventh century. Thus one can put forward the hypothesis that a proportion of the rural aristocracy abandoned this type of cemetery from that time on, building instead funerary chapels or churches (often future parish churches) on the periphery of – or near to – the settlement. These benefited from the subsequent transfer of cemeteries from outside the settlement.

Other cemeteries, fewer in number, did not experience such a change at the end of the Merovingian or beginning of the Carolingian period, but survived for a long time – even to the present day – on the same spot, fixed by a parish church that had not been built at the very heart of the settlement. As far as one can judge, this situation often seems to have been the logical consequence of the building by the local aristocracy of a private funerary chapel, later converted into a parish church. Nowadays the presence of a parish church outside a village can indicate the existence of an ancient cemetery, which is frequently Merovingian. In other instances, for reasons of convenience or security a parish church on the outskirts was transferred into the village itself, without the cemetery necessarily moving with it; the former parish church could then exist as a cemetery chapel. Thus at St. Martin-de-Boscherville (Seine-Maritime), it was not until the eleventh century that the cemetery – established after the end of the sixth century in and around the restored *cella* of a small Gallo-Roman temple – was moved to the parish church of St. Martin in the village. However, the topographical isolation of a parish church may have another explanation, such as a subsequent shift in settlement during the later Middle Ages – such as occurred at Landen in Brabant following the creation of a new medieval town.

In a general survey of this kind, it is not possible to express nuances or to linger over particular examples that merit more discussion. We could have included cemeteries belonging to religious communities; often a specific funerary church was created for a monastic or canonical complex. At Nivelles, where an abbey connected with the aristocratic family of the Pippinides (the future Carolingians) was founded in the mid-seventh century, one of three churches of the monastic complex, the church of St. Pierre, was built as a funerary church; archaeological excavation has revealed that the burial vaults were part of the original structure, but that they were not all used following the development of the cult of the first abbess, Gertrude. Other examples are equally revealing.

Within the geographical area under consideration, the fourth to seventh century saw the predominance of 'extensive' cemeteries, closely linked to the desire to individualise the grave in perpetuity in order to ensure the immortality of the body. Belonging to a world that was still pagan in outlook, which, from then onwards, preferred the inhumation of the dead as opposed to their cremation, this type of cemetery – as well as the funerary customs practised there – did not disappear with the arrival of Christianity in the towns. Indeed, in the beginning the Church did not seek to innovate in funerary matters, for such burial rites were essentially familial and private in nature and scarcely held any religious resonance. Thus, the Church did not modify the arrangement of such cemeteries, apart from the introduction of funerary basilicas, the earliest of which were established over the graves of martyrs or local saints, and soon attracted inhumations *ad sanctos*.

These burial grounds kept their 'antique' appearance throughout the Merovingian period, while their character, from then on considered to be Christian, served as a funerary model for several religious centres in the countryside before being adopted by the majority of rural cemeteries in the seventh century and the beginning of the eighth. It was during the eighth century that the extensive cemeteries disappeared. In the towns, cemeteries moved from the periphery and graves were regrouped around churches. The same phenomenon occurred in the countryside, whether the cemeteries were moved or remained on the same site, and became for the most part indissociable in their turn from parish or cemetery churches.

This striking evolution of the urban and rural funerary topography was accompanied by a radical change in the methods of burial. Until then, graves had accumulated in a random fashion around cult-places, as can be seen with urban inhumations *ad sanctos*; the graves were no longer as carefully individualised as they had been previously; sarcophagi and carefully constructed tombs gave way to simple graves, which were rapidly disturbed or destroyed by subsequent burials. The most important consideration was that the bones of the dead, eventually stacked in ossuaries, remained within the parish close, under the protection of the church, while they awaited the Day of Judgement.

NOTES
1 Werner 1935.
2 Böhner 1958.

ACKNOWLEDGEMENT
The authors would like to thank Cathy Haith, who translated this paper.

Cult and worship in east and west

Averil Cameron

At the beginning of our period the Roman empire still spanned the Mediterranean lands from Gibraltar to the borders of Iran. This was so even though the two sons of the emperor Theodosius I (died AD 395) divided the task of rule into western and eastern zones, with courts based respectively at Milan and Constantinople. Very soon, however, the western half began to fragment: within a decade Britain was given up, and after 476 no more Roman emperors ruled from Italy. The eastern empire, too, lost much of its territory to the Arabs in the seventh century, and began to look to the north, towards the Balkans and the Crimea, where new peoples – Slavs, Turks, Bulgars, Khazars – were making their impact. Already in the sixth century, mainland Greece, the islands and the hinterland of Constantinople were subject to successive raids and Slavic settlement. By 900 Islamic rule from Baghdad had long been a reality; the initial phase of Muslim expansion was over and an Islamic empire stretched from the east and the former Byzantine provinces of Syria, Palestine and Egypt across to the Maghreb and Spain. The three eastern patriarchates, Alexandria, Antioch and Jerusalem, were all within the sway of the Abbasid caliphate, while in the west the papacy in Rome coexisted with, or rivalled, the Holy Roman emperors (Charlemagne's coronation in Rome on Christmas Day 800 was now a century old) and a host of minor kingdoms further afield.

This was an age of discovery and rediscovery, when profound importance attached to local attachments and individual contacts in religious matters. People learned what they could from whoever they happened to meet; old practices and old memories coexisted with new experiences. Thus the earliest, proto-Bulgarian, inscriptions at the new capital of Pliska used the Greek alphabet. It took many years and a new, Glagolitic, alphabet and new literary language, Church Slavonic, before the liturgy and the Scriptures were accessible in the vernacular; when this happened, it took place as a result of the missionary activity of two ninth-century Byzantines, the brothers Saints Cyril and Methodius. The sense of a distant empire lingered long even in far-away places, through prestige objects and diplomatic gifts, like the seventh-century Byzantine silver in the Sutton Hoo treasure (fig. 29). But when St. Patrick set sail to minister to the Irish in the fifth century, 'in the scattered farmsteads of Ireland, how many persons had ever heard of Constantine?' Patrick must have used the knowledge of Irish he had acquired earlier as a slave to communicate with his flock; however, unlike the east, where there were already Christian literatures in Coptic, Syriac, Armenian and

Ethiopian, there was as yet nothing for them to read. The period was one of immense local variation. In the Maghreb, for example, some of the Moorish, or Berber, tribal groups which become more prominent in our written record during the late Vandal period (late fifth–sixth centuries) were already christianised and themselves used Latin. In Byzantine North Africa the relics of eastern saints were formally deposited in seventh-century ceremonies in this most Latin and western of Roman provinces. After the Arab conquest, however, Christianity leaves few traces in North Africa; the same Berber groups may have found the ways of Islam more congenial than the rule of the Greek-speaking Byzantines who after A D 534 reimposed an eastern, 'orthodox', Christianity in the name of Roman restoration and backed it by military force. Nor is it surprising if different types of worship and religious practice coexisted in one place.

The formal end of Roman rule in the west is no longer conceived of as a catastrophic event. On the contrary, the end of the first millennium seems a more plausible point at which to posit a real break in long-term patterns of settlement and exchange. Yet the geographical span now embraced Ireland, Scandinavia and southern Russia. Britain, having been lost to Christianity with the withdrawal of the Romans, was reconverted and had already in the seventh century become a centre of monastic life and learning. In the east, the Khazars in the Crimea and around the Sea of Azov presented the unusual phenomenon of a kingdom which adopted Judaism as its religion while negotiating dynastic marriages with the Christian court of Constantinople, and the Church of the Holy Sepulchre at Jerusalem, even under Abbasid rule, continued to entice intrepid pilgrims who returned with travellers' tales and souvenirs.

Although one by one most of the new peoples came under the influence of Christianity, the process was neither even nor necessarily rapid. By the sixth century the conversion of foreign peoples went hand in hand with political interest: the Greek chronicler John Malalas tells how Tzath, the king of the Laz in the area of modern Georgia, a critical border area in the power struggle between Byzantium and Iran, came to Constantinople to receive baptism and the hand of a Byzantine noblewoman in marriage. Conversion, or at least the proclamation of Christianity, was a central part of the emperor Justinian's church-building in the newly regained province of North Africa. The same emperor sent the Syrian Monophysite John, later titular bishop of Ephesus, on a mission to convert rural pagans in Asia Minor; thousands were claimed for Christianity. Ulfila, the fourth-century bishop responsible for the conversion of the Goths to a version of Arian Christianity, had been consecrated under imperial auspices and met with what seems to have been political resistance from Gothic leaders; nevertheless, Goths, Vandals and other Germanic peoples owed their later Arianism as well as their Gothic Bible to his mission. Mission was also a deep concern for local bishops such as Caesarius, bishop of Arles in the early sixth century, for whom concern for the religious welfare of the many captives taken during this period made the attempt to ransom them a major episcopal duty.

In AD 391–2 legislation issued by the emperor Theodosius I officially declared pagan cults illegal, and from time to time his successors, notably Justinian in the sixth century, attempted to purge suspected pagans from the higher ranks of society. But within the empire as without, pagan practice continued, often coexisting with Christian cult. In sixth-century Lycia, a local holy man and bishop, Nicholas of Sion, found his rural flock devoted to tree-cults and sacrifice. The collections of miracle stories attached to particular Christian shrines such as that of Saints Cyrus and John near Alexandria, or the Church of St. John Prodromos in the quarter of Oxeia at Constantinople, which possessed the relics of St. Artemios, witness to the continuing attraction of astrology and magic practices and the Christian adoption of the pagan practice of incubation, while St. Theodore of Sykeon successfully exorcised a demon identified with the pagan goddess Artemis. The Quinisext Council, or Council in Trullo, held in Constantinople in 692, was at pains to condemn pagan festivals and cult practices; this may reflect the traditional concerns of ecclesiastical legislation, but there is no reason to doubt that competing religious attachments coexisted then just as they do today. Constantine had not attempted to outlaw paganism, still the religion of the vast majority of the inhabitants of the empire at the time of his death in 337, and had contented himself with putting an end to pagan cult at only a few notable temples. Nevertheless, as time went on both the state and local bishops had an interest in converting prominent pagan temples and shrines into churches. Famous cases such as the destruction of the temples of Serapis at Alexandria in 392 at the instigation of Christian monks, and of Zeus Marnas at Gaza in 402 by an alliance between the local bishop and imperial troops acting on the emperor's orders, found numerous parallels on a smaller scale elsewhere. It was expected of a holy man that he would combat paganism: thus a saint's life probably translated from Syriac into Greek and reworked in the sixth century claims that a Syrian monk, Alexander the 'Sleepless', having prepared himself by a sojourn in the desert, destroyed a pagan temple and converted, among many others, the future bishop Rabbula of Edessa. Some urban centres were particularly resistant: the first church at Athens did not appear before the fifth century, and Harran (Carrhae) and Heliopolis (Baalbek) in Syria retained their pagan character long after neighbouring towns had become Christian. Even in Christian circles, the repertoire of classical imagery was retained: textiles from late antique and even Islamic Egypt show the continued popularity of the Dionysian motifs found on fourth-century mosaic floors from Cyprus and Syria, and which also appear on Sassanian silver (pl. 25). In late fifth- and early sixth-century Alexandria, pagan and Christian students rubbed shoulders and sometimes brawled in rowdy displays of male aggression. We should imagine the period as one of immense variety; there was no clear dividing line.

(*Right*) Fig. 41 Monastery of St. Catherine, Sinai, seen from the east. It was built by Justinian and later fortified against the Arab incursions from Palestine. Third quarter of the sixth century.

Fig. 42 Panagia Angeloktistos (Church of the Virgin), Kiti, Cyprus: mainly eleventh century.

As well as combating paganism, it was also essential for Christian writers and preachers to instruct their flocks on the difference between orthodoxy and heresy. Despite, or sometimes indeed as a result of, imperial attempts to restore unity, communities became increasingly divided in the eastern provinces in the sixth and seventh centuries along confessional lines, with Monophysites, Chalcedonians and Monothelites vying for the same churches and the same congregations. The patriarchate of Antioch passed from one group to another more than once; there were rival patriarchs in Alexandria, and eastern monks in exile were sheltered in the capital by the empress Theodora. Another wave of easterners fled from the Persian invasion of Egypt and the east in the early seventh century to settle in Sicily and south Italy, where they brought not only their Greek language but also their doctrinal loyalties.

While the public spaces of classical cities round the Mediterranean were everywhere contracting, large churches continued to be restored and repaired, and even newly constructed. The emperor Justinian is credited with a large-scale building programme: it extended from Palestine, where he built the monastery later known as St. Catherine's (still a functioning Orthodox monastery) at the foot of Mount Sinai and the great New Church of the Mother of God in Jerusalem, to the newly conquered province of North

(*Right*) Fig. 43 Apse mosaic, the Virgin Hodegetria between archangels, Panagia Angeloktistos; late sixth–first half of the seventh century.

Africa (fig. 41). The present church of St. Sophia in Istanbul, known to Byzantines for centuries as the 'Great Church' (pl. 27), was built by him when the earlier church on the spot had been destroyed by fire in the riots of AD 532, and here the pomp of imperial liturgy reached a height still apparent from the tenth-century Byzantine *Book of Ceremonies*. Here in the sixth century, Justinian and Theodora, whose appearance is best known from the mosaic in the church of San Vitale, Ravenna, dedicated by the local bishop in 547 while the Gothic War was still going on, participated regularly in an elaborate ritual of imperial and religious show (pls 26, 36).

Some eastern churches managed to keep their decoration intact through the period of iconoclasm in the eighth and ninth centuries; one was the small church of the Virgin at Kiti in Cyprus, with its sixth-century apse mosaic (figs 42, 43). Local church building and reconstruction went on through the Vandal and into the Byzantine periods in modern Tunisia, where the large basilica of St. Cyprian in Carthage first fell into Arian control and was then recovered by the Catholics. The funerary inscriptions of many ordinary Christians attest to their desire, here and elsewhere in the empire, to reserve a spot close to their favourite saint. During this period the typical large basilical church of late antiquity began to be replaced in the eastern empire by much smaller buildings, often with a dome over a square construction. But at Thessaloniki, for example, the large basilica of St. Demetrius was still the centre of the saint's cult during the attacks on the city by Slavs and Avars in the seventh century, as we read in the contemporary *Miracles of St. Demetrius*; though the present church is mainly modern, the young saint is still to be seen on the wall in late Roman official costume, flanked by the bishop and town officials (pl. 29). In Bostra in Syria and elsewhere, new inscriptions continued up to the seventh century, when their numbers are much reduced. But local communities in what is now Jordan were still prepared, even in the second half of the eighth century, to pay for and dedicate elaborately classicising mosaic floors in their churches.

Churches varied greatly in size and layout to suit local and liturgical variation. Some Roman churches had libraries attached, like the fifth-century church of San Giovanni Evangelista at Ravenna; adjoining baptisteries and rooms for storage and preparation of sacred vessels were also common. Bishops and their episcopal complexes continued to be central to the religious life of cities, and at the start of our period they were also dominant in the liturgical life of Christians through their virtual monopoly of baptism, preaching and the celebration of the Eucharist. But as the number of Christians and the number of rural churches increased, so also did pressure for the ruralisation of church life. The growth of rural baptisteries and parish churches can be detected in Gaul from the fifth century, and by the sixth century there was a class of clergy identified as 'parish priests'. The Sunday liturgy could be celebrated in a variety of kinds of churches, and the rural clergy were gathered together annually by their urban bishop. This was the beginning of the system of rural parishes and country churches.

In the east, in fifth-century Syria, one priest could have charge of numerous villages (*kōmai*); in the sixth century the term *chorion* is used in a similar sense, and the Lycian world of Nicholas of Sion in the same period is a rural world.

The location of Christian sacred sites was often determined by, or benefited from, the existence on the same spot of a pagan shrine or holy place. Cyril of Alexandria transferred the relics of Saints Cyrus and John to Menouthis precisely because this was the site of a famous temple of Isis; the shrine of Thecla at Seleucia was near the tomb of the Greek hero Sarpedon; monks installed themselves in the remains of disused pagan temples. Mamre, where Abraham received his three visitors (Gen. 18.1–22), was a pagan shrine before Constantine claimed it as a Christian one, and the process could also be reversed: the cave of the Resurrection in Jerusalem, site of Constantine's church of the Holy Sepulchre, was claimed to have been found only after the excavation of a pagan temple. Every town and every bishop now claimed the relic of at least one saint, and preferably more. Places which could claim a major saint, like Tours, the centre of the cult of St. Martin, had a major advantage, as did their local bishops. Eufronius, bishop of Tours in the sixth century, repaired and built churches, established the foundation of Queen Radegund's convent at Poitiers and reroofed the church of St. Martin. Two festivals of St. Martin were celebrated each year; during the liturgy, there were readings of miracle stories from the saint's *Life*, episodes from which were also depicted on the walls of the church, which was built round his tomb. But Martin was also commemorated in dozens of other places in Gaul, either where he was believed to have performed miracles, or which themselves possessed relics of the saint. These relics were extremely powerful, as can be read in the late sixth-century account of some of the miracles they performed written by Bishop Gregory of Tours; prayers to the saint could cure the blind and deaf, and two blind men from Bourges had their sight restored simply by listening to the miracle stories in his *Life*.

Martin's shrine at Tours was also a place of pilgrimage. Gregory tells us about nearly three hundred individuals known to him who made the pilgrimage; others went to other shrines and tombs in Tours, or at nearby Pernay. Many came from Clermont and Limoges, others from Paris, Reims, Soissons and Metz, or from Normandy. Building on more ancient pagan traditions, associated, for instance, with the great oracles and shrines of Apollo and Aesculapius in Asia Minor, pilgrimage was now a major religious activity. A Christian sacred geography in the Holy Land developed during the fourth century during the Constantinian and post-Constantinian periods, encouraged by the building of impressive churches on the holiest sites of the life of Christ and fuelled by the convenient discovery of relics to fill them. These included the body of the first martyr, Stephen, which was solemnly interred in the basilica on Mount Sion on 26 December 415. A new genre, that of pilgrims' diaries, grew up to record the experiences of the travellers. Late in the fourth century a woman religious from Spain made a long and at times dangerous journey to the sites mentioned in the Scriptures, and wrote down her impressions in vivid and straightforward Latin for the sisters in the community she had left behind.[1] Still in the same vein, in the early 680s an Irish abbot from Iona recorded the stories he had heard from Arculf, a shipwrecked bishop from Gaul who had recently travelled to the Holy Land, Alexandria, Crete and Constantinople, and returned via Sicily and Rome. Arculf stayed in Jerusalem, by now under the Abbasid caliphate, for nine months, and described its relics and holy places in detail; he also told the Irish monk, Adomnan, about Constantinople and its icons, and about the ceremony of the veneration of the cross in which the imperial court took part.[2] Pilgrims liked to return with souvenirs, if not with actual relics; the most typical were *ampullae*, small pottery vessels filled with earth from a holy place more often than with water or oil, and typically bearing a holy symbol or effigy of the saint. There were also *eulogiai*, literally 'blessings', clay tokens similarly decorated, which proved that the pilgrim had actually been to the holy place. Thousands of these small pilgrim souvenirs survive in today's museums, testimony to the huge volume of pilgrim traffic in our period. Not only was there need of souvenirs: many shrines themselves needed to be enlarged, and provided with accommodation and hospital needs for hundreds of visitors and their animals. The great shrine of St. Symeon at Qal'at Seman in northern Syria was one such centre (fig. 44).

Fig. 44 Monastery of St. Symeon Stylites, south facade, Qal'at Seman, Syria; last quarter of the fifth–first quarter of the sixth century.

Even more visible and numerous than pilgrims during this period were the many thousands of monks and nuns. Monasticism began sporadically at the end of the third century, and seems to have arisen more or less at the same time in Egypt and in Syria. By the beginning of the fifth century a wide variety of forms of monastic life were already being practised in the eastern empire, from that of the solitary to that of large communal (cenobitic) monasteries with highly developed economic ties with their surrounding areas. A common pattern, however, was that of the *lavra*, a name retained by many later monasteries such as the Great Lavra on Mount Athos today. In monasteries of this type, the monks would live separately, but come together on Sundays for the celebration of the liturgy and for a common meal. Nearly seventy monastic sites have been securely identified in the Judaean desert; some are very large communal monasteries, others consist of single cells built into the sides of cliffs, with only a small central chapel. The network survived into the Islamic period, and declined in the face of economic change when the supporting Byzantine trade and communications systems were weakened. In the west, major monastic centres had developed by the fifth century in southern Gaul; one of the most famous was Lérins, on an island near Cannes. In Italy, Cassiodorus, the former minister of the Ostrogothic kings, founded the monastic establishment of Vivarium on his estate at Squillace; it became an important centre for copying manuscripts and for the transmission of classical learning. Whereas in the early stages monasticism owed much to the general appeal of Christian asceticism, monasteries soon became important establishments and monks played a crucial role in the dissemination of culture in the Middle Ages.

Nuns were perhaps not as numerous as monks, and for predictable reasons they played a less prominent role in society at large. This was certainly true in the eastern empire for most of our period; but aristocratic and royal women in the west often founded convents and became abbesses, like Queen Radegund at Poitiers. They might be learned themselves and act as patrons of letters; they sometimes had close friendships with the male bishops who ministered to them. Nunneries were also places where the surplus daughters of aristocrats could be safely deposited, and many of them went on to become abbesses, like Hilda of Whitby, whose uncle was King Edwin of Northumbria. In the sixth century, King Charibert's daughter Chlotild led a revolt among the nuns at the convent at Poitiers, and complained bitterly that moral standards (as well as the standards of comfort) were lax. But in contrast, convents in ninth-century Byzantium are depicted in the written sources as havens of domestic respectability.

Both in east and west the cult of the Virgin rose to paramount importance. One of the earliest and grandest depictions of her is to be found in the fifth-century mosaics on the arch of the apse in the church of Santa Maria Maggiore in Rome, where she is shown in the garb of an imperial lady. From the sixth century onwards she is more often depicted holding the Christ child, and dressed in simple and flowing robes; the Great Church of St. Sophia in Constantinople and the Church of the Koimesis (Dormition, or falling asleep, of the Virgin) at Nicaea both had such mosaic images in the apse which suffered from the eighth-century iconoclasts who objected to the depiction of religious figures in this way. A cycle of liturgical feasts of the Virgin gradually developed, including the Purification, the Presentation in the Temple, the Annunciation and the Assumption or Dormition on 15 August, when she was believed to have been miraculously taken up to heaven; by the end of our period a regular pattern of celebration was firmly established, and illustrated in frescoes and icons. Literary texts echoed this visual and liturgical attention: collections of miracles ascribed to her appeared in the west, and many similar stories can be found in eastern sources, especially after the late sixth century. In Constantinople, which claimed the relics of her robe and girdle, a miraculous icon of the Virgin kept in her church at Blachernae was believed to have saved the city during the great siege of 626.

The relics of saints are perhaps the most characteristic sacred objects in this period. Their collection and ceremonial 'deposition' in their own shrine was a development of the fourth century; when the emperor Constantine built his own mausoleum in Constantinople with a sarcophagus for each of the twelve apostles, they remained purely commemorative until the AD 360s, when relics allegedly of Saints Timothy, Luke and Andrew were installed. The greatest of all relics was the wood believed to be of the True Cross, to be seen already in the fourth century enshrined on what was claimed to be the very site of Golgotha in the Church of the Holy Sepulchre at Jerusalem; from the end of the fourth century it was universally believed that Constantine's own mother Helena had found it when she visited the Holy Land in 327. In the course of time the original relic fragmented into dozens of others claimed by cities, monasteries and churches in far-flung parts of the empire; one of the most famous was that encased in a cross-shaped reliquary which the emperor Justin II and his wife Sophia sent to the convent at Poitiers after their accession in 565. Pilgrim sites, and especially those around the burial-places of saints, also gave rise to the proliferation of less prestigious relics: Thecla's shrine at Seleucia was an exception, since she was believed to have miraculously disappeared into a cleft in the rock, but a fifth-century collection of miracle stories associated with her shrine attempted to compensate for the lack. But relics were also transferred simply by pious people, or to satisfy the ambitions of local churches. Sometimes the circumstances are known from literary or other evidence, but at other times we have only the archaeological or epigraphic record. The iconoclast emperors were accused of hostility to relics and an early ninth-century account records how Leo III ordered the relics of St. Euphemia to be taken from her shrine at Chalcedon and thrown into the sea; in the story, however, they were rescued and taken to the island of Lemnos. Relics also needed reliquaries, either imposing and splendidly adorned, for use in churches and monasteries, or smaller, though often still richly made, for use by individuals; a large number of such objects still survive.

Alongside relics, many other surviving objects demonstrate the growing power of

Fig. 45 Silver-gilt and niello-inlaid paten with the Communion of the Apostles, ? Constantinople, A.D. 565–78; from a hoard said to have been found at Riha, Syria.

religious images in visual art. Large-scale mosaic programmes on the walls or in the apses of churches, as at Ravenna in the fifth and sixth centuries, demonstrate a desire to teach and to proclaim the Christian ideology. The monastery founded by Justinian at Sinai has a complex mosaic scene of the Transfiguration in the apse of its basilical church. Many small objects – ivory boxes, liturgical silver – carried narrative scenes derived from the New Testament, or showed popular contemporary saints. Much impressive church silver survives from this period, with important hoards found in Britain and the west as well as in Syria, where churches were still receiving gifts of this kind in the seventh century. Many of these items are massive, and some carry figural decoration, particularly notable examples being the liturgical plates ('patens') from Stuma and Riha in Syria with finely executed scenes of the Communion of the Apostles, and which were presumably intended for use during the Eucharist (fig. 45). Carved ivory panels in the form of diptychs (book covers), adapted for religious use the traditional iconography which often showed officials in consular dress on the occasion of their taking up office; Christ or the Virgin and Child took the place of the emperor or secular official, while a very fine example in the British Museum collection depicts an archangel, probably Michael (pl. 28).

Best known of all, though few survive from the period before iconoclasm, when there was a campaign to destroy them supported by certain eighth-century emperors in Constantinople, are the icons, portraits of Christ, the Virgin or the saints, painted on wood or fashioned in other media such as carved ivory, which became the object of fierce devotion from their adherents. Only after the formal ending of iconoclasm in AD 843, however, did Byzantine churches begin to take on the richly pictorial appearance that Orthodox churches still have today; of the few surviving early icons, the most spectacular are the portraits of Christ, the Virgin and Child with angels and saints, and St. Peter, from the monastery at Sinai, which was too remote to suffer iconoclast damage. The western church, led by a series of Greek popes, also supported icons in this period, and there are a number of important examples of religious images in Roman churches such as Santa Maria in Trastevere and Santa Maria Antiqua (fig. 46). The eventual ending of the long controversy over images in 843 stimulated other ecclesiastical developments, including the production of decorated liturgical manuscripts, commissioned for use in particular monasteries; many monastic houses now developed their own books of readings for the liturgical calendar and the main feasts. Perhaps surprisingly, the century of iconoclasm saw the evolution of an elaborate and beautiful hymnography in the eastern church, poetic homilies in complex metres and musical settings, which took over in popularity from the choral odes (*kontakia*) associated with the great sixth-century hymn-writer Romanos. A strong influence from Palestine, brought about by the arrival of a number of eastern monks in Constantinople, combined with the freedom won by the monastic movement after 843 to give a new direction to Byzantine liturgy.

Fig. 46 Detail of the palimpsest fresco with the Angel of the Annunciation, the enthroned Virgin and Child, and with Solomon and the Maccabees below; from the apse of Santa Maria Antiqua, Rome; seventh century.

Throughout this period emperors and bishops attempted to control dissension and pluralism in the church by the medium of church councils. The so-called Second Council of Nicaea in A D 787, which temporarily halted the iconoclasts, was the seventh and last such 'ecumenical' council to be recognised by both east and west. But there were as many breakaway councils and synods as there were official ones; there were also regional councils, such as the Synod of Whitby, held in 664 to settle the date on which Easter should be observed. The ties between Rome and England, reconverted by Augustine's mission, armed with service books, liturgical vessels and relics, of 597, were strong (pl. 30); they were reinforced in the seventh century by the then Archbishop of Canterbury, Theodore of Tarsus, himself from the east, and by Benedict Biscop, abbot of Wearmouth, who made many journeys to Rome, from which he brought Roman liturgy, music and manuscripts to England. Directly or indirectly, the papacy encouraged other such initiatives, and in this way Roman texts and Roman devotion reached the Picts, while monasteries such as Bobbio, Ripon and Canterbury received their charters from the popes, and from missionaries such as Willibrord, archbishop of the Frisians, their sanction and encouragement.

Conversion is a major theme of the period. For the first time, Byzantine emperors legislated for the enforced baptism of all Jews; the measure could hardly be enforced, and perhaps was not even intended to be, yet it was an ominous sign of real hostility towards Jews and Judaism. A growing intolerance marked the eastern empire in its dealing with religious minorities, together with dark fears of the coming of Antichrist. The period saw not only the gradual christianisation of the Roman, and later the Byzantine, empires, but also the entry on to the European stage of many new peoples and centres of civilisation; their conversion often served as a badge of acceptance. The religious and political map of the Mediterranean was transformed by the Arab conquests and the establishment of Islam as the religion of vast areas of formerly Christian territory; this time it was Christians who converted to Islam. Yet the formal split between east and west, in ecclesiastical terms, did not come until 1054, and when it did, the reasons had as much to do with custom and politics as they did with belief. Even in 900 it was still just possible to think, if a trifle optimistically, in terms of a united Christendom.

NOTES

1 (In translation) Wilkinson J., 1981, *Egeria's Travels*, 2nd edn, Warminster.

2 (In translation) Wilkinson J., 1977, *Jerusalem Pilgrims Before the Crusades*, Warminster, 93–116, 192–7.

The transmission of ideas

Ian Wood

The late fourth and early fifth centuries, that is the last century of the Roman empire, were marked by a formidable outpouring of scholarly writing, much of it theological. This was the age which saw some of the greatest Fathers of the Church: Hilary, Basil, Ambrose, Chrysostom, Jerome and Augustine among others. Four centuries later there would be something of an intellectual revival in both the Byzantine east and the Latin west, where Charlemagne and his descendants were the most notable patrons of the so-called Carolingian Renaissance. Again, much of the scholarship would be theological, although intellectually the period was much less innovative, being perhaps more important for the transmission of patristic and classical texts and ideas than the writing of new works. The centuries in between have no such scholarly reputation. They constitute the period which saw the fall of the western Roman empire, the establishment of Germanic kingdoms, many of which would be the foundations of the modern states of Europe, the Avar and Slav invasion and settlement of the Balkans, as well as the conquest of the southern and eastern Mediterranean and much of Spain by the forces of Islam.[1] These centuries are the classic Dark Ages – yet they too were important for the transmission of ideas, indeed in many respects they anticipate the Carolingian period, even though sixth- and seventh-century written culture cannot be seen as forming an intellectual programme in the way that the writings of the late eighth and ninth centuries can.

Nevertheless the two centuries following the collapse of imperial government in the west witnessed the transcription of texts and the classification of earlier knowledge in such handbooks as the *Institutiones* of Cassiodorus and the *Etymologiae* of Isidore of Seville. In the seventh and eighth centuries the eastern Mediterranean was provided with its equivalents in Anastasius of Sinai's *Viae Dux* and John of Damascus' *Source of Knowledge*. Books, however, were not the only ways by which ideas were transmitted: objects and buildings could convey Roman or barbarian ideas to posterity, and they did, even if they transformed them in the meantime.

It is as well to begin with the writers. In the early sixth century Cassiodorus, drawing on his own experience of government, compiled a body of model administrative letters, known as the *Variae*: subsequently, as the founder of the monastery of the Vivarium in southern Italy, he turned his mind to the transmission of religious learning, and in so doing played a particularly important role in the cultural history of early medieval Europe.[2] A complementary role was played by the Spanish ecclesiastic Bishop Isidore of Seville, whose *Etymologiae* were something of an encyclopedia for the early Middle Ages.[3] Writers from the sixth to the ninth centuries made a virtue of passing on established ideas. Eugippius, sixth-century abbot of the south Italian monastery of the Lucullanum, made an abridgement, and therefore an interpretation, of some of Augustine's teachings. Two centuries later Defensor of Ligugé, near Poitiers, made his own compilation out of existing theological writings. His near-contemporary, John of Damascus, created the most important of the Greek florilegia in the *Corpus Canonum*.

It would be wrong, however, simply to see the 'Dark Ages' as a period in which other people's ideas were transmitted in a more or less satisfactory fashion. There were writers with new ideas, or who developed established ones. In early sixth-century Italy Boethius wrote a series of philosophical treatises, dependent for the most part on and indeed transmitting the ideas of classical Greek philosophers, but achieving his own remarkable Christian stoicism in *The Consolation of Philosophy*.[4] At the end of the same century Pope Gregory the Great, drawing heavily on earlier patristic writers, added his sensitivities to theirs, as did Bede in the early eighth century. It is arguably, however, in the writing of narratives, whether of the *Lives* of saints (hagiography) or more generally of history, usually the history of the working out of God's plans, that the early medieval west found its own voice. In the fourth century it was the Greek east which established a tradition of hagiography, notably with the *Life of Saint Antony*, and subsequently with accounts of the stars of Egyptian and Syrian monasticism. Sulpicius Severus made a counter claim on behalf of one of the great saints of the fourth-century west with his *Life of Saint Martin* and his *Dialogues*. In the sixth century the same saint was one of the leading figures in the vast hagiographical output of Gregory of Tours. Gaul's early dominance in the field of western hagiography was challenged by Pope Gregory the Great in his *Dialogues*, which recorded the saints of sixth-century Italy, and which became one of the classics of hagiographic literature. In the seventh century, however, it was once again Gaul, or Francia, that saw the most interesting developments in hagiography, most notably in a group of highly political accounts of martyrdoms. Spain, like Italy, lagged behind in the production of hagiography, although it did boast a handful of monastic *Lives*, a well as the remarkable composite *Lives of the Fathers of Mérida*. The early eighth century saw a major outpouring of hagiography from Northumbria (and Mercia), in such Lives as those of Cuthbert, Wilfrid and Guthlac, which capitalised on the Lives of Antony and Martin as well as the writings of Gregory the Great.[5]

Equally substantial were the historiographical achievements of the period.[6] The *Gothic History* of Cassiodorus is lost, but the *Getica* of Jordanes, which was at least partly based on it, survives. There are the *Histories* of Gregory of Tours, concentrating largely on the kingdom of the Franks, but ultimately interested rather in the mysterious workings of the divine, and there is also the *Chronicle* of Fredegar, with its concerns, overt and coded, about the politics of the seventh-century Franks. From Spain comes the remarkably territorial *History of the Goths, Vandals and Suevi* by Isidore, and the *History of King Wamba*, a study of legitimate rule and rebellion, by Julian of Toledo. As regards the English there is Bede's *Ecclesiastical History*, concerned with the christianisation of the Anglo-Saxons, and more immediately with spiritual standards and church reform in the early eighth century. Finally, there is Paul the Deacon's *History of the Lombards*, combining the traditions of a kingdom recently taken over by Charlemagne with precise family and regional interests. These are all individual histories, taking the form of history writing in new ways, even though they took as their models the historical books of the Bible and such Christian histories as Orosius' *Seven Books Against the Pagans*, written in the early fifth century under the influence of Augustine. The sixth-century east also saw the writing of major works of history, both secular and ecclesiastical. The greatest of the Byzantine historians, Procopius, took as the model for his *Histories* of Justinian's wars the classical Greek historian Thucydides, rather than any more recent Christian writer.[7] He was followed by another classicising historian, Agathias, who was himself followed by Theophylact Simocatta.[8] There were also a number of early Byzantine church historians, including Socrates, Sozomen and Evagrius, as well as chroniclers, among them John Malalas and Theophanes. Nor did the east boast only writers of Greek, but also of Coptic and, notably in John of Ephesus, of Syriac.

The narrators of barbarian histories, most notably Jordanes and Paul the Deacon, purport to provide us with accounts of their chosen peoples from their very origins, through a period of migration, to their creation of kingdoms inside what had been the Roman empire. The early parts of these narratives are unquestionably constructs, drawing what they could from Roman sources, and even appropriating material relating to other peoples: as history they are, therefore, notoriously unreliable. Yet the narrators may on occasion have had access to oral traditions relating to individual barbarian leaders. That such traditions existed and were transmitted through the Germanic world may be seen in the strange inscription set up in the ninth century at Rök in central Scandinavia, to a king Theodoric. This is arguably, but not certainly, Theoderic king of the Ostrogoths, who ruled in Italy between AD 493 and 526 (fig. 3). Subsequently Theoderic the Ostrogoth did turn into a fully fledged figure of Germanic legend. How the histories of such early medieval kings were preserved to become the subject matter, however deformed, of medieval German poetry it is impossible to tell: literary works, like the Old English poem *Widsith*, present an image of peripatetic poets, with a repertory of heroic tales – and travelling poets can be traced in the late Viking period. There is also reference to Germanic poetry at Charlemagne's court, but it has not survived, and its subject matter must be a matter of guesswork. For the post-Roman period, however, Procopius may provide a more historical context for the northward transmission of stories relating to Theoderic the Ostrogoth, in his references to the movement of small groups, particularly of Heruli, north of the Danube, and to the journeys of emissaries, who certainly travelled as far as Denmark. Such journeys are also attested in Theoderic's own diplomatic letters, for instance to the Thuringians, preserved by Cassiodorus in his *Variae*.[9]

More basic, but in certain ways more scholarly, than the composition of new histories was the transmission or copying of ancient texts – something which during the fifth and sixth centuries was certainly carried out in private and episcopal households, but which, in the west at least, came increasingly to be associated with monasteries. As a result a substantial number of manuscripts survive from the early Middle Ages. In an age before printing, texts had to be copied by hand, and every copy was liable to introduce errors, not least because the Latin, like the Greek, language was steadily evolving throughout this period, and in so doing was becoming further and further removed from its classical form. In such a context errors of transcription were only too easy; there were, therefore, attempts to establish reliable texts. Already in the fifth century the Roman senator Symmachus set out to provide an accurate text of Livy's *Histories*. It was even more important to produce accurate copies of other texts, such as laws or scripture. Like the Byzantines under Justinian, the Visigoths in Spain and the Longobards (Lombards) in Italy tried to ensure the transmission of correct legal texts through governmental control of the production of lawbooks. Bishop Leodegar of Autun is known to have edited Roman and Frankish laws in the mid-seventh century. The Bible too needed its editors. Although Jerome's great translation of the Bible into Latin, the Vulgate, was only completed in the early fifth century, it required scholarship of a high order to produce first-rate texts of it, for instance at Monkwear-mouth-Jarrow in Northumbria in the late seventh century, and again in Tours in the late eighth.

The task of book production might, however, involve more than the transcription of texts. The actual presentation of those texts could be an art in itself. At its most basic this involved the choice of a style of handwriting, or script, since a variety of majuscule and minuscule hands evolved during the early Middle Ages, notably in a number of major Frankish, Anglo-Saxon and Irish monasteries, including Luxeuil, Corbie, Monkwearmouth-Jarrow and Lindisfarne. Moreover the style of handwriting could carry with it a meaning over and above the words which were written down. Thus when three copies of the Bible (one of them the surviving *Codex Amiatinus*) were made at the most romanising of the Northumbrian monasteries, the twin house of Monkwearmouth-Jarrow, they were written in a particularly beautiful Uncial hand, reminiscent of a hand popular in the Italy of Gregory the Great, the pope who had initiated the christianisation of the English (fig. 47). The choice of script was thus loaded with symbolism.[10]

It was not only through a choice of hand that a book designer could convey ideas over and above his or her text. Another major development of the early Middle Ages

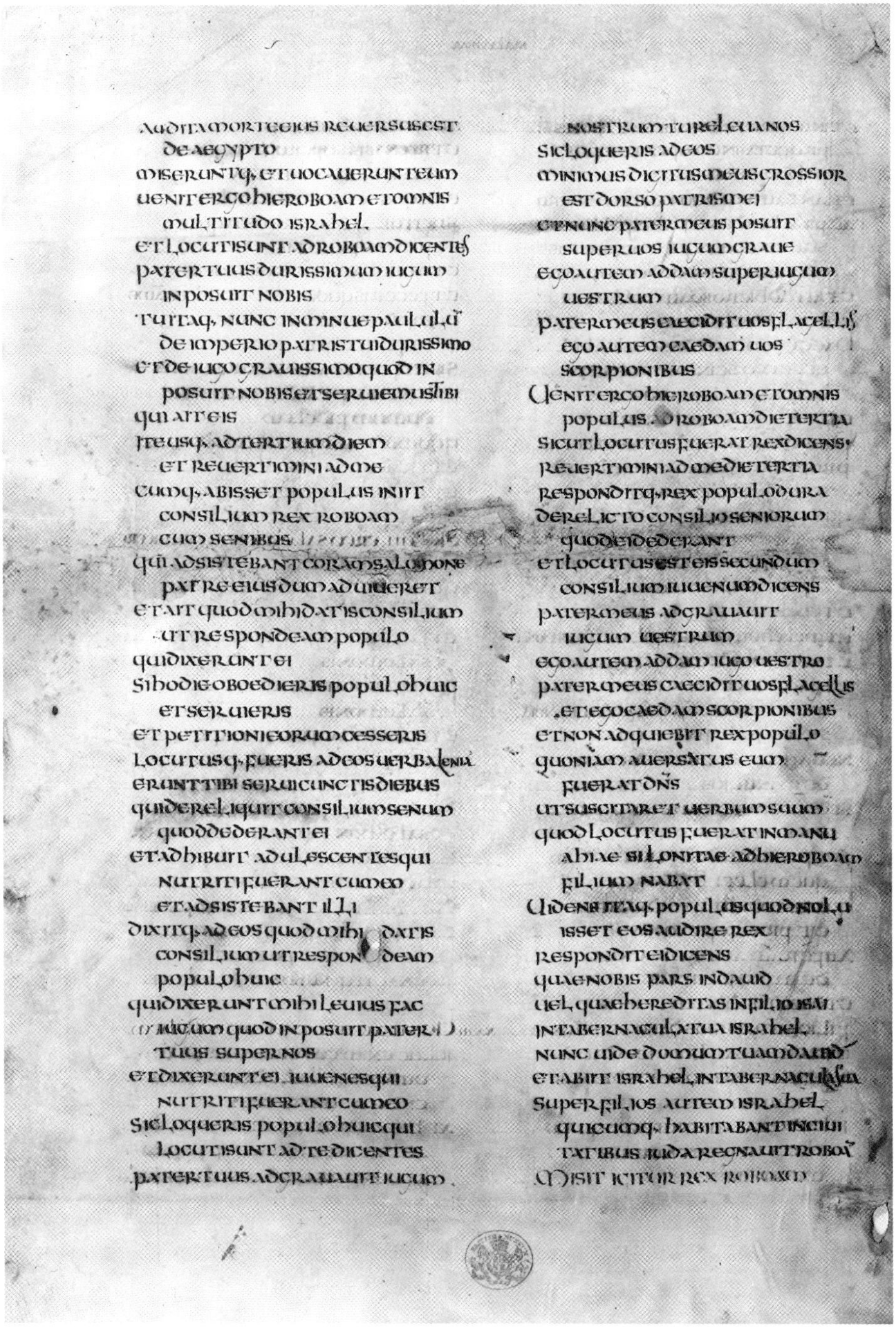

AUDITA MORTE EIUS REUERSUS EST
DE AEGYPTO
MISERUNTQ ET UOCAUERUNT EUM
UENIT ERGO HIEROBOAM ET OMNIS
MULTITUDO ISRAHEL
ET LOCUTI SUNT AD ROBOAM DICENTES
PATER TUUS DURISSIMUM IUGUM
IN POSUIT NOBIS
TU ITAQ NUNC IMMINUE PAULUL
DE IMPERIO PATRIS TUI DURISSIMO
ET DE IUGO GRAUISSIMO QUOD IN
POSUIT NOBIS ET SERUIEMUS TIBI
QUI AIT EIS
ITE USQ AD TERTIUM DIEM
ET REUERTIMINI AD ME
CUMQ ABISSET POPULUS INIIT
CONSILIUM REX ROBOAM
CUM SENIBUS
QUI ADSISTEBANT CORAM SALOMONE
PATRE EIUS DUM ADHUC UIUERET
ET AIT QUOD MIHI DATIS CONSILIUM
UT RESPONDEAM POPULO
QUI DIXERUNT EI
SI HODIE OBOEDIERIS POPULO HUIC
ET SERUIERIS
ET PETITIONI EORUM CESSERIS
LOCUTUSQ FUERIS AD EOS UERBA LENIA
ERUNT TIBI SERUI CUNCTIS DIEBUS
QUI DERELIQUIT CONSILIUM SENUM
QUOD DEDERANT EI
ET ADHIBUIT ADULESCENTES QUI
NUTRITI FUERANT CUM EO
ET ADSISTEBANT ILLI
DIXITQ AD EOS QUOD MIHI DATIS
CONSILIUM UT RESPONDEAM
POPULO HUIC
QUI DIXERUNT MIHI LEUIUS FAC
IUGUM QUOD IN POSUIT PATER
TUUS SUPER NOS
ET DIXERUNT EI IUUENES QUI
NUTRITI FUERANT CUM EO
SIC LOQUERIS POPULO HUIC QUI
LOCUTI SUNT AD TE DICENTES
PATER TUUS ADGRAUAUIT IUGUM

NOSTRUM TU RELEUA NOS
SIC LOQUERIS AD EOS
MINIMUS DIGITUS MEUS CROSSIOR
EST DORSO PATRIS MEI
ET NUNC PATER MEUS POSUIT
SUPER UOS IUGUM GRAUE
EGO AUTEM ADDAM SUPER IUGUM
UESTRUM
PATER MEUS CECIDIT UOS FLAGELLIS
EGO AUTEM CAEDAM UOS
SCORPIONIBUS
UENIT ERGO HIEROBOAM ET OMNIS
POPULUS AD ROBOAM DIE TERTIA
SICUT LOCUTUS FUERAT REX DICENS
REUERTIMINI AD ME DIE TERTIA
RESPONDITQ REX POPULO DURA
DERELICTO CONSILIO SENIORUM
QUOD EI DEDERANT
ET LOCUTUS EST EIS SECUNDUM
CONSILIUM IUUENUM DICENS
PATER MEUS ADGRAUAUIT
IUGUM UESTRUM
EGO AUTEM ADDAM IUGO UESTRO
PATER MEUS CECIDIT UOS FLAGELLIS
ET EGO CAEDAM SCORPIONIBUS
ET NON ADQUIEUIT REX POPULO
QUONIAM AUERSATUS EUM
FUERAT DNS
UT SUSCITARET UERBUM SUUM
QUOD LOCUTUS FUERAT IN MANU
AHIAE SILONITAE AD HIEROBOAM
FILIUM NABAT
UIDENS ITAQ POPULUS QUOD NOLU
ISSET EOS AUDIRE REX
RESPONDIT EI DICENS
QUAE NOBIS PARS IN DAUID
UEL QUAE HEREDITAS IN FILIO ISAI
IN TABERNACULA TUA ISRAHEL
NUNC UIDE DOMUM TUAM DAUID
ET ABIIT ISRAHEL IN TABERNACULA SUA
SUPER FILIOS AUTEM ISRAHEL
QUICUMQ HABITABANT IN CIUI
TATIBUS IUDA REGNAUIT ROBOAM
MISIT IGITUR REX ROBOAM

Fig. 47 The 'Greenwell Leaf'; a page from one of the great bibles produced at the twin monastery of Monkwearmouth/Jarrow for Abbot Ceolfrith, before he left for Rome in AD 716. This copy was presented to Worcester Cathedral by King Offa, but broken up following the Reformation. BL, Add. MS. 37777, f. 1r. (see also p. 247).

came in the illustration of the text.[11] Portraits of authors and pictures illustrating narratives seem to have been known in the de luxe volumes of classical antiquity. This tradition continued in the early Middle Ages, in the portrait of the Byzantine princess Juliana Anicia in her copy of the *Dioskurides*, now in Vienna (pl. 34), in the representations of imperial lawgivers (pl. 33), and more frequently of the evangelists. Alongside the evangelists are their symbols – angel, lion, bull and eagle. More spectacular is the decoration of text itself. Illustration of narrative is not common in western manuscripts of the fifth to seventh centuries, although it can be found in late antique and Byzantine works: the sixth-century Augustine Gospels, from Italy, are unusual in having two pages of narrative illustrations (pl. 30). Nevertheless, in Frankish manuscripts of the mid-eighth century the initial words of texts or sections of text are invaded by representations of birds and fish. In the British Isles similar passages had already become subsumed into highly decorated schemes, which add up to a pictorial revelation of the Word of God. The Books of Durrow, Lindisfarne and Kells are among the glories of this revelatory art – and in the Book of Kells this art is also employed to depict narrative.[12] For such decoration scribes had to find new models, and for this they turned as often to metalwork as to earlier manuscripts.[13] The animal ornament and abstract designs of Insular gospel books look to the zoomorphic interlace and cloisonné patterns on metalwork, while the lion of St. Mark which leaps across the page in the Echternach Gospels (pl. 32) may well have been inspired by an animal akin to that from the Hoxne hoard, which once was a handle on late Roman vase (pl. 31).

Images and decoration carried ideas and meaning alongside and even independent of words. This is not just true of manuscripts. Coins and jewellery were clearly intended to convey ideas – though here the ideas were often secular, looking back to Roman imperial, rather than religious, ideology. For the most part the coinage issued by barbarian rulers copied Roman coinage, and to start with at least an image of Roman hegemony was conveyed, because the kings of the new western kingdoms avoided putting their own portraits on coins. When the Merovingian king Theudebert put his portrait on an issue of gold coin the Byzantines noted the action and decried it. Later in the sixth century changes in the royal ideology and style of Visigothic Spain were reflected precisely in its coinage, which mirrored developments in the Byzantine east. As the style of the Visigothic kings became more imperial, so they developed their own imperial-style coinage.[14] The imagery of imperial coinage was not just borrowed by moneyers. For about two generations, beginning in the late fifth or early sixth century, medallions, known as bracteates, were produced both in the Danube basin and also in southern Denmark, although the relative chronology of the two centres of production is unclear. They were modelled on the imperial portraits of late Roman coinage, and whatever meaning they came to have, it must originally have had some reference to imperial power.

Imperial imitation was certainly not the only intention of the bracteates – some of the more complex or less identifiable images may depict Germanic legends, and they may have had religious significance (fig. 48). Such pagan images are more obviously present on several silver-gilt brooches from sixth-century Scandinavia. Here there appears to be reference to such stories as that of Sigurd the Dragon-slayer and of Odin himself. The presence of these images is of vital importance for establishing the antiquity of some of the Germanic myths, which were only written down considerably later, notably in the twelfth century by Snorri Sturluson. In England Sigurd appears on ninth-century Northumbrian sculpture, and another figure of legend, Weland, appears on the eighth-century whale bone box known as the Franks Casket (pl. 35). So too does Egil, although, as in the case of other named heroes, his legend has not survived. On the other hand the most famous of the Old English poetic legends, that of Beowulf, presents us with some of the problems to be found in the sagas written by Snorri. Although the story draws on genuine historical events, and on figures of early legend, the author of the poem that has come down to us was no simple transmitter of an ancient tale, but a writer structuring and inventing material for literary reasons, and doing so perhaps not much earlier than the year 1000, the approximate date of the sole manuscript of the work.

Fig. 48
Germanic gold bracteate, imitating a fourth-century Trier 'Urbs Roma' coin, with the head of Roma above the symbol of the city, the she-wolf suckling Romulus and Remus; later fifth–early sixth century (see also p. 237).

Fig. 49 Gilt-bronze plaque, possibly from a helmet, identified by an inscription as King Agilulf (AD 591–615) enthroned with attributes and acolytes; Val de Nievole, near Lucca, Italy.

Imperial ideology was transmitted on objects other than coins and bracteates. Certain types of brooches seem to have carried particular imperial connotations. Some brooches appear to have been appropriate for the imperial family, or favoured beneficiaries, perhaps barbarian kings acting as federates for the empire. Imperial-style objects were also copied, not always very well, presumably to imply imperial-style power, as in the famous treasure from Pietroasa. At a slightly lower level a type of fibula indicative of high status in the Roman army and administration was also conferred on or copied by barbarian rulers, one of the finest being that from the grave of the Frankish king Childeric (d. AD 481) at Tournai (pl. 2, and see also fig. 16). Dress could symbolise status as clearly as title, and sub-Roman and barbarian leaders relished Roman-sounding titles; even in the depths of south-west Wales Vortipor was proclaimed in stone as a 'Protector' in the early sixth century, and lower down the social scale, and in some ways yet more remarkably, in the uplands of Snowdonia a man proclaimed himself to be a citizen (*civis*) of Gwynedd at approximately the same time.

Many aspects of imperial style were borrowed from the empire by barbarian rulers. This is clear from Isidore's account of King Leovigild of the Visigoths as being the first to sit on a throne in royal robes. An image of a king seated on a throne is presented by a Longobard visor inscribed with the name of King Agilulf: the inspiration for the scene is apparently an image of a late Roman or Byzantine emperor surrounded by subject people (fig. 49). Although we have no such pictorial representation for the Frankish kingdom, we have panegyrics delivered at court, praising a king's virtues often in classical or biblical terms, and thus continuing the traditions of the later Roman empire, and paralleling those of Byzantium.[15] The great gold votive crowns of Visigothic kings found at Guarrazar in Spain are best seen as offerings of a kind made initially in a Christian context by Constantine (pl. 18 and cover). Even a treasure as far removed from the centres of imperial power as that from Mound 1 at Sutton Hoo includes objects best understood in terms of Roman models:[16] the famous helmet – like those from Vendel and Valsgärde in Sweden – has its origins in parade helmets of the Roman cavalry (see pl. 48), and it may be that the whetstone should be set alongside some of the ritual objects depicted in the *Notitia Dignitatum*, a late Roman list of officers which also illustrates the insignia of their offices (pl. 1).

Objects could gain connotations over and above their original meanings. The connotations associated with surviving objects are lost to us, though written sources tell us of pieces whose histories were well known, and which as a result gained a particular cachet. A gold missorium given by the consul Aetius to the Visigothic king Thorismund was kept in the Visigothic treasury, and King Sisenand was later prevented from giving it to the Frankish king Dagobert in return for military assistance, because the nobility of Spain objected to its alienation. Gregory of Tours tells how Chilperic I had an enormous gold salver created, to the glory of the Frankish people – and probably in deliberate response to Byzantine treasures. Such objects would have been produced at feasts, and their histories retold. Paul the Deacon reveals that the Longobard king Ratchis displayed a cup reputedly made out of the skull of King Cunimund, on the orders of Alboin, on such an occasion. It was a cup with a particular history, since it was thought to have prompted the murder of Alboin at the instigation of his wife, Cunimund's daughter. The Avar treasure distributed by Charlemagne was perhaps produced and discussed in a manner similar to Alboin's skull-cup. That objects and their display was one aspect of the transmission and interpretation of the heroic past is implied by what is related about treasure and weapons in *Beowulf*, not least about the gold collar worn by Hygelac during the historically attested Frisian raid (see pl. 51).

Ideas implying imitation of or even rivalry with the Roman or Byzantine empire were thus conveyed in images and objects. They were also conveyed in panegyrics and, more dramatically, in ritual actions.[17] Much of the imperial ceremony of the late Roman and early Byzantine empires took place in the circus or hippodrome, which in the case of Constantinople was actually attached to the imperial palace (fig. 50). When in the later sixth century the Frankish king Chilperic I restored circuses in Soissons and Paris, the two cities which he regarded as his capitals, he was probably not doing so simply in order to please the people by providing them with horse-races, but rather to enhance his imperial image. Similarly, when Adaloald was elevated to the Longobard kingship in AD 604 the ceremony took place in the circus at Milan. A generation earlier the Visigoths had gone one step further when King Leovigild founded a complete city for his son Reccared, calling it Reccopolis, in an imperial manner.

Buildings and their decoration bring us to another medium for the transmission of ideas, and here ecclesiastical and imperial ideas could and did merge. Some churches

(*Left*) Fig. 50 Ivory diptych panel, the emperor in triumphal costume, holding sceptre and *mappa* and presiding over a circus scene of four *quadrigae* racing round a *spina*; inscribed for the senatorial families of the Lampadii and Rufii, first half of the fifth century.

(*Right*) Fig. 51 Anglo-Saxon crypt with Roman *spolia* from the church built by St. Wilfrid at Hexham, Northumberland, England; late seventh century. The crypt may be a deliberate evocation of the Holy Sepulchre at Jerusalem.

were built with very specific resonances in mind.[18] Charlemagne's Palatine chapel at Aachen, at least in certain respects, was modelled on the Church of San Vitale in Ravenna, which with its imperial portraits of Justinian and Theodora could easily be mistaken as an imperial church (pls. 26, 36). Moreover, for the cognoscenti the imperial nature of the Palatine chapel would have been enhanced by the fact that much of its marble seems to have been brought as *spolia* from the buildings of Ravenna. More prosaically the churches of Northumbria enhanced their links with the city of St. Peter by reemploying Roman stonework (fig. 51). In Rome itself it was relatively easy for the popes to draw physically on the past: most papal buildings of the early Middle Ages made use of *spolia* of earlier buildings. The entrance to the Zeno chapel in Santa Prassede, built by Pope Paschal in the early ninth century, employs highly decorated antique columns and capitals (and copies) to create the effect of an ancient, jewel-like edifice, whose interior certainly looked back to papal and possibly imperial buildings

of the fifth century.[19] In the Byzantine world it was not only *spolia* that carried meaning: to have access to the stone of certain quarries was a recognisable mark of a patron's status and connections.

Like Charlemagne's Palatine chapel, other Carolingian buildings were designed so as to prompt comparisons with imperial and papal Rome (fig. 5). The main church at the monastery of Fulda, begun in the ninth century by abbot Ratgar but never finished, was intended to be a copy of St. Peter's, and just as St. Peter's was built to house the body of an apostle, so too Fulda had the body of the apostle of the Germans, Boniface. The crypt of St. Peter's was copied at much the same time at San Vincenzo al Volturno: there too the bones of a martyr, St. Vincent, were supposedly enshrined. At Ripon and Hexham in the seventh century bishop Wilfrid built crypts which seem to have been intended to recreate the world of the Roman catacombs, while at the same time, perhaps, echoing the sepulchre of Christ at Jerusalem (fig. 51).

The Church of the Holy Sepulchre seems in fact to have been the inspiration behind many centrally planned churches. The parallels could be brought out in sermons, and in the liturgy, which together provided a constant commentary on ecclesiastical buildings and the rituals which took place within them. In addition to the Church of the Holy Sepulchre the Temple of Solomon, which no longer existed, but which could be recreated from biblical descriptions, was another source of inspiration. Justinian is said to have claimed that he surpassed Solomon's work in building the Church of the Holy Wisdom (Santa Sophia) in Constantinople: he was certainly determined to eclipse Juliana Anicia's church of St. Polyeuktos, with its Solomonic symbolism. The biblical description of the Temple perhaps underlies the proportions of the church at Monkwearmouth in Northumbria. Again sermons could make the connections apparent, for all churches were theoretically representations of the Temple. At Germigny-des-Prés, outside Orléans, bishop Theodulf made the association of his chapel and Solomon's Temple explicit by having an image of the Ark of the Covenant set up in mosaic in the apse. Four centuries earlier, in about AD 400, Jerusalem itself was evoked in the Church of Santa Pudenziana in Rome, where the apse mosaic shows Christ as a divine philosopher teaching his disciples in the forum of Jerusalem, whose skyline is instantly recognisable from the portrayals of the complex of the Holy Sepulchre, with its massive jewelled cross. Rome and Jerusalem could be recreated anywhere in the Christian world by a careful use of space, imagery and materials.

Santa Pudenziana and Germigny-des-Prés stand near the beginning and end of a period in which apse mosaics were the chief glories of the decorative schemes of basilican churches. The vast expanse available for decoration at the east end of such churches allowed for the development of a whole range of iconographic schemes,

(*Right*) Fig. 52 West portal jambs (south) of the church of San Miguel de Liño, Naranco, Spain, decorated with circus scenes; ninth century.

among them some radically different treatments of the single topic of the Transfiguration of Christ: the vision of Ezekiel at Christ Latomos in Thessaloniki, the Transfiguration
at St. Catherine's, Sinai, the very spot at which Moses is said to have seen the burning
bush – itself an antecedent of the Transfiguration – and the exactly contemporary
portrayal of the Transfiguration at San Apollinare in Classe in Ravenna. While the
image of St. Catherine's can be seen largely as biblical narrative, that at Ravenna,
with the intrusive figure of Apollinaris, adds a political element, relating to conflict
between Ravenna and Rome then current. Even more complex is the iconography of
the eucharist which swamps the east end of another Ravenna church of the mid-sixth
century, San Vitale.

Although it was rarely used to convey so complex an intellectual scheme, sculpture,
whether architectural or freestanding, could likewise transmit complex ideas through
a set of highly loaded iconographic systems. As in the classical world, the style of
capitals used in a church could carry meaning.[20] In the Church of Santa Maria Maggiore built by Pope Sixtus the capitals were Ionic, an archaic style which deliberately
looked back to an earlier Rome, and which had once been appropriate for the temples
of goddesses, but was now presented as that appropriate for Mary, the Mother of God.
More direct iconography could also be used. The door-jambs of the ninth-century
Church of San Miguel de Liño on Monte Naranco, in the Spanish kingdom of the
Asturias, are decorated with images apparently taken from a late Roman consular
diptych, showing the consul beginning the consular games (figs 52, 53).[21] The diptych
may have been kept in the royal treasury, to be produced, like the skull-cup of Cunimund, at banquets, but it was also a resource for a stone mason. The scene may seem
totally inappropriate for a church, but for a royal church, founded in a kingdom with
imperial pretensions, in opposition to those of its Muslim neighbours, it might have
carried all sorts of complex meanings of triumphal Christian rulership. What San
Miguel de Liño shows is something of the way in which images and ideas were used
in the early Middle Ages. There was nothing necessarily slavish about the borrowing,
whether in stone, metalwork or on parchment. Images and words were resources,
which were adapted to transmit a variety of ideas, often more than one at once.

Infinitely more complex than the carvings at San Miguel de Liño are those on the
monument at Ruthwell, in Dumfriesshire in Scotland, probably carved towards the
middle of the eighth century. The iconographic scheme of this monument, its narrative
images, its vinescroll, its Latin inscriptions in Roman capitals and its Old English
inscriptions in runes, is of extraordinary complexity.[22] One of its most prominent images
is of Christ being adored by beasts in the desert (fig. 54). The image of Christ could be
derived from that of a Roman emperor or senator, his *mappa* (cloth) for starting the

(*Right*) Fig. 53 Diptych of the consul Rufus Gennadius Orestes, Rome, AD 530. The latest
surviving consular diptych from the western empire (see also p. 123).

consular games transformed into a scroll. His antecedent, however, is not the consul of San Miguel de Liño, but a figure closer to the tremendous Christ appearing as judge in the apse mosaic of Sts Cosmas and Damian in Rome, and copied in a number of Roman churches during the ninth century. Sts Cosmas and Damian was built by Pope Felix IV in AD 526, possibly within what had been the audience hall of the city prefect. Christ as judge was an image perfectly suited to such a building: where the city prefect had judged, Christ now towered in judgement – and his judgement is not imperial, but otherworldly, dispensed by a bearded deity, who is set against a background of apocalyptic clouds. At Ruthwell a related figure was used in different circumstances to different effect – he is adored by beasts in the desert, itself a symbol of monasticism.

Another Northumbrian monument, at Bewcastle, also presents a figure of Christ, which although formally similar to that at Ruthwell has a different context, and must have had a different meaning. It is apparently balanced not by other religious figures, but by a man with a hawk, and in so far as the runic inscription can be read it suggests a primarily commemorative monument rather than a theological one. The combination of religious and secular imagery, which is also present at San Miguel de Liño, is perhaps best exemplified by the eighth-century Franks Casket, again from Northumbria. It has its religious imagery – Christ and the Magi – and it looks to the Holy Land in a depiction of the sack of Jerusalem by the emperor Titus. It also remembers classical Rome with a scene of Romulus and Remus, as well as the pagan Germanic past, with two scenes whose meaning is no longer entirely clear, and with a depiction of Wayland the Smith (pl. 35). He is shown fashioning a skull-cup, like that commissioned by Alboin. Perhaps more than any other single object it gives a hint of the range of ideas transmitted in the early Middle Ages, and of the determined attempt made by some to synthesise the wealth of traditions to which they were the heirs.

NOTES

1 Brown, 1996.
2 Momigliano, 1955.
3 Fontaine, 1959.
4 Chadwick, 1981; Gibson, 1981.
5 Berschin, 1986–91.
6 Goffart, 1988.
7 Cameron, 1985.
8 Cameron, 1970.
9 Moorhead, 1992.
10 Wood, 1996.
11 Hubert *et al.*, 1969.
12 Henderson, 1987.

13 Wilson, 1984.
14 Grierson and Blackburn, 1986.
15 George, 1995.
16 Bruce-Mitford, 1975–1983.
17 MacCormack, 1981; MacCormick, 1986.
18 Heitz, 1980.
19 Krautheimer, 1980.
20 Onians, 1988.
21 Fontaine, 1973.

Fig. 54 The Ruthwell Cross; panel showing Christ adored by the beasts in the desert. Ruthwell, Dumfriesshire, Scotland; Northumbrian, mid-eighth century.

From the Elysian Fields to the Christian paradise

Eutychia Kourkoutidou-Nicolaidou

The end of the ancient world was marked by shifts and changes in a variety of cultural spheres, ranging from the techniques and external forms of art to the ideology and world view that expressed the new era.[1] These changes serve as reference points for an outline and an understanding of the historical period known as late antiquity, as a discrete cultural entity in which the new trends gradually took shape. As a time of creativity and evolution, it also acted as a period of transition to the Middle Ages.[2] Within the framework of these changes, the new religion and the new ecclesiastical practices were a steady focal point around which the new ideological currents and social realignments revolved, as Christianity gradually penetrated the various social strata before becoming the official religion of the state. At the same time, important aspects of the classical spirit and civilisation still survived to complete our picture of late antiquity.

In ancient cultures, a major part of religious and private life (which, after all, constitute the clearest expression of the world view of any period) is a belief in life after death and a preoccupation with the dead. In their minds, the ancient Greeks identified the Elysian Fields with the Isles of the Blest, a paradisal land where, having passed before the supreme judges Rhadamanthus, Aeacus and Minos, the gods' elect enjoyed what ordinary mortals were denied on earth.[3] Late Antiquity was a time of religious inquiry, when a new type of religiosity was evolving, even among the most ardent of pagans.[4] The fundamental question of human existence was not ephemeral happiness, but human beings' relationship with the Divine and the salvation of the human soul. Thus, it is the transformation of the paradise of material and earthly well-being and pleasure (represented by the Elysian Fields) into the Christian Paradise of heavenly life and the salvation of the souls of the 'righteous' that differentiates the spiritual and religious substructure and fundamental semantics of Christian iconography, even though many of the morphological elements and semiotic systems of the ancient world are retained.

In the Christian cemeteries of late antiquity, the changes brought about by the new Christian faith are evidenced in the texts and symbols of tomb inscriptions, the iconography of tomb paintings, burial customs and the contents of the tombs.

The exhibition titled *From the Elysian Fields to the Christian Paradise* is staged in a room in the Early Christian wing of the Museum of Byzantine Culture. The wing comprises three thematic units covering various aspects of the culture of late antiquity up to the eighth and ninth centuries: Christian worship and the Christian Church; public and private life; and burials and cemeteries.

The last unit is designed to shed light on the main aspects of the changes which the new religion brought about in the specific area of belief and speculation about life after death, and in people's preoccupation with the dead as a part of their everyday life and as an expression of their metaphysical anxiety. With this objective in mind, the basic theme of the exhibition has been divided into smaller units: the location of the cemeteries in Thessaloniki and the typology of the tombs; typical examples of tombs which have been removed intact from the cemeteries; paintings which have been detached from the walls of tombs, where they could not be preserved *in situ*; funerary inscriptions; and a rich collection of grave goods, providing substantial information about burial customs that reflect religious beliefs and private life, two areas in which elements of ancient culture still lingered on.

Thessaloniki is a densely populated European city and a major Mediterranean port, whose historical and cultural continuity has remained unbroken ever since its foundation in 315 BC. The first Roman tetrarchy was a particularly significant period in the city's history, for it was then that Galerius Caesar (AD 50–311) made Thessaloniki his seat and built a splendid palace complex. Not long after-wards, when Constantine the Great had con-structed the harbour at the south-west end of the city and the walls had been extended and rebuilt, Thessaloniki achieved its definitive form as a walled city, a form it retained until the end of the nine-teenth century.

The ancient necropolises lay outside the east and west walls. Christian burials from the second and third centuries are found on the same sites, included indiscriminately among the pre-existing pagan burials. Subsequently, special Christian cem-eteries were created around the graves and shrines of martyrs, and later on in areas specified by the city's Church. From the eighth or ninth century onwards, the dead were buried inside the city, either in churches (for important ecclesiastical and political figures) or in the precincts of monasteries and churches. The relocation of the cemeteries to residential areas occasioned major changes in the urban organisation of intramural Thessaloniki and marked a significant stage in its evolution from an ancient Greek city into a Byzantine *kastron*, or fortified city.

In Thessaloniki's cemeteries, the prevalent typo-logy and form of the graves in the early centuries of the Christian era remained much the same for Christians, as also for Jews, who formed a substan-tial community in the city from that time onwards. As in the past, marble sarcophagi were customary

(cat. 1, 2), as were inhumations in amphorae or other vessels for everyday use (cat. 3, 4), tile graves (cat. 5), cist graves (cat. 6) and barrel-vaulted graves, either alone or in groups (cat. 7, 8). The Christian burials are chiefly distinguished by the east–west orientation of the body; apart from those cases, of course, in which the cross, the chi-rho or some other Christian symbol in the painted decoration of the tomb or on any of the objects found inside it clearly attests that the deceased was a Christian.

Many of the tombs had grave-markers in the form of either marble or stone slabs with epitaphs, while others re-used older grave stelae or grave altars.[5] Inscribed stelae embedded in altar-shaped above-ground structures over tombs have recently been found in the east cemetery.[6] There are also funerary inscriptions on sarcophagi (cat. 1, 2).

Certain features and conventional expressions established in late antiquity are found in the earliest Christian funerary inscriptions.[7] One hangover from antiquity is the inclusion of the patronymic with the name of the deceased (cat. 11, 15), while hellenised Roman names and titles attest Roman influence (cat. 12, 14, 16, 18, 19, 44, 46, 48). At the same time, conventional obituary formulae such as 'in remembrance' are found alongside symbols of the new religion such as the chi-rho (cat. 9), the cross, the fish and the dove, together with new expressions which simply and succinctly state the

Fig. 55 Clay vessels from tombs of Thessaloniki, 3rd–4th centuries. (From left: cat. 33, 32, 30.)

believer's new relationship with death: 'memorial', 'sleeping place' or 'sleeping place until the resurrection', which are used to denote the tomb; and 'I believe in eternal life', 'sleeping in peace', 'at rest', 'in salvation' (cat. 10, 11, 15, 16, 20). These formulae reflect the essential belief of the new religion that the grave is a place where the dead sleep, a transitional state until the Last Judgement, when it is expected that the dead will rise, the righteous will inherit the Kingdom of Heaven and the human soul will be saved. In addition, the word 'brothers' is also used to signify members of the Christian community (cat. 1). The Christian grave inscriptions supply abundant data for the prosopography of the period, and also information about people's occupations and the social structure of the city (cat. 9, 12, 13, 14, 15, 17, 18, 19), the ownership and purchase prices of tombs and the custom of permitting a privately-owned tomb to be used for the burial of some other person, even a non-relation (cat. 10, 11, 12, 14, 17, 21, 22, 44, 45, 47). Graves in Thessaloniki were markedly more expensive than in other, smaller, towns. The inscriptions also suggest that grave robbery was rife at this time (cat. 13), and threats and curses are inscribed on many tombstones to deter thieves.[8]

The Christian tombs from the third to the sixth century have yielded a rich collection of some of the most important wall-paintings in the Christian world. The subject matter either comes directly from the Old or New Testament or makes symbolical or allegorical allusion to the beliefs of the new religion, such as life after death, the salvation of the soul and so on.[9]

A large number of early Christian tombs from the third century and the first half of the fourth are covered with floral decoration. The motifs reflect the ancient perception of material well-being and delight in the Elysian Fields: trees and plants, flowers and fruit, birds and garlands (cat. 36), *canthari* flanked by peacocks (cat. 8), all composing a picture of paradisal bliss. In some cases, the imagery verges on the extreme, with mouth-watering foodstuffs, slaughtered animals, fish and game, fruit, and brimming drinking vessels (cat. 39, 40). These subjects bring to mind the ironic and exaggerated description of the Isles of the Blest in Lucian's *True History*.[10]

Another group of tombs, dating from the third to the fifth century, are decorated with a painted imitation of marble cladding reminiscent of the sumptuous polychrome marble and inlaid decorative compositions with which the walls of contemporary public buildings were faced, in the *Incrustationstyl*. One typical example is a double barrel-vaulted tomb in which one chamber is decorated with elaborate imitation marble revetment and the other with themes from the Old and New Testaments (cat. 34).

Scenes from the Old and New Testaments make up the thematic repertory of another important group of tombs, their common denominator being allegorical allusions to the redemptive work of Our Lord. The main Old Testament subjects include Daniel in the Lions' Den, Abraham's Sacrifice, Shadrach, Meshach and Abednego in the Furnace, Noah's Ark, Jonah and the Whale, and Adam and Eve in the Garden of Eden. The New Testament themes are taken from the life of Christ, and their content is eschatological, rather than narrative or historical: the Adoration of the Magi, the Baptism of Christ, the Wedding in Cana, the Miracle of the Loaves and Fishes, the Healing of the Paralysed Man, the Raising of Lazarus. We also find the Martyrdom of St. Thecla at the stake and her vision of Christ in the form of St. Paul.[11] This thematic repertory is enriched by symbolic representations reflecting the ideology of the Christian faith, such as Christ the Good Shepherd and the Praying Soul, and also by new logograms and symbols of the new religion, such as the chi-rho and the cross. Other subjects, such as the lamb, the lion, the dove, the deer approaching the water to drink and the peacocks flanking a *cantharus*, are symbolic expressions of religious concepts originating chiefly in the Psalms and alluding to Paradise and life in heaven.[12]

One third-century tomb (cat. 35) juxtaposes such Old Testament themes as Daniel in the Lions' Den, Abraham's Sacrifice and Noah's Ark with an allegorical representation of Christ as the Good Shepherd and a rare iconographical type of the Raising of Lazarus. The Old Testament story of Susanna (cat. 41) is also interesting for its allegorical symbolism: the figure of Susanna praying among the condemnatory Elders symbolises the Church, which is persecuted, yet triumphs. Another allegorical scene shows a sailing-boat with a lone occupant, voyaging across a sea teeming with fish (cat. 37); the other walls and the ceiling are illustrated with the landscape of Paradise. The scene may be interpreted as an allegory of humanity sailing towards the heavenly haven of salvation.

The so-called tomb of Eustorgios (fourth century; cat. 7) contains a family scene set in a flowering paradisal landscape which includes a building. One of the most unusual examples of Christian tomb painting, it is believed to illustrate a ceremony of homage to the family's dead, during which libations of oil, wine or milk would have been made on the grave or on a funeral altar.[13]

The cross, the supreme symbol of the Christian religion because of Christ's sacrifice upon it, is presented in various forms in the decoration of the early Christian tombs: Greek, Latin, Maltese or polyactinal, ornamented with leafy tendrils at the base, or flanked by birds, plants and flowers. No less frequent a motif is the chi-rho, often surrounded by floral ornamentation (cat. 38). Other subjects that decorated the Christian tombs in the third and fourth centuries started to fade out, until, by the sixth century, the principal motif in tomb painting was the cross, the triumphal weapon in the believer's struggle with death (cat. 42, 43).[14]

As well as the varied iconography which refers to and expresses the new, Christian, belief in life after death and the soul's progress towards salvation, the frescoes in Thessaloniki's Christian tombs also illustrate the evolution of the painting of late antiquity – tomb painting being a genre, furthermore, that demands speed and skill in its execution. Christian tomb painting is a major aspect of the pictorial creativity of late antiquity, and reveals the basic elements of the change that accompanied the departure from the aesthetics of the Classical period[15] and the emergence of a dynamic art that combined symbolism with realism. Certainly, many of the paintings in the Christian tombs are hardly works of great inspiration; but some of them clearly betray the hand of major artists, who must have been commissioned to paint the tombs of the city's wealthiest families. The work of these important painters reflects the main features of the painting of the time: bright colours, with a predilection for red and green; broad brushstrokes; bold outlines, which nonetheless do not detract from an overall impressionistic effect in the figures and in the composition as a whole; and finally the absence of any connection between the painted landscape and the human figures.[16]

Apart from their considerable value as genuine reflections of art, craft, industry, daily life and commercial relations, the finds from the tombs give, above all, some very useful information about the most prevalent burial customs in the first centuries of the Christian era. The tomb contents can be divided into three categories:

1. Jewellery, fabrics, gold thread and other accessories used in dressing the dead, as well as objects belonging to the deceased which were placed in the tomb by the family. The dressing up of the dead in their jewellery was an ancient custom that survived in Thessaloniki's Christian tombs until the fifth century. It then died out, probably because the Church demanded greater frugality in burials.

The jewellery and other objects in this category presented in the exhibition include gold and bronze earrings; gold, iron, bronze, lead and clay finger rings; bronze, glass and jet bracelets and necklace beads; fibulae and buckles; bone pins and gold belt-plates; small cylindrical caskets and looking-glasses; metal earpicks for cosmetic use; strigils; daggers; and iron nails from the shoes of the dead.

2. Objects used during the burial and objects connected with the funerary cult. This category includes ceramic and glass vessels for the oil, wine, milk and honey used in the funeral libations, *unguentaria* and lamps. These vessels had specific shapes and were usually small in size and manufactured in pottery workshops near the cemeteries exclusively for funerary use.[17] The ordinary pottery vessels – cooking utensils or amphorae – containing the various liquids for the libations or the funeral suppers were generally smashed after use, either inside or outside the tomb.

3. Coins and coin hoards. The placing of a coin upon the corpse was a surviving ancient custom that was frequently, if not invariably, practised in the early Byzantine period until the sixth century, after which it virtually disappeared.[18] The coins were of bronze and were placed in the mouth or on the chest of the deceased. Gold *danakes* – gold foil bearing the impression of a coin – were sometimes used in the late Roman period, being placed in the mouth of the deceased instead of an obol, as payment for Charon. In addition to these single coins, hoards of coins are also found in Thessalonian tombs up to the sixth century, either inside a pot or heaped up somewhere in the tomb. Excavations also indicate that it was sometimes custo-

mary to throw down coins outside the tombs or in burial courtyards (cat. 24).

The exhibition also presents a selection of typical pottery from the third to the sixth century from graves in Thessaloniki (cat. 33), a collection of jewellery and various small objects from the second to the sixth century (cat. 50–55) and a collection of typical glassware (cat. 56). Apart from these, in order to demonstrate how much the contents of these tombs have contributed to our archaeological and historical knowledge, a considerable part of the exhibition is taken up by grave groups, in which the finds are presented as an inseparable component of the tomb from which they came, if possible, or even of the burial courtyard as well, as in the case of the Axios burial complex (cat. 24). Finds from the latter include a marble statue of the Good Shepherd (possibly a table support) and a large number of coins.

Another way of displaying tomb contents is to group them in small units, one for each tomb in which they were found. The finds from the excavation of the site of the Museum of Byzantine Culture (cat. 29, 30, 31, 32) are presented in this manner, as are those from the excavation of the Lyssiatrion site (cat. 25, 26, 27, 28).

NOTES

1 Marrou 1977, 12–13.
2 See Παπούλιας 1994, 245.
3 Κακριδής 1986, vols 2, 333 and 3, 264.
4 Marrou 1977, 21.
5 Τσιγαρίδα – Λοβέρδου – Τσιγαρίδας 1979, 2–29.
6 Ελευθεριάδου 1989, 271–82.
7 Λοβέρδου – Τσιγαρίδα 1994.
8 Feissel 1980, 459–72.
9 Μαρκή 1990, 171–94.
10 Scholia in Lucianum 1906, 2–4.
11 Παζαράς 1981, 383–5.
12 Velmans 1969, 39.
13 See Pelekanidis 1965, 215–35.
14 See Πελεκανίδου 1994.
15 Grabar 1966, 43–51.
16 Pelekanidis 1965, 229–30.
17 Μακροπούλου 1994.
18 Μακροπούλου 1994.

ACKNOWLEDGEMENTS

The author would like to thank Elena Angelidis for translating this paper.

Catalogue of the exhibition 'From the Elysian Fields to the Christian Paradise'

Museum of Byzantine Culture, Thessaloniki

K. Eleftheriadou,
A. Loverdou-Tsigarida,
D. Makropoulou,
E. Marki, D. Nalpantis,
E. Pelekanidou

1–8 Tomb Typology

1

4th century.

Sarcophagus from the Church of St. Demetrius. Three pieces of the cornice with the inscription:

'Julios Julianos the beloved, (from) the brothers'

ΑΓ 3188 (ΜΘ 6126)

Τσιγαρίδας – Λοβέρδου 1979, no. 26.

2

3rd century.

Sarcophagus from the Eastern Early Christian Cemetery with a saddleback cover, stylised acroteria and the inscription:

'Tomb of Aurelios Sabbatios, son of Marcus'

ΑΓ 3187 (ΜΘ 5675)

Πέτσας 1966, 338.

3

3rd century.

Inhumation and cremation burial in cooking utensils from the Eastern Cemetery.

ΒΚ 4467/149, 24

4

4th century.

Inhumation in an amphora, which is covered by another one, from the Eastern Cemetery.

BK 4467/191, 192

5

3rd century.

Tile grave from the Eastern Cemetery.

It contained a bronze coin (BN 2146/37) and three clay vessels (BK 4467/25, 27, 62).

6

4th century.

Cist grave from the Western Early Christian Cemetery, the walls of which are painted with geometrical motifs and with imitation marble cladding.

BT 158

The tomb contained two clay vessels and sherds of two others (BK 4518/12, 13, 67, 85), a glass flask and fragments of a second (BY 217/7, 23).

Ναλπάντης 1987, 405

7

4th century.

Barrel-vaulted tomb from the Western Cemetery with an externally flat surface, a horizontal entrance, a headrest and painted decoration with representations of a family funeral cult and symbolic scenes (pl. 37).

BCH 1931, 494; Pelekanidis 1965; Μαρκή 1990, 174–7.

8

4th century.

Barrel-vaulted tomb from the Eastern Cemetery with a vertical entrance on the western side, marble revetment and painted decoration representing peacocks on either side of a two-handled drinking cup, and trees.

BT 165

BCH 1962, 814; Pelekanidis 1965, 229–30.

9–23 Funerary Inscriptions

9

4th–5th centuries.

Tomb inscription.

chi-rho

'Kopryllou'.

Name usually given to foundlings.

BE 30

Τσιγαρίδας – Λοβέρδου 1979, no. 20; Feissel 1983, no. 122.

10

5th century.

Tomb inscription from the Eastern Cemetery.

'Tomb of Dionysios and Zoson where Dionysios rests, sleeping soundly'.

BE 14

Τσιγαρίδας – Λοβέρδου 1979, no. 3; Feissel 1983, no. 166.

11

5th–6th centuries.

Tomb inscription.

'Double tomb in which rests Demetrios, son of Andreas and Beroe ΧΜΓ (Christ born of Mary)'.

BE 162

Τσιγαρίδας – Λοβέρδου 1979, no. 11; Feissel 1983, no. 165.

12

AD 507.

Tomb inscription.

'Tomb of Aurelios Gerontios, the "upright", which was purchased for him by Flavia Maria during the consulship of our master Flavios Anastasios in the third (year) of the fifteenth indiction. In here his son Philip has been placed'.

BE 184

Τσιγαρίδας – Λοβέρδου 1979, no. 13.

13

5th–6th centuries.

Tomb inscription from the Western Cemetery.

'Tomb of Eutychios, the teacher, newly baptised Christian, which no one must dare to disturb in order to place another body. He who dares such an action must not ignore the risk he is running'.

BE 241.

Τσιγαρίδας – Λοβέρδου 1979, no. 8; Feissel 1983, no. 123.

14

AD 525 and 535.

Tomb inscription.

'Double tomb belonging to Martinos the admirable employee of the eparch who served under the previous eparch . . . ., in which lies . . . who passed away on the 27th . . . third indiction during the consulship of the most distinguished Flavios Philoxenos and Flavios Probos. The fortunate Antoninos who passed away on . . . during the consulship of the most illustrious Belissarios lies here'.

The bodies were buried ten years apart.

BE 17

Τσιγαρίδας – Λοβέρδου 1979, no. 6; Feissel 1983, no. 134.

15

5th century.

Tomb inscription from Eptapyrgion.

'This tomb belongs to Andreas, the most devout reader, son of Aresias of excellent memory'.

BE 18

Τσιγαρίδας – Λοβέρδου 1979, no. 7; Feissel 1983, no. 142.

16

5th century.

Tomb inscription.

'Jesus Christ, you who created everything with one word, may you give consolation and forgiveness for the sins of your servant Fortunatos'.

BE 238

Τσιγαρίδας – Λοβέρδου 1979, no. 22; Feissel 1983, no. 180.

17

5th century.

Tomb inscription.

'Tomb of Paramonos, servant of the illustrious Trifoniane, which was purchased at the cost of four gold coins and one gramma. Here lies Demetrios who passed away 15 days before the Kalends of March on the day of Kronos' (Saturday 15 February).

BE 240

Τσιγαρίδας – Λοβέρδου 1979, no. 24; Feissel 1983, no. 159.

18

5th–6th centuries.

Tomb inscription from the area of the Church of St. Demetrios.

'Monument of Bardion Palatinos' (functionary of financial services).

BE 28

Τσιγαρίδας – Λοβέρδου 1979, no. 19; Feissel 1983, no. 151.

Fig. 56 Tomb inscription of Chionis, cat. 20.

19

5th–6th centuries.

Tomb inscription.

'Monument to Martirios, employed by the *magister militum* and *curiosus*'.

BE 237

Τσιγαρίδας – Λοβέρδου 1979, no. 25; Feissel 1983, no. 150.

20

5th century.

Tomb inscription from the Eastern Cemetery.

'For my salvation and my pains, having received the word of God she was named Chionis, without stain, having been married, and I consigned her to the place where pain ends, and in my grief I accepted as a reward innocent children, sons and a daughter with the same zeal'.

An inscription written by a mother for a daughter; very clumsily expressed.

BE 31

Τσιγαρίδας – Λοβέρδου 1979, no. 21; Feissel 1983, no. 179.

21

6th century.

Tomb inscription from the excavation of the Rotonda.
a 'Tomb which belongs to Alexander and Tetradia'.
b 'Here lie the sister and brother Zenobia and Thalassios'.

BE 32

Τσιγαρίδας – Λοβέρδου 1979, no. 15; Feissel 1983, no. 164.

(*Right*) Fig. 57 Marble table-support representing a youth as the 'Good Shepherd', cat. 24a.

22

3rd–4th centuries.

Tomb inscription from the Eastern Cemetery.

'Elpis to Thrasson, her husband, in his memory, and while she is still alive'.

BE 115

23

A damaged inscription re-used as flooring in another tomb in the Eastern Cemetery.

BE 215/1

24–32 Groups of Finds from Tombs

24 Axios Tomb complex

Burial structure in the Western Cemetery. It consists of an oblong vaulted antechamber with three vaulted burial chambers on each long side. There are three more independent vaulted tombs, attached to the east side of the main building. The whole is surrounded by an oblong yard. The complex was used in the second half of the 4th century for the burial of fifty bodies.

Μακροπούλου 1990.

a Finds from the outer courtyard
One hundred and four bronze coins
BN 1764–1867
Μακροπούλου 1994.

Marble table-support with a representation of a youth as the Good Shepherd.
ΑΓ 2491

b Finds from the chambers

Antechamber
Clay lamp
BK 4501/1

Chamber B
Three clay lamps
BK 4501/2–4

Clay juglet
BK 4501/5

Bronze cylindrical container
Βχ 240/10

Fig. 58 Miniature terracotta lamps and gold funerary coin, cat. 27.

Chamber Γ

Clay lamp
BK 4501/6

Clay plate
BK 4501/7

Chamber ΣΤ

Clay bowl
BK 4501/8

Clay jug
BK 4501/9

Chamber Z

Clay bowl
BK 4501/10

Clay plate
BK 4501/11

Clay jug
BK 4501/12

Cylindrical bronze container with chain
Bχ 240/11

Six glass beads
BYμ 15/1

Chamber H

Marble relief slab used to cover the entrance
AΓ 1808

Clay jug
BK 4501/13

Chamber Θ

Clay lamp
BK 4501/14

Clay plate
BK 4501/15

Two clay jugs
BK 4501/16, 18

Clay vessel with three handles
BK 4501/17

Bronze finger ring
Bκο 220/3α

Lead earring
Bκο 220/3β

Jet bead
BΛμ 17/3

Pointed amphora containing a
cremation burial
BK 4501/19

25–28 Finds from the 'Lyssiatrion' excavation (Eastern Cemetery)

25 Burial monument I

3rd century.

Cist grave covered by a
rectangular stone structure,
measuring 4 × 3.70 m, and
containing a cremation burial.

FINDS:

Gold funerary coin
BNδ 8

Clay juglet
BK 4467/87

Glass *unguentarium*
BY 227/31

Gold finger ring
Bκο 214/12

Gold earring
Bκο 214/13

Gold leaves
Bκο 214/15

Bronze crossbow brooch
Bκο 214/30

Bronze buckle
Bκο 214/31

Lead earring
Bκο 214/68

Bronze decorative objects
Bχ 234/15

Cylindrical lead container
Bχ 234/41

Iron nails
Bχ 234/43

Remnants of gold braid
Bυφ 42/2

Shell
BO 65/7

A large number of bone objects
BO 65/17

26 Tomb 122

3rd-century pit grave containing
the remains of a woman.

FINDS:

Clay *unguentarium*
BK 4467/92

Clay lamp
BK 4467/93

Two glass *unguentaria*
BY 227/13, 14

Fragments of a glass vessel
BY 227/15

Gold earring
Bκο 214/10

Gold and bronze jewel
Bκο 214/21

Fish made of rock-crystal
BYμ 10/2

Necklace beads made of amber
BΛμ 12/1

Bone pins
BO 65/4

Bone necklace bead
BO 65/3

27 Tomb 148

Late 3rd-century pit grave.

FINDS:

Bronze coin
BN 2146/55

Gold funerary coin
BNδ 17

Thirteen miniature terracotta
lamps
BKμ 11/2–14

28 Tomb 229

3rd-century cist grave.

FINDS:

Three gold funerary coins
BNδ 13–15

Clay lamp
BK 4467/153

Glass *unguentarium*
BY 227/32

Bronze buckle
Bκο 214/52

Bronze earring
Bκο 214/53

Bronze pin
Bκο 214/54

Bronze strigil
Bκο 214/55

29–32 Finds from the 'Museum of Byzantine Culture' excavation (Eastern Cemetery)

29 Pottery from various tombs

Group of nineteen vessels of
different types dating from the
3rd–4th centuries:

Twelve jugs
BK 4506/1, 2, 5, 14, 18, 24, 25,
26, 28–30, 38

Four flasks
BK 4506/22, 27, 31, 37

Small amphora
BK 4506/3

Cooking pot
BK 4506/19

Cup
BK 4506/23

30 Tomb 89

End of the 3rd century.

Cist grave.

FINDS:

Two hoards, one consisting of
twenty-five and another of
fifteen bronze coins, minted in
AD 292–9 and AD 294–310

Fig. 59 Bronze coin of Severus minted in AD 305–6, cat. 30.

respectively. BN 2020/79–103, 104–18 (fig. 59)

Bronze coin of AD 276–82
BN 2020/119

Five clay vessels
BK 4506/32–6

Fragments of glass vessels
BY 244/7

Gold finger ring
Bκο 215/13

31 Tomb 35

First half of the 4th century.

Cist grave.

FINDS:

Six bronze coins of AD 330–40
BN 2020/55–60

Two clay flasks
BK 4506/16, 17

Glass flask and fragments of another
BY 244/2, 5

Bronze crossbow brooch
Bκο 215/9

Iron finger ring
Bκο 215/10

Bronze key-ring
Bκο 215/18

Cylindrical bronze container
Bχ 235/7

Two bronze rings
Bχ 235/8α–β

32 Tomb 16

First half of the 4th century.

Cist grave with at least three burials.

FINDS:

Nine bronze coins of AD 317–48
BN 2020/35–43

Six clay vessels
BK 4506/7–12

Fragments of two glass vessels
BY 244/12, 13

Double gold finger ring
Bκο 215/2

Iron finger ring
Bκο 215/3

Jet bracelet
BΛμ 22/4

Cylindrical bronze container
Bχ 235/5

Part of a nail
Bχ 235/4

196 iron cobbler's nails
Bχ 235/3

Iron tool
Bχ 235/2

33 Pottery

3rd–6th centuries.

Thirty-six clay pots from tombs in Thessaloniki. They were used in funeral ceremonies, or as funeral offerings for the dead. They take various forms and represent the following types:

Fourteen jugs
BK 4499/1, 3α, 4500/9, 22, 23, 27, 4518/2, 15, 20, 23, 24, 26, 47, 4544/5

Five cups
BK 4499/5, 4500/32β, 4518/30, 35, 42

Eight plates
BK 4518/25, 33, 57, 59, 60, 70, 84, 4547/6

Flask
BK 4518/14

Three bottle-jugs
BK 4499/2, 4518/19, 45

Two small amphorae
BK 4500/28, 4518/38

Two cooking pots
BK 4522/1, 4544/11

Vessel with three handles
BK 4547/1

34 Double barrel-vaulted tomb

4th century.

Double barrel-vaulted tomb from the Western Cemetery. It has a flat cover, a horizontal entrance, stones projecting from the wall to facilitate descent into the tomb, and a headrest. The walls are painted with scenes from the Old and New Testaments and with imitation marble cladding (pls 38, 39).

BT 156 A-B

Μαρκή 1995, 32–7.

35–43 Wall Paintings from Tombs in Thessaloniki

35

3rd century.

Wall paintings from a cist grave in the Eastern Cemetery. The paintings depict Daniel in the Lions' Den, the Raising of Lazarus and Abraham's Sacrifice.

BT 116,119

Πέτσας 1966, 336; Γούναρης 1990, 245–57; Μαρκή 1990, 178.

36

3rd century.

Wall paintings from a barrel-vaulted tomb in the Eastern Cemetery: three interwoven garlands, held up with ribbon.

BT 91A

37

3rd century.

a Wall paintings from a barrel-vaulted tomb in the Western Cemetery: a man sailing a ship, parrots holding a garland and three gourds.

BT 65A, 68A–Γ, E

b Four clay pots from the previous tomb dating from the 3rd century.

BK 2467, 2469, 2473, 2474

Παζαράς 1981, 373–9.

38

4th century.

Wall painting from a barrel-vaulted tomb in the Eastern Cemetery: imitation marble cladding and a chi-rho within a circle.

BT 95A, B

Μακροπούλου 1990, 194–7.

39

3rd–4th centuries.

Wall paintings from a barrel-vaulted tomb in the Eastern Cemetery: fish and carcasses, vases and birds on either side of a fountain on a field of flowers and fruit (pls 40, 41).

BT 139

40

3rd–4th centuries.

Wall paintings from a barrel-vaulted tomb in the Eastern Cemetery: fish and carcasses, vases and birds on either side of a fountain on a field of flowers and fruit.

BT 170

41

5th century.

Wall painting from a barrel-vaulted tomb in the Eastern Cemetery depicting imbricated

Fig. 60 Tomb wall painting of a cross flanked by plants, cat. 43.

closure slabs, colonnettes and Susanna and the Elders (pl. 42).

BT 17

Μαυροπούλου-Τσιούμη 1983, 247–58.

42

6th century.

Wall painting from a barrel-vaulted tomb in the Western Cemetery depicting a cross flanked by plants and birds.

BT 128Δ

Ναλπάντης 1992, 314.

43

Wall paintings from barrel-vaulted tombs in the Eastern Cemetery: crosses flanked by plants.

BT 99A, 102E, Z

Ναλπάντης 1988, 381–3.

44–8 Marble Tomb Inscriptions from the Eastern Cemetery (Hospital of St. Demetrius)

44

5th–6th century.

'The tomb of Marcella, where lies my son Phocas'.

BE 171 (ΑΓ 2812)

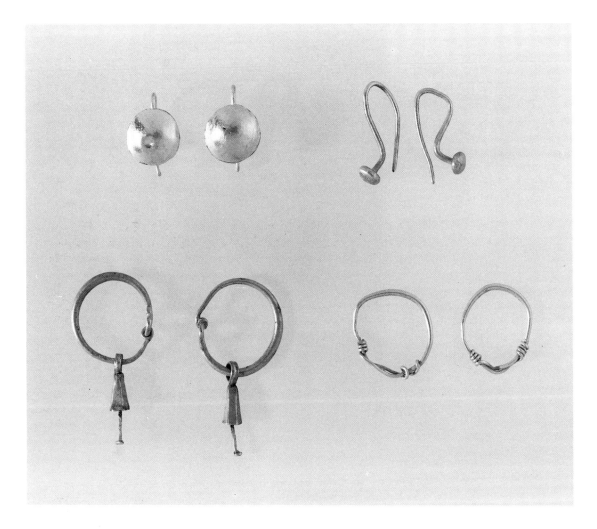

Fig. 61 Earrings from Thessaloniki tombs, cat. 50.

45

5th–6th century.
'The tomb of Theophilos, where Marcella also lies'.
BE 167 (AΓ 2808)

46

5th–6th century.
'The single burial tomb of Victoria'.
BE 170 (AΓ 2811)

47

5th–6th century.
'The tomb which belongs to Euphemios and Sabbatis'.
BE 166 (AΓ 2807)

48

5th–6th century.
'Single burial tomb, where Florentis lies'.
BE 163 (AΓ 2804)

49 Mosaic flooring

4th century.

Mosaic flooring decorated with overlapping circles, from a barrel-vaulted tomb in the Western Cemetery.

BΨ7

50–55 Jewellery

Various types of jewellery from the 2nd–6th centuries, from tombs in Thessaloniki.

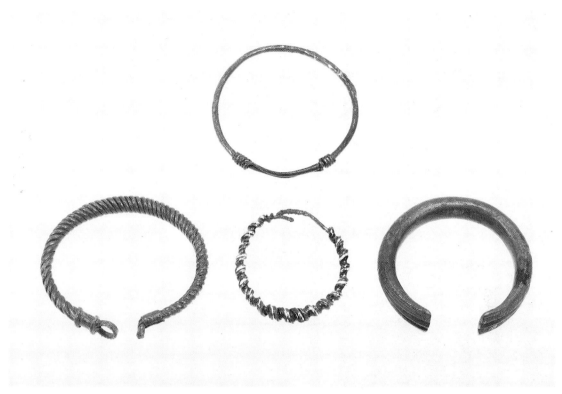

Fig. 62 Bracelets from Thessaloniki tombs, cat. 52.

(*Right*) Fig. 63 Bronze
cross-bow brooch,
cat. 53.

50

Single or paired gold and bronze earrings of three distinct types:

a With an S-shaped hook terminating in various decorative motifs
Βκο 36, 141, 214/14, 56β, 215/1, 225/6

b Plain hoops
Βκο 13/8,42, 45, 136/2, 215/8, 11, 225/2β, γ

c Hoops with fixed or suspended ornaments
Βκο 30, 13/6, 15, 44, 219/5, 225/ 4β, 13, 228/1, 5, 57

51

Gold, iron, bronze, lead and terracotta finger rings of the following types:

a Plain band or beaded profile
Βκο 13/2, 32, 214/22β, 228/44

b With a plain bezel
Βκο 136/1, 214/43, 215/14α, 262/8 (ΜΘ 5448), Βκμ 11/1

c With a bezel containing semi-precious stones
Βκο 3/2, 13/1, 35, 214/8, 22α, 36

52

Bronze bracelets, of either thick or thin wire,
with twisted (Βκο 228/34, 35, 36) or plain (Βκο 225/3, 10, 221/9, 228/56) ends
or of twisted wire with a plain clasp (Βκο 196/1, 228/21, 24, 33).

Two bracelets made of glass (ΒΥμ 10/3, 58/1) (fig. 62).

53

Bronze dress-fittings of two basic types:

a Crossbow brooches, including one which is gilded and another with an inscription.
Βκο 214/37, 228/3, 20, 23, 26

b Belt-buckles, one with matching fittings for the belt.
Βκο 13/9, 214/1, 4, 50, 60, 61β, 228/77

54

Necklace beads made of glass, jet or gold, and amulets made of glass and wood.
Βκο 13/13, 17, 214/56α, 228/38, ΒΥμ 10/1, 12/4, 18/1, 21/5, 8, 9, 12, 15, ΒΛμ 17/4, 22/1, ΒΞυ3/1

55

Various objects.
Bone and copper pins
ΒΟ 65/5, 15, Βκο 214/45, 228/22
Gold pin head
Βκο 13/37
Small knives
ΒΟ 65/12, Βχ 152/1
Bronze mirror
Βχ 234/48
Gold and gilded decorations from embroidered fabrics
Βκο 140, 261

Gold belt-end with geometrical filigree ornament
Βκο 262/5 (ΜΘ 5449)

56 Glass Vessels

3rd–5th centuries.

Forty-two glass vessels from tombs in Thessaloniki and from the Louloudia settlement in Pieria. They contained oil or were used for libations of wine, milk, oil and more rarely honey. See pl. 43. They fall into the following categories, based on their form:

Twelve *unguentaria*
BY 5, 250, 217/5, 227/2, 3, 41, 42, 49, 251/3, 255/1, 257/1, 2
Three bottles
BY 191, 213/1, 217/8
Fifteen flasks
BY 174, 180, 207/4, 209/2, 213/2, 217/1, 6, 9, 12, 227/1, 238/2, 3, 244/3, 247/2, 253/2
Three jugs
BY 173, 217/32, 244/1
Three cups
BY 214/2, 217/41, 227/18
Four jars
BY 207/3, 214/1, 227/17, 255/2
Two small amphorae
BY 217/40, 192

57 Coins

3rd–6th centuries.

Thirty bronze coins from tombs in Thessaloniki.

BN 2020/4, 5, BN 2021/8, 14, 24, 26, 41, 63, 64, 68, 69, 71, 73, 75, 81, 108, 113, 116, 117, 120, 124, 169, BN 2094/1, 15, BN 2145/24, 30, BN 2168/47, 133, 176, 266

Fig. 64 Gold-embroidered belt-end, cat. 55.

Death on the Rhine: changing burial customs in Cologne, 3rd–7th century

Friederike Naumann-Steckner

A stranger approaching Colonia Claudia Ara Agrippinensium (Cologne), the provincial capital of Lower Germania, from Bonna (Bonn), Augusta Treverorum (Trier), Iuliacum (Jülich) or Novaesium (Neuss) would have found his route lined by a multiplicity of graves. Old, well-preserved circular tombs stood alongside unkempt tower tombs, new grave stelae amidst overgrown burial gardens, derelict temple-tombs between grave-altars and those adorned with figurative sculptures. Remnants of foundation stones pointed to dismantled burial monuments. Here and there a newly installed sarcophagus could be seen. Walking along the main street the traveller would pass through what almost amounted to a city of the dead and could discover from the stelae and monuments the name, origin, family status and, in many cases, the profession of the deceased. Less easy to decipher were the inscriptions on the graves of the second or even third row back. Some 300 m from the city wall only freshly dug graves and newly erected grave stelae were to be seen (fig. 65).

Remnants of these grave monuments, together with more recent graves, have been discovered frequently since the Middle Ages. It is only in recent times, however, that attempts have been made to describe comprehensively the finds unearthed during the last hundred years following excavations or archaeological digs. Substantial monographs and articles have been written on individual cemeteries, and the different types of graves and tombstones; these include the studies by Päffgen of the St. Severin cemetery, by Friedhoff of the Jakobstrasse graves, the research of Noelke into gravestones with depictions of funeral feasts and busts, and on grave altars, and by Schmitz on the grave inscriptions of late antiquity and the early Middle Ages; a structural analysis of the Roman necropolis on the Aachener Strasse by Spiegel has recently been published. Although about 6,500 Roman graves have been electronically registered since 1989 (as part of the programme for registering all

the Cologne cemeteries), a systematic analysis has still to be undertaken.

The third to seventh centuries AD constituted a period of unrest, insecurity and upheaval across the entire Roman empire. Weaknesses in the emperors' foreign policy and military defeats repeatedly encouraged revolts and the installation of rival emperors; the separate Gallic empire was proclaimed in Cologne in AD 259. Foreign peoples applied mounting pressure to the boundaries of the Roman empire; on the Rhine border the emperors relied on military measures and fortifications as well as on pacts of alliance with the Germanic princes and on the settlement of Germanic prisoners of war. The history of the events and circumstances surrounding the Frankish acquisition of land has yet to be understood in detail. Political, economic and social insecurity were a fertile breeding ground for mystical oriental cults and religions offering salvation – including Christianity, which was tolerated by emperors from Constantine I onwards and subsequently actively supported. The political, economic, ethnic and religious changes are also reflected in the changes in burial and funeral customs.

In what follows, the changes in burial and funeral practices in the Roman *colonia* and the surrounding areas between the third and seventh centuries will be outlined, whereby the circumstances prevailing in the first and second centuries will be borne in mind as a necessary starting point. The surviving evidence is, however, extremely fragmentary given that the grave monuments, stelae, altars and also sarcophagi once visible above ground have now, for the most part, collapsed, been removed, rebuilt or reused, and a large proportion of the subterranean burials, both in antiquity and more recent times, have been looted or plundered. Moreover, most of the graves without grave goods can only be dated in terms of their location, if indeed they were spotted, recognised or deemed worthy of recording in the first place. One is thus

Fig. 65 The country road from Cologne, in the Roman period, lined with grave monuments. Reconstruction by E. Meissl senior, 1950.

dependent on precise observation of the finds and 'correct' interpretation of what has survived.

No ancient literary sources dealing with the preparations and sequence of events at a funeral in Cologne have come down to us. Accordingly it is necessary to turn to texts which are more often than not concerned with the burials of outstanding personalities either in republican Rome or during the early period of the empire. It is only with substantial reservations that it is possible to draw conclusions from these texts about the conditions for citizens living in the provincial city of Cologne.

Epigraphic evidence either from or about Cologne mostly dates from the first and second centuries and there is little from the late antique period; in the early medieval period the literary and epigraphic sources are even thinner on the ground.

The population of Cologne in the first century AD was a motley crowd: descendants of the Ubians who were settled here by Agrippa; Roman government officials and, from time to time, even members of the imperial family; tradesmen and craftsmen who had moved into the area from all across the Roman empire and who had their home town, *tribus* and their tribal membership recorded on their grave monument; as well as soldiers, veterans, freedmen and slaves. Consequently it is possible to identify at the outset a range of different burial rituals in close proximity. Before long Italo-Roman habits were imitated and cremation burials soon replaced the burial of bodies.

Cemetery sites

In the mid fifth century BC the Twelve Tables Law prohibited the burial of bodies within the boundaries of the city of Rome: this law was complied within all cities of the Roman empire into the late empire. Thus in Cologne the graves were located outside the municipal protection zone (*pomerium*) along the major state thoroughfares: anyone entering or leaving the city would be reminded of the departed by the inscriptions on the gravestones which commemorated them. Five cemeteries have been identified: one stretched along the road heading upstream along the Rhine to Bonn (now Severinstrasse/Bonner Strasse); another along the road to the south-west from Cologne towards Trier (now Luxemburger Strasse); another along the road to the west in the direction of Aachen, Jülich, Tongeren, and Bavai (now Aachener Strasse); a fourth stretched along the road leading downstream to the north in the direction of Neuss (now Neusser Strasse). During the first century the graves were not sited immediately in front of the city gates, but rather at a distance of 300–400 m. From the third century onwards, however, burials also took place right up to the city wall.

Cologne's oldest necropolis, located on the north-west corner of the city (around St. Gereon) and probably along a side road, is an exception. Here the graves reached right up to the city wall from the outset. Given that a particularly large number of burials unearthed here have been of uncremated bodies interred in the first century it is likely that this cemetery was favoured by the Ubian population.

The Roman graves were laid down next to the roads and initially followed their path closely; later the cemeteries were gradually extended until they reached a depth of 400 m on either side of the road. Side roads linked these areas to the main artery: they have been identified in the cemetery on the road to Bonn (Jakobstrasse, Corneliusstrasse excavations), in the cemetery on the road to Aachen (Richard Wagner-Strasse excavations) and in the cemetery on the road to Neuss with a concentration of graves in what is today the area around St. Kunibert.

The location of the grave

It is not known what criteria were employed for choosing a particular burial site and acquiring it 'for all time' as a *domus aeterna* ('eternal domicile'). It may well be that proximity to living quarters played a part. It is also conceivable that certain groups of the population favoured particular burial sites – in the necropolis at the north-west corner of the city, for example, a unusually large number of grave stelae for cavalrymen have been found. Each burial site was bought by a private individual and there were no prescribed norms relating to size or orientation. It is not known who owned the land and how the sale of burial sites was organised. The acquired plot was often fenced off or walled in: thus the husband of Florentia Crispina could record on the grave inscription that the gravestone had been erected in his burial garden. Details of size are rarely given,. although in the case of a grave for three people in the cemetery on the road to Bonn an area of about 5.35 × 5.35 m is mentioned. It was open to each Roman to design the grave monument as he wished; he could also state in his will which members of the *familia* – which included the servants of the house as well as close relatives – could in due course be buried in the grave. Clearly, financial considerations must have played a part both in the choice of location and in the organisation of the grave: grave sites close to busy roads were undoubtedly more expensive than those in the second or third rows or on side roads. Initially burials took place close to the road and as near as possible to the city, then in the second row and further away from the city, and finally in areas further back from the road.

Provisions for burial

In many cases Roman citizens made sure that provision for their tomb – possibly for the whole *familia* – was taken care of while they were still alive, and they gave precise instructions regarding the grave monument, as in the description of Trimalchio's Feast.[1] Provision of this kind can be identified in Cologne in the case of burial chambers with several recesses for urns (for example the Weiden burial) or those with several burials (for example the burial chamber in Efferen, and on the Severinstrasse), or where gravestones have remained unused. On the Aachener Strasse, for example, a number of gravestones were discovered close together which had all been hewn from the same block, were of the same size and had almost identical decoration (inv. nos 401, 402, 403, 404, 405). Bienus, who originally came from north-east France, had three of the gravestones erected for himself, his wife, for his parents and brothers and sisters as well as his wife's family; a fourth gravestone remained without an inscription. Codicils to inscriptions such as *testamento fecit sibi et suis, heres ex testamento faciendum curavit* or *titulum posuit* on grave monuments also indicate provision for death. As in other Roman cities there would also have been funeral organisations in Cologne, possibly separate ones for different professions, to which one could make payments during one's lifetime and which would organise a suitable burial, possibly in the organisation's own plot.

Burial rites

In the case of Cologne there are neither literary nor epigraphic sources giving information about customs practised at the deathbed and immediately after death, although it is unlikely that they differed greatly from the practices in Italy in the republican period and the early years of the empire, for which we have written evidence. Although the priests, who themselves were not allowed to see the dead, were responsible for burial practice as a whole, the carrying out of burials was an entirely private affair which matched the social standing and marital status of the deceased and the financial circumstances of the bereaved family.

Close relatives and, in the case of soldiers, possibly former colleagues, assembled at the deathbed. The eyes of the deceased were closed and he was addressed repeatedly by name before the funeral director, the *libitinarius*, was sent for. The deceased was washed with oils, anointed and made up either by the relatives themselves or the *pollinctor* (undertaker). The corpse was then dressed in accordance with its station – the Roman citizen dressed in his toga, the woman adorned with jewellery – and finally laid out to rest on the high funeral bed, the *lectus funebris*, with feet facing the door. Oil lamps and torches were lit. Extravagant displays of flowers were forbidden. Assisted by their servants and professional mourners, the relatives kept a wake by the deathbed and mourned the deceased with loud lamentations in his or her honour.

As is still common practice today in oriental countries, the funeral procession escorted the deceased to the funeral pyre or grave within a few hours of death; given that it is recorded in *Cod. Theo.* IX 17,5 that in the middle of the fourth century the emperor Julianus prescribed that funerals had to take place at night, presumably until that time they had normally taken place during the day. Large funeral processions were organised by the *dissignator*. Musical accompaniment and actors with the *imagines*, ancestral portraits, together with freemen were undoubtedly the exception rather than the rule in Cologne. The bier was borne by at least six bearers to the site of the cremation or the grave. A burial with only four bearers was considered impoverished. In the case of high-ranking personalities, the funeral procession may well have made its way through the forum where, following the Roman model, a funeral oration was delivered.

The funerary trade

A burial always incurred costs. Whilst the safekeeping of the corpse, the funeral procession, organisation of the funeral ceremony and subsequently of the monument gave the bereaved kin, on the one hand, the opportunity to demonstrate the social status and wealth of the deceased, as well as their own high regard for him, on the other it may well have also landed some families in debt for a considerable amount of time.

Many profited from a bereavement, however. The *libitinarius* and his employees had to be paid. The *lecti funebri*, the high funeral beds with bronze ornamental fittings or bone trimmings, were presumably kept in stock by dealers. From the locality, woodcutters provided dry local wood for the pyres which was most probably stored near the cemetery. The grave plot had to be purchased and measured out. Some workshops probably specialised in producing objects used for laying out the corpse and for the burial itself: the coarse pottery with applied face motifs may well have been made specially as cremation urns. 'Tear vessels' – *alabastra* made of clay or glass – were presumably thrown or blown specifically for the burial cult. In the case of some lamps found in graves no hole was made in the lip, whilst others are so small that they could barely have been threaded with a wick: they too were made for the burial cult. Some amber jewellery was not suitable for everyday use, for example, rings of extremely small internal diameter. The black jet doubtless imported from England may well have been particularly suitable as a burial gift, although the armbands, necklaces, pendants and finger rings made of this material could also have been worn in life.

Working together with quarries and importers of stone, the stonemasons turned out cremation urns, gravestones, burial monuments and, later, sarcophagi; the sarcophagus of a *negotiator artis lapidariae*, a trader dealing in stonemason's products, has been found in Cologne on the road to Bonn. However, urns, sarcophagi and grave decorations made of imported marble have only rarely been identified. Cremation urns chiselled from Lorraine limestone or cut from tufa from the Eifel were undoubtedly kept in stock in workshops or by dealers. Sarcophagi were probably supplied half-finished to Cologne by quarries and were completed by workshops near to the cemeteries. Stonemasons fashioned gravestones and grave altars according to the taste and pocket of the customer and perhaps had grave stelae in the most 'popular' styles in stock. At the client's request architects would have worked together with stonemasons and builders to design and construct elaborate monuments.

Cremation burials in the first and second centuries AD

During the first and second centuries cremation burials were the norm. The cremation always took place outside the city walls. In the vicinity of the cemeteries there were special cremation sites (*ustrinae*); two such cremation sites were partly excavated in 1974 in the cemetery on the road from Cologne to Trier, some 1250 m outside the city wall; one of these sites consisted of a walled area measuring 13 × 12 m with a platform and a pit at the centre still discernible. The pyre was built up above the pit and the bier with the body lying on it was placed on top, together with small ointment vessels containing perfumes and burial offerings. After the

cremation, which lasted around two hours, the flames were extinguished with wine and water and the remains collected.

The funeral ashes were not always picked over, but sometimes buried together with the remains of the pyre (a cremation pit grave). In most cases, however, the ash was separated out and either buried together with the burnt grave-goods or separately from them. The bones and ashes of the very poor were doubtless simply collected in linen or cloth bags and on excavation can be identified only as a dark discoloration; in some cases the ashes

(*Right*) Fig. 66 Gravestone with relief depicting a funeral feast for M. Val. Celerinus, born in Astigi, subsequently a citizen of Cologne, veteran of the 10th legion Gemina Pia Fidelis. *c.*100 AD. Inv. RGM 86.

were covered by shards of pottery. Wooden caskets were presumably also affordable cremation containers. Besides pottery urns, glass jars and glass urns with lids were also popular in Cologne, as were both round and rectangular lead urns. These ash containers were often protected by stone packing, a set of brick slabs or stone urns and stone caskets. The round stone urns were either buried in the earth unprotected or were deposited in niches within underground or overground tombs.

During the period of the early empire so-called *bustum* cremation was also practised: in this case the pyre was built directly over the open grave pit. The task of collecting the ashes did not apply as they fell directly into the pit, together with the ash from the fire, cremated furnishings and burial gifts. Since the heat of the pyre burnt the walls of the pit until they were red and hard, *bustum* graves can easily be identified during excavations (for example grave 8 from the section of the cemetery on the road from Cologne to Trier excavated in 1974).

The funeral and the commemorative meal

Funeral meals were also an integral part of the burial. The first, the *silicernium*, took place on the day of the burial. The deceased received his portion, was addressed by name once again and bidden farewell three times with the word *vale*. Vessels found in Cologne containing remnants of food next to urns and deliberately broken crockery are evidence of this custom. After a nine-day period of mourning, the family, which according to religious practice had become impure following the death, met at the grave to offer up a sacrifice to the dead and to partake of a second commemorative meal, the *cena novemdialis*. Annual days of commemoration served to preserve the memory of the dead (fig. 66).

The grave goods

In graves from the ancient world archaeologists often find objects buried with the dead person. These grave goods include the deceased's clothing and jewellery, personal belongings, objects used in the burial ceremony, offerings from relatives, friends and neighbours, possibly equipment for life beyond death, as well as the tableware and food from the funeral meal. The type, number, quality and position of the gifts depend on a number of factors, including the date of the grave, the location, the burial rites and the wealth of the deceased or his heirs. In terms of archaeological finds Cologne, like the entire province of Germania Inferior, is 'rich in gifts' in comparison, for example, with the city of Rome itself. A richly furnished grave does not necessarily imply, however, that the deceased was also wealthy; it can also be a sign of the times. Moreover, the bereaved relative's passion for pomp and display may have played a part. Likewise, wealth may manifest itself in a magnificent monument on a prominent spot, but be accompanied by a burial with few grave goods.

Nevertheless it is possible to identify some typical grave goods. The most common of all is tableware, consisting of eating and drinking utensils together with the hand-washing equipment that went with them. A set of three white-ware jugs from a local pottery is typical of graves in Cologne. In addition there is imported tableware such as the *terra sigillata* from Gaul and the inscribed beaker made in Trier. From the middle of the first century onwards, the glass tableware commonly found in graves came almost exclusively from Cologne glassworks.

Based both on the evidence of what are often high-quality eating and drinking utensils, sometimes unearthed with remnants of food and traces of dried liquids on them, and what can feasibly be inferred from gravestones depicting funeral meals, the tableware was probably mainly intended to benefit the deceased in the next world. However there are also finds which indicate that the tableware was left behind, following a funeral meal at the graveside.

Even in graves which are otherwise devoid of burial gifts there are pottery lamps, the so-called *firma lampen* bearing the factory's stamp, and lamps with relief decoration on the upper surface. Some lamps are fresh from the factory whilst others have traces of soot. Their function, whether as illumination for the laying out of the corpse or the funeral ceremony, or their symbolic value as light for the *domus aeterna* cannot normally be deduced from the finds themselves.

Coins have been found in several graves, generally singly near the head or in the hand of the deceased, presumably based on the Greek custom of paying an obol to Charon the ferryman for the journey across the river of the underworld. In cremation graves the coins were generally deposited uncremated. Less commonly, beginning in the second century, a number of coins were deposited in the grave, sometimes in a purse. The coins are not always newly issued and some had been in circulation for a considerable time. Old coins were also deposited; some coin motifs, such as the Consecratio or Hercules, appeared to be particularly suitable. The coins are nonetheless useful aids to the archaeologist in dating a given grave, as they provide a date before which the grave could not have been constructed.

Writing equipment – stylus, wax spatula, writing case and inkpot – as well as tablet knives with iron blades and decorative handles have been found in the graves of both men and women and testify to the social status of the deceased.

Bone and jet hairpins, gold and glass earrings and necklaces, jewellery caskets of wood or bone with bronze ornamentation, as well as cosmetic equipment and mirrors, are typical of women's graves. Iron razors are sometimes found in the graves of men. There are also graves with equipment specific to some profession or other, for example medical instruments or a barber's equipment. Amulets have been found in numerous children's graves. Metal vessels and clay or metal figurines are rare, and only a very small number of graves contain statuettes of gods.

The marking of graves at ground level

The sites of Roman graves were marked at ground level and there are hardly any cases of overlap between burials of roughly the same period. There would have been wooden planks or plaques to mark the position of the grave, but they have all been lost. In the first and second centuries stone grave altars and gravestones were popular. They bore inscriptions: D.M. for *dis manibus*, 'to the gods of the dead', then name, family, sometimes birthplace, age and profession of the deceased and usually also of the person who had the stone erected. The gravestone was sometimes enriched with a picture in relief; during the first and second centuries a portrait bust of the deceased or the funeral meal were common motifs. In the case of cavalrymen who died in action a representation of the horse was also added.

Specially constructed grave monuments were of course very expensive: wealthy people often had a tomb, a mausoleum or a grave monument con-structed for themselves and their family during their lifetime. Only a very few of these large grave monuments have survived. The collapse soon after construction of the monument for L. Poblicius in the cemetery on the road to Bonn has resulted in its preservation. There must, however, have been a large number of comparably luxurious and expensive burial monuments along Cologne's main roads in the second half of the first and second centuries AD. The foundations of some have survived, for example on the road to Bonn near St. Severin. Evidence of other lost grave monuments was provided by the limestone relief blocks uncovered in 1980 during the construction of the Wallraf-Richartz-Museum: probably at the beginning of the fourth century numerous grave monuments were dismantled and the stone blocks, which were valuable in a city short of stone, reused as foundation stones. From this one building alone it is possible to identify reused blocks from at least twenty-one grave monuments including mausoleums with one or more storeys, some of which had a temple-like upper storey, grave towers, grave monuments with deep *aediculae* and at least one rotunda.

Cremation in the third century AD

Until the middle of the third century the dead were generally cremated. As in the first and second centuries, there were several ways to bury bones and ashes; two graves on the road to Bonn are typical and show the variations: in the first (St. Severin IV 63) a container (no longer identifiable) containing the cremated bones was placed in the northern half of the grave, and six clay vessels and a glass *balsamarium* were deposited next to it without any special protection. In the other grave (St. Severin V 208), however, a wooden casket filled the entire grave and the glass and clay tableware was placed inside it directly on the ashes. In second- and third-century graves square or rectangular tufa caskets with sides about 60 cm in length are often found; they are sealed by a flat slab of tufa or a hipped tufa lid. Many of them have a ledge for grave goods inside and some have been found with two niches for goods. It was now usual for goods to be placed inside and outside the casket. Three graves in the necropolis along the road to Aachen will serve here as examples. In one of the graves, that of a woman, the deceased's jewellery was found in the tufa casket together with a mirror, two knives, a coin and a valuable glass drinking cup decorated with a figurative painting; next to the casket there were four white-ware jugs, a miniature oil lamp and a glass bottle. The tufa casket in another grave contained hairpins and silver pendants as well as five coins; outside the casket there were medical utensils, a small box of bone, a stone for grinding cosmetic pigment or ointment, three white-ware jugs and a glass drinking cup decorated with a snake-thread ornament. Finally, in a third grave, two out of a total of six white-ware jugs had been placed in the tufa casket, whilst the others had been deposited next to the cremation casket along with other ceramic and glass vessels.

Whilst these valuable burial gifts also bear witness to the wealth of individual families in the third century, the large and hence expensive tombs and grave stelae become increasingly rare. Perhaps it was possible for some citizens to forgo a lavish memorial without losing credit in society; according to Trebellio Pollio[2] even the graves of Victorinus, emperor of the separate Gallic empire, and his mother Victorina were 'modest, with a small marble monument'. During this period older gravestones start to be reused, as for example in the case of the second-century gravestone of C. J. Maternus for Liberalinius and his daughter who died in the second half of the third century. Cremation burials also die out in Cologne towards the end of the third century although there are rare exceptions through to the fourth century.

Burials in the third and fourth centuries AD

The number of inhumation burials increases during the second century and, in particular, from the middle of the third century inhumations are often found next to cremation burials in the same area of a cemetery. A definitive explanation for this change in burial custom has yet to be found; it is possible that various factors played a part. It has been suggested, for example, that concepts of the next world may have changed, for example through the introduction of eastern religions; the theory put forward earlier, that uncremated burials were the graves of the Christian population, is certainly no longer tenable. Social causes have also been considered, given that many of the inhumation burials contain few grave goods or none at

all; however a number of such burials from the fourth century are particularly rich in such accompaniments.

The cemeteries continue to follow the course of side roads. The graves are in rows and for the most part parallel or at right-angles to the road. The west–east alignment of graves without grave goods is not in itself sufficient evidence to identify them as Christian; there are no graves in Cologne prior to the fourth century which can be identified unambiguously as Christian from their inscriptions or from pictures or symbols on the gravestones.

Most uncremated bodies were buried in wooden coffins, which can now often be identified only by the coffin nails. Instead of being placed in the centre of the grave many of the coffins were positioned right up against one of the side walls. In the third century the gifts were normally deposited in the coffin itself, whilst in the first half of the fourth century additional recesses for grave goods were dug out of the earth in the side walls of the grave above the level of the floor. Niches of this kind are found on the long side, the short side and, not infrequently, on two sides. Some recesses were lined with wood and had drawers (fig. 67).

A good example of a grave with a wooden coffin and niches for grave goods is grave 227 from the Jakobstrasse excavations on the Roman road to Bonn, dating from the second quarter of the fourth century. The dead woman's cosmetic utensils and a large number of glass vessels had been placed in the coffin itself, which stood at the centre of the large grave, whilst eating and drinking utensils, mostly pottery, had been deposited in two recesses, one at the head end of the grave and one to the right; eggshells and poultry bones were found on the plates.

Some wooden coffins were lined with lead. The lead lining was soldered together from a number of individual sheets and the edges – sometimes decorated with beaded or leaf patterns – bent over. The coffin lid was also fitted with lead furnishings. Wooden coffins lined with lead in this way were used in Cologne from the middle of the third century through to the middle of the fourth. Since this type of coffin lining must have entailed considerable expense, it is mistaken to conclude that the relative scarcity of accompanying objects in graves of this kind implies that the deceased was impoverished.

Stone sarcophagi were undoubtedly expensive and the more so the further they had to be

Fig. 67 Burial of a woman in a wooden coffin. The remains of the coffin can be recognised as soil stains. A niche for grave goods has been inserted in the eastern wall of the grave shaft. Mid-4th century, Cologne, Jakobstrasse, grave 216.

transported, and the more opulent the execution. Most stone sarcophagi are made of sandstone and a few are of tufa; in Cologne only one imported marble sarcophagus has been discovered. A small number of stone sarcophagi are decorated on one side with a tablet of text held by two cupids; only one bears reliefs depicting mythological subject matter. In fact the majority are unadorned, simply rough-polished. The sarcophagi were covered with one-piece lids in the form of a hipped, saddle or arched roof. Both decorated and undecorated stone sarcophagi were buried directly in the ground or placed in burial chambers.

Burials also took place in built-in grave ledges, the so-called *formae*. Burial chambers containing up to twelve *formae* were spanned by barrel vaulting whilst others were surmounted by a prestigious superstructure, presumably for commemorative ceremonies.

A further type of grave is the brick-built, in which a rectangular box with a floor, walls and roof was generally constructed out of roofing tiles or, more rarely, smaller wall bricks. Most of the brick slab graves found in Cologne contain few grave goods; this also makes them difficult to date, but many of them may have been constructed towards the end of the fourth century, at which time there were generally fewer burial goods.

Finally, simple burials in the ground without any identifiable container must be mentioned; the deceased was probably simply wrapped in a cloth and placed on a bier (for the purposes of transport).

In Cologne there are also occasional examples of the burial of a number of people in the same grave, but the finds are not conclusive enough to be able to infer that they were, for example, burials following an accident, epidemic or act of war.

In a few burials it seems that quick-lime was poured over the body. Presumably the lime was used as a disinfectant (perhaps for plague victims?).

As far as grave goods are concerned, inhumation burials do not differ substantially from cremation ones. In inhumations objects are also found which can be classified as personal gear and possessions, equipment used in laying out the body, grave goods from the bereaved family, and food and tableware possibly for use in the next world or from the funeral meal. In the case of cremations, grave goods are found both within the cremation container and alongside the urn; in the case of inhumations they are also found both within the coffin or sarcophagus and alongside it. In the first half of the fourth century table services, jugs and goblets were mainly deposited outside the coffin, in some cases in one or more recesses. From the middle of the fourth century there is, however, a decline in the number of goods deposited in graves within the cemeteries along the main roads. This may have been a result of an overall impoverishment of the city population.

Because almost all the gravestones in Cologne have been discovered without an associated burial, it is in most cases unclear whether they were erected above a cremation or an inhumation; from the fourth century onwards, however, the standard inscription *hic iacet* allows a gravestone to be identified as marking an inhumation burial.

Burial in the countryside surrounding Cologne

The large agricultural estates outside the city and the suburban villas had burial sites on their own land. In accordance with the wish to keep alive the memory of the departed, graves were located at places clearly visible from the principal estate buildings, either on the main road or on a connecting road. In those cases where the main house of the estate and burial site have been identified, the graves were invariably situated at least 30 m or so from the principal buildings.

The graves in these small cemeteries differ in their outward appearance: there are subterranean burial chambers both with and without prestigious superstructures, as well as burial gardens with isolated graves. Three examples will be discussed here.

The burial building in Köln-Weiden, situated close to the road to Aachen, presumably belonged to a *villa rustica* situated about 9 km west of the city gates which has not yet been identified. The monument was built in the middle of the second century as a family tomb. The subterranean burial chamber holds twenty-nine recesses to accommodate cremation urns; the portrait busts of some of the deceased were also placed here, together with stone imitation wicker chairs, of the kind known from reliefs depicting funeral meals (fig. 68). Only fragments of two columns have survived from the overground monument, as well as a marble drum-shaped sarcophagus, imported from Italy in around AD 300, which was probably placed in it. The owner of the estate clearly followed the change in

Fig. 68 Limestone funerary chair from the burial chamber in Köln-Weiden (cat. 26).

burial custom from cremation to inhumation burials and had the financial wherewithal to acquire a sarcophagus of the kind popular in Rome at the time. The coins verify that the burial site was used until the middle of the fourth century.

Approximately 7 km west of the city in Köln-Müngersdorf there is an estate dating back to Claudian times. Nearby there are a number of private cemeteries belonging to the estate. In the east, outside the perimeter wall of the villa, there is a small cemetery with sixty-one cremation graves from the first and second centuries. The location of the third-century cemetery is not known. To the north-west of the principal building six fourth-century stone coffins have been found loosely grouped together. They were all opened during excavations and found to have been looted. The fact that in one of the stone coffins there were no human bones has led Fremersdorf to surmise that it was never used. Grave goods were discovered, however, outside the other stone coffins on one or both of the long sides and, in one case, underneath the sarcophagus itself. In each case the goods consist of a sizable dining service containing numerous bronze and glass vessels. Traces of food, eggshells and chicken bones were identified in three graves. Two of the graves contained silver spoons with the inscription DEO GRATIAS ('Thanks be to God').

Six burial sites have been discovered close to the *villa rustica* in Köln-Braunsfeld. In this private cemetery cremations and inhumations were placed side by side, and burials occurred in stone sarcophagi as well as in wooden coffins. In four of these burials the grave goods were placed in the coffin. In grave 5 they were placed beside the sarcophagus at head and waist height. Each grave contained an exceptionally valuable glass vessel. One of these shows scenes from the Old and New Testaments.

It is essential to exercise caution before identifying graves containing grave goods with Christian iconography as being the burials of Christians. For example, three identical segmental bowls have been found in three separate Cologne graves; they were probably engraved in the same workshop in the second third of the fourth century, but depict completely different motifs: a boar hunt, Apollo and Diana, Adam and Eve. The criteria for choosing an object with a particular motif as a grave-offering are not yet understood.

Germanic graves

A number of cremations and inhumations of the second to fourth centuries contain a series of objects which stand apart from normal Roman burial gifts of the period by including a belt set and a massive axe, a sword, shield and large shears or whetstones. Graves of this kind are to be found in the cemeteries on the Roman roads to Bonn and Aachen as well as in the cemetery on the estate in Bickendorf in between graves with exclusively Roman contents. However, graves with similar contents have also been excavated in Germania Libera, for example in Leverkusen-Rheindorf. They can be interpreted as the graves of members of Germanic tribes who were buried with their weapons in accordance with Germanic law, which stated that weapons belonged to the dead man and that he had a right to his 'movable property'. The Germanic population was fascinated by Roman cultural possessions, which they were able to acquire, for example, through trade, and they imitated Roman customs. A considerable number of Teutons had been settled around Cologne as *laeti* or had perhaps served in the Roman army as *federati*. This was the only category of the population to be buried with belt sets and the gold crossbow brooches which served as Roman badges of rank.

Graves from the fifth to seventh centuries AD

An abrupt end to Roman rule on the Lower Rhine is not visible in the archaeological remains. Following the extensive withdrawal of regular troops the Franks took on the task of protecting the Rhine border; according to Salvian,[3] Cologne was 'overrun by enemies' around AD 440. With the death of Valentinian III in 455, Roman policy vis-à-vis its allies disintegrated and the *Liber Historiae Francorum 8* reports that Cologne was captured by the Franks at the time of the military commander Aegidius (around 460). The first king of the Ripuarian Franks whose name has been recorded was Sigibert the Lame, who declared Ripuarian Gaul as his own autonomous territory. Other minor Frankish kings also strove for expansion: at the instigation of the Merovingian Clovis, Sigibert was removed by his own son Chloderic in around 510; as a result Cologne stopped being the permanent

Fig. 69 Frankish graves in the cloisters of St. Severin.

royal centre from the Merovingian period onwards, but remained a metropolis within the eastern Frankish domain.

Only a very small number of fifth-century graves can be identified archaeologically. This is a result of the fact that the graves of the remaining Roman population of the city were generally scant in grave goods, or even entirely devoid of them, from as early as the second half of the fourth century; this makes them hard to recognise. The graves of those of Roman origin can only be identified from names on gravestones. Some Roman cemeteries were no longer used for burials: in the cemetery on the road to Trier there are no furnished burials, and thus no datable graves, beyond the fourth century.

Burial of the city population

In the fifth century, plots were used for burial which were later to become sites for churches. The most conspicuous example is St. Gereon in the north-west corner of the city. Vestiges of a building from the fourth century have survived here; the function of this building remains open to question; from the end of the sixth century it was associated with the martyrdom of Theban legionaries. Numerous fourth- and fifth-century gravestones fashioned from limestone and sandstone have been discovered here which can be identified as Roman graves from the inscriptions: examples include the gravestone for the soldier Viatorinus erected in around 400 and gravestones for Martinianus and for the girl Optata. Many of the gravestones bear a Christian symbol or idioms typical of Christian gravestones such as *in Deo ivit* ('he is with God'), or *in albis recessit* ('he died in his christening robe'). According to old literary sources, very richly furnished graves dating from the Frankish period were opened here in the eleventh and twelfth centuries.

In the south cemetery on the Roman road to Bonn there is a continuity of use. Various burial constructions dating from late antiquity have been archaeologically identified. One of these was probably extended and the memorial converted into a Christian memorial church in the fourth century. Severin, a bishop of late antiquity, was later venerated here as a saint. Burials both inside and outside this much-extended church typically took place in graves made of limestone or trachyte slabs, and *spolia* from local Roman graves, or alternatively in reused stone coffins. Many of the graves have few grave goods or none at all; some contain traces of gold-woven fabric, suggesting that the deceased was dressed in expensive clothes.

Some graves, however, have plenty of grave goods. Some male graves can be identified by weapons, belt fittings and shoe buckles. Some women's graves were uncommonly richly equipped and have been found to contain headbands of gold braid, silver earrings with semi-precious stones, necklaces of glass beads, gilded brooches, silver bracelets, shoe buckles, bags with handles containing iron knives, bone combs and keys, cosmetic cases and, at the foot of the grave, glass goblets, large bronze bowls for hand-washing and earthenware pots. Only a very small number of graves show signs of having been looted.

Bishop Kunibert (died AD 663) had himself buried in the north of the city in a church building which he himself may have established and which today still bears his name. A number of further graves were subsequently sited near his grave. It would seem that churches were very desirable places to be buried, especially if they contained the graves of saints or martyrs.

In accordance with the old Roman decree, all cemeteries were situated *extra muros*. For this reason the graves within the Roman city wall under what is today the Cathedral are unusual. Two graves of royal status have been unearthed and other burials have also been identified, although they have been looted. The two princely burials were deposited soon after AD 525 in chambers made of limestone slabs.

One of the chambers contained a wooden coffin with a woman facing east in full traditional costume and wearing her jewellery. The dead woman wore a headband of gold braid, earrings and brooches set with garnets, three necklaces, one of which was set with seven Byzantine gold coins (the latest dating from AD 518), and a Roman ring. As well as an iron knife with a gold handle, her bag contained two Ravennate silver coins dating from the time of Theodoric the Great or Athalaric. The grave goods, deposited at the foot of the deceased outside the coffin, are typical of the period but more extensive and finer. The grave has been linked to the Longobard wife of the Merovingian king Theudebert I, who reigned from 534 to 548.

The second grave chamber was the final resting place of a young boy. It was situated against the woman's grave at its eastern end. The chamber was constructed out of Roman *spolia*; any cracks had been carefully filled with clay. On the western side of the chamber lay the small wooden bier and a matching chair, on which most of the grave goods were placed or hung. Like the woman, the boy was dressed in traditional costume; fragments of fabrics and leather, clasps and buttons have survived. As well as tableware, the boy had been given all the equipment of an adult warrior as grave goods; only the helmet and throwing-axe (*francisca*) appear to have been made for a child. Five silver bracteates were also left in the grave. The boy's grave would have been deposited at about the same time as the woman's (fig. 32).

The cemeteries near village settlements

The Frankish row-grave cemeteries are associated with single farmsteads or small village settlements which today can no longer be identified, as they have become the basis of more recent villages. The starting point is normally the grave of the landowner followed by those of his relatives and servants. In the case of graves from a closed community of this kind it is possible to establish with a reasonable degree of accuracy the social standing of the deceased on the basis of the effects in the grave. Examples include the row-grave cemeteries at Köln-Junkersdorf and Köln-Müngersdorf, and in Rodenkirchen and Godorf. The 149 graves in Köln-Müngersdorf could have belonged to the cemetery of a hamlet, and the 543 burials in Köln-Junkersdorf to the cemetery of a small village.

Frankish cemeteries have also been discovered on the right bank of the Rhine. In Köln-Poll a Merovingian cemetery has been discovered with eighty mostly undisturbed graves facing east, the majority unfurnished, and in Köln-Deutz a single Frankish inhumation grave has been excavated.

Ten inhumations belong to four Frankish houses in Porz-Grengel; Frankish graves with few grave goods have also been identified in Porz-Zündorf and Porz-Langel.

The laying out of the corpses and the burial

Few documents describe burial procedures during the Merovingian period. In his *Ten Books of Histories* VII,1 Gregory of Tours reports as follows on the supposed death of Bishop Salvius in the French town of Albi: 'He raised his hands to the Heavens and breathed his last with a word of thanksgiving. At this point the monks united with his mother in their lamentations, lifted out the corpse, washed him, dressed him and placed him on a bier. They then spent the night singing psalms and shedding tears. When day broke however . . . they prepared themselves for the solemn burial . . .'. This report on the death of a bishop catalogues all of the characteristic components. The dead man was mourned, washed, combed, dressed and laid out on the bier. The position of objects belonging to traditional costumes in the row-grave burial grounds implies that the corpse was laid out with abundant gifts and buried in everyday clothes or, perhaps, festive dress.

Chapter 55,1 of the Laws of the Salian Franks stated correspondingly that: 'Anyone who is found to have robbed the body of a dead man before it is laid to rest in the earth will be liable to forfeit 2500 pence.' Flower displays have rarely been identified, although in the 'Minstrel's Grave' (St. Severin III, 100) – constructed of sandstone slabs and trachyte – organic substances have survived: the wooden bier had a lining of rye straw and was decorated with box, lavender and dog-rose. A burnt-out torch was also found in the grave.

Types of coffins

In the Merovingian period inhumation burials were compulsory; the few cases of cremation must be linked with non-Frankish groups in the population (Frisians and Saxons). The grave pit was dug in relation to the size of the body and the deceased buried either on a wooden bier or in a wooden coffin; the bier or coffin also served to transport the corpse to the grave. A number of graves are distinguished by special furnishings: wide graves were reinforced with chamber-like wooden braces (chamber graves) and contained the coffin and grave goods. Another special grave type is exceptionally long and usually dates from the middle of the sixth century. The two graves under Cologne Cathedral fall into this category. Luxury items could be deposited at the foot of the dead body. Stone grave containers remained popular. Scrap material from Roman cemeteries was often used: sarcophagi were recycled and slab graves, characteristic of the Merovingian period, were constructed using *spolia* as well as limestone and sandstone slabs. Walled grave chambers, in some cases plastered, have been identified from the later Merovingian period. Unlike in France, there is no evidence in Cologne that sarcophagi were produced locally. Only after the transition to the Carolingian period were trapezoid sarcophagi produced using limestone from Lorraine traded in Cologne.

Contents of the graves

For generations archaeologists have prized the rich furnishings of Merovingian graves. The objects deposited provide insights into everyday life at the beginning of the Middle Ages. Moreover, traditional costumes and weaponry of the period can also be deduced from these finds.

In the case of objects found in women's graves, it is the brooches which are most striking, and which also provide a useful guide for dating purposes. In the late fifth and early sixth centuries costumes with four brooches were in fashion: two small bird brooches or S-shaped brooches held the garment together at the shoulders and a heavy pair of bow brooches served as a skirt- or cloak-fastener in the waist area (an example is to be found in grave 33 in Köln-Junkersdorf). Small garnet-inlaid disc brooches with a divided central zone are typical shoulder fasteners on costumes dating from AD 550 onwards (an example in this case is grave 41 in Köln-Junkersdorf). Towards the end of the sixth century the pairs of brooches disappear and a larger disc brooch takes their place as a shoulder fastener (the women in graves 49 and 337 at Köln-Junkersdorf wore a later costume of this kind).

The graves of men can be identified by the silver, bronze or iron belt buckles produced either locally or in the Mediterranean area. In the first half of the sixth century thin belts with a simple unornamented buckle were common. Belts with two-part cast buckles were worn in the second half of the sixth century and belt sets decorated with silver inlay only after about AD 600 (Köln-Junkersdorf grave 397). Iron weapons are also typically found in men's graves. Seaxes with narrow blades are found in the earliest graves; after about 600 they are replaced by broad seaxes (Köln-Junkersdorf grave 397). Long swords (*spatha*) only entered general use from the second half of the sixth century. Throwing axes – the *franciscae* – are characteristic of the late fifth and early sixth centuries and after that were no longer deposited in graves. Spears served as grave goods from about 520 (Köln-Junkersdorf grave 198). Sets of two or more weapons are typical of the sixth century. Weapons were deposited considerably less frequently in the graves in and around St. Severin than in the local burial grounds.

Some graves are notable for their deposits of used objects. In Cologne objects dating from Roman times are often found. Pottery lamps (Köln-Junkersdorf grave 336) can be considered curiosities. This is not the case with Roman coins. With holes punched in them they could be added to the bead necklaces worn by Frankish ladies. Moreover they still served as currency. The Merovingians did not use small denomination coins and only minted coins from precious metals. The old Roman coins served as small change in the everyday transactions of the Ripuarian Franks and ended up as personal belongings in their graves (Köln-Junkersdorf grave 527, Köln-Müngersdorf grave 122).

Pottery vessels are standard accompaniments in the graves of both sexes, although there were no complete services. In the first half of the sixth century there were up to three clay or glass vessels (Köln-Junkersdorf graves 159, 49), later only one pot (Köln-Junkersdorf graves 564, 216). Various forms of *Knickwandtopfe* are the most common. As was the case in Roman Cologne, so too in the Frankish city there is a high percentage of glass vessels, to begin with spherical bottles and, later, bell-beakers (Köln-Junkersdorf graves 159, 49, 564). In some cases traces of food and drink have been identified, including birch must, bird and poultry bones.

Towards the end of the seventh century the custom of placing gifts in graves died out, and it disappeared altogether in the first third of the eighth century. In the Carolingian period the burial procedure appears to have been completely reorganised: the dead were buried in their local parish cemetery.

Marking of graves and commemorating the dead

Frankish graves were undoubtedly identified at ground level, in the row-grave cemeteries with a mound of earth and possibly a wooden grave marker. In the tradition of late antiquity graves continued to be furnished with a gravestone and provided with an inscription. The limestone grave stelae discovered around St. Gereon and St. Severin, and the isolated examples near St. Ursula, are difficult to date. Stones with inscriptions and the chi-rho monogram, including for example the gravestones for Fugilo and the girl Rusufula in the cemetery by St. Gereon, were presumably erected in the fifth or sixth centuries.

The wording of inscriptions appears to be very simple. What mattered was the name of the deceased and his or her dates, which are often given with utmost precision in years, months and days. The fundamental attitude of Christians towards death is expressed in formulations such as *fidelis in pace recessit* ('he died a religious and peaceful death'); it is expressly noted on the grave of the girl Rusufula that she lies 'with the martyrs'. Gravestones without inscriptions but bearing a volute or etched cruciform decoration – in most cases made of red sandstone or, less commonly, limestone or *Muschelkalk* – were common from the later Merovingian period onwards.

Ceremonies to commemorate the dead, together with funeral meals, may well have normally taken place a few days after the burial. According to Gregory of Tours (*Histories* II,23) one of the priests close to Bishop Sidonius organised 'a meal and invited all the citizens to the church' following the death of his companion. In the Carolingian period ceremonies of this kind were deemed to be unchristian *sacrificia mortuorum* and forbidden.

Grave robbery

The disadvantage of depositing rich grave goods in row-grave cemeteries is grave robbery. Numerous Merovingian and Carolingian laws made the desecration of a grave a punishable offence; despite this, 87 per cent of graves in Köln-Junkersdorf and 31 per cent in Köln-Müngersdorf have been disturbed. Most common was partial looting soon after the burial: the grave robbers knew whether a particular grave was rich or not and were wise to the location of the contents. Precious metals were much sought after; gold jewellery and brooches from women's graves, weapons from men's graves. Jewellery consisting of glass beads was generally left in the grave, just as pottery or glass vessels and even valuable bowls were not stolen. The thieves tended to leave the golden crosses, which in any case were extremely rare, and other objects with Christian symbols. The early graves from the Merovingian period were not looted, whilst in the sixth century the desecration of graves appears to have been common practice. In the middle of the seventh century, as the number of grave goods dwindled, grave robbery also came to an end.

Numerous strands of continuity link Merovingian burial customs back to the rites of Roman late antiquity, whilst the late Merovingian age itself fed the burial customs of the Middle Ages. Many centuries later they in turn shaped our own burial customs and, in some cases, are still observed today.

NOTES

1 Petronius, *Satyricon* 71.
2 *Tringinta Tyranni* 7.
3 Salvianus, *De Gubernatione Dei* 6,39.

ACKNOWLEDGEMENTS

The author wishes to thank
Prof. Dr. H. Hellenkemper and Dr. B. Paffgen for substantial discussion of the manuscript and much helpful advice; and also Martin Brady for translating this paper.

Catalogue of the exhibition 'Death on the Rhine'

Römisch-Germanisches Museum, Cologne

Cremation graves of the first and second centuries

1 Grave of brick slabs in the cemetery on the road to Neuss

On the ancient overland route to Novaesium/Neuss there was an extensive cemetery which was used for burials from the early 1st century AD. In 1924 a grave of brick slabs was discovered dating from the 1st or 2nd century AD: five large bricks protected a 30 cm high cremation urn of blue-green glass containing a small quantity of funeral ash which was buried next to a simple factory-produced lamp.

Glass urn with two handles and lid inv. no. 24,57. *Alongside*: Lamp inv. no.24,58.

Römer am Rhein. Exhibition in Cologne 1967, 261 D 31; F. Fremersdorf, *Wallraf-Richartz-Jahrbuch* 3/4, 1926/27, 4f.

2 Cremation grave with stone urn from the cemetery on the road to Neuss (Niehlerstrasse/Innere Kanalstrasse)

A further cremation grave was discovered in 1990 in the same cemetery. The container for the ashes was a round stone urn with a lid, 68 cm high. As well as the funeral ashes it also contained two small glass *balsamaria* and nails from a small wooden casket; three white-ware jugs, a child's drinking vessel and further pots and fragments were deposited next to the urn. It may well be that the ashes are those of a woman who died in confinement; in accordance with an old custom, children who died before their milk teeth had come through were not cremated. The burial probably occurred in the middle of the 1st century AD.

Large stone urn with lid inv. no. 91,16. *Containing*: Glass *balsamarium* inv. no. 91,13; glass *balsamarium* inv. no. 91,14; nails from a small wooden casket inv. no. 91,15.
Alongside: Terra rubra plate inv. no. 91,3; white-ware jug inv. no. 91,4; white-ware jug inv. no. 91,5; white-ware jug inv. no. 91,6; child's drinking vessel inv. no. 91,7; colour-coated cup inv. no. 91,8; ceramic fragment inv. no. 87 91,9; pottery cup inv. no. 81,10; lid inv. no. 91,11; fragment of a lid inv. no. 91,12.

Excavation report 90,27 (P. Otten); unpublished.

3 Cremation grave with lead urn from the cemetery on the road to Aachen

Numerous early cremation graves were discovered in 1902 during sewerage construction in the large cemetery along the main road in the direction of Aachen, Tongeren, Bavai, some 1200 m outside the city wall. Grave 52 contained a round, shallow lead urn with a lid which held ash and cremated bones; the grave goods were alongside, either upright or lying on the ground. The inclusion of three white-ware jugs of local origin is characteristic of graves from the Cologne area dating from the 1st and 2nd centuries.

Lead urn with cremated bones, 28 cm diam., 12 cm high, inv. metal 1334.
Alongside: Pear-shaped white-ware jug inv. no. 4077; pear-shaped white-ware jug inv. no. 4078; spherical white-ware jug inv. no. 4079; tall, conical pottery cup inv. no. 4080; small hemi-spherical pottery bowl inv. no. 4081; small hemi-spherical pottery bowl inv. no. 4082; pottery lamp with an indecipherable maker's stamp inv. no. 4083; green glass *aryballos* inv. no. 903; bronze key inv. no. metal 1332; bronze slate pencil inv. no. metal 1333.

J. Hagen, *Bonner Jahrbücher* 114/115, 1906, 418 no. 52 with pl. XXV.

Cremation graves of the third and fourth centuries

4 Cremation grave from the cemetery on the road to Bonn (St. Severin IV, 63)

A large cemetery stretched for around 3 km along the road from Cologne to Bonn. It was used for burials continually from the 1st century AD through to the Frankish period. The area around the church of St. Severin was investigated with particular thoroughness between 1925 and 1957 and around 1200 graves have been found in this part of the cemetery.

The cremation grave (St. Severin IV, 63) was discovered close to other contemporaneous cremation graves. It stood out on account of a rectangular discoloration of the ground over an area of 40 × 88 cm. The funeral ash was deposited in the northernmost part of the grave; it may possibly have been collected and buried in a small cloth bag. The funeral gifts – six pottery vessels and two small glass bottles – were deposited in the southern part of the grave.

Single-handled jug inv. no. 55,19; colour-coated pottery indented beaker inv. no. 55,20; cup of colour-coated ware inv. no.55,21; bowl of

coarse-ware inv. no. 55,23; plate of smooth ware inv. no. 55,22; plate, colour-coated ware inv. no. 55,24; small glass bottle inv. no. 55,26.
A second glass vessel has entirely disintegrated.

G. Strunk, *Kölner Jahrbuch* 6, 1962/63, 145; W. Binsfeld ibid., 152; Päffgen, 1992, vol. II, 438ff.

5 Cremation grave with wooden casket from the cemetery on the road to Bonn (St. Severin V, 208)

The cremation grave was identified in the ground as a grave (75 × 64 cm) with vertical walls; discoloration and iron nails suggest that the ashes were buried in a wooden casket. The grave also included the remains of a small child; the contents indicate that this was the grave of an adult woman who was buried together with her child. The precious grave goods were all found in the casket, whilst the jewellery was evidently interred in a small wooden case of which a buckle has survived. The miniature ladder may have been a toy, amulet or symbol of affiliation to a particular sect; miniature implements of this kind have been found only in Cologne and the surrounding area.

The *dupondius* of Marcus Aurelius provides a *t.p.* of AD 161–80; the grave was probably laid down in the first half of the 3rd century AD.

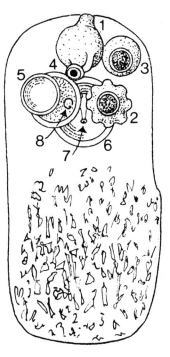

Fig. 70
Cremation burial in the cemetery on the road to Bonn (St. Severin IV, 63), cat. 4. After Päffgen 1992. Drawing H. Stöcker.

Necklace: three jet beads, a black glass bead and a silver *lunula* pendant inv. nos 57,63; 57,67; 57,66; two bone pins inv. nos 57,64; 57,65; jet medallion depicting Medusa and a married couple inv. no. 57,62; glass mirror inv. nos 57,68; single-handled jug inv. no. 57,50; single-handled jug inv. no. 57,51; single-handled jug inv. no. 57,52; coarse-ware pot with a handle inv. no. 57,55; coarse-ware lid inv. no. 57,56; colour-coated cup inv. no. 57,54; coarse-ware bowl inv. no. 57,53; glass bottle with dolphin handles inv. no. 57,58; glass beaker with cut grooves inv. no. 57,59; bronze pyxis inv. no. 57,60; bronze pyxis inv. no. 57,61; miniature ladder made of sheet silver inv. no. 57,66; buckle (presumably from a jewellery case) inv. no. 57,67; *dupondius* of Marcus Aurelius inv. no. 57,57.

Kölner Jahrbuch 8, 1965/66, 109–12; Päffgen, 1992, vol. II, 592ff.
On the miniature implements: P.Noelke, *Germania* 62, 1984, 2nd half vol. 413ff.

6 Cremation grave with tufa casket from the cemetery on the road to Bonn (Severinswall 3, grave 1)

In 1986 a number of graves of differing dates were discovered in the same cemetery but in an area further away from the main road.

Grave 1 contains the buried remains of a cremated woman in a tufa casket (62 × 48 cm). Some of the grave goods had been cremated on the pyre and placed in the tufa casket along with the ashes; further grave goods were deposited alongside the casket. Comparable writing equipment – a combination of inkpot and quill for writing on parchment, and a stylus and wax spatula for writing on wax tablets – is not uncommon in Cologne cremation graves dating from the middle period of the Roman empire. Writing equipment of this kind is clearly an expression of the self-image projected by the provincial upper social stratum. The grave can be dated to the latter part of the 3rd century AD.

Tufa casket inv. no. 86,3513.
Probably cremated grave goods: Silver bell-shaped pendant inv. no. 86,3505; tubular silver bead inv. no. 86,3506.1; tightly folded sheet silver inv. no. 86,3506.2; silver ring with carnelian intaglio inv. no. 86,3507; bone-handled folding knife inv. no. 86,3501.2; bronze inkpot inv. no. 86,3501.1; handle of a wax spatula inv. no. 86,3501.3; bronze stylus inv. no. 86,3501.4; base of a white-ware jug inv. no. 86,3501.5; two small glass jugs with lateral spouts inv. no. 86,3502.1/2; fragments of a glass goblet inv. no. 86,3503.2 and of a glass *balsamarium* inv. no. 86,3503.1.

Excavation report 86,22 (U. Giesler); unpublished. Writing equipment as grave goods: D. von Boeselager, *Kölner Jahrbuch* 22, 1989, 221ff.

7 Cremation grave with tufa casket from the cemetery on the road to Bonn (Severinswall 3, grave 2)

This grave is a cremation burial of a woman in a tufa casket (60 × 44 cm). It also contained both cremated and uncremated goods. The bronze probe, small bronze spoon and grinding stone with traces of red pigment are a woman's cosmetic utensils. The small box made of bone could be a container for cosmetics or jewellery. Cases of this kind - *arca* or *arcula* – were often buried in the graves of women during the second half of the 3rd and first half of the 4th centuries; two Cologne gravestones show a picture of a woman holding a container of this kind.

Tufa casket.
Cremated and uncremated gifts: Glass beads, possibly from a hairnet; bone hairpins; pieces of the sides and lid of a small bone box; bronze probe; small bronze spoon; grinding stone; scraps of textile with gold flecks; bronze key; colour-coated cup; fragment of glass.

Excavation report 86,22 (U. Giesler); unpublished. Cosmetics and jewellery cases: U. Friedhoff, *Der Römische Friedhof an der Jakobsstrasse zu Köln*, 1991, 185ff.

8 Cremation grave with tufa casket from the cemetery on the road to Aachen (Richard-Wagner-Strasse 47, find location 103)

In 1991 an area on the Richard-Wagner-Strasse was subjected to archaeological investigation, a section of the cemetery along the Roman road to Aachen which was presumably reached by a side road. Tufa sarcophagi, tufa cremation caskets, a wooden coffin with a lead lining and simple burial plots with no surviving evidence of a coffin were discovered here in close succession.

Find location 103 marks the grave of a woman. The tufa casket (63 × 50 × 42 cm) had a lid and on the ashes were placed the dead woman's jewellery, two knives and a glass cup with figurative painting. Ceramic objects and a small glass bottle were laid alongside the casket.

The colourful enamel painting on the stemmed cup depicts the unmasking of Achilles by Odysseus in the Palace of Lykomedes on Skyros. In size, shape and glass material the goblet resembles other Cologne products, but the decoration is unique.

The grave can be dated to the late 2nd or early 3rd century AD.

Tufa cremation casket.

Grave goods in the casket: Bone hairpins; jet finger ring with a gold bead; rock crystal bead set in gold; chain of blue glass beads and small natural pearls; colourless glass disc, possibly a mirror; knife with a silver handle; amber handle of a folding knife in the form of a running dog; glass goblet with figurative enamel painting; gold flecks; well-worn bronze coin dating from the 1st century.

Outside the casket: Four identical white-ware jugs; miniature oil lamp; bulbous glass bottle.

S. Neu, *Archäologie in Köln*, 1, 1992, 69f. Neu, 1994, vol.1, 54ff.

9 Cremation grave with a tufa casket from the cemetery on the road to Aachen (Richard-Wagner-Strasse 47, find location 100/101)

Find location 100/101 is the cremation grave of a woman buried in a cremation casket (85 × 60 cm). Inside the tufa casket there is a two-tiered ledge into which has been worked a semicircular aperture. To the cremation casket had been added the woman's jewellery, a mussel shell and five bronze coins dating from the 2nd century AD. A cup with snake-thread decoration and pottery vessels were found standing upright outside the casket. Here were also an ivory casket, a porphyry dish, two round bronze containers and various other equipment in bronze. These objects were interpreted as her cosmetic instruments. Among the equipment, however, there was also a long, slender bronze cylinder, open at the end – possibly an enema syringe. It may thus suggest that other items should be interpreted as medical instruments. Perhaps a female doctor was interred in this grave. The graves of doctors are well represented in Germania Inferior, and also in Cologne itself. The combination of medical instruments varies, though medicine boxes, grinding dishes for the preparation of medicaments, various probes and a scalpel are almost always present. Female doctors feature in ancient literature and on grave reliefs, and seem often to have practised as midwives.

Glasses with colourful snake-thread decoration are typical products of Cologne glassworks during the last third of the 2nd and first half of the 3rd centuries. A large number of glasses with this decoration have been found in graves in the cemeteries along the roads to Bonn and Trier. A fragment of a glass with a snake-thread ornament came to light in a sarcophagus with coins of the emperors Alexander Severus, Gallienus and Galerius Maximianus

(emperor from AD 305 to 311), implying that it must have been hoarded for a long period of time as a precious possession. However, these glasses are also to be found in graves that otherwise contain objects of only average value.

Tufa casket.

Grave goods in the casket: Bone hairpins; two small silver amulet bottles for amulet texts on sheet silver; five bronze coins from the 2nd century; mussel shell. *Next to the casket*: two round bronze containers, small ear-scoop; spoon-shaped probe; spatula probe; scalpel handles; large spoon with lateral lips; hemispherical small bronze bowl scissors; knife with silver and jet handle; porphyry dish for grinding cosmetics or preparing medicines; glass beaker; goblet with snake-thread decoration; three white-ware jugs.

S. Neu, *Archäologie in Köln*, 1, 1992, 67f; Neu, 1994, vol. 1, 54.
On glasses decorated with snake-thread decoration: F. Fremersdorf, *Römische Gläser mit Fadenauflage in Köln*, 1959, 44ff.
On medical equipment and practice: E. Künzl, Medizinische Instrumente aus Sepulkralfunden der römischen Kaiserzeit, *Bonner Jahrbuch* 182, 1982, 1ff; A. Krug, *Heilkunst und Heilkult*, 1985, esp. 195ff.

10 Cremation grave with tufa casket from the cemetery on the road to Aachen (Richard-Wagner-Strasse 47, find location 107)

Find location 107 marks a cremation burial in a tufa cremation casket (71 × 61 × 32 cm). Some of the grave goods – in all, thirteen pottery and three glass vessels – were found in the cremation casket, whilst the majority were deposited alongside it.

Vessels intended for the conservation and preparation of food such as amphorae, *mortaria* and cooking pots are sometimes found in graves, but are not part of the typical drinking sets and dining services.

Cremation casket inv. no. 91,203
Inside the casket: Two white-ware jugs; two goblets. *Alongside the casket on the outside*: Four white-ware jugs; three bowls; plate; *mortarium*; glass bottle; glass vessel.

S. Neu, *Archäologie in Köln*, 1, 1992, 70.

11 *Bustum* cremation from the cemetery on the road to Trier

In 1974, 89 graves of differing dates were discovered in the cemetery along the Roman road to Trier. Cremation grave 8 is a *bustum* grave, i.e. one in which the pyre was constructed directly over the grave itself. During the cremation the ash, cremated bones and burnt gifts fell directly into the grave. The grave shows the poor state of preservation of grave goods typical for this kind of burial. The grave can be dated to the late 3rd or early 4th century AD.

Burial ashes inv. nos 74,517–74,518 with: *terra sigillata* bowl with rosette stamp on the inside base; fragment of a double-handled jug; fragments of a white-ware jug with a pattern of painted stripes; fragment of a cup with notched decoration; fragment of a white-ware plate; fragment of a white-ware jug; fragment of a conical dish.

M. Riedel, *Kölner Jahrbuch* 17, 1980, 99.

Inhumation burials of the third–fourth centuries

12 Burial in a wooden coffin from the cemetery on the road to Bonn (Jakobstrasse grave 128)

Excavations in the Jakobstrasse area have revealed that during the 2nd and 3rd centuries AD the cemetery in the south of the city along the road to Bonn was closed to the west by a wall. Grave 128 was located near to this wall. The skeleton was unearthed from a pit (2.25 x 0.7 m); iron nails at the sides of this shaft suggest that the body was buried in a wooden coffin. A sestertius of Marcus Aurelius and a glass beaker were found close up against the head, and a pottery plate by the feet of the deceased. The coin provides a *t.p.* of AD 168/169. The grave was disturbed during the laying down of grave 126 in the middle of the 4th century, but it is unlikely that it originally contained further valuable objects.

Blue-green glass beaker inv. no. 29,1772; *sestertius* of Marcus Aureleus for Lucius Verus inv. no. 29,1773; plate made of pale clay inv. no. 29,1771.

U. Friedhoff, *Der römische Friedhof an der Jakobstrasse*, 1991, 252.

13 Burial of a small child in a wooden coffin (St. Severin IV, 68)

The wooden coffin, measuring a mere 97 × 48 cm, was easily identified in the 110 × 60 cm grave by reason of discoloration and iron nails found at the sides of the grave. A glass beaker lay next to the skull and beside the right upper arm there was a coin; seven coins and five pendants were placed in a leather bag near the child. A small glass bottle stood at the feet.

Although the coins were found in a purse they can scarcely be construed as the property of the child. It is possible that they were given to him as a payment for Charon. Together with the pendants, which include a silver Hercules club, they may well have served as magical protection.

The coins provide a *t.p.* of AD 290–94 for the burial.

Cylindrical beaker of colourless glass inv. no. 55,46; small greenish glass bottle inv. no. 55,47; silver club-shaped pendant inv. no. 55,37; three bronze pendants in the shape of vessels inv. no. 55,36; pendant of black glass inv. no. 55,45; *as* of Marcus Aurelius, *sestertius* of Lucius Verus, *antoniniani* of Gallienus, Probus and Maximianus Herculius inv. nos 55,35; 55,38–55,44.

B. Päffgen, 1992, vol. II, 442ff.

On the custom of giving coins as grave goods see: J. Gorecki, *Studien zur Sitte der Münzbeigabe in römerzeitlichen Körpergräbern zwischen Rhein, Mosel und Somme*, Bericht der Römisch-Germanischen Kommission 56, 1975, 179ff.

14 Burial in a wooden coffin or directly in the earth from the cemetery on the road to Bonn (Severinswall 7–13, grave 11)

Archaeological excavations along the Severinswall in 1991 included a section of the cemetery situated along the Severinstrasse comprising 17 burials. Grave 11, which had been disturbed, was the burial place of a woman either in a wooden coffin or directly in the ground. The surviving grave goods comprised glass goblets, jewellery and cosmetic utensils as well as two shells.

Oyster shells were also found in grave 17 and a cockle shell in grave 107 of the Roman cemetery on the Jakobstrasse. As with the much more commonly found animal bones, in particular those of poultry, they derive from gifts of food.

The grave is dated to the first half of the 4th century.

Plate 37 Wall painting, tomb of the Western Cemetery, Thessaloniki, representing a family in funeral worship, fourth century. (*Elysian Fields* cat. 7.)

Plate 38 Adam and Eve in a wall painting from a tomb of the Western Cemetery, fourth century. (*Elysian Fields*, cat. 34.)

Plate 39 (*Above*)
Wall painting, tomb of the
Western Cemetery, Thessaloniki,
imitating marble cladding,
fourth century. (*Elysian Fields*,
cat. 34.)

Plate 40 (*Left*)
Wall painting, tomb of the
Eastern Cemetery, representing
a lamb and a bird in a garden,
third-fourth century. (*Elysian
Fields*, cat. 39.)

Plate 41 (*Above*)
Wall painting, tomb of the Eastern
Cemetery, Thessaloniki, representing
seafood and carcasses on a floral
background, third-fourth century.
(*Elysian Fields*, cat. 39.)

Plate 42 (*Above, right*)
Wall painting, tomb of the Eastern
Cemetery, representing Susanna, fifth
century. (*Elysian Fields*, cat. 41.)

Plate 43 (*Right*)
Glass vessel from a tomb of the Eastern
Cemetery, third century. (*Elysian
Fields*, cat. 56.)

Plate 47 Grave goods from a stone cist grave under St. Severin, Cologne (III,73). (*Death on the Rhine*, cat. 42.)

Plate 44 (*Opposite, above*) Part of the grave goods from a grave in the cemetery on the Bonn road (Jakobstrasse grave 227), Cologne. (*Death on the Rhine*, cat. 15.)

Plate 45 (*Opposite, below left*) Circus dish, the most valuable grave good in grave 3 in the family cemetery from the villa in Köln-Braunsfeld. (*Death on the Rhine*, cat. 27,3.)

Plate 46 (*Opposite, below right*) Cage cup, the most precious item from grave 5 in the family cemetery at the villa in Köln-Braunsfeld. (*Death on the Rhine*, cat. 27,5.)

PLATE 47

Plate 48
Gilt silver helmet of
a Roman officer
from a peat-bog
deposit, *c.*320,
Deurne. (*Elite
Lifestyle*, cat. 1.)

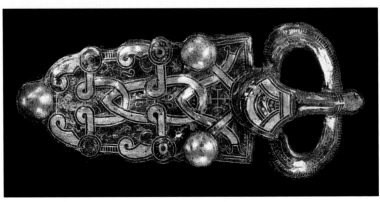

Plate 49
Iron military belt
buckle, *c.*600, Lent.
(*Elite Lifestyle*,
cat. 15.)

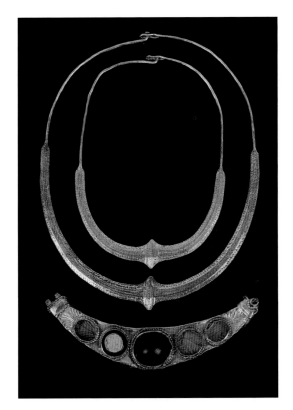

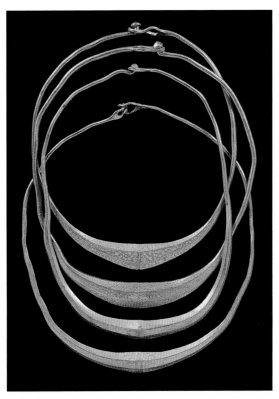

Plate 50 (*Above, left*) Gold neck-rings, *c.*375/400, Rhenen. (*Elite Lifestyle*, cat. 6.)

Plate 51 (*Above, right*) Gold neck-rings, *c.*400, Olst. (*Elite Lifestyle*, cat. 7.)

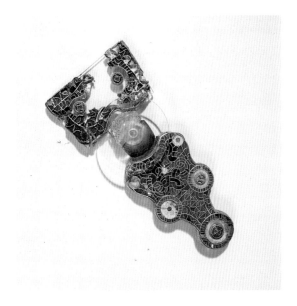

Plate 52 (*Right*) Gold brooch with all-over garnet cloisonné in geometric and zoomorphic patterns, *c.*630, Wijnaldum. (*Elite Lifestyle*, cat. 20.)

Plate 53 The gold hoard of a Frisian king? Jewellery and mounted coins, c.630, Wieuwerd. (*Elite Lifestyle*, cat. 21.)

Plate 54a, 54b Frankish *solidus* from Huy, by the moneyer Landegisilus, c.600. (*Elite Lifestyle*, cat. 45c.)

Plate 55 The Remmerdem hoard: 101 gold and 146 silver coins of Frankish and Frisian origin, *c*.650–700. (*Elite Lifestyle*, cat. 44.)

Plate 56 Buckle from a sword belt, *c*.630/640, Rijnsburg. (*Elite Lifestyle*, cat. 36.)

Plate 57 (*Left*)
Gold bracteate
from Gerete;
sixth-seventh
century.

Plate 58 (*Below*)
Silver gilt brooch
from Ekeby,
Malsta, Uppland;
early sixth
century. (*Firebed
of the Serpent*,
cat. 2.)

Plate 59 (*Above*)
Silver gilt brooch
with garnet
inlays;
unprovenanced,
När, Gotland; late
fifth century.
(*Firebed of the
Serpent*, cat. 3.)

Plate 60 (*Right*)
Roman gold and
silver coins from
the Hoxne hoard,
deposited in the
early fifth century.
(*Heirs of Rome*,
cat. 5a.)

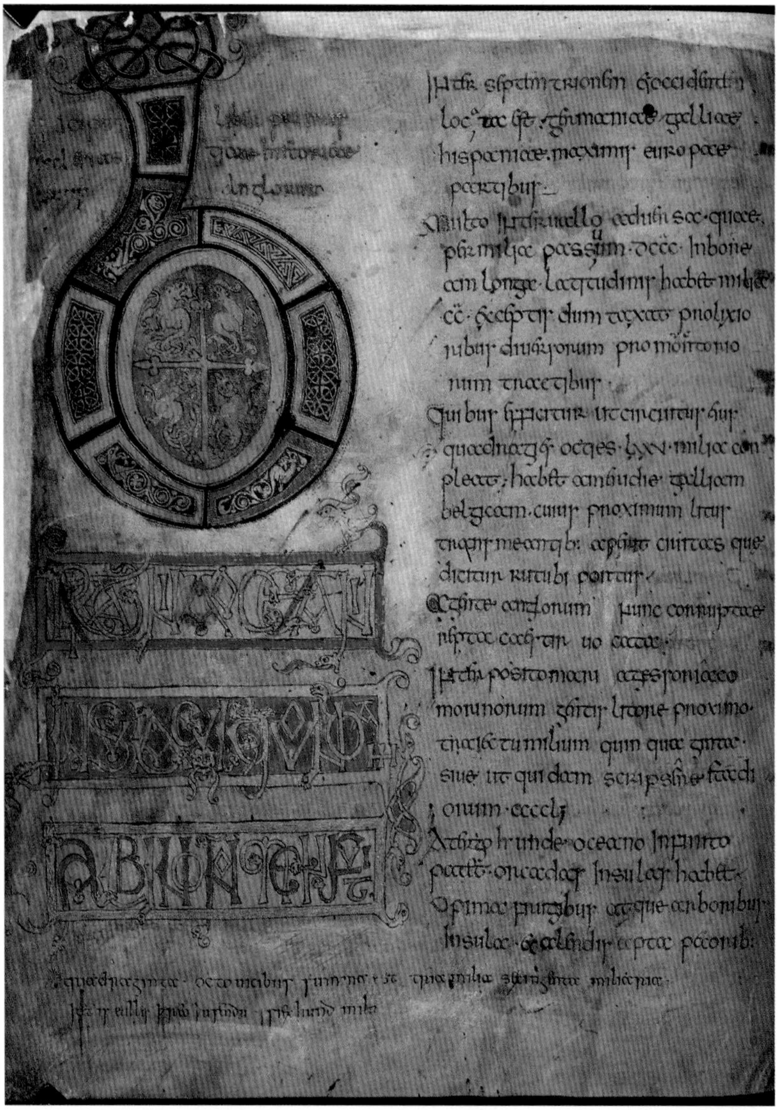

Plate 61 (*Left*) Copy of Bede's *History of the English Church and People* (BL Cotton Tiberius C. ii, f.5v), Anglo-Saxon, first half of ninth century. (*Heirs of Rome*, cat. 31.)

Plate 62a, 62b (*Below*) Imperial-style shoulder clasps from Sutton Hoo Mound I, Anglo-Saxon, early seventh century. (*Heirs of Rome*, cat. 53c.)

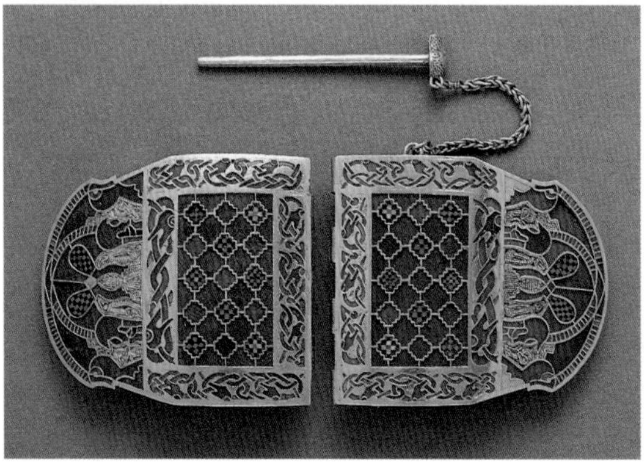

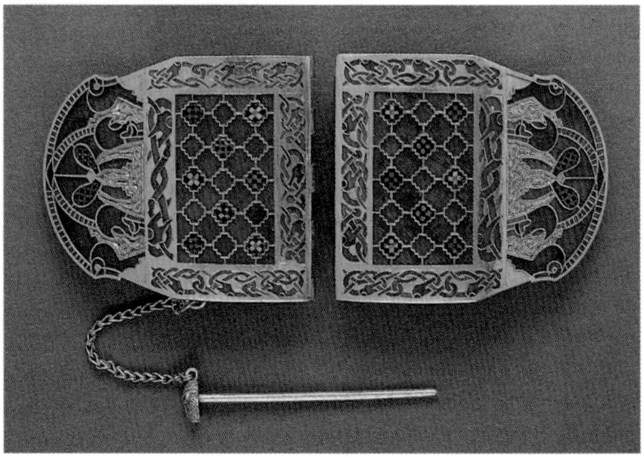

Plate 63 (*Above*) David as psalmist (f. 30v) and as warrior (f. 31r) *The Vespasian Psalter* (BL Cotton Vespasian A.i, ff. 30v–31r), Anglo-Saxon, second quarter of eighth century. (*Heirs of Rome*, cat. 67.)

Plate 64 (*Right*) King David as warrior and Christ's precursor, *The Durham Cassiodorus* (Durham Cathedral Library, Ms B.II.30, f.172v), Anglo-Saxon, second quarter of eighth century. (*Heirs of Rome*, cat. 65.)

Plate 65
Detail of the St. Andrew's sarcophagus, showing David as king and image of salvation, and a royal hunt. Pictish, late eighth or early ninth century. (*Heirs of Rome*, cat. 66.)

Plate 68 Opening of St. Luke's Gospel from *The Royal Bible* (BL Royal MS i.E.vi, f.43), Anglo-Saxon, c.820–840. (*Heirs of Rome*, cat. 118.)

Plate 66 (*Opposite, below left*) General view of the Dupplin cross. Pictish, ninth century. (*Heirs of Rome*, cat. 72.)

Plate 67 (*Opposite, below right*) Anglo-Saxon gilt-bronze brooch, Chessel Down, Isle of Wight, first half of sixth century. (*Heirs of Rome*, cat. 106.)

PLATE 68

Plate 69 Evangelist miniature of St. Luke from *The Book of Cerne* (Cambridge University Library, MS Li. 1. 10. f.21v), Anglo-Saxon, *c.*820–840. (*Heirs of Rome*, cat. 124.)

PLATE 69

Wooden casket.
Jet arm ring; six bone pins; two silver pins, one of which is decorated at the end with a leaf pattern; bronze pins with fragments of textile; jet handle of a tool with two gold foil bands; two conical glass beakers; cockle shell; oyster shell.

U. Giesler, *Archäologie in Köln* 1, 1992, 77.

15 Burial in a wooden coffin from the cemetery on the road to Bonn (Jakobstrasse grave 227)

Burial of a young woman in a wooden coffin (about 2.16 × 0.50 m) sunk into a shaft (2.60 × 1.47 m). The coffin contained jewellery and a mirror belonging to the woman, together with a number of glass vessels. Niches to hold gifts had been constructed to the west, at the head end, and to the south next to the coffin. They contained drinking and eating utensils, in some cases with remnants of food. The contents indicate that the grave dates from the second quarter of the 4th century (pl. 44).

Graves with niches to hold gifts are to be found in many places in the north-western provinces of the Roman empire; they are not unique to Cologne. Haberey surmised that a grave with a recess for gifts was a money-saving substitute for a stone burial chamber with recesses in the wall.

In the coffin: Bone hairpin inv. no. 30,493; fragment of a bone hairpin inv. no. 30,494; glass mirror with a lead frame inv. no. 30,491; folding knife with bone handle inv. no. 30,494; glass beaker with engraved decoration inv. no. 30,483; small bottle of brown-green glass inv. no. 30,485; small bottle of violet glass inv. no. 30,487; brown glass bowl with indentations inv. no. 30,484; single-handled jug of brown-green glass inv. no. 30,482.
In the western niche: Terra sigillata plate inv. no. 30,476, with eggshells on it; *terra sigillata* plate inv. no. 30,478 with poultry bones on it; jug with a handle inv. no. 30,481; glass bowl inv. no. 30,488.
In the southern niche: Inscribed goblet inv. no. 30,477; two jugs with handles inv. nos 30,479 and 30,480; spherical bottle inv. no. 30,486.

U. Friedhoff, *Der römische Friedhof an der Jakobstrasse*, 1991, 283f.
On recesses for grave goods see: W. Haberey, *Germania* 18, 1934, 274ff.

16 Burial in a wooden coffin with lead lining in the cemetery on the road to Aachen (Richard-Wagner-Strasse 47, find location 105)

In the area excavated in 1991 a scattering of burial graves were found amidst numerous cremation burial urns. Find location 105 denotes a burial in a wooden coffin with a lead lining. Inside the lead casing the well-preserved skeleton of a young woman was discovered; even a tuft of hair had survived. The woman had been laid in the coffin wearing simple gold earrings; she had only an octagonal glass bottle as a grave good.

Lead lining from a wooden coffin.
Contents: Gold earrings; octagonal glass bottle.

S. Neu, *Archäologie in Köln*, 1, 1992, 70f.

17 Burial in a wooden coffin with lead lining in the cemetery on the north-west corner of the city (Königin Luise-Schule, find location 6)

The graves discovered in 1957 during the construction of the Königin Luise-Schule between the Albertusstrasse and Alte Wallgasse are part of the cemetery on the north-west corner of the city.

Find location 6 denotes a wooden coffin with lead lining: the coffin (1.92 × 0.47 × 0.45 m) was aligned on a north–south axis. Besides the skeleton, it contained three coins placed by the head, next to the right hand and by the toes, as well as a so-called Mithras symbol, ceramic fragments and fragments of a cup with snake-thread decoration. The coins provide a *t.p.* of AD 295–305.

In Cologne lead lining was used in wooden coffins as well as in stone sarcophagi in the second half of the 3rd and first half of the 4th centuries. The wooden coffin and lead lining were joined by iron nails hammered in just below the top edge. In some cases the lead lining is decorated – here with a beaded pattern.

Lead lining of a wooden coffin.
Contents: Bronze model of a yoke, a so-called Mithras symbol inv. no. 57,262; fragment of a cup with snake-thread decoration inv. no. 57,264; bronze coin of Galerius Maximianus inv. no. 57,259; *denarius* of Severus Alexander inv. no. 57,260; *antoninianus* of Claudius Gothicus inv. no. 57,261; small pieces of a plain fabric inv. no. 57,263; fragments of a plate inv. no. 57,265.

P. La Baume, *Kölner Jahrbuch* 5, 1960/61, 87.
On lead linings see: U. Friedhoff, *Der römische Friedhof an der Jakobsstrasse zu Köln*, 1991, 48ff; Päffgen, 1992, vol. 1, 80ff.

18 Burial in a wooden coffin with lead lining in the cemetery on the north-west corner of the city (Königin Luise-Schule, find location 7)

This wooden coffin with lead lining lay at a right angle to the coffin at find location 6. The coffin, measuring only 1.24 m x 33 cm × 34 cm, contained the skeleton of a 2- or 3-year-old girl with strawberry blonde hair. A coin had been placed in the child's mouth. The child was dressed, adorned with an arm ring and had been given three small glass jugs as grave goods. The burial probably occurred around AD 300.

The child was buried in a small coffin befitting her size. Children's coffins have also been discovered in the cemetery along the road to Bonn. Given that the individual sheets of lead making up the lining had to be soldered together, it can be assumed that coffins for children were also kept in stock.

Lead lining of a wooden coffin.
Contents: *Antoninianus* of Gallienus 57,271; fragments of three glass vessels.

P. La Baume, *Kölner Jahrbuch* 5, 1960/61, 87f.

19 Burial in a sandstone sarcophagus from the cemetery along the road to Aachen (Am Hahnentor, grave 12)

The area just beyond the city wall was used during the late 1st and 2nd centuries by commercial enterprises, in particular pottery workshops. However, the construction of industrial and domestic buildings came to an end during the 3rd century, and cemeteries were subsequently established here. In the course of archaeological excavations near the Hahnentor in 1989 a number of burial sites were discovered dating from the 4th century.

Grave 12 is a burial in a red sandstone sarcophagus (2.15 × 0.70 m) with a hipped lid which was sunk into the sand. The sarcophagus contained the skeleton of a man 1.71 m in height. His garment, made up of two different fabrics, was pinned together on the right shoulder by a crossbow brooch. Remains of a glass bowl were found near the pelvis and in his hand the deceased held a coin. A niche for grave goods had been dug into the wall of the shaft at the level of the sarcophagus lid.

Crossbow brooches served to pin together the *paludamentum*, the military mantle worn chiefly by high-ranking individuals. They were always worn singly. As Roman citizens were normally buried in a toga, this grave may perhaps be interpreted as the grave of a non-Roman in official Roman service.

The coin provides a *t.p.* for the burial of AD 305/307.

Red sandstone sarcophagus with a hipped lid.
Contents: Bronze cross-bow brooch with remnants of a dark brown wool fabric and a light coloured thin fabric attached to it; *follis* of Galerius Maximianus; glass bowl.
In the recess for grave goods: Plate with poultry bones; white-ware jug; colour-coated cup; two small glass bottles.

R. Thomas, *Kölner Jahrbuch* 23, 1990, 407f.

20 Burial in a sandstone sarcophagus from the cemetery along the road to Trier (Barbarossaplatz)

In 1991 a red sandstone sarcophagus was unearthed on the Barbarossaplatz in the cemetery along the Luxemburgerstrasse. The sarcophagus had clearly been discovered and robbed during the nineteenth century. Grave goods next to the sarcophagus remained unnoticed at the time: two glass jugs and a glass bowl.

Deposits of grave goods in recesses next to the coffin or sarcophagus are common in 4th century burials. In this case, however, it is not entirely clear from the position of the find whether the goods belong to the burial in the red sandstone sarcophagus.

Red sandstone sarcophagus.
On the outside in a recess: Glass jug; glass jug with applied trails; fragment of an engraved bowl depicting a circus scene.

R. Thomas, *Archäologie in Köln* 1, 1992, 58f.

Grave stelae and grave monuments of the 1st–4th centuries

21 Gravestone of the Marsacian Lucius

A typical 1st-century gravestone for a cavalryman who died in action. Above the inscription is a depiction of the deceased lying on a couch. He holds a drinking cup and napkin. In front of him is a small food table with a fruit bowl and goblet. On the floor there is a wine jug. The servant at the foot of the couch is ready to pour wine with a ladle.

Below the inscription there is a picture of a soldier leading the bridled horse of the deceased.

The inscription states that Lucius, son of Crispus, of Marsacian lineage, and a cavalryman in the North African cavalry unit, died aged 28 after 9 years in service. His heir had the gravestone erected.

The gravestone was discovered in 1885 in the Gereonstrasse; it may well have stood in the cemetery in the north-western corner of the city. Grave stelae for six other cavalrymen who served in the North African and Noric cavalry regiments and that of Sulpicius (Galba) derive from the same cemetery.

Probably dating from the 1st century AD. Height 197 cm; width 78 cm; depth 17 cm. Inv. no. stone 90.

B. and H. Galsterer, 1975, no. 245, pl. 53.

22 Fragment of the grave monument of Julius Speratus

On the front of the block there is a scale pattern to the left, and the remains of an inscription to the right which states that the donor had the grave built for himself during his own lifetime and for his dead brother Julius Speratus. On the left short side there are the remains of a sacrificial scene. The monument, dating from the end of the 1st or 2nd century AD was destroyed and this single block was clearly reworked in the 3rd century to form a cremation urn.

Height 54 cm; width 97 cm; depth 81 cm. Inv. no. stone 203.

B. and H. Galsterer, 1975, no. 410, pl. 89.

23 Fragment of a grave monument

The block depicts a fluted corner pilaster and on the front a relief: a man wearing leggings, possibly Attis, stands on a pedestal in an alcove; only the feet and lower legs have survived. The block originally came from the side of a medium-sized monument and can most likely be dated to the middle of the 1st century AD.

The block was discovered in 1980 during excavations between Cologne Cathedral and the Rhine. It had been built into the foundations of a building made up of blocks with reliefs on them. They are all, without exception, *spolia* derived from grave monuments generally dating from the 1st and 2nd centuries. Given that very few of the blocks can be pieced together, it is clear that the building material for the foundations was not taken from one single dismantled grave; rather it would appear that already by the end of the 3rd century a large number of grave monuments had been dismantled and the resulting blocks stored in a stone depository.

Height 75 cm; width 1.27 m; depth 45 cm. Inv. no. 79,400.99.

S. Neu, *Kölner Jahrbuch* 22, 1989, 253f, ills 15–17.

24 Grave inscription for Aprilius and Innocentia

The limestone slab is simply framed and bears a ten-line inscription: 'Verinius Friattius and Apra erected this monument to their children who died at the ages of 9 months and 11 days and 7 years and 48 days'. The slab dates from the 2nd or 3rd century AD. It was discovered in 1893 in the Monastery of St. Severin and was reused during the Merovingian period as the lid of a tufa sarcophagus.

Width 59 cm; height 49.5 cm; depth 11 cm. Inv. no. stone 408.

B. and H. Galsterer, 1975, no. 284, pl. 62; Päffgen, 1992, vol. 1, 36f.

25 Gravestone for Julia Burspra

The sandstone stela was dedicated by Julius Kalvisius to his sister Julia Burspra that she should rest 'in eternal peace'. At the top of the stela between the invocation to the gods of the dead D(is) M(anibus), there is a portrait of the deceased in a roundel. The stela was discovered in 1897 at the junction of the Innere Kanalstrasse and Aachener Strasse near to a burial chamber from the Trajan period, albeit without any connection to it. It can in all likelihood be dated to the 3rd century AD.

Width 77 cm; height 44 cm; depth 12 cm. Inv. no. stone 458.

B. and H. Galsterer, 1975, no. 368, pl. 82; P. Noelke, Niedergermanische Grabstelen des 3. Jahrhunderts, *Kölner Jahrbuch* 29, 1996 (in preparation).

Cemeteries of the 3rd and 4th centuries near villas outside the city

Both the large agricultural estates outside the city and the suburban villas had burial plots in their own grounds. In accordance with the wish to keep alive the memory of the departed, graves were set down at locations clearly visible from the estate house or on the roads connecting with the main road. The graves differed in their outward appearance: as well as burial gardens and isolated monuments there are subterranean burial chambers both with and without prestigious superstructures. Without exception the graves were situated at least 30 m from the principal building or villa.

26 Grave in Köln-Weiden

The country estate to which the grave on the road to Aachen belonged has not been identified. It is situated approximately 9 km west of the city. The grave was probably built in the middle of the 2nd century as a family tomb to accommodate funeral urns containing cremated ashes. The subterranean chamber has survived with two couches and twenty-nine recesses for cremation urns and, possibly, grave goods. During excavations of the burial chamber in 1843, two Tuscan columns and fragments of a marble tub-shaped sarcophagus were unearthed as well as urns, portrait busts, limestone chairs and other contents of the grave. The final resting place and width of the sarcophagus (which could not pass through the door), along with the position of the columns, suggest that the sarcophagus was installed in an architecturally designed superstructure. The coins confirm that the burial chamber was used up until the middle of the 4th century.

The sarcophagus was imported from Italy. On the front it is adorned with a medallion bearing portrait busts of the deceased held by Victories surrounded by genii of the four seasons. The lid bearing a depiction of a sea *thiasus* originally belonged to a larger sarcophagus and was cut down to size in a rough and ready manner. This sarcophagus is to date the only irrefutable example of an imported late Roman sarcophagus in the German provinces, and is evidence both of the wealth and *romanitas* of this landowning family. It dates from around AD 300.

Marble tub-shaped sarcophagus
Length 200 cm; width 90 cm; height 90 cm.

Pottery cremation jug and fragments of further cremation jugs.
Equipment and gifts found in the grave (these cannot be related to the individual burials): Two wickerwork chairs made of limestone; portrait bust of a woman; portrait bust of a girl reworked from an idealised head; portrait bust of a man; amber chain with a pendant; five small pieces of tortoise shell, probably ornamental fittings from a jewellery case; four ivory relief plaques depicting goddesses; Mercury bottle bearing the workshop name 'Hilarius et Hylas', with traces of oil; shallow glass plate; fragment of a glass goblet with an engraved toast; base and neck fragments from a number of glass bottles with engraved figurative decoration: 'medicine bottles'; handle of a glass drinking cup; fluted silver bowl with an eight-pointed star at the centre with twisted gold threads; handle of a silver implement, probably the remains of a mirror; bone knife handle with the inscription ENTI ZESES ('Enties, thou shalt live'); silver ring with chains (presumably from a lamp); bronze chain from a lamp;

chalcedony statuette of a goddess, presumably the handle of an implement; five blue glass gaming pieces and one of white glass; four or five coins from the period AD 260–340.

F. Fremersdorf, *Das Römergrab in Weiden bei Köln*, 1957. J. Deckers and P. Noelke, *Die römische Grabkammer in Köln-Weiden*, 1980.

27 Family cemetery next to the Roman villa in Köln-Braunsfeld

Approximately 6 km from the gates of Roman Cologne there was a Roman estate close to the road to Aachen. Built in the 2nd century AD, it was repeatedly rebuilt and occupied until late in the 4th century. The private cemetery was situated approximately 70 m west of the house; the graves face in different directions and it is possible that some of them were aligned to a road leading onto the Aachenerstrasse. Seven graves have been discovered since 1907.

Grave 1. Burial in a sandstone sarcophagus
The sarcophagus, which was fully intact, was broken open in 1907 and has since disappeared; the position of the finds was not documented. The sarcophagus contained a pottery jug with a handle and a spherical bowl of cobalt blue glass with figurative decoration and gold overlay: five large medallions depict scenes from the Old Testament and there are four small medallions of boys' heads in the spandrels. It is no longer possible to ascertain whether two coins that turned up at a later date really belong to this burial.

For iconographic reasons the gold-glass bowl cannot be dated prior to the second third of the 4th century. Signs of wear and tear on the underside of the glass suggest that it may have been in the possession of the deceased for a long time prior to being deposited in the grave. The question remains as to whether this grave was laid down before or after the Frankish invasion of AD 355/356.
Finds in the sarcophagus: Jug with a handle of the 'Niederbiber' type no.95; glass bowl with gold overlay inv. no. glass 991; possibly a coin of Hadrian inv. no. metal 2079; follis of Maximinianus Herculius inv. no. metal 2080.

On gold glass: D. Harden *et al.*, *Glas der Caesaren*. Catalogue of the exhibition Corning – London – Cologne – Rome, 1987, 25 no. 5.

Grave 2. Burial in a stone sarcophagus
Stone sarcophagus no. 2 was discovered in 1908: details of material and size have not come down to us. The skeleton could still be recognised in the sarcophagus; a segmental glass bowl lay on its chest.

The layout of the other grave goods was not recorded. A gold coin of Emperor Gratianus provides a *t.p.* for the burial of AD 373.
In the sarcophagus: Gold coin of the Emperor Gratianus inv. no. metal 1944; glass bowl with cut-glass decoration inv. no. glass 997; three spherical glass goblets inv. nos glass 994, 995, 996; two spherical glass bottles inv. nos glass 992, 993; handled pot made of coarse ware inv. no. clay 4229; ten bronze rings inv. no. metal 1438.

Grave 3. Burial, presumably in a stone sarcophagus
The inventory states categorically that coffin 3, discovered in 1910, was not lifted from the ground: it was therefore most probably a stone sarcophagus. Given that two hairpins were found in the grave, it is likely that the deceased was a woman. A valuable grave good was placed on her chest: a segmental glass bowl with a wheel-cut figurative decoration depicting a chariot race in a circus around Helios holding a whip in the central medallion. The position of the other grave goods is not known.

The circus bowl (pl. 45) was probably made between AD 320 and 340 in a Cologne workshop and perhaps modelled on an original from Rome. The burial probably dates to shortly before the middle of the 4th century.
In the sarcophagus: A pair of bronze hairpins inv. nos metal 1512, 1513; circus bowl inv. no. glass 1002; a spherical glass bottle inv. no. 1003; a glass jug with a handle inv. no. glass 1004; a glass ointment vessel inv. no. glass 1005; *antoninianus* of Tetricus; *follis* of the sons of Constantine.

On circus bowls: Harden, ibid., 210 no. 117.

Grave 4. Burial in a wooden coffin (?)
Burial 4, discovered in 1953, was probably in a wooden coffin; the shaft could still be discerned. A *terra sigillata* plate bearing a spherical greenish glass goblet was positioned on the left lower leg.
Spherical glass goblet inv. no. 53,58; *terra sigillata* plate inv. no. 53,57.

Grave 5. Burial in a sandstone sarcophagus
This plain red sandstone sarcophagus, scored on the outside and topped with a hipped lid, had been lowered through the outcrop of clay into the gravel beneath; it was positioned precisely on an east–west axis (with head pointing west). The sarcophagus contained only the bones of the deceased; all of the gifts were deposited to the south of the sarcophagus on a narrow strip of earth approximately 50 cm wide, level with the bottom of the grave. At head height there was a cage-cup already damaged when buried and a small bone die and, in the lower third, an opulent table service including a large number of glass vessels.

The cage-cup (pl. 46) consists of a colourless goblet in a delicate mesh of coloured glass: close to the lip, in purple Greek letters, is the phrase 'drink and live happily ever after', which leads into a yellow neck and green glass mesh. The cage-cup was the most prized glass object during the late antique period, not least on account of the high level of risk involved in its production. It is not certain which of the known glass manufacturers produced this piece.

Dice, knuckle-bones and gaming pieces are often found in Roman graves. They bear witness to the lifestyle of the upper social stratum.
Sarcophagus, length 210 cm, breadth 73 cm, height 73 cm (including lid).
Grave goods next to the sarcophagus:
At head height: Cage-cup inv. no. 60,1; bone die inv. no. 60,2.
At body height: Iron knife with bone handle inv. no. 60,3; three pottery jugs inv. nos 60,4–60,6; three glass cups inv. nos 60,7–60,9; greenish glass cup with blue and green bull's eyes inv. no. 60,10; cylindrical jug of greenish glass inv. no. 60,11; two cylindrical jugs with engraved pattern inv. nos 60,12, 60,13; shallow glass plate inv. no. 60,14 with poultry bones; oval glass bowl inv. no. 60,15.

On the cage-cup: Harden, ibid., 240, no. 135; on dice: E. Strauch, *Merowingerzeitvertreib?*, 1994, passim.

Grave 6. Cremation burial in an urn
Amongst the burial sites in this private family cemetery there was also a cremation grave: the cylindrical lead ash container was set in a tufa urn. The urn was sealed with a lid, laid in the grave and then walled in. The grave goods – a table service – were all deposited in the tufa urn together with the leaden container for the ashes (fig. 71).

From the design of the black slip-ware beaker and the three white-ware jugs the grave can be dated to the late 3rd century AD.
Tufa cremation casket, 76 × 66 × 34 cm (remains in the possession of the landowner).
Contents: Cylindrical lead urn inv. no. 60,20a (lost); three double-handled pottery jugs inv. nos 60,21–60,23; black slip-ware beaker inv. no. 60,24; glass goblet inv. no. 60,25.

Grave 7. Burial
Burial (with skeleton facing east) without goods in a wooden coffin. Rusty nails indicate the existence of the coffin.

O. Doppelfeld, *Kölner Jahrbuch* 5, 1960/61, 7ff.

Fig. 71 Grave goods from the cremation grave
(grave 6) in the family cemetery of the villa in
Köln-Braunsfeld, cat. 27.

28 Family cemetery next to the Roman villa in Köln-Müngersdorf

The estate with its principal dwelling and numerous
outbuildings was situated approximately 5.2 km
outside the gates of the city close to the road to
Aachen. It was probably occupied from Claudian
times until around AD 400 and was enlarged and
rebuilt on numerous occasions.

The 4th-century cemetery was situated to the
north-west of the principal house within the perimeter
wall. It was not encircled by a wall of its own. Six
stone sarcophagi were discovered. They were all
aligned on an east–west axis, but were buried at
different depths in the ground.

Grave A
Neither bones nor gifts were discovered inside or next
to this red sandstone sarcophagus measuring 2.17 m
× 83 cm × 61 cm. Fremersdorf tentatively suggested
that the sarcophagus was never used. It could thus
be interpreted as evidence for the preparations made
for death.

Grave B
The white sandstone sarcophagus measuring
2.2 m × 86 cm × 65 cm was sealed by a somewhat
larger lid of grey sandstone. The lid had been
damaged and the sarcophagus looted. Grave goods
had survived outside the sarcophagus at the level of
the underside: a patched bronze bowl, a pottery jug
and, between them, the bones of two chickens.
Beside the sarcophagus: Oval bronze bowl inv. no.
26,963; pottery jug with handles inv. no. 26,965.

Grave C
Tufa sarcophagus C, similar in size to sarcophagus
B, had also had its lid smashed and been looted. On
the south-facing long side, however, there was a
wealth of grave goods deposited at the same level as
the sarcophagus base: at least seventeen glass
vessels, bronze implements and a silver spoon with
the inscription DEO GRATIAS. This last gift suggests
that this was the grave of a Christian. There are,
however, also signs of superstition and magic: one
of the glass bottles contained the heads of nine small
rodents; since there were no other rodent bones, it
is clear that the heads must have been cut off and
deliberately placed in the vessel.

Based on the composition of the gifts this grave
can be dated to about AD 370.

Fig. 72 Part of the grave goods from grave C in the family cemetery of the villa in Köln-Mungersdorf, cat. 28.

Beside the sarcophagus: Three conical glass beakers (one survives: inv. no. 26,973); six cylindrical glass bottles (one survives: inv. no. 26,972); three glass cups; glass jug with a handle; glass bowl with a depiction of hare-coursing inv. no. 26,975; glass plate inv. no. 26,974; numerous fragments of glass vessels; silver spoon inv. no. 26,977; bronze jug inv. no. 26,971; fittings from a wooden bucket inv. no. 26,970; bronze dish inv. no. 26,969; oval bronze bowl; the skulls of seven field shrews and two field mice in one of the bottles.

On the hare-coursing bowl: D. B. Harden, *Journal of Glass Studies* 2, 1960, 74; K. Painter, *Kölner Jahrbuch* 22, 1989, 95.

Grave D
Tufa sarcophagus D (2.18 m × 79 cm × 50 cm), which stood adjacent to sarcophagus C but was buried at a lower level, had also been looted: it was found to contain only human bones. Grave goods lay outside the sarcophagus in the north-east corner and along

the eastern narrow side at the same level as the sarcophagus base. They included a bronze dish and a silver spoon with the inscription DEO GRATIAS, as in the case of grave C. One of the three coins could be identified as having been minted under the emperor Valens and provides a *t.p.* for the burial of AD 364–78.
Beside the sarcophagus: Bronze dish inv. no. 26,987; small glass bottle inv. no. 26,980; silver spoon inv. no. 26,986; lead jar, possibly an inkpot, inv. no. 26,976; three coins inv. nos 26,990, 26,988, 26,989; two iron knives; iron ring; bronze tweezers; small bronze button; bronze pin; pottery bowl; fragment of a cooking pot; fragments of a black slip-ware cup; remains of a conical glass beaker; fragments of a number of glass vessels.

On the spoon: S. Hauser *Spätantike und frühbyzantinische Silberlöffel*, 1992, passim.

Grave E
The red sandstone sarcophagus had been smashed and looted; the lid was completely missing but about half of the sarcophagus survived; it contained some human bones. Grave goods mixed with charcoal and cremation ash were discovered on both long sides

and beneath the sarcophagus: this means some were placed in the grave before the sarcophagus was lowered into it.

Sets of three identical spherical glass bottles and glass cups, differing only in size, were deposited in the grave; discoloration of the glass bottles indicated that they had been filled with liquid. Bones, presumably from prepared dishes, had survived in one of the cooking pots and there were chicken bones on the plate.

Burial goods on the northern long side: Cooking pot inv. no. 26,992; cooking pot inv. no. 26,993; white-ware jug inv. no. 26,999; white-ware jug inv. no. 26,1000; white-ware jug inv. no. 26,1001; goblet inscribed with the (incorrectly spelled) word VIVAS inv. no. 26,994; black slip-ware cup inv. no. 26,995; spherical bottle inv. no. 26,996; spherical bottle inv. no. 26,997; spherical bottle inv. no. 26,998; four plain bronze rings inv. no. 26,991 a–d.

Burial goods on the southern long side: Glass cup inv. no. 26,1002; glass cup inv. no. 26,1003; glass cup inv. no. 26,1004.

Partially beneath the sarcophagus: Glass cup with indentations; pottery plate inv. no. 26,1006 with chicken bones; short iron knife.

Grave F

Sandstone sarcophagus F (2.09 m × 69 cm × 44 cm) had also been damaged and looted in ancient times. The gifts lay outside the casket along both long sides and included three spherical glass bottles with ribbon handles of the kind popular in the Rhineland during the 4th century, in some cases with bull's eye decoration.

On the northern long side: Double-handled spherical bottle of greenish glass inv. no. 26,1011; eggshells.

On the southern long side: Two double-handled spherical bottles of greenish glass inv. nos 26,1010, 26,1009; cooking pot inv. no. 26,1012; cooking pot inv. no. 26,1013; cup inscribed with the word VIVAS inv. no. 26,1014.

Black slip-ware cup inv. no. 26,1015; glass bowl with indentations inv. no. 26,1015 with chicken bones; iron knife inv. no. 26,1016.

F. 'Fremersdorf, Der römische Gutshof Köln-Müngersdorf', *Römisch-Germanische Forschungen* 6, 1933, 93ff.

Germanic graves of the 3rd–4th centuries

In archaeological literature there has been considerable debate about the ethnic affiliation and status of those buried with weapons or Germanic jewellery on the left bank of the Rhine: in the 3rd century the Roman border on the Rhine was increasingly threatened by Germanic tribes, and the Roman emperors attempted to secure the boundary by entering into contractual agreements with the Germanic leaders. The Teutons were obliged to serve in the Roman army and could even attain high-ranking positions; soldiers who had completed their period of service received fallow land.

G. Behrens, *Mainzer Zeitschrift* 14, 1919, 1ff; F. Fremersdorf, *Prähistorische Zeitschrift* 18, 1927, 284f; K. Böhner, *Jahrbuch des Römisch-Germanischen Zentralmuseums Mainz* 10, 1963, 144f; H. W. Böhme, *Germanische Grabfunde des 4. bis 5. Jahrhunderts zwischen unterer Elbe und Loire*, 1974, passim; M. Schulze-Dörrlamm, *Jahrbuch des Römisch-Germanischen Zentralmuseums Mainz* 32, 1985, 509ff.

29 Burial in a sarcophagus on the road to Bonn (Severinswall grave 3)

Discovered in 1986, this burial of a man in a limestone sarcophagus differs from other graves in the surrounding area on account of the gifts: as well as a silver spoon with the inscription UTERE FELIX and a purse containing ten coins, the sarcophagus also contained a silver cross-bow brooch and a rider's spur. The most recent of the coins was minted at the time of Postumus, who founded the separate Gallic empire in AD 259.

It is possible that the dead man was the leader of an auxiliary Germanic troop, buried with his equipment.

In the sarcophagus: Silver spoon with niello inscription UTERE FELIX; cross-bow brooch, silver with scroll ornament; iron spur; ten coins in a purse.

In front of the sarcophagus: Two incense burners; fragments of pottery vessels.

Excavation report 86,22 (U. Giesler), unpublished.

30 Burial in a wooden casket in the cemetery on the road to Bonn (St. Severin I, 69)

The grave could be identified from a layer of burnt material (70 × 70 cm) with bone deposits. The presence of iron nails indicates that the burial probably took place in a wooden casket. Along with pottery vessels and coins, the deceased was buried with a heavy iron axe, a large pair of iron shears, two whetstones and two razors.

Axes are found in many of the graves of Germanic men on the right bank of the Rhine. Large shears were grave goods in Germania Libera in particular.

The coins provide a *t.p.* of AD 211; grave I, 69 overlaps with burial I, 113 in a wooden coffin and the Merovingian grave of stone slabs I, 109.

Handled jug inv. no. 25,1012; handled jug inv. no. 25,1017; handled jug inv. no. 25,1018 (lost); small jug inv. no. 25,1014; small jug inv. no. 25,1015; small jug inv. no. 25,1016; handled pot inv. no. 25,1013; whetstone inv. no. 25,1023; whetstone inv. no. 25,1024; iron shears; iron razor with bronze dolphin handle inv. no. 25,1028; bronze razor handle in the shape of a griffin's head inv. no. 25,1028a; axe inv. no. 25,1026; copper ring inv. no. 25,1025b; four *sesterces* of the emperors Hadrian, Antoninus Pius and Caracalla inv. nos 25,1019–25,1022.

F. Fremersdorf, *Prähistorische Zeitschrift* 18, 1927, ill. 24; Päffgen, 1992, vol. I 128 and vol. II 60ff.

31 Grave on the road to Bonn (Dreikönigenstrasse/An der Eiche)

These finds were acquired from the art market by the Altertumsmuseum (Museum of Antiquities) in Mainz in 1894; the dealer stated that the find location was 'Cologne, in front of the Severinstor'. Besides a substantial set of eating and drinking utensils made up of pottery and glass vessels, the dead man's weapons (a sword and shield) were also placed in the grave. The contents of the grave have been identified as the 'equipment of a Germanic warrior of the first half of the 4th century who probably came originally from central Germany and served in the Roman army'. The finds are now kept in the Rheinisches Landesmuseum, Bonn.

Bronze cross-bow brooch; square silver belt buckle; ten ornamental silver rivets; six bronze slides; two small bronze wire rings; iron long sword; silver chape with niello decoration; remains of an iron shield boss and grip; three white-ware jugs; terra sigillata plate; goblet with the inscription BIBAMUS PIE; colourless glass bottle with a funnel-shaped neck; glass goblet.

G. Behrens, *Mainzer Zeitschrift* 14, 1919, 1ff; *Catalogue Gallien in der Spätantike*. Exhibition Mainz/Paris 1980/ I, p. 147 no. 215; Päffgen, 1992, 127.

Gravestones of the 5th–9th centuries

The majority of gravestones of the 5th–9th century were discovered near churches and many of them had been used as *spolia*. Their original locations often remain obscure, but they can be regarded as having served as grave stelae or memorial slabs on the ground or set into church walls.

S. Seiler in: *Ein Land macht Geschichte*. Catalogue of an exhibition in Cologne, 1995, 297ff.

Fig. 73
Grave inscription for Valentiniano, cat. 33.

32 Memorial slab for Rusufula (?)

The 50 cm high limestone slab had been reused as a gravestone. In a circle above a chi-rho and between two doves a clumsily written text states 'For anyone who cares to know my name I was called Rusufula and died aged four years and eleven months. I have joined the martyrs'.

The slab was already in the museum by 1839. Its origin is unknown. However, the martyrs of the Theban legion associated with St. Gereon were the only ones to be worshipped in Cologne before the 8th century. By reason of the reference to the martyrs and the chi-rho, Schmitz dates the slab to the 6th century A D.

Inv. no. stone 283.

B. and H. Galsterer, 1975, 105 no. 499 ill. 103; S. Breuer, *Kölner Jahrbuch* 25, 1992, 102; W. Schmitz, Die spätantiken und frühmittelalterlichen Grabinschriften der Stadt Köln (manuscript 1995).

33 Gravestone for Valentiniano

A piece of architecture has been reused as a gravestone: beneath the *cymatium*, a chi-rho and inscription have been added. The inscription states that Valentiniano died at the age of 3 years, (?) months and 16 days and that he had been baptised only shortly beforehand (fig. 73).

The gravestone was discovered in 1821 on the square in front of St. Gereon together with other gravestones and sarcophagi and walled up in the Nikolauskapelle. The gravestone can be dated to the 6th century. A cast of the gravestone is shown here.

B. and H. Galsterer, 1975, 105 no. 500 ill. 103; S. Breuer, *Kölner Jahrbuch* 25, 1992, 102; W. Schmitz, Die spätantiken und frühmittelalterlichen Grabinschriften der Stadt Köln (manuscript 1995).

34 Gravestone with incised crucifix

A crucifix has been scratched into the red sandstone of this trapezoid gravestone. The lower third is flanked by circles.

The gravestone (70 × 40 × 8 cm) was found near to St. Caecilien in Cologne. It can be assumed that there was a cemetery next to this church, which itself is mentioned in a document as early as A D 941.

A. Nisters-Weisbecker, *Bonner Jahrbuch* 183, 1983, 248 no. 13.

35 Gravestone with a cross decorated with volutes

This slightly trapezoidal limestone gravestone, 53 cm high, has an incised cross on its obverse with terminal volutes of equal size.

The gravestone was found near the church of St. Maria im Kapitol. In Roman times there was probably a temple of the Capitoline Trias here, and it is surmised that this is where the Frankish landlords had their seat. The founding of a church on this site probably resulted from an endowment by Plectrudis, wife of the Maior Pippin II; she was also buried in St. Maria im Kapitol. The cemetery around St. Maria im Kapitol cannot have been set out before the first quarter of the 8th century.

A. Nisters-Weisbecker, ibid., 258 no. 42.

36 Gravestone with an inscription

This rectangular slab of limestone is divided by two bands of text which cross one another. In the upper fields circles are engraved with an omphalos and Latin crosses in circles. The inscription cannot be precisely deciphered. It is not known where the slab was found and a date in the 9th century is possible.

A. Nisters-Weisbecker, ibid., 267 no. 63.

Graves of the 5th–8th centuries from St. Severin and the adjacent cemetery

In the cemetery on the Severinstrasse a *memoria* of the late antique period has been enlarged to a cemetery church. From the 6th century at the latest the church was connected with the Cologne bishop Severin, who was worshipped as a saint in this area; and shortly after A D 700 the Cologne bishops Giso and Anno were buried in the church. Burial in close proximity to these saints, either within or near the church of St. Severin, was highly desirable.

37 Grave next to St. Severin (V, 21)

In 1950 a grave was uncovered on the inside of the southern part of the cloisters of St. Severin. The skeleton was lying supine on the base of the tomb, which measured 2.18 m in length and was 70 cm wide at the bottom and 1.5 m wide at the top. No remains of a wooden coffin were found. Amongst the scant grave goods there was a silver pin on the skull and pottery and glass vessels at the foot of the tomb. A late antique stratum of pottery soil had been dug through in order to excavate a pit for the grave. At a later date a grave of stone slabs had been added to the northern part of the tomb. Consequently the

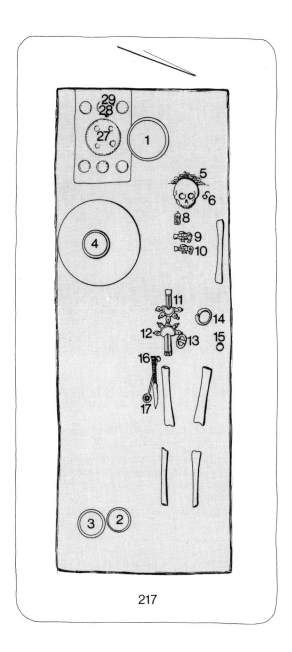

217

Fig. 74 Furnished burial in wooden coffin in
St. Severin (v, 217), cat. 38. After Päffgen 1992.

grave must have been deposited in the second half of
the 5th century.

Burials with a small number of pottery and glass
vessels, in particular glass bottles, are typical of early
Frankish burial sites in Cologne.

Handled pot inv. no. 50,258; glass bottle inv. no.
50,259; silver pin inv. no. 50,260.

Päffgen, 1992, vol. II, 484ff.

38 Burial in a wooden coffin next to St. Severin (v, 217)

In 1957 the grave of a woman was discovered in the
south-west corner of the cloisters. In the tomb (2.34
× 1.10 m) a wooden coffin could be identified. The
1.5m long skeleton was lying supine, facing east, in
the northern part of the coffin. Remains of a gold
braid headband were identified around the head;
precious jewellery – including four brooches – was
found in the position of traditional costume. A knife
with a gold handle and a perforated spoon (sieve)
lay on the right thigh. At the head end a wooden
casket had been placed in the tomb in which it was
still possible to identify a clove and fragments of moss.
In addition, the woman had also been buried with
a large and a small pottery pot, a bronze dish and a
glass bowl. A coin (without any indication of origin)
provides a *t.p.* of AD 388–423; on the basis of the
jewellery gifts, in particular the small bird brooch at
chest height and the massive bow brooches near the
pelvis, the burial can be dated to around 500 or the
early part of the 6th century.

Gold threads from a headband inv. no. 57,99;
earring, silver wire with moonstone bead inv. no.
57,86; earring, silver wire with a carnelian bead
inv. no. 57,87; necklace: gold foil pendant, small gold
foil tubes, amber bead and melon bead of glass frit
inv. nos 57,100, 57,107, 57,109; a pair of bird
brooches, gold with garnets and glass inv. nos 57,88
and 57,89; a pair of silver-gilt bow brooches, set with
garnets inv. nos 57,90 and 57,91; silver buckle
inv. no. 57,93; silver bracelet inv. no. 57,92; gold
finger ring inv. no. 57,94; knife with a gold foil
handle and silver chape on the (former) sheath
inv. no. 57,95; silver sieving spoon inv. no. 57,96;
pendant: pyrite nodule set in silver inv. no. 57,101;
pair of buckles inv. nos 57,104 and 57,105; two strap
ends inv. nos 57,102 and 57,103; small silver knife
inv. no. 57,106; silver pin inv. no. 57,111; silver
buckle inv. no. 57,110; bronze ring inv. no. 57,112;
wooden casket with buckles, containing a clove and
fragments of organic material inv. no. 57,82;
Knickwandtopf inv. no. 57,81; small *Knickwandtopf*
inv. no. 57,97; glass bowl inv. no. 57,98; bronze dish

inv. no. 57,84; bronze coin of Theodosius I (presumably AD 388–423) inv. no. 57,108.

Kölner Jahrbuch 8, 1965/66, 115–18 ill, 15–17; Päffgen, 1992, vol. II, 599ff.

39 Burial of a child in a stone sarcophagus next to St. Severin (II, 18)

Burial of a girl in a tufa sarcophagus. The grave was disturbed during the laying of the stone slab grave St. Severin II, 17, although needless damage was avoided. When discovered the sarcophagus, originally measuring about 1.40 × 0.7 m, was sealed by a flat lid. Inside there was a skeleton of the upper part of an approximately 3-year-old girl; the pelvis, leg bones and lower arms had been deposited on top of the upper body bones during the construction of the later grave. The jewellery and the other gifts, including a small bronze key, lay near the head. The burial took place around AD 500.

Keys without an accompanying casket are found in a fair number of Frankish graves. They are particularly common in the graves of children – in the cemetery of St. Severin there is also one in the grave of a child (II, 38). The keys probably served as amulets.

Two silver polyhedral earrings set with garnets (one survives) inv. no. 30,184; 80 out of 88 glass beads, presumably from a necklace inv. no. 30,189; glass bead with thread pattern inv. no. 30,190; glass bead with applied trailing inv. no. 30,191; three tesserae inv. no. 30,192; bronze key inv. no. 30,188; bronze rod of unknown use inv. no. 30,186; *antoninianus* of Tetricus inv. no. 30,193.

B. Päffgen, 1992, 102f.
On keys as grave goods: U. Arends, *Ausgewählte Gegenstände des Frühmittelalters mit Amulettcharakter*, 1978, 29ff.

40 Stone slab grave next to St. Severin (V, 59)

A stone slab grave (21.14 m × 65 cm) made of sawn-up Roman grave monuments and remnants of sarcophagi was erected on the inside of the cloisters of St. Severin. A knife and seax were placed next to the skeleton at hip-height and a *francisca* under the right foot, and a pot and a jug at the feet of the deceased.

The depositing of a number of weapons as grave goods is a characteristic of Frankish graves of men in the 6th century AD. Given that throwing axes were no longer placed in graves after the middle of the 6th century, this grave can be dated to the first half of the 6th century.

Roman spolia used in the construction of the grave: Fragment of a pilaster; gravestone of Egnatia Libera inv. no. 50,130; fragment of a gravestone inv. no. 50,311.
Grave goods: Bronze buckle inv. no. 50,302; iron buckle from a seax belt inv. no. 50,301; iron seax with remnants of a leather sheath inv. no. 50,300; iron *francisca* inv. no. 50,306; three iron arrowheads inv. nos 50,303–50,305; iron knife inv. no. 50,296; bronze ring inv. no. 50,299; *Knickwandtopf* inv. no. 50,308; fragment of a pottery jug inv. no. 50,307; bronze coin from the 1st century AD; bronze coin of Constantinus I (AD 315/316).

Päffgen, 1992, vol. II, 505ff.

41 Stone slab grave under St. Severin (III, 73)

This stone slab grave of a woman is situated under the floor of the nave of St. Severin along the axis of the church. The base of a Roman tufa sarcophagus was reused for the base of this grave; the long sides consist of four sandstone slabs each 1.20 m long and slabs of trachyte form the short sides. An oak and beech wood coffin (1.88 × 65 cm) was placed in this container. The grave was sealed with two slabs of trachyte.

The deceased was dressed in her traditional costume and buried with valuable pieces of jewellery. Remnants of fabric were observed on top of the corpse. At the foot of the deceased there was a wooden casket containing linen and silk cloths, a leather bag with a silk cloth, a 'powder puff' and two glass vessels. Outside the wooden coffin, at the foot of the stone slab container, there was a bronze dish.

The woman was not only buried in a prominent position within the church itself, but also very lavishly equipped. The gold headband in particular, the *vitta*, marks her out as a lady of the highest social standing. The short gold braid was probably extended on the back with fabric or leather – as in the case of the gold braid from the grave St. Severin V, 217 – whereas the gold braid of the princess buried beneath the cathedral stretched all round the head. Jewellery caskets, fine linen and cosmetics have only been found in a small number of richly furnished graves. Unlike other caskets from Frankish graves in and around Cologne, this one is not decorated with bronze sheeting.

The grave dates from around AD 570.

In the wooden coffin: Headband made of gold foil threads; a pair of polyhedral earrings, gold with garnets and glass paste; bronze pin with a polyhedral head; glass spindle-whorl; pieces of a chain: 3 cross-shaped gold pendants set with garnets, 2 gold disc-shaped pendants and 94 glass beads; necklace of

32 glass and 27 amber beads; garnet and silver disc brooch; silver and garnet rosette brooch; pair of silver-gilt bow brooches, gold finger ring; two pairs of bronze buckles; open-work bronze disc, probably from a bag; pair of silvered bronze strap ends; iron knife; iron shears; small beechwood casket with bronze mounts; spherical dark green glass bottle; bell-beaker of yellow-green glass.
Outside: Bronze dish.

F. Fremersdorf, *IPEK* 15/16, 1941/42, 124ff.; Päffgen, 1992, vol. II, 232ff.

42 Walled-in grave beneath St. Severin (III, 81)

Beneath the nave of St. Severin a grave was constructed using a Roman sarcophagus: after breaking away two sides of the sarcophagus, the grave (2 m × 88 cm) was constructed using fragments of sandstone, tufa and limestone and covered with slabs of trachyte and sandstone.

The dead man was buried supine and facing east. He wore a finger ring set with a gold coin of Marcian. In the pelvic region a bronze buckle, a strap end from a sword harness and a knife were discovered together with rusty pieces of iron; in the chest region an iron silver-inlaid buckle from a seax belt was discovered (pl. 47). Two flints, an animal bone and a shell lay close to the head.

Ornamented buckles with silver inlay were also discovered in graves of the row-grave cemeteries of Köln-Müngersdorf and Köln-Junkersdorf. The leather strap had to be arranged skilfully in order that the ornamented buckle-plates were visible. Buckles of this kind were only used in the period around AD 600.

The grave can be dated to the late 6th or early 7th century AD.

Grave goods: Finger ring set with a gold coin of Marcian (AD 450–57); silver-inlaid iron buckle; bronze buckle; bronze belt tongue; iron knife; two flints; shell.
Between the covering slabs: Silver-inlaid iron plate.

Päffgen, 1992, vol. II, 244ff.

43 Burial in a sarcophagus in St. Severin (III, 74)

St. Severin grave III, 74 came to light beneath the floor of the church to the south of the grave of stone slabs St. Severin III, 73 and below the sarcophagus St. Severin III, 75. It is a grey sandstone sarcophagus (2.18 m × 74 cm) sealed with two segments of a tufa lid. Traces of a wooden coffin were identified inside the grave. The dead woman had been buried wearing her traditional costume and her jewellery: she was wearing a twisted silver neck ring, which may be a clue to the deceased's origin or ethnic affiliation. Apart from the jewellery, she was buried only with a wooden vessel and a glass beaker, which were placed at the foot of the grave.

The grave dates from the late 7th century AD.

Silver wire neck-ring; a pair of silver polyhedral earrings; silver strap-end; bronze buckle; bronze strap-end; three small gold stars with a fastening clip; four triangular gold pendants; eight glass and two amethyst beads; goblet of clear glass; wooden vessel (lost).

Päffgen, 1992, vol. II, 240f; on the neck ring see vol. I, 425f.

44 Stone slab grave in St. Severin (III, 100)

This grave (measuring 2.20 m × c. 80 cm) was constructed beneath the nave of St. Severin of sandstone, tufa and trachyte slabs and sealed with two trachyte slabs. The dead man was buried in full costume, although the remains can only be identified with reservations: he apparently wore a silk robe and a cloak with a wide hem woven with gold threads, leather gauntlets, stockings or leg bindings and shoes with leather soles. His six-stringed oak lyre accompanied him. At his feet there were a leather bag, a wooden bottle, folding knife, comb, shears, a steel for kindling fire and flint. Plant remains were found on the skeleton and on the lyre: a box tree twig, dog-rose, lavender and flower stalks.

Music making, especially playing the lyre and reciting one's own songs, was part of the lifestyle of the Frankish upper social stratum: at festivities the lyre was passed from hand to hand.

The grave dates from the late 7th or early 8th century AD (fig. 75).

Gold braid; remnants of leather and textile (now lost); a pair of silver shoe buckles; two silver strap ends; silver belt buckle; five silver belt mounts; wooden water bottle; iron shears; iron folding knife; iron knife in a leather sheath; flint; fire-steel; bone comb; wooden lyre (copy: original destroyed); torch (?).

Päffgen, 1992, vol. II, 280ff.
On the lyre: J. Werner, Leier und Harfe im germanischen Frühmittelalter. *Festschrift Th. Mayer* vol. I, 1954, 9ff.

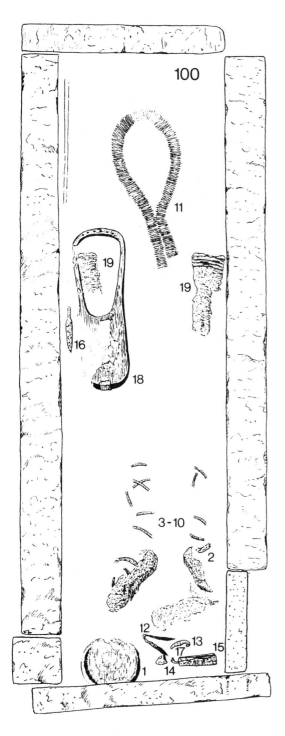

100

11

19

19

16

18

3 - 10

2

12

13

15

17

1

14

Fig. 75 So-called 'Minstrel's Grave' from St. Severin (III, 100), cat. 44. After Päffgen, 1992.

The row-grave cemetery at Köln-Junkersdorf

Two Frankish cemeteries have been unearthed within 1000 m of each other in the immediate hinterland of Cologne: in Köln-Müngersdorf and in Köln-Junkersdorf. The settlements to which they belonged have not yet been discovered, probably because they became the nuclei of medieval villages.

The Frankish cemetery at Köln-Müngersdorf was excavated between 1926 and 1929 and 149 burials were recorded. The majority of the finds were lost during the Second World War.

The cemetery in Köln-Junkersdorf was considerably larger: in 1940, 1943, 1950 and 1951 Fremersdorf uncovered 587 sites, including 541 Frankish graves; the publication of the details of the graves and finds was undertaken by La Baume in 1967.

The Frankish cemetery was built on top of a small number of Roman cremation and cremation debris graves that probably belonged to a local Roman estate. Most of the dead were buried in wooden coffins and only a small number in wooden tombs and graves of stone slabs. The graves rarely overlap or touch one another, so one can assume that they were marked at ground level by a sign, most probably made of wood. This theory is supported by the fact that a large number of the graves, especially the most richly furnished, were looted soon after they were laid down by people who had knowledge of the locations of the objects within the graves. Burials took place in this cemetery from the middle of the 5th century AD; of the earliest a number are aligned on a south–north axis, whereas all the others are aligned east–west. The more recent graves to the east and south were grouped in a semicircle around the older ones in the north-west; later the cemetery was expanded step-by-step to the south. Burials no longer took place at this cemetery after AD 700.

La Baume, 1967; Päffgen, 1992, vol. I, 289ff.

45 Köln-Junkersdorf grave 33

Grave 33 is an intact grave of a woman; in the grave shaft (2.25 m × 80 cm) only a few traces of the wooden coffin were identified. The dead woman was buried in her traditional costume with a complete set of jewellery. She wore a costume involving four brooches: two bird brooches lay in the chest area and two silvered bronze bow-brooches with semicircular headplates were found in the lower body region. Apart from an iron knife, which may well have hung from her belt, she had only a bronze coin with a hole in it for use as a pendant, and a key. Päffgen dates the grave to about AD 500–530.

Necklace of 20 glass beads inv. no. 40,265; bronze

coin with a hole in it (Constantine?) inv. no. 40,266; pair of small bird brooches of bronze inv. nos 40,267 and 40,268; bronze ring inv. no. 40,269; pair of silvered bronze bow brooches with semicircular headplates inv. nos. 40,271 and 40,272; iron buckle with tongue (lost); iron knife (lost); bronze key inv. no. 40,270.

La Baume, 1967, 146, pl. 55. Päffgen, 1992, vol. I, 291.

46 Köln-Junkersdorf grave 159

The grave of a woman, no. 159, is no longer intact: the length of the 90 cm wide coffin in the only marginally wider, 2.60 m long shaft could not be ascertained. Grave robbers clearly knew of the location of the valuable accessories associated with the traditional costume: there is no silver or gold jewellery, although a part of a necklace of glass beads, ornamental bronze fittings and the burial goods deposited at the foot of the grave survive.

The grave can be dated to the period between AD 520/30 and 550/60 on account of the form of the bell-beaker.

Four beads inv. no. 51,278; 3 triangular bronze ornamental fittings inv. no. 51,279 and inv. no. 51,280; bone comb with two rows of teeth inv. no. 51,281; greenish glass bell-beaker inv. no. 51,282; bronze bowl with beaded rim (lost).

La Baume, 1967, 181 plate 69,2; Päffgen, 1992, vol. I, 314.

47 Köln-Junkersdorf grave 41

In a pit measuring 2.45 × 1.45 m traces were found of a large coffin or wooden tomb (2.10 m × 87 cm). The dead woman had been buried in her full traditional costume and was pushed close up against the northern wall of the coffin (or had perhaps slipped into that position?). A thin-walled bronze dish and a bone comb with two rows of teeth had been placed at the foot of the coffin by the bereaved.

On the basis of the bow-brooches with chip-carved decoration and the rosette brooches, Päffgen dates the grave to the period between AD 550/60 and 580/90.

A pair of silver polyhedral earrings inv. nos 40,314 and 40,315; necklace of 46 beads and a small silver plate inv. no. 40,318; pair of rosette-shape garnet-inlaid disc brooches inv. nos 40,316 and 40,317; bi-conical glass bead or spindle whorl inv. no. 40,319; bronze coin of Constantine II inv. no. 40,320; pair of silver bow-brooches with rectangular head plate and chip-carved ornament inv. nos 40,321 and 40,322; silver bracelet inv. no. 40,323; glass disc-shaped spindle whorl inv. no. 40,325; iron knife (lost); remnants of a bag (?); double-handled bronze dish inv. no. 40,328; bone comb with two rows of teeth (lost).

La Baume, 1967, 148f, pl. 56; Päffgen, 1992, vol. I, 314.

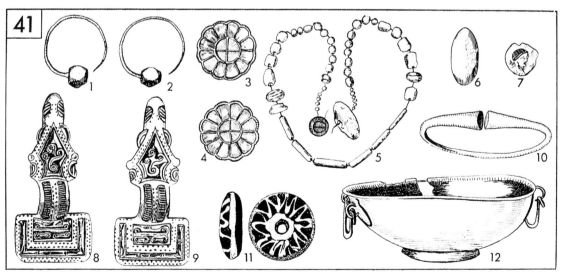

Fig. 76 Grave goods from a female grave (41) in the Frankish cemetery at Köln-Junkersdorf, cat. 47. After La Baume 1967.

48 Köln-Junkersdorf grave 49

Like its immediate neighbour grave 41, grave 49 also dates from the period between AD 550/60 and 580/90. A coffin (2 m × 48 cm) had been placed on thick wooden boards in the 2.12 m long shaft. In this intact grave of a woman the jewellery was also found in place on her traditional costume, whilst the other gifts had been placed at the foot of the body. A pottery bottle was found below the level of the coffin. The characteristic shape of the (lost) bell-beaker permitted the grave to be dated.

Pair of polyhedral earrings, silver with garnets inv. nos 40,364 and 40,365; silver-gilt and garnet disk brooch inv. no. 40,368; necklace of ten glass beads inv. no. 40,366; small necklace of six glass beads inv. no. 40,367; coarse-ware bowl inv. no. 40,370; greenish glass bell-beaker (lost) with seven glass beads around it in a semicircle inv. no. 40,372; red-ware bottle inv. no. 40,369.

La Baume, 1967, 152f, pl. 57; Päffgen, 1992, vol. I, 314.

49 Köln-Junkersdorf grave 337

This grave of a woman was discovered intact: traces of the wooden coffin (2.35 m × 66 cm) were discovered in a pit 2.80 m × 1.12 m. The woman was buried with all the jewellery belonging to her traditional costume; her necklace consisted of glass, meerschaum and amber beads. A glass beaker placed, as usual, at the foot of the coffin was the only grave good.

Meerschaum beads are rare; there was also a meerschaum bead in the grave V, 198 in St. Severin. Amber beads, on the other hand, were quite common on necklaces, particularly in the mid 6th century.

The bow brooches with rectangular headplate provide evidence to date the grave to between AD 550/60 and 580/90.

Necklace of 57 glass and amber pearls, inv. no. 51,680; silver and garnet disc brooch inv. no. 51,681; necklace of nine meerschaum, glass and amber beads inv. no. 51,682; oval iron buckle inv. no. 51,683; pair of gilt-bronze bow brooches with rectangular headplates inv. nos 51,684 and 51,685; iron knife with a wooden handle inv. no. 51,685a; yellow-green glass beaker inv. no. 51,686.

Germania 30, 1952, 459 ill. I pl. 31, 11–12; La Baume, 1967, 215f, pl. 80, 1.

50 Köln-Junkersdorf grave 564

Grave 564, that of a woman, was laid down in the south-east of the cemetery. Traces of a wooden coffin measuring 1.75 m × 0.80 m were discovered in the 2.30 m × 1.20 m tomb. The grave had been disturbed. Beads from a necklace were found in the neck region and the remaining gifts at the foot of the grave. On the basis of the bell-beaker and the combination of gifts Päffgen dates the grave to *c.* AD 580–610.

Necklace of 15 glass beads inv. no. 51,1141; biconical clay pot inv. no. 51,1142; bell-beaker of yellow-green glass inv. no. 51,1143.

La Baume, 1967, 253; Päffgen, 1992, vol. I, 314.

51 Köln-Junkersdorf grave 125

Traces of a wooden burial chamber (2.25 m × 1.20 m) were easily identified in the very large grave pit (2.70 m x 1.52 m). The contents of the chamber had been completely ransacked by grave robbers; however the thieves had decided that not everything was worth taking: the surviving remains of a traditional costume and goods indicate that this was the grave of a woman. The woman was buried with a wooden casket with ornamental iron fittings on the corners. According to Päffgen the grave was deposited in about AD 580–610.

Necklace of 18 glass beads and a bronze coin of Constantine the Great inv. no. 51,148; an arm band of 11 glass beads and a bronze coin of Constantine the Great inv. no. 51,149; pair of silvered bronze buckles inv. nos 51,153 and 51,154; pair of bronze strap ends inv. nos 51,151 and 51,152; ornamental iron fittings from a wooden casket inv. no. 51,155; bone fittings, presumably from the same wooden casket inv. no. 51,156.

La Baume, 1967 173f; Päffgen, 1992, vol. I, 314.

52 Köln-Junkersdorf grave 160

For this man's grave a pit 3.30 m × 1.55 m had been excavated; no remnants of a coffin could be identified. Traces of a fire were discovered about 50 cm above the base of the grave. The dead man was dressed and was buried with his weapons – a long sword and an arrowhead. The gift of weapons implies a date between AD 580 and 610.

Iron arrowhead inv. no. 51,283; iron long sword (*spatha*) inv. no. 51,285; iron knife in a wooden sheath inv. no. 51,286; iron buckle inv. no. 51,287; round iron mount with bronze rivets from the belt inv. no. 51,288.

La Baume, 1967, 181f, pl. 69,3; Päffgen, 1992, vol. I, 314.

53 Köln-Junkersdorf grave 216

No remnants of a wooden coffin were identified
in the 2.80 × *c.* 1.40 m grave pit. The burial
had been ransacked, and all that remained were
accessories to a traditional costume together with
iron, bronze and pottery equipment. The belt buckle
makes it possible to date grave 216 to about
AD 580–610.

Iron fire-steel (lost); rectangular bronze mount with
studs inv. no. 51,450; large oval belt buckle with triangular ornamental plate inv. no. 51,451; fragments
of a biconical pot (lost).

La Baume, 1967, 193 pl. 74,4; Päffgen, 1992, vol. 1,
314.

54 Köln-Junkersdorf grave 198

As in grave 160, also that of a man, no remnants of
a coffin were discovered in the 2.10 × 1.14 m pit of
grave 198. The dead man was buried with a shield,
spear and a very large pair of shears; the shears were
not hanging from the belt, as is normally the case,
but were deposited near the head. The grave had been
disturbed, but the wood and iron implements were
not stolen. On the basis of the design of the shield
boss Päffgen dates the burial to about AD 610–630/
40.

Iron shears inv. no. 51,381; iron shield boss inv. no.
51,382; iron spear head inv. no. 51,383 and remnants
of the wooden shaft.

La Baume, 1967, 189; Päffgen, 1992, vol. 1, 315.

55 Köln-Junkersdorf grave 438

The grave had been disturbed; in the relatively short
grave (1.95 m long) there were hardly any traces of
the wooden coffin. All that was left, in the middle of
the grave, was an iron knife with a lightly rounded
back and similarly rounded blade. The grave lies
between graves that can be dated to the first half of
the 7th century.

Iron knife inv. no. 51,910.

La Baume, 1967, 233.

56 Köln-Junkersdorf grave 514

Both the skeleton and coffin had entirely
disintegrated; the jewellery lay at what was probably
the head end and the other grave goods were
discovered at the foot of the grave. A few fragments
of iron in the chest region cannot clearly be
identified. On the basis of the jewellery the grave was
that of a woman. The deceased was given a fragment
of a blue-green glass bowl as a burial gift; given the

colour it was perhaps an amulet. The grave was
deposited around AD 610–630/40.

Bronze hairpin inv. no. 51,1053; 202 mostly glass
beads from a necklace inv. no. 51,1054; bronze coin
with a hole through it serving as a pendant inv. no.
51,1055; wheel-shaped bronze pendant inv. no.
51,1056; fragment from the edge of a blue-green
ribbed glass bowl (lost); glass fragments (lost); oval
buckle loop (lost); coarse-ware bowl inv. no. 51,1063;
biconical pot inv. no. 51,1062; red-ware bottle inv. no.
51,1061.

La Baume, 1967, 246 pl. 84,6; Päffgen, 1992, vol. 1,
315.

57 Köln-Junkersdorf grave 397

This man's grave had been disturbed; the 2.20 m
long and *c.* 60 cm wide wooden coffin was lowered
into a pit only marginally longer, but twice as wide.
The ornamental mounts from the belt set and the
grave goods at the foot of the grave – a sword in its
sheath and a *Knickwandtopf* – are the only things to
have survived. The decoration on the belt fittings
and the type of seax allow the grave to be dated to
the period around AD 630/40–670/80.

Silver-inlaid iron plate, counterplate and rectangular
fitting from a belt inv. nos 51,812, 51,816, 51,817; iron
seax inv. no. 51,813; remnants of the leather sheath,
decorated with bronze studs inv. no. 51,814; globular
pot inv. no. 51,815.

Kölner Jahrbuch 4, 1959, pl. 11,5; La Baume, 1967,
226 pl. 82,4; Päffgen, 1992, vol. 1, 315.

ABBREVIATION USED IN CATALOGUE

*Kölner Jahrbuch = Kölner Jahrbuch für Vor- und
Frühgeschichte*

Elite lifestyle and the transformation of the Roman world in Northern Gaul

Monica Alkemade

In the late Roman period a remarkable change occurs in the nature of the archaeological record from the region between the Seine and the Rhine (Northern Gaul). From the middle of the fourth century AD onwards, archaeologists are confronted with a boom in objects from graves, watery contexts (rivers and bogs) and hoards. Until the end of the eighth century this material culture – especially weapons, accessories (brooches, belts, buckles) and tableware (ceramics, glass, metal, wood) – constitutes the main source for the study of transformation processes in this north-west periphery of the Roman world.

In the archaeology of late Roman and early medieval Northern Gaul it has become customary to refer to this material culture as 'Germanic', on the basis of an assumed 'un-Roman' appearance and use. Subsequently, the occurrence of these artefacts within the borders of the Roman empire has been interpreted as the archaeological witnesses of the Germanic influx from the north in late Roman times. In this way, archaeological evidence was supposed to fill the gap in our knowledge of the sequence of events leading up to the ultimate fall of the Roman empire. After all, written sources from the centuries between the disintegration of Roman authority in the fifth century and the rise of the Carolingian empire in the eighth century are scarce and often ambiguous.

In the Roman period the area now known as the Netherlands was intersected by the Roman *limes* or frontier, in this case the Rhine. The southern part of the Netherlands belonged to the Roman province of Germania Secunda, whereas north of the river Germania Libera ('free Germania') began. Thus the Netherlands has traditionally come to be regarded by those studying the decline of the Roman empire as the setting for a dramatic encounter between various powers which, to modern eyes, seem contrasted (Romans vs Germans, Christians vs pagans, civilised people vs barbarians). However, the question arises: how 'Roman' or 'Germanic' were the

societies in this north-west periphery of the Roman world? Was the Roman frontier really the 'Iron Curtain' envisaged by generations of researchers? After all, for centuries prior to the final fall of Roman authority, groups of very different kinds had maintained intensive contacts on both sides of the *limes*, not only in the form of trade but also at an aristocratic level and by providing troops to the Roman army.[1]

It is doubtful whether the traditional archaeological approach to the material culture of this period will be able to stand the test of criticism any longer. As an introduction to the catalogue of Dutch finds from this period, it is useful to consider changes which have taken place in the past decades in the research into the late Roman and early medieval periods.

In a long tradition of historiography of the emerging European nation-states (notably France and Germany) much energy has been invested in the writing of a political-military history (*histoire événementielle*) of late Roman and early medieval societies. In the course of the nineteenth century the image of a massive and dramatic migration of peoples (*Völkerwanderung*) and the consequent fall of Roman civilisation became firmly anchored in the modern perception of the end of the Roman empire and the beginning of the early Middle Ages. Many of us can remember from childhood those stirring pictures of this period, of Germanic barbarians dragging down Roman civilisation into obscurity (the 'Dark Ages'), which only receded step-by-step; or conversely, of heroic Germanic folk breathing new life into a degenerate Roman society.

But all such notions are subject to change. The perception of the past as a confrontation of cultures has long been considered outdated by historians. Instead, there has been growing interest in viewing those transitional centuries between antiquity and the Middle Ages as a period of social, religious and economic transformation. This altered perspective

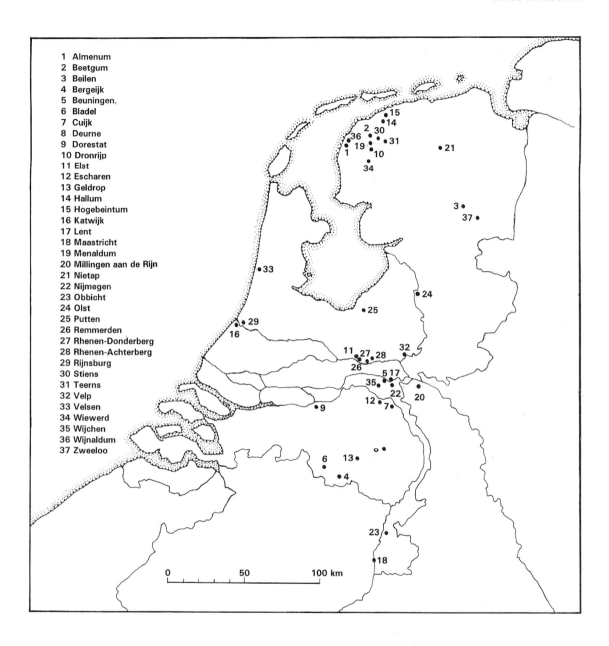

1 Almenum
2 Beetgum
3 Beilen
4 Bergeijk
5 Beuningen,
6 Bladel
7 Cuijk
8 Deurne
9 Dorestat
10 Dronrijp
11 Elst
12 Escharen
13 Geldrop
14 Hallum
15 Hogebeintum
16 Katwijk
17 Lent
18 Maastricht
19 Menaldum
20 Millingen aan de Rijn
21 Nietap
22 Nijmegen
23 Obbicht
24 Olst
25 Putten
26 Remmerden
27 Rhenen-Donderberg
28 Rhenen-Achterberg
29 Rijnsburg
30 Stiens
31 Teerns
32 Velp
33 Velsen
34 Wiewerd
35 Wijchen
36 Wijnaldum
37 Zweeloo

Fig. 77 Map of find-spots.

has counterbalanced the earlier preoccupations with migrations, invasions and battles with an approach more closely related to the *histoire des mentalités*.

For archaeologists concerned with the transition from the Roman period to the Middle Ages, this would seem to offer the opportunity to escape from the streamlined narrative accounts that traditionally allude to 'The Fall of the Roman Empire', 'The Spread of Civilisation', 'The Birth of Europe' or 'The Coming of Christianity', into which their unruly data were too often squeezed.

In late Roman and early medieval archaeology, however, a paradoxical situation arises in which the transition between Roman and medieval times is too often still couched in terms of a confrontation between Roman and Germanic culture. While the traditional historical framework with its – mostly ethnic – schematisations has been discarded, current typologies of material culture from this period have been left unaltered. The special character of the majority of the archaeological data from this period is rarely addressed, even though in many cases a very specific use of the objects is involved: the deliberate disposal of one or more artefacts in specific contexts such as hoards, graves and wet sites (rivers or bogs).

In my view, this reflects a fundamental problem. Archaeologists are often too hesitant in accepting that this material culture not only relates to daily life (trade, technology, possession and status) but also to the *histoire des mentalités*. Thus archaeologists nowadays are confronted by the question of what the study of material remains (objects, settlements, graves etc.) can actually contribute to our insight into man and society in this period. What type of history can and will we as archaeologists write?

The goal of the Dutch contribution to the theme of 'The Transformation of the Roman World' – presented by the Royal Coin Cabinet with the National Museum of Antiquities in Leiden – is to display the undeniably splendid Dutch finds from this period in a context that would be more in keeping with recent thinking in history, anthropology and sociology. Instead of a streamlined chronological or narrative account, the visitor is encouraged to consider how people use material culture to order their world and to define their position within a network of relations – in the social, natural and supernatural sphere. In the presentation of finds from this period in the Netherlands ethnic contrasts are avoided in favour of the 'communal' canon – the new lifestyle that emerges in this period and which, in our view, is a distinctive characteristic of the Netherlands as part of a frontier zone.

In the late Roman period social changes took place both in and outside the Roman empire, by means of which persons and groups redefined their identities within a changing world. The way in which this occurred varied from place to place and from era to era, and was partly dependent on the traditions of the particular region and on how new elements were incorporated in them. In this creative process of appropriation, integration and interaction between new and existing ideas, the use and exchange of material culture plays a major role. This social/anthropological approach to material culture and its forms of use recognises the importance of material culture as a medium that all human beings, whether individually or as groups, actively use to explore and shape their social, natural and supernatural surroundings and (consciously or unconsciously) to construct meaningful identities. In other words, material culture is no passive reflection of human behaviour: objects are, like language, gestures and even writing, indispensable to human beings in actively shaping their reality.

However, a modernist approach to material culture from this period severely hampers any historical insight into what, in our view, is really at stake in this period: the transformation of social and ideological structures and their articulation in the design and use of objects, space, language etc. Therefore, if we really want to penetrate this world by way of material culture, we will have to take the obviously ritual context of our archaeological data as a major concern, instead of brushing it aside as a negligible or irrelevant peculiarity of archaeological research. For this reason, the archaeological data should be studied from the departure point of looking at how conceptualisations of the relation between man and the material world differed in past eras from those of our own modern one. The modern separation and isolation of the mental and the material dimensions of life are the product of a long process of demystification of the surrounding world that ran parallel to the rise of capitalism in early modern Europe.[2]

From this perspective it is preferable for archaeologists to study those historical processes that were traditionally alluded to as 'The Fall of the Roman Empire', 'The Birth of the Occident', 'The Conversion to Christianity', 'The Barbarisation of the West', and so on, as 'a mental and social process that becomes tangible to the archaeologist via new rituals and a specific association with material culture'.[3]

To return to the concerns of this exhibition: the point of departure is that the deposition of material wealth in ritual contexts in this world is obviously considered a form of 'appropriate use'. Instead of treating this as the peculiarity of a specific ethnic group, the exhibition avoids the traditional Roman vs Germanic dichotomy and attempts to present the objects found in ritual contexts as part of a more general contemporaneous *discours* in which various groups (Germans, Romans, Christians, pagans) participate – for example to define and shape new cultural identities that rise above socio-political and economic practice.

For this reason the exhibition has chosen to concentrate on the changing lifestyle of elites that emerges in the archaeological record in the north-west periphery of the Roman empire. From the material culture connected with this elite lifestyle (body ornaments, weapons, tableware) we can deduce that, in this lifestyle, three aspects keep recurring: the emphasis on warrior values, feasting and personal adornment. Through these main themes, much of the archaeological information can be presented so that it can be seen to articulate, in various ways: the design and use of objects; the lay-out of houses, cult places and settlements; burial ritual; iconographic and narrative sources; and even Christian liturgy.

By examining elite lifestyle, the aim is to approach society from the participants' perspective rather than by using static models imposed from the outside. Especially in older publications, the striking visual appearance of 'Germanic' material culture (light-and-shade effects, polychromy, animal decoration, and/or a glittering quality) is often equated with 'barbarian taste' – a predilection for pomp and splendour, drinking and fighting. This is, however, a stereotyped association, originating from modern notions about an assumed under-developed control of passions and impulses in 'primitive' societies.[4]

First and foremost, it needs to be emphasised that these objects point to a set of interconnected contemporary ideas about taking an active part in society; they are the focus of transactions and events by which society is shaped. Here the crucial factor is a shared experience or knowledge of how to participate in the relationships that underpin society: how to think and act, and correspondingly to use these objects in an appropriate way – which means how to use them in rituals and ritualised events in which significant relationships between people and their surrounding social and supernatural world are expressed and defined. For other people living alongside the elite, knowledge of the elite lifestyle offers a source of information about society and its constituents. Within an elite lifestyle, meaningful behaviour and events are defined, valued and articulated through a hierarchy of objects. By using this particular theme the archaeological record is no longer a random collection of isolated objects found by chance, but a coherent material construction – a contemporary native model of human orderings of the surrounding world.

These rather abstract ideas are focused by means of quotations from the *Beowulf* epic, which act as a guide throughout the exhibition. This poetic account of (more or less) historical persons and their behaviour, preserved in a volume compiled *c*.1000, enables the different elements of the exhibition to be knitted together in a natural way and evokes the right atmosphere – even though it must be admitted that there are some basic differences between the content and background of the story and our subject.

The exhibition begins with a short introduction to the late Roman period and the early Middle Ages in the Netherlands. Then the visitor is confronted with forms of use of objects from these periods which may seem puzzling to modern eyes. This is achieved by reconstructing the original find-contexts of some of the most spectacular finds, such as the late Roman parade helmet from the Peel bog and the gold hoards from Rhenen, Beilen and Velp. In this way, attention is drawn to the fundamental question: what is this splendid object doing in a bog? in the earth? in a grave?

After these questions in the first section, the visitor is taken through an audiovisual presentation where the deposit of splendid possessions in (to modern minds) negative contexts such as a bog or a grave can be seen from the 'native' perspective to be a rational and appropriate choice, however different this may seem from current perceptions of the uses of wealth. By explaining our views on the meaning of these objects within the elite lifestyle, the visitor is offered an inside view of the life of early medieval elites. The three themes – warrior values, personal adornment and feasting – are introduced and explained here as an introduction to the material culture presented in the next three sections. There, each of the themes is represented in more depth, by means of weapons, vessels, articles of clothing, ornaments and coins – categories of objects which recur throughout the exhibition in a variety of contexts, whether grave, river or bog deposition.

With regard to the first theme, warrior values, it is important to stress that, in this world, being a warrior is not to be put on a par with actual participation in combat – the use of weapons in warfare and feuding. Warrior-culture is first and foremost a complex of *ideas* about the appropriate behaviour of young men in society. From this perspective it is apparent that weapon-finds from this period do not necessarily reflect functional fighting equipment. Many finds shown are prestige-goods – carefully decorated weapons and accessories which, in some cases, were not fit for actual use.

The second theme, personal adornment, is treated by presenting various objects that, in one way or the other, are related to the human body. However, there is more to these objects than just functional dress items or ethnic markers. In the early medieval world the body may be seen as the natural point of reference in contemporary human experience, and a reflection on a person's position in the surrounding world. Thus the objects connected with the body are not mere symbols of social status, they are constituents of a person's being, of his/her fame and reputation. We could call this 'identity', but should be aware not to use it in its modern, individualist sense – as something fixed and static. The notion of the human being as a clearly bounded and indivisible entity is a relatively young, modern Western notion, the universal applicability of which is highly debatable. For example, the medieval practice of disarticulating the bodies of holy men and women in order to produce relics would certainly suggest an alternative view – that of the human being consisting of elements temporarily put together.[5] From the perspective of an elite lifestyle, the body is the crucial connecting link between the realms of thinking

and doing: everything the body does – when and where and how it dresses up, fights, feasts and so on – is guided by an overall image of life itself, its nature and continuity.

The last theme of our treatment of elite lifestyle, feasting, is presented by evoking the atmosphere of a feast in a banqueting hall (something like the one described in *Beowulf*). With the help of archaeological objects from different find-contexts it is shown how, at an event like this, societal relationships are defined and 'materialised' through the highly ritualised use and exchange of material objects. In the hall the warriors gather in their best attire to eat and drink, to commemorate brave deeds, to listen to the song of the bard and to exchange gifts. In short, here a number of people define themselves as a particular group. Under the banner of harmony and laughter there is, however, a strong element of competition: the rank of every person present in the gathering is contested – by the place he is awarded in the distribution of mead,[6] by the gift the host presents to him and by the way his actions are mentioned in the epic sung. 'Now, go to your seat and enjoy the pleasures of the banquet as one honoured for his prowess. A very great quantity of treasures is to change hands between us when morning comes' (*Beowulf* 1782–4).

NOTES

1 E.g. Roymans 1995.

2 Appadurai 1986.

3 Theuws 1995, 134.

4 See Kuper 1988.

5 See, e.g., Geary 1994.

6 See Enright 1996.

The author wishes to thank the European Science Foundation for the opportunity to participate in the sessions of Working Group 5 ('Power and Society'). I am most grateful for inspiring discussions with the members of this group: Javier Arce (Rome), Lotte Hedeager (Göteborg), Frans Theuws (Amsterdam), Heinrich Härke (Reading), Janet Nelson (London), Jos Bazelmans (Leiden), Mayke de Jong (Utrecht), Regine Le Jan (Valenciennes), Christina La Rocca (Padua), Pablo Diaz (Salamanca) and Stefano Gasparri (Venice).

Catalogue of the exhibition 'The Lifestyle of the Elite'

Rijksmuseum Het Koninklijk Penningkabinet, Leiden:
'National Museum, Royal Coin Cabinet'
with the assistance of
Rijksmuseum van Oudheden:
'National Museum of Antiquities'
Arie Peddemors and Arent Pol

Introduction

1

Deurne 1910

Rijksmuseum van Oudheden (Leiden)

Hoard, *c.*320

a gilt silver helmet (pl. 48) with inscriptions: STABLESIA VI ('6th cavalry unit of the equites Stablesiani') and M TITVS LVNAMIS LIBR I-L ('M Titus Lunamis, weighing 1 pound 1½ uncia')

k 1911/4.1–6

Braat 1973, 56–61

2

Maastricht 1953–4

Schatkamer Basiliek van Sint-Servaas (Maastricht)

Grave, *c.*450

a sepulchral stone with inscriptions: crosses, Christ's monogram, Alpha and Omega, doves and epitaph:
[HIC IACET IN]NOCEN[S QVI VIXIT ANNOS ......VIVERE] DVM POTV[IT.........
..........E?..F]VIT CAR[ISSIMA POST DIES P]AVCOS DVLCISSI[MA FIDELIS IN] PACE RECESSIT
('Here lies innocent ..., who lived ... years, as long as she could live. ... She was the dearest. After a few days she passed away sweetest and faithfully and in peace')

Timmers 1955; Cense/Werner 1984

3

Nijmegen-Mariënburg 1953

Provinciaal Museum G. M. Kam (Nijmegen)

Female grave, *c.*350

a gold wedding-ring, with inscription: OMONOIA ('Harmony')

b pair of gold earrings

c jug of smooth surfaced ware

d dotted glass bowl

BE.III.159, BE.III.157–8, BB.VI.105, BC.I.162 (grave 53)

Koster 1989

4

Obbicht 1905–76

Bonnefantenmuseum (Maastricht)

Coin hoard, *c.*400

a 17 Roman *solidi* of Valentinian I, Gratian, Valentinian II, Eugenius, Theodosius I, Honorius, Arcadius (364–423)

2526A–2533A

Bloemers 1969; Van der Vin 1988, 267–71

5

Beilen 1955

Drents Museum (Assen)

Hoard *c.*400

a 23 Byzantine *solidi* of Valentinian I, Valens, Gratian, Valentinian II, Theodosius I and Honorius (364–423)

b 5 gold neck-rings with stamped ornamentation

c 1 gold bracelet with stamped ornamentation

M1955.7, M1986.9, 1955/IV.1–6

Waterbolk/Glasbergen 1955; Van der Vin 1988, 264–6; Martin 1996

6

Rhenen-Achterberg 1938

Gemeentemuseum Het Rondeel (Rhenen)

Hoard *c.*375–400

a 2 gold neck-rings with stamped ornamentation (pl. 50)

b link of gold necklace with five inlaid stones and inscription: ERE F[ecit] [Unciae] V D[enariorum] XXII M[ilia] PROCLV[S] ('Ere (?) made this, at a weight of 5 unciae and a value of 22,000 denarii, by order of Proclus')

A6.27–9

Glazema/Ypey 1956, nos 1–2; Heidinga 1990, 14–19

Fig. 78 Wooden bucket, bronze bowl and iron
weaponry from Rhenen, cat. 11.

7
Olst 1953
Rijksmuseum van Oudheden (Leiden)
Hoard c.400
a 4 gold neck-rings with stamped ornamentation
   (pl. 51)
d 1953/2.1–4
Braat 1954

8
Velp 1715
Bibliothèque Nationale de France (Paris),
Rijksmuseum Het Koninklijk Penningkabinet (Leiden)
Hoard (consisting of several pieces of jewellery, at
least five medallions and a large number of coins),
c.450
a Roman gold medallions of Honorius and Galla
   Placidia (393–450) (pl. 17)
(Paris) L14, L55; (Leiden) 12790, 12844
Van der Vin 1989

9–15 Warrior Culture

9
Cuijk 1955
Rijksmuseum van Oudheden (Leiden)
River-deposit, c.400
a spatha
k 1955/1.1
Ypey 1962/3, 169–71, 174 ill. 10

10
Rhenen-Donderberg 1951
Rijksmuseum van Oudheden (Leiden)
Male grave, c.400
a incrusted iron javelin
Rh 839 A
Ypey 1980, no. 224d ill. p. 151; Heidinga/Offenberg
1992/3

11

Rhenen-Donderberg 1951

Rijksmuseum van Oudheden (Leiden)

Male grave, *c.*600

a wooden bucket with bronze mountings

b iron angon

c iron spearhead

d iron hilt

e iron shield boss

f bronze bowl with beaded rim

Rh 763 A–F

Ypey 1973a, 302–3 ill. 9; Heidinga/Offenberg 1992/3

12

Elst (U) 1981

Centraal Museum (Utrecht)

Male grave with complete armour, *c.*600

a iron angon

b iron horse bit

c iron belt-fittings

— (grave 178)

Van Es/Hessing 1994, 244–8

13

Hallum 1913

Fries Museum (Leeuwarden)

Context unknown, *c.*650

a two ornamental pieces with animal heads from the crest of a Vendel-type helmet

FM 27aa/270

Bos 1995, 158–60

14

Geldrop 1992

Rijksmuseum van Oudheden (Leiden)

Male grave with full armour and belt-set, *c.*600

a iron spatha with mountings

b iron seax with sheath

c iron spearhead

d iron shield boss with fragment of the grip

e iron knife

f iron buckle with silver-inlaid belt-plate

g iron counter-plate with silver inlay

h silver-plated iron ornamental belt-fitting

i bronze buckle

j rectangular bronze buckle

k bronze ring

— (grave 19)

15

Lent 1972

Provinciaal Museum G. M. Kam (Nijmegen)

Male grave with military belts, *c.*600

a iron belt-fittings with brass and silver inlay (pl. 49)

b iron mount from a horse harness

— (grave 24) ROB 1972/24 [1–70]

Van Es/Hulst 1991, 101, 233–9, 260–1, 270–5; Hulst 1989

Personal Adornment

16

Maastricht 1954

Schatkamer Basiliek van Sint-Servaas (Maastricht)

Female grave, *c.*600

a gilt silver brooches with four bead-stringlets

b gilt silver disc brooch with garnet inlay

c rock crystal ball in silver mounting

d gold pendant with garnet

e gold earring

f silver buckle

g string of glass and amber beads

—

Glazema/Ypey 1956, no. 47; De Grooth/Quik 1989, 74

17

Beuningen 1955

Provinciaal Museum G. M. Kam (Nijmegen)

Female grave, *c.*650

a string of amethyst beads and gold pendants

12.1970.84–109

Ypey 1973b, 422–4, 451–5

18

Geldrop 1992

Rijksmuseum van Oudheden (Leiden)

Male grave, c.650

a 24-part silver belt-fittings, mostly strap-ends of
Alamannic/Bajuvaric type, partly set with sheet
silver, partly with garnets *en cabochon*

— (grave 14)

Theuws 1993, 97–100

19

Hogebeintum 1909

Fries Museum (Leeuwarden)

Deposit in terp mound, c.630

a gold brooch with filigree ornament

FM 28/1254A

Boeles 1951, 328–32, 558, pl. XLIII.2; Kramer/
Taayke 1996, 22–3, ill. on cover

20

Wijnaldum 1954/1994

Fries Museum (Leeuwarden)

Deposit in terp mound, c.630

a gold brooch with garnet cloisonné in geometric
patterns (pl. 52)

FM 144/56

Bruce-Mitford 1954; Bos 1991; Besteman/Bos/
Heidinga 1992, 33–40; Jager 1996, 84–5, no. 87

21

Wieuwerd 1866

Rijksmuseum van Oudheden (Leiden), Fries Museum
(Leeuwarden)

Hoard, c.630 (pl. 53)

a large gold brooch

b four gold pendants

c three gold rings

d three gold bracteates

e 7 Byzantine *solidi* of Justin I, Mauricius Tiberius,
Phocas, Heraclius and Heraclius Constantine
(518–632)

f 6 Germanic imitations of Byzantine *solidi* and
tremisses, with the names of Anastasius, Justin I,
Justinianus I and Justin II (491–578)

g 1 Visigothic *tremissis* of Sisebut (612–621)

Fig. 79 Gilt silver brooch of the 'princess of Zweeloo',
cat. 22.

h 13 Frankish *solidi* and *tremisses* of Clotarius II (613–
29)

i 2 Frankish *tremisses*, struck at Maastricht by the
moneyers Ansoaldus and Thrasemundus

(Leiden) Bn.W. 1–37 [1866/10]; (Leeuwarden) FM
62a/2, 62a/37

Lafaurie/Jansen/Zadoks-Josephus Jitta 1961; Grier-
son/Blackburn 1986, 124

22

Zweeloo 1952

Drents Museum (Assen)

Female grave (with strings of beads and several other
ornaments), c.450 (fig. 22)

a gilt silver stylised animal brooch

1952/III.26b (grave 87)

Van Es/Ypey 1977, 105, 125

23

Maastricht c.1980

Rijksmuseum van Oudheden (Leiden)

Stray finds from redeposited excavation dump
(1953/4), c.500–650

a gold bird-shaped pendant with garnet cloisonné
work

b silver-sheeted clad bronze buckle and buckle plate
with garnet in silver cloisonné

c cuttle-fish bone buckle with bronze tongue with
garnet inlay

d silver eyes with garnet inlay: fragments of a larger animal ornament

e bronze buckle with stylised bird heads, inlaid with red glass eyes

f silver bracelet

l 1995/4.1, l 1995/12.2–5

Peddemors 1995, nos a.1, a.3–6

24

—

Rijksmuseum van Oudheden (Leiden), Fries Museum (Leeuwarden), Schatkamer Basiliek van Sint-Servaas (Maastricht)

Accessories and toilet requisites from female graves, c.600

a bronze axe-brooch (Bladel)

b gilt silver hair-pins (Rhenen)

c bronze belt-set (Rhenen)

d bronze buckles (Rhenen)

e bronze pair of tweezers (Rhenen)

f bronze ear-picks (Hogebeintum)

g antler combs (Maastricht)

(Leiden) k 1949/12.2, Rh 356B, Rh 696B, Rh 699Ba–g, Rh 445Ea–b, Rh 652C-D, Rh 702Ba–c, Rh 593E, Rh 716D; (Leeuwarden) FM 28W/202; (Maastricht) —

Glazema/Ypey 1956, nos 12, 16, 18, 22, 62–4; Braat 1959, no. 135a pl. XXVIII

Feasting

25

Putten 1928

Rijksmuseum van Oudheden (Leiden)

Male grave c.550

a bronze tripod hanging-bowl

e 1928/10.1

Peddemors/Kempkens 1997

26

Wijchen 1940

Rijksmuseum van Oudheden (Leiden)

Context unknown, c.650

a 'Coptic' bronze jug

e 1940/4.1

Peddemors/Swinkels 1989

27

Millingen aan de Rijn 1946

Rijksmuseum van Oudheden (Leiden)

Context unknown, c.650

a 'Coptic' bronze bowl

e 1946/7.41

Peddemors/Swinkels 1989

Fig. 80
Bronze vessels
Wijchen and
Millingen,
cats 26, 27.

28

Rhenen-Donderberg 1951

Rijksmuseum van Oudheden (Leiden)

Graves, c.600

a glass vessels

b wooden buckets with bronze mountings

Rh 758, Rh 775

Glazema/Ypey 1956, nos 27–8, 31–4, 38–43

29

Maastricht 1954

Schatkamer Basiliek van Sint-Servaas (Maastricht)

Graves, c.600

a glass vessels

—

Glazema/Ypey 1956, nos 85–9

30

Nijmegen

Provinciaal Museum G. M. Kam (Nijmegen)

Graves, c.600

a glass vessels

b globular glass beaker

c glass bowl

d glass tumblers

e glass bell-beaker

XX.a.116–117, XX.a.121, XX.a.121a–e, XX.a.215

Isings 1959

31

Katwijk 1912

Rijksmuseum van Oudheden (Leiden)

Male graves, c.650

a glass vessels

h 1912/1.28, h 1912/1.58, h 1912/1.65, unknown

Isings 1959

32

Bergeijk 1957

Museum Eicha (Bergeijk)

Grave, c.675

a glass bag-beaker

— (grave 30) nr Q

Ypey 1957/8, 85–7 no. Q, 91 no. 7

33

Rhenen-Donderberg 1951

Rijksmuseum van Oudheden (Leiden)

Female grave, c.600–50

a glass claw-beaker

Rh 413P

Peddemors/Carmiggelt 1993, 39

34

Rhenen-Donderberg 1951

Rijksmuseum van Oudheden (Leiden)

Male graves, c.600

a iron shield bosses, mounted on wooden shields

Rh — (various grave numbers)

Ypey 1973a, 298

35

Netherlands 1940

Rijksmuseum van Oudheden (Leiden)

Context unknown, c.640

a iron display seax with gold and bone inlay

U 1940/9.1

—

36

Rijnsburg 1913

Rijksmuseum van Oudheden (Leiden)

Male grave, c.630–40

a bronze sword-belt buckle with twisting animal-figures and interlace in gold filigree and garnet cloisonné (pl. 56)

b bronze belt-slide with blue and white glass and garnet cloisonné

c Byzantine bronze coin-weight for 1 *uncia*

h 1913/11.88–90

Peddemors/Carmiggelt 1993, 28–30

37

Teerns, Hallum and Hogebeintum 1905–25

Fries Museum (Leeuwarden)

Settlement finds from terp mounds: musical instruments, c.600

a bone tail-piece (Teerns) and tuning pegs (Hallum) from a lyre

b bone flute (Hogebeintum)

Fig. 81
The Escharen
hoard:
Byzantine and
Frankish gold
coins, cat. 41.

FM 16D/234, FM 26A/26–38, FM 28/669
Boeles 1951, 535, pl. XXXI.2; Van Vilsteren 1987, 56;
Brade 1975

38

Hogebeintum 1905
Fries Museum (Leeuwarden)
Settlement find from terp mound
a 10 knucklebones
FM 28/333
Knol 1987

39

Menaldum, Almenum, Beetgum, Hallum and Stiens
Fries Museum (Leeuwarden)
Settlement finds from terp mounds
a 5 bone dice, each with 2-3-4-5 dots
FM 23/16, FM 26/84, FM 46/127, FM 77/22, FM 45/
135
Roes 1963, 52–4, pl. XLIV.1–14

40

Velsen 1866
Rijksmuseum Het Koninklijk Penningkabinet
(Leiden), Koninklijke Bibliotheek Albert I (Brussels)
Coin hoard, c.575
a 2 Byzantine *solidi* of Justinian I (527–65)
b 4 Germanic imitations of Byzantine *solidi*
c 2 Visigothic *tremisses*
d 9 Frankish and Frisian *tremisses*
(Leiden) 17347–17359; (Brussels) 7003
Van der Chijs 1866, 351–60, pls XXII.11–15 and
XXIII.1–11

41

Escharen 1897
Rijksmuseum Het Koninklijk Penningkabinet
(Leiden), Koninklijke Bibliotheek Albert I (Brussels)
Coin hoard in a container, c.600
a 5 Byzantine *solidi* of Zeno, Justin I, Justinian I and
   Mauricius Tiberius (474–602)
b 1 Frankish *solidus* with the name of Anastasius
   (493–518)
c 11 Frankish *solidi* and *tremisses* from various mints
   in France

Fig. 82 The Dronrijp Hoard: Frankish and Frisian
gold coins and buckle fragment, cat. 43.

d 26 Frankish *solidi* and *tremisses* from various mints
   along the river Rhine

e 3 Frankish *tremisses* struck along the river Meuse

f 19 Frankish or Frisian *tremisses*

g ceramic globular pot, copy of the lost original

(Leiden) 17444–17482, M462; (Brussels) 7102–7111

Lafaurie 1959/60; Grierson/Blackburn 1986, 124

42

Nietap 1900

Rijksmuseum Het Koninklijk Penningkabinet
(Leiden), Drents Museum (Assen)

Coin hoard, *c.*630–35

a 1 Byzantine *solidus* of Heraclius and Heraclius
   Constantine (613–632)

b 5 Frankish *tremisses*

c 7 Frankish or Frisian *tremisses*

d 8 *tremisses* from Maastricht plus imitations

e 15 Frisian *tremisses* of the so-called
   Dronrijp-type

(Leiden) 17424–17441, 1986.202, 1988.201–202;
(Assen) M1901.14–15, M1937.5–5d, M1967.13,
M1978.1, M1986.13, M1990.1–6

Pol 1975/77; Grierson/Blackburn 1986, 125

43

Dronrijp 1876

Fries Museum (Leeuwarden)

Coin hoard, *c*.640

a 5 Frankish *tremisses* struck in France

b 10 Frankish *tremisses* struck along the rivers Rhine and Meuse

c 21 Frankish or Frisian *tremisses* (2 of the pseudo-Dorestad/Madelinus-type)

d 8 Frisian *tremisses* of the so-called Dronrijp-type

e gold pendant

f 3 fragments of a (deliberately) broken gold buckle

g gold ingot

NDR.1876

Dirks 1887; Boeles 1951, 309–10, 514–21, 588 pl. XL; Grierson/Blackburn 1986, 125

44

Remmerden 1988

Rijksmuseum Het Koninklijk Penningkabinet (Leiden)

Coin hoard, *c*.700. (pl. 55)

a 2 Frankish *tremisses* struck in France

b 15 Frankish *tremisses* struck along the Meuse

c 13 *tremisses* struck at Dorestad

d 50 Frankish or Frisian *tremisses* of the pseudo-Dorestad/Madelinus-type

e 18 *tremisses* from the Rhine region

f 3 Frisian *tremisses* of the Dronrijp-type

g 2 Frankish *denarii*

h 134 Frankish or Frisian sceats of the continental runic type

i 10 Frisian sceats of various other types

j 2 pieces of broken silver

1991.239–497, 1994. 1036–1037, 1994.1049

Pol 1989

45

—

Rijksmuseum Het Koninklijk Penningkabinet (Leiden)/Bibliothèque Nationale de France (Paris)/Koninklijke Bibliotheek Albert I (Brussels)/Fries Museum (Leeuwarden)

A selection of gold coins from the Meuse, Rhine and Magna Frisia regions, 6th–7th centuries

a 2 *tremisses* from unidentified Frankish and Frisian mints (pseudo-imperial coins)

b 7 *tremisses* from Dinant and Namur (moneyers Adeleus, Bertelandus, Tullius, Abolinus, Amerinus, Cusane and Haroaldus)

c 1 *solidus* and 7 *tremisses* from Huy (moneyers Bertoaldus, Bertelinus, Bobo, Gandebertus, Landegisilus and Rigoaldus). (pl. 54a, b)

d 15 *tremisses* from Maastricht (moneyers Adelbertus, Ansoaldus, Boso, Chagnomirus, Chrodebertus, Domaricus, Godofridus, Grimoaldus, Madelinus, Magno, Rimoaldus and Thrasemundus)

e 3 *tremisses* from Dorestad (moneyers Rimoaldus and Madelinus plus imitation)

f 4 *tremisses* from unidentified mints in Magna Frisia ('Dronrijp-type')

(Leiden) M441, 17393, 17402, M482, 17413, 17460, 17416, R22305, 17339, 17342, 17466, 1991.241, 1959.221, 1991.275, 17337, 17334, 17306, 17316; (Paris) Prou: 1221, 1216, 1213, 1204, 1199, 1190, 1189; (Brussels) Vanhoudt: 66, 64, 62, 50, 49, 56, 97, 109, 84; (Leeuwarden) 411, 381

Belfort 1892–1895, nos 1522–54, 1726–33, 1758–1805, 2333–4, 3123–5, 4417–68, 5375–429; Grierson/Blackburn 1986, nos 362–75, 493–7, 517–21

(*Right, above*) Fig. 83 Frankish *tremissis* from Dorestad, cat. 45.

(*Right, below*) Fig. 84 Frisian *tremissis* of the so-called Dronrijp-type, cat. 45f.

The Firebed of the Serpent: myth and religion in the Migration period mirrored through some golden objects

Bente Magnus

The stream of gold which reached Scandinavia during the late Roman and the Migration periods was instrumental in the consolidation and expansion of the local chiefdoms or petty kingdoms based on tribal divisions. The power of the king was based on his wealth, his group of armed warriors and the number of people who supported him. Gold probably was the most important factor in transactions between local elite groups, in creating and keeping alliances, in creating and maintaining the standing war band for the kings, and as gifts given during the large ceremonial feasts demonstrating the king's hospitable and generous nature. Gold was important as sacrifice to the gods, and it figures in central Germanic myths such as Sigurd the Dragonslayer and Weland the Smith. Gold has many metaphors and there exist numerous kennings for gold, one of which is 'The Firebed of the Serpent'. Kennings are metaphorical circumlocutions such as 'ring giver' for king, '*beowulf*' (literally, 'bee-wolf') for bear, 'Gallic grain' for gold; they are known from Viking age skaldic poetry, but also from runic inscriptions from the Migration period.

Gold came to the northern Germanic kingdoms as Roman gold coins, in the early empire as *aurei* and, after the imperial monetary reform of AD 324, as *solidi*. Several hoards of minted gold, mostly *solidi* from the late empire, have been found in Scandinavia, especially on the Baltic islands Öland, Gotland and Bornholm. The imperial portrait on the coins, as well as on the more ceremonial double and triple *solidi*, inspired the Nordic kings to order something similar for themselves. After a short period of experiment with a specifically Germanic type of golden medallion connecting the elite to the gods, the first gold bracteates were created in the fifth century with symbolic pictures in an ornamental, figurative style related to the early phase of the Scandinavian ornamental style, Style I. The magic character of the gold bracteates was occasionally strengthened by runic inscriptions in the early futhark. Other golden objects which functioned in the gift-giving system of the Germanic kings were gold neckrings, armrings and finger-rings, as well as gold scabbard mountings. The sacral character of the three large golden collars found in Sweden and the tiny stamped gold figure foils, the so-called *gullgubbar*, is undisputed. (*Gullgubbar* is Swedish for golden men, originally a term from the late eighteenth century in Scania, where the local population from time to time found such tiny foils in the sand dunes.)

Both the handicraft and the decoration of the golden objects testify to the important position of the goldsmith in the king's household. During the Migration period the large Scandinavian relief brooches became the playground for artistic expression. They were decorated with symbolic motifs executed in sharp relief, much like chip-carving. The sharp ridges reflect light and shadow and give the surface of the brooches a three-dimensional impression. The best pieces are unique, moulded in silver, heavily gilded, and often further embellished with borders of niello as well as filigree and garnets or pieces of coloured glass. These brooches were soon copied in bronze by other craftsmen and new forms were created. The excavations of the settlement on the island of Helgö in Lake Mälaren near Stockholm have revealed nearly 1,100 fragments of moulds for relief brooches and clasp buttons decorated in Style I. Relief brooches were used by women all over Germanic Europe from the fifth to the seventh century. Judging from grave-finds, Scandinavian and Anglo-Saxon women wore only one such brooch, maybe to close their cloak. On the Continent, however, women usually wore two to fasten the dress on the shoulders, or sometimes hung them from the belt on long, decorative straps. The relief brooches

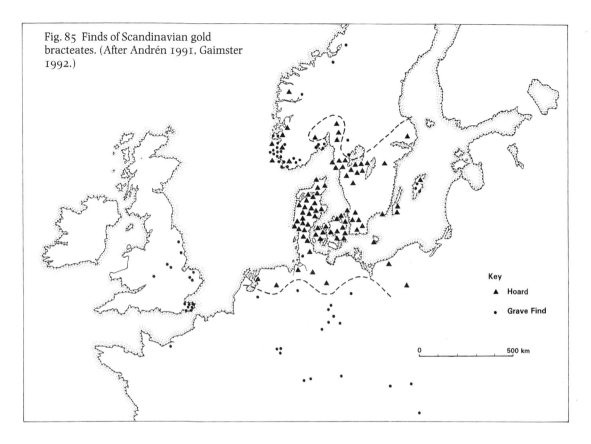

Fig. 85 Finds of Scandinavian gold bracteates. (After Andrén 1991, Gaimster 1992.)

Key

▲ Hoard

• Grave Find

0   500 km

originated in Scandinavia, and the finest pieces, seen from an artistic viewpoint, have been found there.

In the following, three different types of gold and gilded objects with a very special ornamentation are discussed: gold bracteates, the gold foils (*gullgubbar*) and the relief brooches. Their dates range from the fourth to the ninth centuries AD and they were found in Scandinavia. They demonstrate how the northern Germanic elites were inspired by Roman imperial ceremonial when they built their early kingdoms on the basis of tribal structures.

The gold bracteates

These pendants of gold foil were designed for suspension from a necklace. They carry iconographic scenes and symbols and were made and used for nearly five generations. About nine hundred bracteates have been found all over Germanic Europe, some in graves and some in sacrificial

hoards. Most of the hoards have been discovered in southern Scandinavia and on the Baltic islands (fig. 85) and seem to indicate trading routes, cult centres and major settlement areas, while gold bracteates, especially in Anglo-Saxon England and in south and south-west Norway, have been found in women's graves of the late fifth and early sixth century and so give a rather different picture. These women may have had a special position in their local society to judge from their monumental graves and the composition of their grave goods: a gilded relief brooch of high quality decorated in animal Style I, two or more smaller brooches, often gilded, a glass beaker, decorated well-made pottery, a weaving batten and several stone spindle whorls. Admittedly, gold bracteates are not common even in these graves, but when they occur, they are often found in pairs. Runic inscriptions also occur in this group of graves, either on the gold bracteates or on the back of relief brooches. This female dominance stands in contrast to the mainly male motifs of the iconography of both the grand brooches and the gold bracteates themselves.

The Roman legacy is easily discernible in the forerunners to the gold bracteates of the Migration period in Scandinavia, the Roman imperial coins. Through service in the auxiliary troops of the Roman army, through plunder or payments or widespread contacts with friends and relatives among the Germanic tribal aristocracies on the Continent, the Scandinavian elites early became acquainted with the sacral nature of the Roman imperial portrait. The large imperial golden coins (medallions) presented by the emperor to friends, high military officials who had served the empire well, or to ambassadors, had a rather restricted circulation and must have been much sought after by the Scandinavian elites; only six specimens have been found so far, four in Denmark and two in Norway. One such precious *nummus maximus* (large coin) made for the emperor Valentinian (AD 367–75) was provided with a gold frame and a loop for suspension and followed its owner, a local chieftain in south-west Norway, to the grave.

Soon imitations of imperial medallions were being made for the Scandinavian aristocracy. We know of twelve pieces, most of them found in graves, both women's and men's. The portrait is no longer the emperor's, but an artistic rendering of a male face in profile with certain features – such as the hairstyle, the strong chin and the bejewelled diadem – of unmistakable Roman origin (fig. 86). The reverse shows a man riding a horse. Small symbolic signs of unknown meaning are strung out on both sides of the medallion in the manner of the Latin inscription of the large coins. Who does this portrait represent? Obviously a sovereign, since Roman imperial insignia such as the diadem and the shoulder brooch was used also to mark his status. We may suspect that he is the supreme god of the Germanic tribes, Woden (Odin), the Allfather who could cross all barriers, between life and death, between male and female, between humans and animals. He is not the only god of the Germanic pantheon symbolised on the barbaric medallions, but he seems to be present on most of them.

It is clear that these golden medallions inspired the goldsmiths to depict scenes from Germanic mythology in a symbolic form, and also gave them a chance to show off their artistry by giving them a gold frame and a loop for suspension. The way

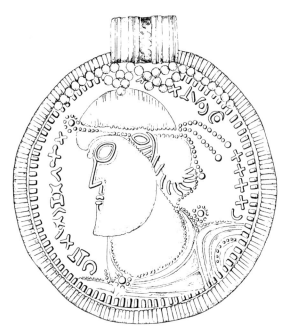

Fig. 86 Obverse of gold bracteate from Midtmjelde, Norway; fifth century. (After Hauck 1970.)

of presenting important religious myths compressed into one small picture surface becomes the hallmark of the artists of the Migration period, especially in Scandinavia.

On a medallion found in a cremation grave at Viken, north of modern Trondheim in Norway, the obverse shows a woman holding a staff in her right hand and gripping the left hand of a man coming towards her holding a ring in his right hand (fig. 87). Between them is a small tree or a plant. On the reverse is a lone rider armed with spear and shield. In front of his face there is a swastika. In the view of the German scholar Karl Hauck, who for many years has worked on the iconography of the barbaric medallions and the gold bracteates, the front scene alludes to the myth of the death of Balder. The story is from the collection of Viking skaldic poetry known as the Edda, which the Icelander Snorri Sturlusson wrote down for posterity in the thirteenth century.

In the story, Woden and Frigg's only son, the kind and beautiful Balder, is killed by his half-brother, the blind god Hoder, who is induced by the giant Loki, the trickster, to shoot a fatal arrow made of mistletoe at him. Balder must descend to

Fig. 87 Gold bracteate from Viken (obverse and reverse); fifth century.

the realm of the dead where he is received by the goddess Hel. The bracteate probably shows the moment when he is about to step over the border between life and death, possibly symbolised by the plant. The ring he is carrying is the famous Draupnir, which Woden placed on Balder's funeral pyre and from which nine new gold rings drip every night. Hermod, also a son of Woden, volunteers to go to Hel, to ask her to let Balder return to the gods. She agrees on condition that all things cry for Balder. Hermod returns with gifts from Balder for the gods, among others the golden ring Draupnir to be given to his father. But on his way back Hermod meets an old giantess (maybe Loki in one of his disguises) who refuses to cry for Balder, and so Balder has to remain with Hel in her realm of the dead. The rider on the sad-looking horse on the reverse of the medallion from Viken may be Woden realising that his beloved son is lost. In spite of all his secret and sacred knowledge, even the supreme Woden cannot recall his own son from death. The myth of Balder's death must have been vital for the southern Scandinavian aristocracy of the Migration period: it says that death is final, and not even the greatest of gods could alter the fate given at birth by the Norns, goddesses of fate.

In the fifth century no more imitations of Roman imperial medallions were made, one of the many signs that the north Germanic tribes were entering a more independent phase in their contact with the Romans. The gold medallions were substituted by thin circular gold foils with a motif on one side only, made with a die. Since one matrix could be used to produce several pieces of foil, these gold bracteates can have a number of close parallels which have sometimes turned up in finds located several days' journeys apart. The bracteates are equipped with a loop and a frame, often of high artistic quality (pl. 57), but the motifs used on them are not numerous. By far the most popular motif is a man's head above a horse or another quadruped, both shown in profile. This is probably a depiction of a Woden myth related to the one seen on the medallion from Viken (fig. 87). (If one combines the 'portrait' of the god with the representation of him riding his horse the result could be something like this.)

On most of the bracteates there are several other creatures present in the picture as well – one or two birds of prey with large, curved beaks, another quadruped and a number of symbolic signs. Runic

inscriptions, mostly very short but occasionally
long ones which are often difficult for modern
scholars to interpret, strengthen the feeling of the
sacral character of the gold bracteates. According
to Hauck, the myth behind this most common motif
(on the so-called C-bracteates) is another one connected with Woden and Balder and shows Woden
as the healer. He blows into the ear of Balder's
horse to revive him. The birds are probably one
raven and one eagle, maybe symbolising two help-
ing spirits of Woden. In the Viking age these birds
of prey became two ravens and were known as
Hugin and Munin.

Another, rare, type of bracteate with a motif
also believed to be connected to the cult of Woden
presents the picture of a dancing man, his two legs
swung behind him, his head thrown back. This is
interpreted as Woden, god also of magic and poetry,
in his role as shaman and shows him in an ecstatic
dance, having worked himself into a frenzy in order
to rid the world of the monster lying in front of
him. From his mouth slips a symbol in the form of
a curl. There are five bracteates made from the
same die showing the bearded, dancing god. Four
of them are part of a gold hoard from Uppland in
Sweden (fig. 88a and 88b). The myth behind this
motif is unknown to us. Two of the bracteates from
a gold hoard found at Sletner on the east side of
the Oslofjord, Norway, show the ecstatic god in
two different versions. The first represents him in
wild movement, with one hand gripping his ankle;
the other shows him stretched forward with his
thumb pointing upwards, and the head thrown
back with a curling breath slipping out of his
mouth. This representation of breath, seen on
many gold bracteates, and most often on the large
relief brooches, is thought to indicate the free soul
of Woden. The Germanic peoples believed that
humans as well as the gods had two souls; one
was bound to the body, the other was free. The
free soul could leave the body as breath during
sleep, fever or hallucinations, and venture out seek-
ing new knowledge or to fight against evil. Woden,
being the greatest of all shamans, sought wisdom
about the future in a state of trance. In the old
Norse poem *Hávamál*, the Speech of the High One
(i.e. Woden), the god relates how he became master
of poetry and magic. Many of the Norse skaldic
poems conjure up visions of Woden as the ruler,
the almighty god, lord of the dead and the embodi-
ment of the uncertainty of fate.

Fig. 88 a and b Gold bracteate with dancing Woden
figure from Söderby Karl, Uppland, Sweden, and
interpretative drawing by J. Thorne.

(*Right*) Fig. 89 *Gullgubbar* from Eketorp, Öland, Sweden; sixth–seventh century.

(*Below*) Fig. 90 Gold foil with possible representation of the god Thor, from the Sorte Muld ('Black Earth'), Bornholm, Denmark; sixth–seventh century.

As the bracteates indicate, the court life of the Germanic tribal kings must have been inspired by Roman life and rituals. We must presume that the iconography and the mythical scenes found on the gold jewellery also were present on their buildings, on their various pieces of equipment and on their ceremonial clothing.

The *hieros gamos* (sacred marriage) and other foils

Gullgubbar are tiny, mostly rectangular gold foils with a stamped picture on one side. But there are also some depicting naked men or animals which have been cut out from the gold foil like silhouettes. The most widespread motif of the square foils is a woman and a man embracing. She wears a long dress partly covered by another long garment and topped by a short cape. He is dressed in a tunic sometimes seen to cover narrow long trousers. Both wear shoes on their feet. The woman's long, straight hair is twisted into a large knot rather high up on the head with the loose end hanging down on her back, whereas the man's hairstyle is simple with shoulder-length hair cut straight. This special motif could be connected with engagement or marriage. In contrast to the gold bracteates, the gold foils have hitherto nearly always turned up on large, central settlement sites, in or close to houses. The latest find of fifty-five *gullgubbar* turned up in 1994 in a settlement at Slöinge, in western Sweden. Several were found together in a posthole of a large house foundation with remains of the original roof-supporting oak post covering the hoard. Earlier another hoard was found underneath the medieval church at Mære, south of Steinkjer in northern Trøndelag, Norway. But the settlement site of the Sorte Muld (Black Earth) on the island of Bornholm in the Baltic overshadows all other sites. Here 2,300 *gullgubbar* of all shapes and sizes have been found, thanks to the wet sieving of all the excavation debris.

The function of figure foils is not known to us. Many archaeologists believe that the embracing couples refer to the myth of the fertility god Frey and the giantess Gerd narrated in the Eddic poem *Skírnismál*. But it may equally be the fertility goddess Freya in one of her more spectacular erotic adventures hinted at in many of the Eddic poems. The scene may allude to a sacral marriage, *hieros gamos*, and the tiny gold foils may be interpreted as 'temple money', i.e. small symbolic sacrifices to the gods within a cultic sphere of a special, erotic nature.

The small hoard of fifteen *gullgubbar* unearthed within the Iron Age fortress of Eketorp on the island of Öland can hardly belong to the same ritual as the 'love-foils' (fig. 89) as they represent either a single man or a woman. The foils showing a man in profile facing towards the right are of two kinds. One is dressed in a seemingly pleated tunic reaching to his knees. His arms are not visible and he seems to be bound with a rope below the shoulders. He is bareheaded with straight, medium-length hair, and under a prominent nose his open mouth gives the impression that he is singing. The other man is wearing a short garment, possibly a tunic, either pleated like the other one or of a furry material, a pelt of some kind. He is tied with a rope as well, and is standing on the tip of his toes as if dancing. The small woman may be the goddess Freya or Frigg. Among the numerous single figure foils from Sorte Muld there are about 400 which depict a man carrying a rod. He has long, straight hair and wears a caftan with elaborate trimming (fig. 90). The number of foils with this motif points to its ritual importance. The motifs of the gold foils may seem stereotyped at first glance. But the body language of the figures and their differing attributes make up a kind of hidden text which was well understood by those who took part in the rituals. The long-haired male figure is also found on the relief brooch from Häste, Jämtland, and on some foils embellishing the glass goblet and the sword of a local chieftain or king from Snartemo in south-west Norway.

Although the figurative motifs of the gold medallions and the gold foils are simple, the interpretation is often highly conjectural. The material itself, gold, makes it probable that the objects belong to the upper strata of the local or regional societies where they must have functioned on many levels, both secular and sacred. When the flow of gold into the Scandinavian lands dried up in the early sixth century due to the course of events on the Continent, gilding became a way of economising with the precious metal while at the same time giving the impression of solid gold. This is the case with the relief brooches, the most exciting of the Germanic jewellery of the Migration period.

Relief brooches

In the fourth century large silver sheet brooches, mostly gilded and decorated sparingly with stamped ornaments, made their appearance in Scandinavia. Their very special tripartite form, consisting of a rectangular plate connected to a 'foot' by an arched bow, made room for sparingly executed stamped decoration. At the beginning of the fifth century the number of stamps used was increased and the shoulders of the brooches were embellished with a stylised horse head on each side, the so-called Sösdala style. The inspiration for this two-dimensional ornamentation came from metalwork current in the Roman military camps along the *limes*. Soon out of fashion, these beautiful brooches were replaced by brooches of the same form but cast by means of clay moulds, which gave the artisans a new freedom in decoration. The first of the Nordic relief brooches were created somewhere in southern Scandinavia and quickly became important as part of some wealthy women's outfits. Both the new moulding technique and the patterns of the earliest relief brooches were taken over from provincial Roman artisans, who made fine buckles for the soldiers' broad leather belts with classical geometric patterns in chip-carving. Mythical beasts and sometimes a human figure are also part of this art associated with the military belts. The early Nordic relief brooches employ classical geometric patterns such as scrolls, spirals and meanders, while strange animal figures crawl along the edges. A few circular human masks or even entire human figures are to be seen, and the relationship with both the figures of the gold bracteates and the gold foils is obvious. The entire surface of the brooches is filled with ornaments, the head plate as well as the bow and the foot. It is obvious that the constellation of motifs is not random decoration, and clearly it alludes to a mythical world. In the latter half of the fifth century the figurative art of the relief brooches changes markedly into abstraction. The classical patterns make way for a maze of animal figures entangled in eternal combat, sometimes with human figures involved. The coherent picture of a mortal battle between a monster and a man, which can be seen on the relief brooch from Grönby in Scania, gives way to a very different, more symbolic concept with a high degree of stylisation. The animal bodies and limbs may be presented as ribbons, not interlacing (which comes later) but in a staccato rhythm. Loose limbs and fantasy monsters, half human and half animal, occur together with birds of prey with dangerously curved beaks. The very best examples are made of gilt silver, with ridges and decorative elements executed in niello. One of the most fascinating relief brooches was found during ditch-digging in the mid-nineteenth century at Malsta in Uppland, Sweden (pl. 58). It was in perfect condition and is probably a sacrifice, as the find locality was wetland. The surface of the brooch is divided into sections by way of ridges embellished with zigzag borders in silver and niello. What we see is a maze of zoomorphic figures crawling along the outer edge in the act of devouring each other. At both ends a demonic animal mask is shown devouring a human head, with puffed up cheeks and a tongue-like triangular figure emerging from the open mouth. Near the bow on both sides lurks a quadruped monster with a jaw full of sharp teeth, ready to pounce. Head to head with the mask at the foot one can see a human head with long hair parted in the middle. The hair turns into two ridges: these delimit the mid section of the brooch which is filled with human arms and legs (fig. 91). Two mini-monsters are in the act of climbing over the ridge as if to get to the limbs. The impression the

Fig. 91 Detail of silver-gilt brooch from Ekeby, Malsta, Uppland, showing mythic images, possibly of Ragnarök; early sixth century, cat. 2.

motifs convey is one of total chaos, and that is a very probable interpretation. In many of the old Norse skaldic poems, but first and foremost that known as the Sibyl's Prophecy, the Germanic conception of the destruction of the world and the pantheon is told. The forces of chaos such as the Fenris wolf, the Midgard serpent and the giants are let loose, brother fights against brother, the human race and the gods are destroyed and the world goes up in flames.

Most of the large relief brooches from the late Migration period can be interpreted within such a context. The monster masks in the act of devouring a human could symbolise the Fenris wolf swallowing Woden represented by the breath emerging from his open mouth. The mini-monsters may be giants' offspring in the shape of wolves eating dying men, and so on.

The art of the Migration period developed within the north Germanic tribal societies which in the course of a few generations underwent great structural changes as a result of, among other things, the fall of the *limes* and the western Roman empire, and with the resulting very unstable barbarian kingdoms coming into existence on the Continent. Religious cults and strict rituals most probably played a key rôle for the kings in their political and economic struggle to increase their power over larger groups of people. But also the ideology of strife and combat, which must have been paramount for the warrior aristocracy, clearly influenced religious life in Scandinavia. The strong male focus that is conveyed to posterity through the late Viking Age skaldic poems was probably not quite as obvious in the Migration period. One argument for this indeed lies in the high quality relief brooches which have been found in women's graves in Scandinavia, in England and on the Continent. On these brooches the symbolic character of the ornamentation and the high degree of stylisation of one or a few motifs give the impression that only those initiated in the religious myths would understand the design. It may have functioned like the skaldic kennings. The ladies who wore the relief brooches were probably the wives of tribal kings, and they may have functioned as priestesses in cult enactments staged at the large ceremonial feasts in the hall of the king's farm, where sacrifices were made to the mighty Woden, Thor, god of weather, to Frey, and to the goddess Freya, who was also a death goddess. In the Anglo-Saxon epic *Beowulf*, scenes of ritual in the king's hall are described, but in a very restrained way as this epic was first written down in a Christian milieu. The forces of chaos, which were everywhere and threatened the cosmos of gods and humans alike, had to be fought and deflected by rituals and sacrifice to the gods. We know of human sacrifice in bogs, of ritual deposits of weapons and ships, of horse sacrifice and hoards of gold weighing up to 11.3 kg (25 lb) which testify to ritual and cultic events built on religious myths of great importance for the tribal kings. But the finds also provide evidence that there was a move from collective towards individual emphasis, and consequently stronger competition between rival kings. At the same time their friends and relatives among the aristocracy of the new Germanic states on the Continent considered themselves to be heirs of Rome and accepted Christianity. Only in the northern Germanic regions did *'forn siðr'*, the beliefs and traditions of old, remain.

When the Icelander Snorri Sturluson wrote down Norse skaldic poems and sagas in the thirteenth century, old traditional myths were still remembered and retold in Scandinavia. But Christian influence had put paid to them and many were forgotten. The golden art of the Migration period embodies myths and traces of cult and rituals that once were known all over Germanic Europe and are worth searching for, in order to enrich our knowledge of past societies.

Monsters and embracing couples

The iconography of late Migration period Scandinavia encompasses zoomorphic creatures with large, open mouths ready to devour other creatures, or anthropomorphic figures often depicted in very cramped positions as well as dancing single persons or couples embracing. On close inspection of the gold or gilded objects – such as relief brooches, clasp buttons, gold collars, gold bracteates or picture foils – a multitude of figures springs to life. It is also very obvious that different styles are used on different types of objects. While personal jewellery, such as buttons and relief brooches, shows a highly sophisticated abstract style, the gold bracteates have a symbolic language that is easier to discern but equally difficult to decipher. Even tiny golden picture foils have a seemingly simple iconography with their pictures of men and women, singly or together.

The iconography of the fifth to seventh centuries in Scandinavia seems to go back to a common treasure of myths and traditions and the decorated gold objects probably fulfilled functions connected with religious rituals.

Catalogue of the exhibition 'The Firebed of the Serpent'

Statens Historiska Museum, Stockholm

1 Square-headed relief brooch

Häste, Rödön, Jämtland

Statens Historiska Museum, Stockholm

Early sixth century

Square-headed relief brooch of gilded silver with zoomorphic and anthropomorphic decoration in Style I. Length 17.1 cm

SHM 19579

The burial mound on the island of Rödön in Lake Storsjön (the big lake) in north-west Sweden was in a border region which was part of Norway until the sixteenth century where the ancestors of the Saamis also had their settlements. The mound was removed before an archaeologist came onto the site, but had obviously covered a female burial in a cist of upright schist slabs. Besides the large brooch were found two buttons decorated in Style I, a belt buckle of bronze and a bronze pin.

Characteristic features of the brooch are the masks at the upper corners of the headplate with their prominent eyebrows and hair, which extends into a long nose. The circular figure with concentric rings in silver and niello inlay is repeated along the sides of the headplate (fig. 92). The foot of the brooch has a number of tonguelike projections along the outer moulding, a late feature within the Scandinavian relief brooches. The masks terminating the lobes have curved, upright ears and a triangular tongue, something which is to be seen on the terminal mask of the foot as well. This is a real monster (fig. 93) with high curving ears, slanting eyes with a square field between them and a long bridge of the nose terminating in a large triangular tonguelike projection. The nostrils are in fact two human heads in profile with one circular eye each, a long, prominent nose and a mouth more in the shape of an open bird's beak. The triangular 'tongue' has a high frame decorated in niello which encloses a small face with round eyes and a number of ridges making up the limbs and head of a human with long hair. On both sides of the 'tongue' is a male face shown in profile with some kind of headgear. The whole surface of the brooch is crammed with ornament in high relief, and prominent

Fig. 92 Silver gilt brooch from Häste, Rödön, Jämtland, Sweden; early sixth century, cat. 1.

mouldings decorated in silver and niello frame the different sections of ornamentation. This *horror vacui* is common on the relief brooches of the Migration period and gives them a very special character. This brooch from Häste in Rödön was probably created by the same craftsman who made a related but bigger relief brooch (24 cm long) found at Dalum in Sparbu, some 100 km north-east of Trondheim in Norway. This brooch, found in the latter half of the nineteenth century, is part of a very poorly documented grave find. Both the Norwegian and the Swedish find localities are strategically placed on a main route connecting the Atlantic with the Baltic Sea. Several square-headed relief brooches testify to the close connection between the two regions during the Migration period.

The relief brooches, with their monsters and stylised crawling and interlaced figures executed in

Fig. 93 Silver gilt brooch from Häste, detail: early sixth century. (Cat. 1.)

high relief, are decorated in Germanic Style I, which is also to be seen on buttons, sword mounts, mounts for glass beakers and drinking horns and on textiles as well. Recent finds in Germany indicate that wooden carved furniture and special wooden household utensils from this period were similarly decorated. The human figures, which are part of the symbolic design almost without exception, are pictured in very cramped and risky positions, mostly related to another figure with a large, open jaw. The late phase of Style I gives a sinister impression which may be connected to a transitional period in barbarian Europe, when the old tribal system with a large number of local chiefdoms based on a redistributive economy had to give way to larger units based on a few families who traced their descent and their legitimacy from the gods. With the help of standing groups of professional warriors, they organised raids and waged war and collected tributes from people who needed

their protection. Through exogamy, by giving precious gifts and organising lavish, ritual drinking feasts in their lofty halls, they created a network of powerful contacts all over Germanic Europe. Their characteristic decorative styles, especially the animal style, Style I as it appears on the relief brooches, illustrate their common myths and traditions very well and testify to the occurrence of a common symbolic language.

2 Equal-armed relief brooch

Ekeby, Malsta, Uppland

Statens Historiska Museum, Stockholm

Early sixth century

Equal-armed relief brooch of gilded silver with zoomorphic and anthropomorphic ornamentation in Style I. Length 23.9 cm

SHM 8284

This is one of the finest examples of Scandinavian goldsmiths' handicraft from the Migration period. The brooch was found in 1888 by a farmhand digging ditches; no more information was given at that time. Most probably the brooch belongs to a group of sacrificial finds in wetland, a ritual tradition which was still alive at the end of the Migration period. The equal-armed relief brooches testify to the existence of a far-reaching social network among aristocratic families, as they have been found in the coastal districts of East Sweden and Finland only. The one exception is a fine specimen which was part of a young woman's funeral dress in Gepidic Hungary. The brooch was most probably manufactured in eastern Sweden, perhaps on Helgö in Lake Mälaren, and may have travelled with the woman when she was married to a Gepid and settled on the river Theiss, a tributary of the Danube. The Gepids were an agrarian Germanic people probably related to the Goths and in the sixth century AD they were centred on the Danube basin with Sirmium as their capital city.

Until now, only seventeen equal-armed brooches are known in all, of which the one from Ekeby is by far the finest (pl. 58). The front side of the brooch is covered with ornament which at first seems unintelligible. Through the raised mouldings, which once were ornamented with geometric inlay in silver and niello, a structure appears. The inner and an outer framework which is thus formed display three scenarios. First, there is the mask at each end of the brooch, then a rather narrow belt of biting monsters with open jaws following the outer contour of the two arms of the brooch, and, finally, the roughly heartshaped field below the bow on each side.

The mask is of a wolflike animal which carries a human male mask in its open jaw. It has characteristic round cheeks, as if filled with air, and its mouth seems to be gagged. On each side crawls a wormlike quadruped with its open jaw interlocked in combat with a similar creature. A second human mask appears head-to-head with the wolf mask. Its long hair is parted in the middle, and forms the frame of the heartshaped picture field. Over this, two small creatures with wide open jaws clamber, one on each side. They are smaller versions of the large quadruped filling the heartshaped space with its big, flat body seen from above; it has four legs and a big head with a large jaw displaying a number of sharp teeth. Below it two pairs of booted human legs and two pairs of human arms with hands are to be seen. The connecting bow of the brooch displays four mini-monsters in high relief.

More than any other relief brooch, this one from Ekeby conveys a myth. But which one? The most obvious candidate is the myth of Ragnarok, the creation and the end of the world found in the epic the Sibyl's Prophecy, known from Snorre Sturlusson's Edda (see p. 201). Perhaps the wolflike mask devouring the human on the Ekeby brooch can be interpreted as the Fenris wolf swallowing the god Woden. All the other creatures depicted on the brooch may be the offspring of Fenris. The human figure with the long hair may also be Woden in one of his many shapes.

3 Semicircular-headed brooch

Unknown provenance, När, Gotland

Statens Historiska Museum, Stockholm

Late fifth century

Relief brooch with semicircular headplate of gilt silver with red garnets. Length 15.5 cm

SHM 1079

The present Swedish islands in the Baltic, Gotland and Öland and the Danish Bornholm, are famous for their numerous and exciting archaeological sites and finds. During the first 500 years AD much precious metal reached the islands and was trans-

formed into marvellous jewellery by skilful artisans. The relief brooch (pl. 59) belongs to a group of closely related brooches found on these three islands only. The brooch from När, Gotland, has a headplate which is framed by two rows of small birds with striated long necks, large, circular eyes and long curved beaks in openwork. Three zoomorphic masks jut out from the frame, the central one being distinctly bovine in character. In the centre of the headplate is placed a rectangular garnet in a gold setting. It has a border of running spirals executed in low relief. The bow is adorned with a garnet as well as with spiral decoration. The footplate of the brooch repeats the same pattern of spirals in chip-carving and garnets, as well as zoomorphic lobes and rows of identical small, long-necked birds. The largest terminal mask has the shape of an eagle's head with slanting eyes and a broad curved beak. Seen in profile the whole brooch is formed like a diving eagle. The brooch is heavily worn along the right side, which indicates that it may have been carried as a cloak fastener on the shoulder close to the neck, as indicated by a picture foil from Helgö. The symbolism which forms the basis for the design of relief brooches of this type is unknown but four related bird frieze brooches are known from former Ostrogothic regions (Hungary and north Italy). The god Woden changed himself into an eagle when, according to the myth, he brought the stolen skald mead from the giant Suttung to the Æsir. Eaglehead, *arnhofdi*, is one of the numerous names for Woden. The bovine head may also refer to Woden, as one of his names, *jormuni*, has been interpreted as 'bull' or 'cattle'. The Gothic tribes, and probably the people of Gotland, as well as the Angles and the Longobards, counted Woden as their mythical ancestor. The bird-of-prey relief brooches may have been worn by women from the leading families in their function as priestesses in rituals to assure these families divine right to land.

The embracing couples

The tiny gold foils are known from all over Scandinavia and have been found on settlement sites dated from the sixth to the ninth century AD. To manufacture such paper-thin tiny square foils and stamp them with an erotic scene seems very foreign to the Germanic martial ideology of power and honour as we know it from later written sources.

The idea must have come from Roman stamped votive foils.

Twenty-nine sites are so far known, of which the Sorte Muld (Black Earth) settlement on the island of Bornholm is the most famous. There more than 2,000 figure foils with a variety of representations have been found during excavations in recent years. On most sites the 'love foils' are in the majority and they may have been connected with marriage rituals in the honour of the fertility god Frey and his sister Freya. Several scholars have interpreted the foils as referring to the myth and later Eddic poem *Skírnismál*: the story relates how the god Frey was sitting one day in Woden's high seat where he had no place to be, looking out over the world. He spotted the beautiful giantess Gerðr and fell at once in love with her. Skirnir, his servant, was sent to demand her hand in marriage to his master, but she refused. Skirnir then threatened her with the prospect of all the horrible things that may befall a young maiden, and frightened her into agreeing to meet Frey in a grove called Barre. The foils are thought to symbolise their meeting. A Norwegian scholar has interpreted the poem as dealing with the myth of *hieros gamos*, the holy marriage between god and giantess. It is connected with the ideology of pre-Christian kingship where the god symbolises the sovereign and the giantess the land that he subjugates. In the following, three of the twenty-six figure foils from the settlement of the island of Helgö (Holy Island) in Lake Mälaren west of Stockholm are described, as they illustrate some of the variety in the artistic expression of the motive of the embracing couple. Most of the foils were found spread out across a small area in one of the many house foundations of Helgö (fig. 94 a–c).

Fig. 94 (a) Gold foil with figures, Helgö, Ekerö, Uppland, Sweden; seventh century, cat. 4; (b) Gold foil with embracing figures, Helgö, Ekerö, Uppland, Sweden, sixth or seventh century, cat. 5; (c) Gold foil with figures, Helgö, Ekerö, Uppland, Sweden, seventh century, cat. 6.

4 Figure foil

Helgö, Ekerö, Uppland

Statens Historiska Museum, Stockholm

Seventh century(?)

Rectangular figure foil of gold showing a man and a woman facing each other in profile. 1.1 × 1.1 cm, 0.01 cm thick

SHM 25075:476

The woman is wearing a full-length undergarment with a broad checked border at the front. A mantle covers her upper arms and is fastened at the shoulder with a disc-shaped clasp (the button of a large disc-on-bow brooch?). Her hair is dressed in a special knot which symbolises her status. The man has shoulder-length hair and a long tunic with long sleeves and a pattern like chain mail. Between their heads is a semicircular shallow figure of unknown meaning. The man is grabbing the woman by her cape and she seems to be pushing him away, as if trying to resist his violent approach.

5 Figure foil

Helgö, Ekerö, Uppland

Statens Historiska Museum, Stockholm

Sixth or seventh century

Rectangular figure foil of gold showing a man and a woman facing each other. 0.9 × 1.1 cm, 0.01 cm thick

SHM 25075:961

The woman's hair is dressed in a knot with the loose end hanging down her back. She is wearing a full-length garment with a trailing pleated mantle or overgarment. A short checked cape covers her shoulders. The man has a knee-length frock-like garment finished with a border. Both man and woman seem to be wearing shoes. The couple is embracing, with their noses touching.

6 Figure foil

Helgö, Ekerö, Uppland

Statens Historiska Museum, Stockholm

Seventh century

Rectangular figure foil of gold showing a man and a woman facing each other in profile. 0.9 × 0.9 cm, 0.01 cm thick

SHM 25726:2593

The woman's hair is dressed in a large knot, with a short loose end hanging down her back. She is wearing a full-length plaited tunic with billowing back, and over this a short coat. The man has shoulder-length hair and a knee-length tunic, trousers and shoes. Both wear neckrings. They are embracing, with their arms intertwining and their noses touching.

Heirs of Rome: the shaping of Britain AD 400–900

Marion Archibald, Michelle Brown, Leslie Webster

Introduction

For the sixth-century British monk Gildas, the barbarian raids and settlements, whether of Picts from the north, Scots from Ireland, or Angles and Saxons from north-western Europe, were a sure sign of darkening times. In his passionate ecclesiastical polemic, *The Ruin and Conquest of Britain* (cat. 10), the fiery assault of the Saxons, which 'licked the western ocean with its fierce tongue', was only the latest in a series of disastrous incursions whereby a just God punished sinful British leaders, secular and ecclesiastical. For centuries, the spirit behind this tract – drawn on by Bede and many other successors – set the scene for an historical perception of the end of Roman rule in Britain. Viewed from perspectives such as this, it was only with the coming of renewed Roman contacts through the Christian missions to the Anglo-Saxons from the late sixth century that the culture of Britain emerges from a long dark age of ignorance, barbarism and brutality. It is a view which has endured well into modern popular history. Yet reassessments of the historical evidence and new archaeological information combine to reveal a very different and more complex version of these times of transformation.

This exhibition is concerned both with the continuity of Roman traditions and continuing, if intermittent, contacts during the aftermath of Roman rule in Britain in the fifth and sixth centuries, and with the subsequent closer relationship with Roman culture which came about through the Christian initiatives of the late sixth and seventh centuries. From this large and complex subject, we have chosen three main themes to exemplify the changing currents of Roman tradition in different parts of Britain in this period: the post-Roman power vacuum; the growth and exercise of power and authority; and, with the coming of Christianity, the communication of ideas and knowledge through images, language and text. The indigenous Celtic peoples and the Anglo-Saxon settlers had all – in different ways – experienced Roman culture before the official withdrawal of Roman administration and defence in AD 410. Some, like the British, had lived mainly within the Roman province; others, such as the Scots in Ireland and the Picts in Scotland had regular contact through trading and raiding (cat. 6); while many of the first settlers from continental Germanic tribes might in addition have served as federate troops in the Roman army (cat. 8). The influence of Roman culture on their lives was profound, if unquantifiable; it is very clear, however, that they seized upon certain Roman concepts with enthusiasm and imagination, reinventing them in their own terms and for their own, sometimes very different, purposes.

Ruin and Resilience

The later fourth century in Roman Britain, although not without its dangers, was a period of prosperity. The luxurious life-style of the wealthy is exemplified by the contents of hoards of gold and silver coins, plate and jewellery such as Hoxne (cat. 5). Further down the social scale, the vitality of commercial life is shown by the large numbers of contemporary bronze coins found on Romano-British sites and in hoards (cat. 3). The very existence of these hoards and, in particular, their non-recovery by the original owners, is evidence that the good times were already under threat. The end came rapidly. A succession of British-based usurpers in the early years of the fifth century culminated in Constantine III who sought to further his imperial ambitions across the Channel by withdrawing army contingents from Britain, which was left with inadequate forces to defend itself against intensified barbarian attack. Early coins of Constantine III from Lyon of AD 407–8 were the latest coins dispatched to Roman Britain (cat. 5a). The Romano-Britons repudiated Constantine, but in a letter to them from the legitimate western emperor Honorius in 410 they were told to look to their own defence. The consignments of new Roman coin which had previously been sent by the imperial government to pay the army and the civil service and to sustain the fiscal system, were sharply cut off (cat. 1–4). In the circumstances, hoarding increased so that currency stocks disappeared and a money economy on the former Roman lines soon ceased to exist. Britain became functionally coinless and the new economic structures, such as they were, operated without coined money. This thesis is not invalidated by the possibility that a few subsequent coins might have reached Britain through Church, trade or other contacts, by the survival of the occasional imperial coin as a treasured relic of *romanitas* or by the respect shown to chance finds (cat. 16). It is, however, only in the second half of the fifth century that there is positive evidence of foreign gold coins beginning to reach England again (cat. 17). This may be only a change in degree, marking an expansion in relations with continental Europe. The Anglo-Saxons, alone among the barbarian peoples settled in the former western provinces, did not at first produce a coinage of their own as they lacked the political cohesion and the economic organisation which made it possible or necessary. In the later sixth century a few blundered copies of imperial gold *solidi* were struck in England but, like the continental imports (cat. 109), they were often made into jewellery. After the reintroduction of Christianity, motifs from Roman coins inspired Anglo-Saxon gold *solidus*-type pendants adapted to devotional purposes as well as display (cat. 101). From the later sixth century, Merovingian gold *tremisses* arrived in increasing numbers (cat. 53f), and were 'current', mainly in south-eastern England, before and for some time after the more sporadic issues of Anglo-Saxon *tremisses* (the gold shillings of the Kentish law-codes, the so-called 'thrymsas', cat. 73 and 102) began to be struck, again using Roman-derived types, around AD 600.

The late Roman hoards from Britain and Ireland illustrate one aspect of the barbarian settlement – raiding and conquest (cat. 5, 6). Late Roman military equipment from Anglo-Saxon graves suggests another – through land-grants awarded for service in the late Roman and post-Roman defensive forces, giving substance to Gildas' and Bede's famous accounts of how the invaders were invited into Britain initially to defend it against other barbarian assaults. Family and tribal settlement followed, as well as more aggressive initiatives. Meanwhile, the Celtic populations of North and West Britain, as well as of Ireland, continued to maintain links with the eastern empire and with western Gaul, as various luxury imports from elite sites show (cat. 12); other contacts with the late Roman world were maintained through the Christian church – by missionaries such as Palladius, Patrick and Ninian. A strong conscious sense of Roman inheritance can be seen in many monuments in the Celtic zones, where Latin, Roman lettering and Roman titles continue into the ninth century (cat. 142); perhaps an echo of this underlies the account, in the *Anonymous Vita* of St. Cuthbert, of the city's *praepositus* who showed the saint round the Roman remains at Carlisle (cat. 9). Increasingly, we can also recognise signs which indicate that significant numbers of the native Romano-British population in eastern England were not annihilated or displaced, but often absorbed into the newly emergent communities, through marriage, slavery or other processes of acculturation; or were able, at least for a while, to co-exist independently. Many graves in Anglo-Saxon cemeteries are likely to be those of Romano-Britons who have simply adopted the prevailing Anglo-Saxon modes of dress and burial (cat. 13, 15).

Power and Authority

One of the primary needs of the successor states was to define and consolidate their authority – often by invoking Roman antecedents. The stages in the transmission of power and authority from the Roman Empire to the successor states in western Europe are particularly clearly exemplified by the coinage. Although familiar with money from subsidy and tribute, none of the barbarian peoples struck coins of their own until they settled in the former Roman provinces where there was an established money economy. The precise form and pace of currency evolution from the fifth to the eighth centuries varied in the different states but, in the main, it followed a broadly similar sequence, seen at its clearest in Italy (cat. 18–21 and 24–7). During the fifth and sixth centuries, the barbarian rulers regarded their kingdoms as belonging to the Roman Empire and their earlier issues, especially gold, were struck in the name of the ruling emperor (cat. 17 and 20). The first overt assertion of independent barbarian authority on the gold coinage is the addition to the existing design of the ruler's initial or monogram, usually consigned to the reverse of a coin still struck in the emperor's name (cat. 28). The growing power of the barbarian kings and their increased perception of their independent authority is shown by their names or monograms appearing prominently first on the reverse of the coins (cat. 21) and then replacing those of the emperor on the obverse of the lower denominations. This is epitomised by the commanding image of Theodahad, king of the Ostrogoths, on his large bronze coins (cat. 47, fig. 96). There was still a limit, however, for the gold *solidus* continued to be regarded as an imperial prerogative. The presumption of the Frankish king Theodebert I in issuing *solidi* in his own name (cat. 48, fig. 97) was censured and the experiment was not repeated in Gaul until the concept of Empire had weakened a century later (cat. 29). There was less of a problem with the gold *tremisses*, a third of a *solidus,* and this factor no doubt helped to make it the standard gold coin of most of the successor states. It was, in any case, more convenient to their economies, and in particular to reviving trade, to have the currency unit of a lower denomination. The most spectacular numismatic declaration of power and imperial pretention extant of any barbarian king is the triple *solidus* of Theoderic (fig. 3). During the seventh century the political independence of the successor states was consolidated and coinage developed along different national lines as required by their individual economies and administrative systems. Acknowledgement of the emperor was abandoned and coins were issued in the king's own name in Italy and Spain (cat. 24 and 30) but rarely in Gaul (cat. 29) where the names of the mint and moneyer were normally substituted (cat. 147). In England, there was no continuity of minting from imperial issues and the early Anglo-Saxon coins adapted the contemporary Frankish model (cat. 73). The *tremisses* were, in contrast to their prototypes, largely anonymous (cat. 102), making it difficult to attribute them to a particular authority and place or to assess the extent to which the coinage was under royal control. By the end of the seventh century, silver coinage had replaced gold in Gaul (cat. 148), Frisia (cat. 74) and England (cat. 58–9, 61, 75 and 96); from the middle of the eighth it

was explicitly regal (cat. 24, 26, 39, 40, 51–2 and 76–7). Charlemagne revived the reality of empire in western Europe and late in his reign struck coins of superficially Roman type including some rare gold pieces (cat. 49). The unified coinage system he introduced for the territories under his direct control was already fully medieval, and little remained of the Roman monetary inheritance outside southern Italy (cat. 25, 26). The concept that proper coins should look like Roman ones has, however, periodically reasserted itself, even down to our own day.

Coins provide a very accessible and direct means of disseminating images of power and political identity. Archaeological evidence shows similar processes at work. The early Anglo-Saxon settlers were drawn from several north-western continental tribal groups, roughly divisible into the three main peoples categorised by Bede as Angles, Saxons and Jutes (cat. 31). They had lived outside the empire, but were in constant contact with it, through, for example, trade and military service; their distinctive ornamental vocabulary and their use of certain signals of status derive directly from Roman traditions (cat. 85–6, 105–7). In the fifth and sixth centuries, perceived tribal affiliations were signalled in the traditional costume of women, which can be reconstructed from burial evidence (cat. 32–5). This need to express identity seems to have become, if anything, stronger, while the emergent polities which were to consolidate into the later sixth- and seventh-century kingdoms were battling it out for control of territory and resources. The kings of this time were also swift to see that the authority of the Church could underpin their claims to power, making them, in a very direct way, the heirs of Rome (cat. 37). Christianisation went hand in hand with the development of new instruments of political power, such as written laws, and charters (cat. 41, 44).

Crucial to all this was the visual presentation of kingship – an issue for Celts and Picts as much as for the Anglo-Saxon incomers. As we have seen, coinage was one of the most immediate ways of generating an image of royal authority; but other symbolic manifestations of royal power, replete with imperial imagery, may be traced in the archaeology and sculpture of this period (cat. 63). In England, the example of Sutton Hoo provides a classic example of how, even on the very fringes of Europe, an ambitious local Germanic dynasty asserted its authority through a powerful mixture of traditional cultural vocabulary and a deliberate evocation of Roman ancestry and *romanitas*; the upwardly mobile Anglo-Saxon as the true heir to Roman rule (cat. 53). The use of a symbolic Christian iconography which embraces elements of imperial descent also plays its part in building images of kingship, as manuscript illustrations and sculpture demonstrate. The sophisticated and multi-layered use of David iconography in Insular art is particularly revealing (cat. 65–70, 72). The great stone shrine from the Pictish royal and monastic centre of St. Andrews, with its David, presents both the Christian message of salvation and the Old Testament warrior king, a mirror for princes in a focal place for Pictish kings (cat. 69).

Word and Image

The readiness with which the Celts, Picts and Anglo-Saxons seized upon the newly introduced imagery of the Roman Christian world owes much to their own long tradition of reading non-verbal messages, which fostered the development of complex symbolic decoration in their native art (cat. 105–6); a trait which was to be readily deployed in the powerful and distinctive Insular tradition of manuscript decoration, in which text and image exist in creative symbiosis (see below) (cat. 124). But it was arguably the impact of the written text in the classical manner that transformed these barbarian cultures more than any other factor.

Of all the traditions of antiquity introduced by the Church, the most radically transforming was the use of writing for the preservation and transmission not only of Scripture and learned commentary, but of group memory and culture. The Celtic and Germanic peoples had, of course, a sophisticated oral tradition, and made limited use of their own, ultimately Latin-derived, alphabetic systems – oghams and runes – in special epigraphic contexts (cat. 135–42). As we have seen, their surviving metalwork and sculpture also shows that communication through graphic symbol and image played a major part in their culture (cat. 107). But it was through the conversion to Christianity, a religion of the Book, that they gained access to the intellectual traditions and communicative processes of the late antique world. Perceptions of the book as icon in a religious context underpinned the use of writing as a means of

expressing and securing political and institutional power, vested in its primary exponent, the Church, and its royal and aristocratic patrons.

Within a decade of the arrival in Kent of Augustine and his fellow missionaries from Rome in AD 597, the processes of cultural synthesis and transformation were under way. King Æthelberht of Kent had recognised the value of the written record as an essential adjunct of the civilised – and successful – ruler. The Kentish laws were codified and committed to 'the safe-keeping of writing', but in Old English, rather than in Latin (cat. 41). Charters and other documents recording property claims and other agreements, and royal pedigrees proclaiming legitimacy through descent from Germanic gods and imperial antecedents quickly followed (cat. 36, 55). This was also the means by which the ecclesiastical establishment was absorbed into the social structure, and its prerogatives established.

Similarly, the promotion of Christianity and accompanying literacy in Ireland and Pictland largely through the missionary endeavours of the post-Roman British church from the fifth century onwards engendered the development of a Christian tradition of learning which played a vital role in preserving and transmitting late antique culture in Britain and Ireland. This process also led to the reinvention of a system of scripts guided by the principles of form and function, in which it is not appropriate to use the same script for a shopping list as for a Gospel book (cat. 154). Fed by renewed Mediterranean influence, this was to form the influential Insular hierarchy of scripts (cat. 150–4). Learning Latin as a foreign language also encouraged Irish scribes to contribute to the development of grammar along antique lines, and of punctuation; and to introduce radical new aids to comprehension such as word separation (cat. 120, 133), which aided the processes of silent reading and meditation advocated by clerics such as Isidore and Bede. The precocious development of the written Irish vernacular accompanied this process (cat. 126).

Within a century of the conversion of the Anglo-Saxons, under Roman and Celtic influence, their schools had become the envy of the west. The task facing the early missionaries and scholar/prelates such as Theodore of Tarsus and Hadrian from Africa, who were appointed to Canterbury in AD 667, must have been a daunting one. Instilling a knowledge of Latin and Greek in students with whose own tongue the teachers were unfamiliar was a formidable achievement. Surviving glossaries and lectionaries bear eloquent witness to the life of the schoolroom, just as the works of internationally renowned scholars such as Bede, Aldhelm and Alcuin, speak of its intellectual achievements (cat. 129–31).

Equally significant was the unique and lasting contribution of the Insular world to book production, through its spectacular promotion of illumination, and the remarkable level of integration of text, script and image. The perpetual tension between word and image which was common to religions of the Book was given new scope in the mission fields of the west, where Gregory the Great's lead was taken in using images to teach. Here, word and image in intimate association offered mutual validation, whether in books or in sculpture and in other artefacts, in a catalytic merging of native traditions with those of late antiquity (cat. 116, 118, 124). In particular, the historiated (story-telling) initials and the striking decorated *incipits* (text openings) of prestigious Insular liturgical volumes mark a new approach to writing – here the Word is made word, and a chi-rho symbol is as much an image of Christ as a crucifixion, but with added spiritual dimensions (cat. 121–3). Likewise, pictorial narrative adapted from classical and early Christian sources acquires new depth and layers of exegetical meaning (cat. 116–5). Simultaneously the decorative and meaning-laden motifs of authority, power and wealth developed over centuries of display in the Germanic and Celtic repertoires are applied to that potent new symbol of authority derived from the Roman world, the book.

The fourth to the ninth century in Britain was a period of profound cultural, religious and political change, yet one central strand binds these societies in the transformational process: the enduring and constantly renewed influence of the Roman world. And as our writing system, books and coinage, and much else, show even to this day, we are still the heirs of Rome.

Catalogue of the exhibition 'Heirs of Rome: The Shaping of Britain AD 400–900'

British Museum in collaboration with the British Library, London

Ruin and resilience

The end of empire

Coin-finds provide unequivocal evidence of when the Roman empire last carried out its monetary obligations towards its British provinces. Cats 1–3 belong to the latest types of Roman coins found in such quantities as to suggest that they were part of official consignments from the legitimate imperial government. Significantly, the latest of them, issued in 402–6 (cat. 1), is the gold used to pay the army. The next issues, exemplified by no. 4, are not found in Britain. Coins of 407–8 of the usurper Constantine III (cat. 5a) formed the latest consignment of Roman coins to reach Britain.

1 *Solidus* of emperor Honorius, 395–423

Gold coin of the VICTORIA AVGGG type struck at Ravenna in 402–3 and 405–6.

BM, CM 1931–8–6–2, presented by H. M. Office of Works. Found in excavations at Richborough, Kent.

Society of Antiquaries Reports: *Richborough* 1–5; *RIC* X, 125–37 and no. 1287; Reece 1981.

2 *Siliqua* of emperor Honorius, 395–423

Silver coin of the VIRTVS ROMANORVM type struck at Milan, 395–402.

BM, CM 1936–6–1–36. From the Shapwick, Somerset, hoard 1936.

RIC X, 125–37 and no. 1228d; Robertson 1936.

3 Bronze coin of emperor Honorius, 395–423

Bronze coin of the SALVS REIPVBLICAE type struck at Rome, 395–403.

BM, CM 1929–4–11–22. From the Weymouth Bay, Dorset, hoard.

RIC X, 125–37 and no. 1248; Salisbury 1929.

4 Bronze coin of emperor Honorius, 395–423

Bronze coin of the VRBS ROMA FELIX type struck at Rome, 404–8.

BM, CM, 1951–11–15–832, J. W. E. Pearce bequest.

RIC X, 125–37 and no. 1280.

5 Troubled times: the Hoxne hoard (selection) (see also pls 31, 60)

One of the largest Roman treasures ever to have been found in Britain, the recently-discovered hoard consists of some 15,244 coins (with recent additions) and around 200 other gold and silver objects. It represents a significant part of the accumulated wealth of a very affluent private family, and was buried for safe-keeping in a chest by its original owners in the early 5th century AD. The selection of objects here illustrates the coins, jewellery and fine tableware which comprise much of the hoard.

BM PRB P.1994, 4–8, 33, 29, 23, 43 and 47, CM 1994, 4–1, acquired with the aid of generous grants from the National Heritage Memorial Fund, the National Art Collection Fund, the British Museum Society, the Goldsmiths' Company, J. Paul Getty Jnr and others.

a Representative group of coins (pl. 60)
Gold and silver coins including one of the two latest coins, clipped silver *siliquae* from the first issue of the British usurper emperor Constantine III, 407–11, struck at Lyon 407–8, which provide the earliest date for the deposit of the hoard.

b Gilded silver 'pepper-pot' in the form of the bust of a late Roman empress. The four pepper pots in the hoard are exceptional survivals. The imperial female depicted here strongly recalls the 5th- and 6th-century bronze Byzantine steelyard weights in the form of Empress busts.

c Gold bracelet with *opus interrasile* (pierced work) decoration incorporating the inscription, VTERE FELIX DOMINA IVLIANE, 'Use (this) happily, Lady Juliana'. Altogether there were nineteen gold bracelets in the hoard, of which those in this intricate technique are among the most impressive. The type was favoured equally in the Eastern empire.

d Gold bracelet with pierced decoration in the form of a procession of speckled animals. The comparatively crude decoration has affinities with the ornament known as the 'quoit-brooch style', which was current in southern England in the 5th century, occurring on objects known from Anglo-Saxon contexts.

e Two gilded silver ladles from a matched set of ten with chip-carved scrollwork and engraved dolphin decoration.

Like the bracelets, these reflect widespread decorative trends in late Roman metalwork. The boldly faceted geometric ornament had a powerful influence on Anglo-Saxon metalwork, and the speckled animal types are ancestral to those in the indigenous 'quoit-brooch style'.

Hoxne, Suffolk. Roman, deposited after AD 407.

Johns and Bland, 1993; Bland and Johns 1993.

6 Barbarian loot: the Coleraine hoard (selection)

Unlike the Hoxne hoard, which was buried for safekeeping, the Coleraine hoard is clearly booty, presumably the spoils of Irish raiders. It contained ingots, *hacksilber* (mostly from tableware and military sword belt fittings), and 1506 coins, deposited after AD 410, possibly after 420. Picts and Scots were as much a threat to Romano-British stability as the Germanic tribes across the sea.

a Gilded silver buckle fragment, with niello inlay and geometric chip-carved decoration.

b Gilded silver rectangular mount from a scabbard mouth, with niello inlay and goemetric chip-carved decoration.

c Gilded silver scabbard bridge with chip-carved rosette, and stamped and punched ornament.

These three items date to the later 4th century, and are all fittings from the military equipment of high-ranking personnel. Their decoration and form are types which were very influential in the Germanic world of the 4th and 5th centuries.

BM, MLA 1855, 8–15, 12–14.

Ballinrees, Coleraine, Northern Ireland. Roman, deposited after AD 410.

Kent and Painter (eds) 1977, nos 211–13 and refs; Edwards 1990, 4–5.

7 The forts of the Saxon Shore from the 'Notitia Dignitatum'; Britain at the end of the Empire

The *Notitia Dignitatum* contains a list, with diagrams, maps and other illustrations, of the offices of the late Roman Empire. Its military dispositions include the coastal defences and naval bases which were constructed during the 3rd and 4th centuries to withstand the growing pressure from Germanic, Irish and Pictish raiders. It shows that the military and civil administration, and the Christian Church's diocesan structure were still functioning, paving the way for a measure of continuity following the formal Roman withdrawal in 410.

Oxford, Bodleian Library, MS Canon. Misc. 378, f. 153. Vellum; ff. 173; 273 × 195 mm. Latin; copy made in 1436 of a Carolingian copy of a Roman original of *c*.395.

Facs., Seeck 1876; Pächt and Alexander 1966, I, no. 666; Campbell 1982, 14, fig. 9; Watson 1984, no. 336.

FIFTH-CENTURY INCOMERS

Germanic troops, including Saxons, were a staple element in the late Roman army; federate soldiers were rewarded on retirement with modest land-grants within the Empire. Some arrangement of this kind may be glimpsed behind the story of the arrival of the first Anglo-Saxons in Kent, as recounted by Gildas (23.1–5) and Bede (Book I, chapters 14 and 15). Certainly the distinctive buckles and other belt-fittings of soldiers in the late Roman army are known from Anglo-Saxon graves; late Roman weapons also occasionally occur. The official settlement of Germanic federate soldiers and their families in Eastern England was augmented and eventually overtaken by unconstrained population movements of Germanic peoples from Southern Scandinavia and North-western Europe.

8 Federate uniform: the military belt-set

Bronze four-piece belt-set (buckle, counterplate and subsidiary strap-hangers) of a type current in the late Roman army, which included Germanic federate troops.
The completeness of this set suggests that it is from an Anglo-Saxon grave.

BM, MLA 1942, 10–7, 5, a–c, given by the N.A.C.F. From Kent. Roman, late 4th or early 5th century.

Hawkes and Dunning, 1961, 10ff, 60, 66, 68, pl. 1.

THE CONTINUING SUB-ROMAN AND CELTIC NETWORK

The withdrawal of official Roman rule in AD 410 did not mean an end either to Roman tradition or to contact with the world of late antiquity and its culture; the independent rulers of Celtic stock in the West and North of Britain kept up regular contacts with the Mediterranean through trading links and, increasingly, through the influence of the Christian church. Despite the lurid (and non-contemporary) Celtic documentary tradition, archaeological evidence is increasingly confirming significant acculturation of Romano-British population groups within the Anglo-Saxon community. Meanwhile, the new settlers had their own independent links with the ongoing traditions of the Roman world on the continent.

9 Carlisle – a Roman town in the post-Roman world

In this image from a 13th-century copy of Bede's *Life of St. Cuthbert*, the 7th-century Northumbrian saint is shown prophesying the fate of Carlisle during a guided-tour by eminent citizens (one of whom is described in the *Anonymous Vita* as a *praepositus*, a late Roman title) who proudly show him a Roman fountain. Carlisle (the Roman city of *Luguvall[i]um*, 'the wall of the god Lugus'; adapted by adding the Welsh *caer*, 'city') played an important role in defence and the continued Christian life of post-Roman Britain, influencing the missions of St. Ninian to SW Scotland and St. Patrick to Ireland.

BL, Yates Thompson MS 26 (formerly Add. MS 39943), f. 55v. Bede, *Life of St. Cuthbert*. Vellum; ff. 150; 135 × 98 mm. Latin; copy of *c*.1200 of an early 8th-century text. Durham.

Morgan 1982, I, no. 12a; Farmer 1983, 77–8.

10 Gildas, The Ruin and Conquest of Britain: a British view

In this impassioned polemic addressed to the rulers of post-Roman Britain and its people, the monk Gildas (writing in the mid-6th century) warns that their immorality and indolence will again open the floodgates to the Germanic hordes who had been held at bay by the British military victories of the late 5th–early 6th centuries (the 'Age of Arthur' as it has become known). This charred volume is the earliest surviving copy of a rare British version of the early history of Britain and the Germanic invasions. Gildas recounts how, during the 5th century, Germanic mercenaries had turned against their British paymasters, rampaging 'from sea to sea' and causing wide-scale British emigration to Brittany.

BL, Cotton MS Vitellius A.vi, f. 16v. Gildas, *De Excidio Britanniae et Conquestu* ('The Ruin and Conquest of Britain'). Vellum; ff. 37; 258 × 202 mm. Latin; 10th century. Canterbury (?St. Augustine's).

Winterbottom 1978; Lapidge and Dumville 1984; Higham 1994.

11 Nennius, The History of the Britons: romanticising the British view

This is the earliest surviving copy of a history of the British written around 830 by a Welsh cleric known as Nennius. His *pot pourri* of sources, including 'the tales of our old men', introduces a mythical and romantic element into the British/Celtic view of their early history and contains much of the early elaboration on the theme of Arthur, such as the list of his battles (including the crucial British victory at Mount Badon of *c*.500). The Romano-British legacy and descent of the British are often alluded to.

BL, Harley MS 3859, f. 187. Nennius, *Historia Brittonum* ('History of the Britons'). Vellum; ff. 365; 267 × 152 mm. Latin; *c*. 1100. Unknown origin.

Morris 1980; Dumville 1985.

12 Catering for the Celtic elite: imported pottery from the Eastern Mediterranean

Fragments of amphorae from North Africa and red slipware from Turkey.
These exemplify the persistence of trading contacts between the Mediterranean and the Celtic peoples of western and northern Britain and Ireland. Though debate persists about the scale of this trade, it clearly signifies that oil, wine, fine tablewares and other luxury commodities associated with late Roman life-styles had a continuing market among the independent post-Roman Celtic elites.

BM, MLA 1949, 5–1, 1, 2, 18; 12, 13. Tintagel, Cornwall; from the high-status settlement. First half of 6th century.

Lane 1994; Campbell 1996.

13 Britons in England: glass cone-beaker

Glass cone-beaker with thickened rim and flattened base with kick. Along with a number of other late Roman artefacts from the 5th–6th-century Anglo-Saxon cemetery at Chessell Down, the presence of this vessel in an Anglo-Saxon style burial probably represents the gradual acculturation and assimilation of elements of the indigenous population within the Anglo-Saxon community, a phenomenon increasingly recognised in Anglo-Saxon cemeteries.

BM, MLA 1869, 10–11, 2. Chessell Down, Isle of Wight, from the Anglo-Saxon cemetery. Roman, late 4th century.

Harden 1956, 135, 158; Arnold 1982, 38, 57, fig. 24.

14 Britons in England: quoit-brooch

Silver quoit-brooch, part-gilded, with zones of engraved animal ornament and three-dimensional doves. This splendid piece typifies the southern English 5th-century 'quoit-brooch style' which survives on objects found in Anglo-Saxon contexts, though arguably not on artefacts of diagnostic Anglo-Saxon type. A derivative of late Roman metalwork styles, it seems probable that it is an indigenous continuation of that tradition, produced for mixed successor populations after the withdrawal

of Roman rule, and indicative of sustained interaction between Germanic and Romano-British cultures.

BM, MLA 1893, 6–1, 219. Sarre, Kent, from the Anglo-Saxon cemetery. Sub-Roman, 5th century.

Haseloff 1974, 5; Ager 1985 and refs.

15 Britons in England: grave-group

a Iron riveted bracelet

b Iron bracelet

c Bronze slip-knot bracelet

d Bronze riveted strip bracelet, with engraved 'quoit-brooch style' geometric ornament.

From a 5th-century grave in Anglo-Saxon cemetery II at Mucking, these personal belongings represent late Roman dress and decorative traditions and were most probably buried with a woman of Romano-British stock.

BM, MLA 1985, 5–1, 631/1–4. Gift of the Trustees of the Estate of F. W. Surridge. Mucking, Essex, grave 631. Sub-Roman, first half of 5th century.

Hirst and Clark forthcoming.

16 Five pierced Roman coins

a Allectus, 293–6,

b Constantine I, *c*.310,

c a contemporary forgery of Constantine I, *c*.318,

d Crispus, *c*.323–4, and

e Constans, 348–9.

These bronze coins, pierced for use as prestige jewellery, were found in the same grave dated to the late 5th or early 6th century. None of them was in circulation at the end of Roman Britain. They belong to three mutually exclusive currency phases: a; b–d; and e; so that they cannot derive from a single hoard, but had been collected as site-finds in Anglo-Saxon times.

BM, MLA 1893, 7–16, 20 (a–e). East Shefford, Berkshire, grave 37.

RIC V 2(2), 129; *RIC* VI, London 121a; -; *RIC* VII, Trier 440; *RIC* VIII, Rome 109.

17 Visigothic *solidus*, 461–*c*.475

Gold coin, struck by the Visigoths in southern Gaul in the name of the western Roman emperor Libius Severus, 461–5. Not all gold coins were made into jewellery; this *solidus* is unmounted and had served a monetary function.

BM, CM 1910, 5–9–1. Found near Sittingbourne, Kent, 1910.

Rigold 1975, no. 23; Webster and Backhouse (eds) 1991, cat. 19; Grierson and Blackburn 1986, 44–6.

Power and authority, its expression and use

Defining kingdoms

COINAGE OF THE BARBARIAN SUCCESSOR
STATES IN MAINLAND WESTERN EUROPE

The stages in the transmission of power and authority from the Roman Empire to the successor states is reflected in their coinage. The evolution is complex, differing from state to state but with much in common. It is illustrated here mainly from Italian examples. The first barbarian coins were struck in the name of the emperor, then the king's initial and later his name were added to the imperial designs. These innovations usually began on the lower denominations, and only later appeared on the gold. During the 7th century distinctive national coinages emerged which were essentially medieval in character rather than Roman. By the time Charlemagne extended his rule over wide areas of continental western Europe, and silver had replaced gold as the chief coinage metal, little of the Roman monetary inheritance survived outside south Italy.

Italy

18 *Solidus* of emperor Priscus Attalus, 409–10 (fig. 17)

Gold coin struck in Rome during its occupation by Alaric in the name of the puppet emperor he appointed.

BM, CM acquired 1799, Revd C. W. Cracherode bequest.

RIC X, 138–42; and no. 1406.

19 Bronze coin of Odovacer, 476–93

Bronze coin struck in his own name at Ravenna in 477 by the Roman general who had, in 476, deposed the last western emperor to rule from Italy. His later coins were struck in the name of the last legitimate western emperor Julius Nepos.

BM, CM pres. Count de Salis c.1860.

BMC Vandals etc, 45, no. 10; *RIC* X, 213–14 and no. 3502.

20 *Solidus* of Theoderic, king of the Ostrogoths, 490–526

Gold coin struck at Rome in the name of the contemporary Byzantine emperor Anastasius, 491–518. Style and design details identify it as Ostrogothic rather than imperial.

BM, CM acquired 1799, Revd C. W. Cracherode bequest.

BMC Vandals etc 55, no. 61; Grierson and Blackburn 1986, 35–6.

21 Quarter-*siliqua* of Athalaric, king of the Ostrogoths, 526–34

Silver coin struck at Ravenna for Athalaric with, on the obverse, the name of emperor Justin I, 518–27; the king's own name (without the royal title) appears on the reverse.

BM, CM 1855, 6–12–482.

BMC Vandals etc 63, no. 28; Grierson and Blackburn 1986, 37.

22 Italian *solidus* of Byzantine emperor Maurice, 582–602

Gold coin of the official Byzantine weight standard struck at the imperial mint of Ravenna.

BM, CM 1904, 5–11–237.

BMC Byzantine I, 155, no. 271.

23 Gallic *solidus* in the name of emperor Maurice, 582–602

Gold coin struck at Marseille and lighter than its Italian counterpart (cat. 22). Pope Gregory I, writing in AD 596 (*Letters* III, 33), said that he would be unable to spend such Gallic *solidi* and asked that his revenues from south Gaul be sent to Rome in the form of commodities.

BM, CM pres. Count de Salis c.1860.

Grierson and Blackburn 1986, 130.

24 *Tremissis* of Luitprand, king of the Lombards, 712–44

Gold coin on the distinctive broad flan used in north Italy with the name and title of the Lombard king on the obverse.

BM, CM 1855, 6–12–489.

BMC Vandals etc 144, no. 3; Grierson and Blackburn 1986, 64.

25 *Solidus* of Luitprand, duke of Beneventum, 751–8

Gold coin in the name of emperor Justinian II, 685–695, with the duke's initial L on the reverse.

BM, CM pres. Count de Salis c.1860.

BMC Vandals etc 165, no. 3; Grierson and Blackburn 1986, 70.

26 *Solidus* of Grimoald III, duke then prince of Beneventum, 788–806

Base gold coin with the duke's name on the obverse, and that of '(Our) lord, King Charles' i.e. Charlemagne, his overlord 788–92, on the reverse.

BM, CM 1855, 6–12–510.

BMC Vandals etc 171, no. 4; Grierson and Blackburn 1986, 70–1.

27 Quarter-*siliqua* of pope Gregory III, 731–41, with emperor Leo III, 717–41

Base silver coin struck at Rome. Although Leo's bust is on the obverse, Gregory's monogram on the reverse reflects the transition of real power in Rome from the Byzantine emperors, still nominally in control, to the popes.

BM, CM 1847, 11–8–108.

Grierson and Blackburn 1986, 259–62.

Burgundy, Francia and Spain

28 *Solidus* of Gundobad, king of the Burgundians, c.473–516 (pl. 6)

Gold coin struck by Gundobad in the name of the emperor Anastasius, 491–518; the king's monogram, of small size, is added to the Byzantine-type reverse design.

BM, CM 1860, 3–30–1005, pres. Count de Salis c.1860.

Grierson and Blackburn 1986, 74–6.

29 *Solidus* of Dagobert I, king of the Franks, 629–39

Gold coin struck at Marseille with a profile bust and the king's name and title. (This coin had been made into a pendant, but the loop has been broken off.)

BM, CM pres. Count de Salis c.1860.

Grierson and Blackburn 1986, 130–1.

30 *Tremissis* of Recceswinth, king of the Visigoths, 653–72

Gold coin of late Visigothic type struck at Toledo with the king's name and title on the obverse.

BM, CM 1849, 6–20–18.

Grierson and Blackburn 1986, 51.

DEFINING POLITICAL IDENTITY IN ENGLAND

The Anglo-Saxon settlers came with their own cultural traditions, characteristically typified in the archaeological record by differing forms of costume, according to tribal and regional groupings. These continued to develop in distinctive ways for two centuries after their arrival in England, in patterns which, roughly speaking, can be associated with areas historically recorded as Anglian, Saxon, and Jutish; though the origins of the settlers, and their subsequent cultural development, are much more complex than those crude designations imply. The gradual development of more organised polities in the course of the later 5th and 6th centuries seems to be accompanied by an enhanced need to give more emphasis to such expressions of cultural affiliation, reflected in ever more dramatic and bold costume accompaniments.

31 Bede, History of the English Church and People: creating English history (pl. 61)

By the early 8th century 'England' had begun to emerge. The scholarly Northumbrian monk Bede, from his monastic home at Jarrow, gathered together material from as far afield as the papal archives in Rome to help him compile what is considered to be a landmark in the writing of history. He sought to create a group identity for the disparate ethnic components of England, acknowledging a British and Celtic contribution but emphasising the role of the Germanic successor kingdoms and of the Roman Church in forging Anglo-Saxon England.

BL, Cotton MS Tiberius C. ii, ff. 5v–6. Bede, *Historia Ecclesiastica*. Vellum; ff. 157; 272 × 216 mm. Latin, with Old English glosses; first half of 9th century. Mercia/Kent (?Canterbury).

CLA ii, no. 191; Alexander 1978, no. 33; Webster and Backhouse (eds) 1991, no. 170; Farmer 1990; Colgrave and Mynors 1991.

32 Dress accessories from the burial of an Anglian woman (selection)

a Bronze cruciform brooch

b Bronze annular-brooch pair

c Bronze sleeve-clasps

d Glass and amber beads

e Bronze girdle-hangers.

BM, MLA 1883, 4–1, 327–30, 332, 334. Gift of A. W. Franks. Sleaford, Lincolnshire, grave 158. Anglo-Saxon, second half of 6th century.

Thomas 1887, 399.

33 Dress accessories from the burial of a Saxon woman

a Gilt-bronze saucer-brooch pair with running scroll ornament, from the neck of a tunic.

b Gilt-bronze square-headed brooch with animal ornament, from an outer garment.

c Glass and amber beads slung between the brooches.

d Iron purse mount.

BM, MLA 1964, 7–2, 394–5; 579; 389; 396. Gift of Mrs D. King and son. Great Chesterford, Essex, grave 126. Anglo-Saxon, middle of the 6th century.

Evison 1994, 5–6, 109, and fig. 49.

34 Dress accessories from the burial of a Kentish woman

a Two gilded silver square-headed brooches of Kentish type, with animal ornament, from the neck of a tunic.

b Glass and amber beads slung between the brooches.

c Silvered bronze small long-brooch, and bronze ring brooch, from the bodice of the garment.

d Iron knife and key hung from the waist.

BM MLA 1963, 11–8, 806–7; 58–60; 61–2, 56. Dover, Kent, grave 13. Anglo-Saxon, first half of 6th century.

Evison 1987, 35–7, figs 9 and 67, text fig. 13.

35 Brooches associated with different regional groups

a Bronze swastika-brooch pair of Anglian type.

b Gilt-bronze saucer-brooch pair of Saxon type.

c Three garnet-inlaid gilded silver disc-brooches of Kentish type, showing the influence of Frankish metalworking techniques.

BM, MLA 1883, 4–1, 174–5. Sleaford, Lincolnshire, grave 95. 6th century; BM, MLA 1893, 7–16, 43–4. East Shefford, Berkshire, from an Anglo-Saxon grave. 6th century; BM, MLA 1046'70, 1043'70, 1040'70. Faversham, Kent, from Anglo-Saxon graves. Mid-6th century.

What a king does

ROYAL PEDIGREES, STYLES AND TITLES

As in the Roman world (and indeed in Celtic society), the ruling families of Anglo-Saxon England sought to confer prestige and legitimacy on their rule through their ancestry. The Christian Church assisted them in this and clerics seem to have been involved in drawing up such politically advantageous lineages. In the concoction of such pedigrees heroes were a key ingredient. Bardic accounts of the deeds of one's ancestors, to be sung in the mead-hall, were no longer sufficient – their names were recorded for posterity in the Roman manner, that is, in writing.

Throughout the Anglo-Saxon period there was also a growth in the claims of territorial, ethnic and temporal/spiritual authority on the part of rulers expressed in the title accorded them in documents and, to a limited extent, on coins. For example, the regnal styles, or titles, adopted by that ambitious and expansionist king of 8th-century Mercia, Offa, proclaimed his right to rule by divine appointment, simultaneously reinforcing his attempts to usurp elements of ecclesiastical authority and property.

36 Regnal lists: ancestors and other heroes

This fragment, used in the binding of a printed book, dates from the reign of Alfred and contains the earliest known text of the West and East Saxon royal genealogies. The descent of the kings of Wessex, to Alfred, is traced from Woden via Cerdic and Cynric who are proclaimed as the first to seize Wessex from the British. Likewise, the more obscure East Saxon dynasty is traced via its founder, Sledd, to the Saxon god, Seaxnet. Although such lists are valuable records, comparison with other sources indicates that they are rather untrustworthy and are more representative of a political than an historical view.

BL, Additional MS 23211, ff. 1v–2. West Saxon and East Saxon royal genealogies. Vellum; ff. 155 × 105 mm. Latin and Old English; late 9th century. Wessex.

Webster and Backhouse (eds) 1991, no. 30; Sisam 1953, 287–348; Dumville 1977, 72–104; 1985, 21–66; Yorke 1985, 3–4, 8–24; Dumville 1986, 1–32.

37 Royal 'styles' (titles): what's in a name?

A charter of King Offa 'King ordained by the King of Kings' and 'King by the gift of God'. Earlier rulers had stressed in charters that they ruled by divine grace but, perhaps influenced by contemporary Frankish and Byzantine examples, Offa attempted to consolidate this sacral view of kingship and to exploit its authority. The value of such designations was perceived and developed by the later kings of Wessex and used in promoting a single English monarchy.

BL, Additional Charter 19790. Charter of King Offa of Mercia to his *minister*, Æthelmund, of land at Westbury-on-Trim, Glos. Vellum; 185 × 135 mm. Latin; between 793 and 796. Mercia (?Worcester).

Sawyer 1968, no. 139; ChLA, no. 180; Webster and Backhouse (eds) 1991, no. 158; Brooks 1971, 78; Scharer 1982, 275–8.

REGNAL TITLES ON COINS

Anglo-Saxon gold *tremisses* follow Frankish practice in rarely bearing regal names and titles. The sole English example yet known is Eadbald of Kent (cat. 38). In the early silver series only East Anglian (cats 139–41) and Northumbrian coins (cats 113–15) name the king. After the mid-8th century, kings' names are almost invariably present but the regal title, although normal, is not always used. The names (usually contracted) of the people over whom the kings ruled appear for the first time, although they are often omitted. Only in Kent is a territorial designation found instead.

38 Gold shilling of Eadbald, king of Kent, 616–40

Gold shilling ('thrymsa') struck at London and inscribed: +AVDVARLD[I] REGES ('[coin] of King Eadbald').

Reproduction of coin in the Ashmolean Museum, Oxford (kindly supplied by Prof. Metcalf). From the Crondall, Hampshire, hoard, 1828.

Metcalf I 1993, 41 and 61.

39 Penny of Offa, king of Mercia 757–96

Silver coin by the moneyer Ealhmund inscribed: +OFFA REX MERICIORV[M] ('Offa king of the Mercians').

BM, CM acquired before 1838.

BMC Anglo-Saxon I, 26, no. 16.

Fig. 95 Silver penny of Offa, king of the Mercians (757–96), cat. 39.

40 Penny of Cuthred, king of Kent, 798–807

Silver coin by the moneyer Swefheard inscribed: +CVÐRED REX CANT. The territorial CANT[IAE] was intended, as in contemporary charters, hence 'Cuthred king of Kent'.

BM, CM 1992, 11–33–46, pres. British Museum Society. Found in excavations at Burrow Hill, Suffolk.

Fenwick 1984.

CODIFYING ENGLISH LAW

Dispensing or ensuring justice was a fundamental aspect of kingship. Bede tells us that, with the consent of his counsellors, Æthelberht I of Kent introduced a written law-code 'inspired by the example of the Romans'. The laws are chiefly concerned with procedure and with the levels of compensation to be paid for certain misdemeanours. In its emphasis upon the *wergild* (blood-money) and its treatment of sexual and moral issues it is closer to Germanic than Roman law. The 'Roman' influence presumably related to that of Augustine and his fellow missionaries, who would have been responsible for persuading Æthelberht that a written law-code was an essential attribute of a Christian ruler and assisting in devising written Old English. The code commences with a clause specifying compensation to be paid to the Church, reflecting its influence and the process of its integration into Anglo-Saxon society, but advice sought by Augustine from Pope Gregory the Great on theft of Church property is ignored, indicating that Christian influence was limited. The law-code was probably kept as a symbol of majesty whilst its contents presumably continued to be distributed and applied orally. From Kent the practice of compiling laws extended to Mercia and Wessex and, through King Alfred, contributed to the development of a single English state. Continental Germanic law codes were also strongly influenced by Roman imperial codes.

41 The Laws of King Æthelberht I of Kent (photograph)

The only extant copy of the Laws of King Æthelberht I of Kent, issued soon after his conversion, perhaps in 602–3. It is the oldest known document in English and is preserved in this 12th-century Rochester compilation, the *Textus Roffensis*.

Rochester, Cathedral Library, MS A.35, f. 1. Textus Roffensis (photograph). Vellum; ff. 235; 225 × 155 mm. Old English and Latin; 1122–3. Rochester.

Liebermann 1898, 3–8; Attenborough 1922, 4–17; Sawyer 1957–62; Richardson and Sayles 1966, 1–13; Wallace-Hadrill 1971, 32–46; Whitelock 1979, no. 29; Simpson 1981, 3–17; Cramer 1989, 483–93; Webster and Backhouse (eds) 1991, no. 25; Wormald 1994.

ADMINISTRATION

The right to control the granting of land was an important royal attribute. In property transfers, as with the laws, oral tradition was rapidly supplemented by written records, in the Roman manner, following the conversion to Christianity. The Church promoted this, for it was by means of such records that the new ecclesiastical hierarchy was assimilated into the structure of English society and its property assured. The earliest surviving authentic Anglo-Saxon charters date from the late 7th century (although they are generally thought to have been introduced earlier) and are hybrid instruments displaying Italian and Frankish influence as well as English legal features. In appearance, however, they are very different from the products of the late antique bureaucracy and its Byzantine, Italian and Frankish successors and speak of a higher level of status and perception, emulating the appearance of high-grade books. The new form of tenure was termed 'bookland' as the title was recorded in a 'boc' or charter. Their purpose was to avoid future dispute, with the act of transfer of property continuing to be conducted in the traditional way, before witnesses, by placing turf on an altar or some such symbolic gesture. It was not the grantor (usually a king) but the grantee who was responsible for having copies of the record drawn up by Church scribes and housed in ecclesiastical archives. By the 9th century, however, such was the value of written evidence that it began to challenge that of oral witness.

42 New Roman Cursive: the secretary hand of the Roman world

This example of a Roman document is typical of the sort of administrative record and office hand which would have been found throughout the late Roman Empire. It is written upon papyrus which is made from a plant grown in the southern Mediterranean, especially Egypt. With the Islamic expansion of the 7th century onwards, papyrus supplies became rare and it was replaced by parchment, a form of prepared animal skin which had become increasingly popular from the 4th century when the book (codex) began to seriously challenge the papyrus roll as the prime vehicle for carrying text.

BL, Papyrus 447, recto. Draft petition of Flavius Abinnaeus to the emperors Constantius and Constans, requesting a new posting. Papyrus; 290 × 505 mm (frag.). Latin; *c*.345–6. ?Egypt.

Mallon, Marichal and Perrat 1939, no. 35; Brown 1990, no. 8.

43 Merovingian Chancery Script: the legacy of Antiquity

In post-Roman Gaul the comparative continuity of administration guaranteed by the Church and its converted Frankish rulers is reflected in the output of the royal chancery and in the script used by its clerks. Once compared to the wanderings of a demented spider, this hand represents a somewhat vulgarised version of Old Roman Cursive, the Roman secretary hand, rather as the Romance languages were to evolve from a Latin base.

Paris, Archives Nationales, K.2, no. 3. Confirmation by King Clovis II of the privilege of immunity to the abbey of St. Denis. Papyrus; 318 × 935 mm. Latin; 654. Clichy.

Bruckner and Marichal 1981, no. 558.

44 The English discover bureaucracy

This charter of 679 is the oldest surviving dated example of English handwriting. The charter combines Italian, Frankish and English legal features, but looks very different from Roman and Merovingian documents: it is written on parchment (papyrus may have been used in England initially but has not survived) and in uncials, one of the high-grade book scripts of the Roman world. This reflects the lack of local bureaucratic continuity, for it was the formal script of liturgical books which initially shaped the Anglo-Saxon perception of the status of the written word.

BL, Cotton MS Aug.II.2. Charter of King Hlothere of Kent to Abbot Berhtwald of Reculver of land in the Isle of Thanet. Vellum; 330 × 150 mm. Latin; 679. Kent (Reculver).

Sawyer 1968, no. 8; *ChLA*, no. 182; Webster and Backhouse (eds) 1991, no. 27; Chaplais 1965, 51–4; 1968, 317–27; Whitelock 1979, no. 56; Scharer 1982, 65–8; Wormald 1984, 2–7, 13–14.

45 Promoting written evidence at law

By the early 9th century the use of writing and the sense of authority with which it was imbued was such that Wulfred, Archbishop of Canterbury, could produce an impressively written document in a court of law and claim the proof of written evidence over centuries of oral tradition. As part of his campaign of litigation against the Mercian royal house, and to fend off their encroachments upon his authority, Wulfred encouraged the development of a stylish cursive script (Christ Church, Canterbury's 'Mannered Minuscule') to enhance the appearance of his documents. Once such developments in the perception of the use of writing had occurred, forgeries began to proliferate.

BL, Cotton MS Aug.II.74. Charter of King Coenwulf of Mercia to Archbishop Wulfred of Canterbury of land in Kent (?Kingsland, Faversham Hundred). Vellum; 440 × 228 mm. Latin with Old English bounds; 814. Canterbury (Christ Church).

Sawyer 1968, no. 177; Webster and Backhouse (eds) 1991, no. 169; Brooks 1984, 180–6; Brown 1987, 119–37.

FINANCIAL ADMINISTRATION

The coinage of the successor states implies the existence of a sophisticated financial organisation, built on Roman foundations but adapted to the different economies of the post-Roman world. The allusion on the coins to regal (and church) treasuries confirms the early existence of financial offices.

46 Merovingian *tremissis*

Gold coin inscribed: RACIO DOM[IN]I ('treasury of [our] lord [the king]'), early 7th century

BM, CM 1939–10–3–26, pres. Mrs E. M. Pretty. From the Sutton Hoo mound I burial, 1939.

Kent 1975, p. 626, no. 19; Grierson and Blackburn 1986, pp 145–6.

Outward and visible signs of a king

Imitatio Imperii

Issuing coinage was, in itself, an attribute of emperors and kings. The barbarian rulers' increasing use of their own names and, on occasion, of personalised effigies shows that they appreciated the prestige and status conferred by issuing coins or donatives. Coins were struck for propaganda as well as for fiscal and commercial purposes. The later use by Offa and Charlemagne of antique Roman effigies represents more than the casual copying of chance finds, or even the enduring respect for all things Roman; it is a conscious statement of the ruler's perception of his power as overlord of several peoples, a position approaching that of an emperor.

47 40 *nummi* of Theodahad, king of the Ostrogoths, 534–6

Bronze coin with the king's name and title surrounding a striking icon of him wearing Ostrogothic royal robes and the decorated helmet (*Spangenhelm*) of Germanic rulers.

BM, CM 1853, 7–5–3.

BMC Vandals etc 76, no. 23; Grierson and Blackburn 1986, 38.

48 *Solidus* of Theodebert I, king of the Franks, 534–48

Gold coin of the first barbarian king to place his own name on the *solidus*. Procopius, the Byzantine historian, censured such usurpation of the imperial prerogative. The effigy is unchanged from its Byzantine prototype.

BM, CM 1848, 8–19–164.

Grierson and Blackburn 1986, 115–17; *Procopius*, Loeb Classics edition, VII, xxxiii, 5.

(*Above, left*) Fig. 96 Bronze coin of Theodahad, king of the Ostrogoths (534–6), cat. 47.

(*Above, right*) Fig. 97 Gold *solidus* of Theodebert, king of the Franks (534–48), cat. 48.

49 *Solidus* of Charlemagne, 768–814

Gold coin struck at Dorestad, with Charlemagne's titles for the period 774–812, produced initially for presentation purposes. This example is possibly unofficial.

BM, CM from the collection of King George III, pres. King George IV in 1823.

Kent 1968 and refs, Grierson and Blackburn 1986, 328.

50 Anglo-Saxon penny, *c*.735–45

Silver coin ('sceat'), struck at London. The seated figure on the reverse is copied from that of Roma on late imperial silver *siliquae*. It has been suggested that the Anglo-Saxon figure seated in an elaborate chair, and holding a cross and a bird, is a king.

BM, CM 1860. 11–14–49. From the London (Thames Bank) hoard, 1860.

BMC Anglo-Saxon I, 11, no. 92; Metcalf 3 1994, 409.

51 Penny of Offa, king of Mercia 757–96

Silver coin probably struck at London. The bust is derived from that of a 4th-century emperor but an Anglo-Saxon interlaced serpent is added above, combining Roman and Germanic design elements.

BM, CM 1844, 4–25–2661.

BMC Anglo-Saxon I, 28, no. 27; Stewart 1986.

52 Penny of Queen Cynethryth, wife of Offa of Mercia, 757–96

Silver coin struck by the moneyer Eoba whose name appears on the obverse; the queen's is on the reverse. Coinage for a consort apes Roman imperial practice.

BM, CM acquired in 1802. Found at Eastbourne, Sussex, in the 18th century.

BMC Anglo-Saxon I, 33, no. 60.

The case of Sutton Hoo

The well-known Anglo-Saxon royal ship burial at Sutton Hoo, Suffolk, is the imposing memorial to one of the early kings of East Anglia. The Frankish coins in the dead man's purse suggest a burial date after about AD 625, and he has thus usually been identified as King Redwald (d. after 616/17, and before 627/8), recorded by Bede as the Anglo-Saxon overlord of his day. Whatever his identity, however, there can be no doubt that this is the burial of a ruler from a powerful and ambitious dynasty, which, in the wealth and variety of equipment and regalia symbolically interred with the dead man, as well as in the ostentatious manner of his burial, expresses its claim to rule in no uncertain terms. The burial of the king in a boat, and under a massive earthen barrow, visible for miles, is fully in the Germanic tradition, as is the idea of accompanying the dead with a variety of personal and symbolic objects. So, too, is the iconographical and decorative repertoire of much of the personal equipment in the grave. Indeed, the spectacular gold and garnet jewellery, and the menacing helmet embellished with dragons, serpents and warriors have come to be *the* image of Germanic warrior culture, the Anglo-Saxon hero familiar from readings of *Beowulf* and other early heroic literature. Yet there is another dimension to the reading of this assemblage, and one which the rulers of East Anglia, who claimed their descent from Caesar as well as Woden, deliberately emphasised.

This royal burial comes from a period when rival kingdoms in England were jockeying for domination; so it is no surprise that its contents emphasise the power of an Anglo-Saxon king and his heirs through treasure, tribute, diplomatic gifts and booty gathered from all quarters of the known world: from Celtic Britain in the West to Byzantium in the East, and from Sweden in the North to the neighbouring Frankish kingdoms which ruled in Gaul to the South: a range to rival that of the former Empire, and perhaps thus deliberately intended to deliver a symbolic message about *imperium* as well as the sheer power and wealth of the dynasty. Certainly, the elaborate parade armour, regalia and treasure belonging to the dead king constitute a conscious evocation of the traditions of imperial Rome, and were clearly intended as a visible statement of the East Anglian dynasty's claim to be the authentic inheritors of Roman rule.

53 The royal image: the Sutton Hoo Mound I ship burial (selection)

a Iron helmet with face-mask and a variety of zoomorphic and figural motifs in tinned and gilded bronze, silver wire and garnets (fig. 98).
Like the equivalent 6th–7th-century Swedish helmets, and the later Anglo-Saxon one from York, the Sutton Hoo helmet derives from prestige late Roman parade helmets like that from Deurne, Netherlands (pl. 48). In this respect, all these are quite unlike the normal Byzantine helmet form in use among the continental barbarian aristocracy, the so-called *Spangenhelm*. The peripheral cultures drew on a fossil late Antique tradition different from that current in successor states less remote from the eastern empire.

b Iron sword with garnet-inlaid gold hilt- and scabbard-mounts and other harness fittings.
The sword was the most prestigious weapon of the Roman officer and of the barbarian warrior alike. Here, the heavy two-edged sword of the Anglo-Saxon nobility has a full set of elaborate harness mounts in the Eastern Roman manner.

c Glass- and garnet-inlaid gold shoulder-clasps from a leather cuirass (pl. 62). Unique survivals in Europe, these shoulder-clasps are clearly based on imperial prototypes such as those portrayed on the statue of Augustus at Prima Porta.

d Gold buckle with niello inlay and animal ornament. Imposing buckles, which in late Roman custom were signifiers of rank and position, were increasingly adapted by the Germanic aristocracy to express status. This massive gold buckle, though visually far removed from these models, is a paramount symbol of male supremacy in a defined Roman tradition.

e Glass- and garnet-inlaid gold mounts from the ivory? lid of a leather purse, containing 37 Merovingian gold coins, each from a different mint, together with three unstruck blanks and two small ingots (see following entry). (pl. 19).

f Group of coins from the purse: gold Merovingian *tremisses*, a blank and an ingot.
To possess coins was a sign of wealth and status but the recourse to blanks suggests that the treasury had a limited stock, and that the coins acquired in gift-exchange or trade were still often melted down to make prestige objects.

The gaining and keeping of treasure was a major concern of early medieval rulers; but in the form of coinage, as *largitio*, it played a further role in Roman and barbarian ruling culture. The Frankish king Clovis is described by Gregory of Tours as scattering gold and silver coins in the Roman manner among the populace of Tours, when the emperor Anastasius conferred the consulate upon him (*Ten Books of Histories*, II, 38); thereafter, says Gregory, he was called Consul or Augustus. The Frankish coins in the Sutton Hoo purse certainly represent treasure, not currency, and may also perhaps have carried some overtones of Roman-style *sparsio* or *largitio* – as distributed by emperors, consuls, or even by barbarian kings.

g Stone sceptre with carved and painted anthropomorphic terminals with bronze cages, and, at its upper end, an iron ring surmounted by the bronze figure of a stag. A unique and strange object, the sceptre has attracted more speculation than any other object in the burial. As a manifest symbol of power, however, it is hard to ignore its relationship

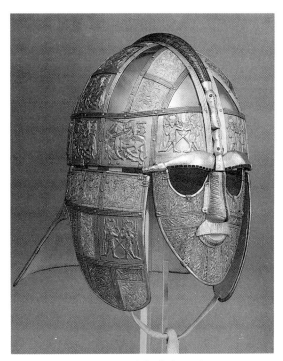

Fig. 98 Reconstruction of the helmet from Sutton Hoo Mound I, Anglo-Saxon, cat. 53a.

to the prominent sceptres depicted in the widely disseminated images of late Roman consuls, some of which also bear eagles and other symbolic images, and incorporate circular wreaths.

h Silver tableware from the Eastern Mediterranean: large dish with engraved decoration and control stamps of the emperor Anastasius (491–518), made in Constantinople; three bowls with engraved and stamped decoration, from a set of ten, of 6th-century date (fig. 29).

These prestigious items of Byzantine silver would have reached Anglo-Saxon England indirectly, as diplomatic or marriage gifts – almost certainly via contacts with the Merovingian courts.

BM, MLA 1939, 10–10, 93, 95, 4, 5, 1, 2, 160, 76, 79, 80, 83; CM 1939, 10–3–1, 4, 7, 10, 20, 22, 24, 30, 38, 42. Gift of Mrs E. M. Pretty.

Bruce-Mitford 1975, 1978, 1983; Evans 1986; Kent 1975; Stahl and Oddy 1992.

54 A prince's pony: bridle mounts, Sutton Hoo, Mound 17

Bridle with decorative fittings of gilt-bronze, silver and iron. Horse-gear is very rare in Anglo-Saxon contexts. This example from one of the lesser graves in the Sutton Hoo royal cemetery is exceptional both in the complexity of the articulating fittings and in the high quality of the animal ornament on the major pieces. The use of roundels and small decorative pendants suggests that its antecedents are to be found in the gear of late Roman equestrian cohorts.

BM, MLA 1991, 12–10, 8173.

Evans A. C., forthcoming, *Horse Equipment in Anglo-Saxon England.*

55 The genealogy of the Kings of East Anglia

From the Anglian collection of genealogies and regnal lists, the earliest and most extensive collection of pedigrees of the Anglo-Saxons. The dynasties represented here were of Angle origin, emphasising the importance attached to establishing distinct ancient origins. Pedigrees, probably concocted by clerics, were a means of establishing the right to rule. Illustrious forebears enhanced a dynasty's prestige, hence the inclusion here of descent from 'Caesar' and, the Germanic god Woden.

BL, Cotton Vespasian B.vi, f. 104v. Vellum; ff. 2; 251 × 388 mm. Latin; between 805 and 814, with later 9th-century additions. Mercia.

Dumville 1976, 23–50; Moisl 1981, 215–48; Webster and Backhouse (eds) 1991, no. 29.

56 Roman symbols of power: consular diptych of Orestes (fig. 53).

Ivory diptych of Rufus Gennadius Orestes, showing the newly appointed consul seated on the *curule* chair with the *mappa* in his right hand, and sceptre in his left, and flanked by personifications of Rome and Constantinople. Portrait busts of the Ostrogothic queen regent Amalasuntha and her son Athalaric (526–34) are above the inscription, and below the consul's feet are figures dispensing *sparsio* (largesse) represented by plate and coins.

Aptly described as ostentatious greeting cards, the consular diptychs were presented to friends and officials on appointment to the office. This is the last known such diptych produced in Rome, and is closely based on a Constantinopolitan diptych of Clementinus dated to 513. The attributes of power represented here – such as the sceptre and disbursement of treasure – would have been familiar to the Anglo-Saxon kings.

Victoria and Albert Museum, 139–1866. Rome, 530.

Delbrueck 1929, no. 32; Volbach 1976, no. 31; Cameron and Schauer 1982, 135–7; Williamson 1982, 7, 22–3; Netzer 1983.

Kings and divinity

ROMAN PAGAN IMAGERY AND CHRISTIAN COGNATES

The Anglo-Saxons in the later 7th and earlier 8th centuries copied some Roman coins simply because they were contemporary types or had turned up as chance finds. In other cases it appears that particular prototypes were selected because their designs were interpreted in a way which gave them a new significance in an Anglo-Saxon political, cultural or religious context. As most of these English coins have no inscriptions, and the issuers and minting places are often unknown, explanations of their types are bound to be hypothetical.

57 Roman coin showing Victory

Bronze coin of emperor Constantius II, 337–61, struck at Trier. Victory advances right holding the traditional wreath and palm.

BM, CM 1865, 9–11–35.

RIC IX, Rome no. 17(b).

58 Anglo-Saxon coin showing Victory

Silver penny ('sceat'), south-east England, *c.*730. The figure is a direct copy of the Roman Victory, advancing right holding a wreath, but an angel may already be intended.

BM, CM acquired before 1838.

BMC Anglo-Saxon I, no. 110. Metcalf 3 1994, 440–3.

59 Anglo-Saxon coin showing an angel

Silver penny ('sceat'), south-east England, *c.*730. The figure has no wreath and is a facing Christian angel. This version was probably inspired by Byzantine coins with a facing Victory which had replaced a profile one about a century earlier.

BM, CM 1995, 6–14–4. From the Woodham Walter, Essex, hoard, 1993.

Metcalf 3 1994, 440–3.

MILITES CHRISTI

Although open to other explanations, some at least of the Anglo-Saxon two-figure types seem to have been intended to represent *milites Christi* (saints), perhaps the patrons of coin-issuing monastic foundations, and in particular Saints Peter and Paul. (See also Two Emperors type below. Archibald forthcoming).

60 Roman coin showing two soldiers

Bronze coin of emperor Constans, 337–50, struck at Trier. The heads of the soldiers are turned towards the cross standard between them.

BM, CM R193, pres. Bank of England, 1877.

RIC VIII, Trier no. 41.

61 Anglo-Saxon coin showing two standing figures

Silver penny ('sceat'), struck in south-eastern England, *c*.730. The heads of the two figures are turned towards the cross between them, like their prototype (cat. 60).

BM, CM 1994–4–2–59. From the Woodham Walter, Essex, hoard, 1993.

Metcalf 3 1994, 440–3.

62 Anglo-Saxon coin showing two standing figures

Silver penny ('sceat'), struck in south-eastern England, *c*.730. The two figures here are full-face and, although a Byzantine prototype has been suggested and other identifications made, two saints are also a possibility.

BM, CM before 1832. Found on Thanet, Kent, in the 18th century.

Kent 1961; Metcalf 3 1994, 440–3.

MOUNTED VICTORS

The image of the soldier for Christ was a potent one, used to depict both saints (as on the coins above) and monarchs, for example in the famous image of Louis the Pious as *Miles Christi* in Hrabanus Maurus, *De Laude Christi* (cat. 64). Anglo-Saxons and Franks drew on Germanic tradition and imperial exemplars to portray the mounted warrior as a soldier for Christ.

Fig. 99 Stone cross-shaft from the Mercian royal mausoleum at Repton, cat. 63.

63 The Christian warrior: the Repton cross

Sandstone cross-shaft, carved on one side with a mounted Germanic warrior, on the other with monstrous creatures, perhaps an image of the Final Judgement.

Found broken up and discarded in an 11th- or early 12th-century pit alongside the great Mercian royal crypt at Repton, this remarkable piece has been interpreted as a monument to the powerful Mercian warrior king, Æthelbald (d. 757). The mounted figure is moustached and equipped in Germanic fashion, but the image clearly owes much to depictions of victorious cavalry officers familiar from Roman tomb monuments in Britain. The secular appearance of the figure gives credence to arguments in favour of this as a royal memorial, in which the image of the warrior for Christ merges with that of the triumphant emperor (fig. 69).

Derby Museums and Art Gallery, DBYMU 1989–59/ 1165. Repton, Derbyshire. Anglo-Saxon, 8th century.

Biddle and Kjølbye-Biddle 1985.

64 Hrabanus Maurus, Carmina Figurata (photograph): the emperor as 'Miles Christi'

The Carolingian emperor, Louis the Pious, as the Christian warrior. This is the earliest surviving illumination depicting a Carolingian ruler. His dress is indebted to imperial Roman models and he forms part of a *carmina figurata* ('figure poem') in which an image superimposed upon a text serves to highlight key phrases (such as the 'You Christ crown Louis' marked by the halo). Such devices were favoured by the late antique intelligentsia, such as Porphyrius, court poet of Constantine the Great.

Vatican City, Biblioteca Apostolica Vaticana, Reg. lat. 124, f. 4v. Hrabanus Maurus, *De Laudibus Sanctae Crucis* ('In Praise of the Holy Cross'). Vellum; ff. 61; 365 × 295 mm. Latin; *c.*840. Fulda.

Mütherich and Gaehde 1977, pl. 12; Nelson 1996.

Images of power: the case of King David

The change from a pantheon of deities to a single, jealous, God left emperor and barbarian kings alike little scope to claim divine status on their own behalf. A new relationship had to be developed in which the special role of the ruler as the earthly representative of the Lord, defender of His people and arbiter of His will, was expressed.

The creation of an 'image' has always played an important part in establishing credibility and authority, and the powerbrokers of the early Middle Ages had a formidable battery of classical and early Christian precedents to draw upon. A ready-made image of ideal kingship existed in David, King of Israel, who, from the 3rd century AD was celebrated in Jewish art as the ideal ruler of the chosen people. In Christian art, he appears as a 'type', or Old Testament parallel, for Christ, in many guises. Enthroned like Christ in majesty, he is earthly ruler and divine symbol. As the victorious warrior, he could represent the ideal, expressed for example, by Bede, of the Old Testament king as a model for contemporary rulers; as the good shepherd who rescues his flock from the jaws of the lion, and defeats Goliath, he is a metaphor of salvation, Christ conquering the forces of evil; as the Psalmist, he symbolises divine inspiration, and speaks of the relationship between God and man.

Classical sources were drawn upon to form such images, including the biographical picture-cycles of pagan gods and the iconography of enthroned deities, which had already been adapted as power-imagery in the figures of enthroned emperors and hellenistic kings. In its Christianised form the iconography of David provided a royal hero for both noble and cleric alike, as the English and their neighbours the Picts, the Irish and the Franks were quick to realise.

65 The Durham Cassiodorus: David, the warrior king and precursor of Christ (pl. 64)

In this image David is shown as the armed warrior trampling on or being adored by the beasts, as in similar contemporary depictions of Christ (on the Bewcastle Cross, for example). David was adopted as an Old Testament 'type' or precursor of Christ in early Christian iconography. These monumental figures were probably inspired by a Mediterranean source, perhaps from Cassiodorus's monastic foundation, the Vivarium.

Durham, Cathedral Library, MS B.II.30, ff. 172v–173. Cassiodorus, Commentary on the Psalms. Vellum; ff. 266; 420 × 295 mm. Latin; second quarter of 8th century. Northumbria (?Monkwearmouth/Jarrow).

CLA ii, no. 152; Alexander 1978, no. 17; Webster and Backhouse (eds) 1991, no. 89; Bailey 1979.

66 The Vespasian Psalter: exploring aspects of King David (pl. 63)

Here David is depicted as a young man enthroned, like Christ, amidst his musicians, like an heroic king in an Anglo-Saxon mead hall – the 'gold-friend', the 'giver of gifts'. The naturalistic figures and exotic plant motifs, as well as the stately uncial script, point to the Italian byzantinising models available in England by the 730s. The iconography of David is explored further in the historiated (story-telling) initials where he is shown with Jonathan, shaking hands, as warrior and peace-maker and as the shepherd guarding his sheep – the ruler protecting his people (again with Christological overtones). A lost initial probably depicted the anointing of David by Samuel.

BL, Cotton MS Vespasian A. i, ff. 30v–31. Psalter. Vellum; ff. 153; 235 × 180 mm. Latin with continuous Old English gloss (added mid-9th century); second quarter of 8th century (*c.*725). Canterbury (St. Augustine's).

CLA ii, no. 193; Alexander 1978, no. 29; Webster and Backhouse (eds) 1991, no. 153; facs. Wright 1967.

67 The Codex Aureus of St. Emmeram (photograph): the king as descendant of David

Here the Carolingian ruler Charles the Bald is identified by an inscription as the descendant, like Christ, of King David. He is enthroned in a church-like setting, flanked by angels, in the manner of Christ in Majesty. The hand of God bestows blessing and protection and he is presented with the weapons with which he is to serve Christ. Female figures depicting Francia and Gotia, like Antique personifications of cities, brandish cornucopias overflowing with the plenty to be guaranteed by his reign.

Munich, Bayerische Staatsbibliothek, Clm 14000, f. 5v. The Codex Aureus of St. Emmeram (Gospels). Vellum; ff. 126; 420 × 330 mm. Latin; 870. Court School of Charles the Bald.

Mütherich and Gaehde 1977, pls 35–8; Nelson 1996.

68 The Tiberius Psalter: King David, a model of royal iconography

By the end of the Anglo-Saxon period, in the Tiberius Psalter of c.1050, the potential of the iconography of David as an expression of royal power had been fully realised. Here David appears crowned and enthroned, holding a sceptre as a symbol of authority and a harp as the sign of his role as prophet. The Holy Spirit, in the form of a dove, converses with him and the hand of God anoints him, recalling the coronation rites of the English monarchy.

BL, Cotton MS Tiberius C.vi, ff. 9v–10. Psalter. Vellum; ff. 129; 248 × 146 mm. Latin with Old English gloss; mid-11th century. Winchester.

Temple 1976, no. 98; Backhouse, Turner and Webster (eds) 1984, no. 66.

69 A Pictish royal shrine: the St Andrews Sarcophagus (fig. 100, pl. 65)

Sandstone rectangular box-shaped shrine, of which three corner slabs and the front and left end panels survive. It probably originally had a flat, rather than coped, lid. The main panel is dominated by an image of the shepherd David, shown at heroic scale grappling with the marauding lion; alongside, at smaller scale, a hunt is in progress. The rider image is based on lion hunt scenes decorating late antique silver plates; awareness of exotic models is also seen in the motif of the griffin, pouncing on a foal. The two frontal corner slabs have elaborate entwined animal designs on their broad faces, interlace on their narrow ones. The end panel bears a cross with dense interlace, bosses encrusted with interlacing snakes, and two figural scenes. The remaining corner slab has key pattern and interlace designs.

Discovered to the west of St Regulus church in the cathedral precincts in 1833, the Sarcophagus was probably originally constructed within a royal chapel or monastic church. St. Andrews (the Pictish Kinrimonth) was an important early Pictish royal and ecclesiastical centre; a monastery existed by the mid-8th century. Although uniquely grand, the Sarcophagus is one of a number of such monuments, while the figural panel is fully in the tradition of Pictish relief sculpture, in which the courtly deer hunt plays an important part. The use of imagery from an imperial lion hunt signals clearly the secular prestige of the Sarcophagus. The dominant image of David, however, gives another dimension, by presenting David both as Christ, saviour of his flock, and, through his classicising grandeur and prestigious hunting weapon, as king of Israel. The mounted Pictish warrior who fights the lion recalls imperial equestrian images; the figure may commemorate a successful Pictish king. Such resonant iconography suggests that this is certainly no average tomb, but had some greater significance; as the burial of a king, perhaps, or as a shrine or altar containing relics of St. Andrew and other saints. It has been associated with the prominent Pictish king. Oengus son of Fergus (d. 761).

Historic Scotland: St. Andrews Cathedral Museum. St Andrews Cathedral, Fife, Scotland. Pictish, late 8th or early 9th century.

Bullough 1975; Anderson 1980, 266; Henderson 1986 and refs; Henderson 1994; Foster 1996, 98, 111.

70 Pictish David iconography: sculptural fragment

Sandstone fragment, possibly from a shrine panel; the pose and dress of the figure rending the lion's jaw closely parallel the St. Andrews David figure. Many other fragments of sculpture from this site confirm its standing as a monastery well into the 9th century, when Picts and Scots had united in the face of Viking pressure.

Elgin Museum and The Moray Society, ELGNM: 1855.1.14. The Manse, Drainie, Kinneddar, Elgin, Scotland. Pictish, late 8th or early 9th century.

Henderson 1986; Foster, 1996, 44.

71 The classical hunt: ivory pyx

Ivory pyx with scenes of hunting. The hunt was as much a prestige pastime of the nobility in late antiquity as it was to be in the Middle Ages, and is often portrayed on luxury items. The hunt scenes frequent in Pictish sculpture have a distinctly aristocratic flavour, and owe an evident debt to late Roman sources. In Irish sculpture, similar hunts also occur on the bases of the high crosses.

BM, MLA 1924, 6–17, 1. Byzantine, 4th century.

Volbach 1976, no. 103.

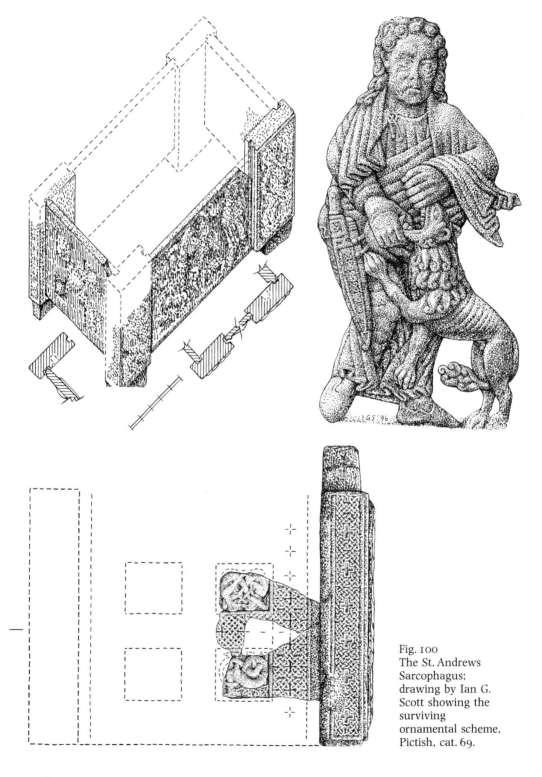

Fig. 100
The St. Andrews
Sarcophagus;
drawing by Ian G.
Scott showing the
surviving
ornamental scheme,
Pictish, cat. 69.

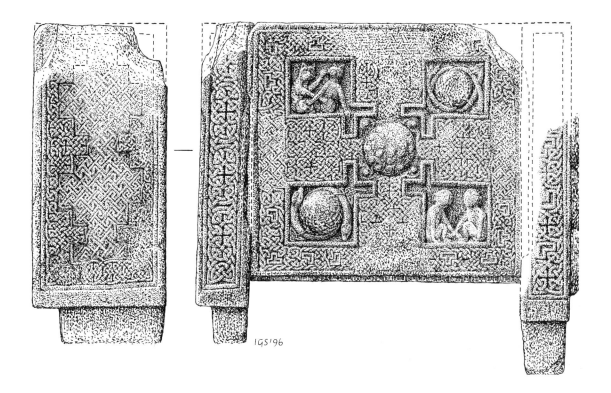

IGS'96

72 A Pictish royal monument: the Dupplin cross (replica) (pl. 66)

Sandstone free-standing cross, with elaborate iconographical programme, and inscriptions in Pictish ogham (on the base), and Roman letters in a panel on the back of the cross. The ogham inscription has not yet been interpreted, but careful study of the main inscription gives a reading: CUSTANTIN FILIUS FIRCUS – meaning 'Constantín son of Fergus'. The decorative scheme includes three David scenes; David the shepherd in combat with the lion and a bear, and David the musician and psalmist portrayed as a harper, as is frequent in Insular art. Other scenes include a mounted warrior heading a procession of armed troops, and elements of a hunt.

The cross stands in a dominant hillside position overlooking the Pictish and, later, Scottish centre of Forteviot. A suggestion (Alcock 1992, 236–41) that it is associated with the final Scottish takeover of the Pictish kingdom in the 840s, and commemorates the new dynastic supremacy through its David iconography and prominent warrior images, has recently been modified due to the partial reading of the Latin inscription. This places it in an earlier context, when Scots and Picts were beginning to coalesce, in which it commemorates the effective Pictish king Constantín son of Fergus (c.789–820). He reigned for a time over both peoples, and had a reputation for sanctity. Images of political might and Christian kingship unite in this most powerful and assertive of monuments.

National Museums of Scotland (replica); original *in situ*, Dupplin, Perthshire. Pictish, 9th century. Alcock 1992 and refs; Forsyth 1995; Foster 1996, 98–9; Henderson forthcoming.

The control and expression of wealth and status

TREASURES

The high individual value of Anglo-Saxon and Merovingian gold coins made them suitable for gift-giving, compensation payments and storing treasure, but for only major commercial transactions. The later silver coinage was produced in greater quantity and had an increasing role in trade. At a rough estimate, the silver penny was the equivalent of what about £20 means to us and the gold shilling of 50 per cent gold, about £100. On this basis, the Crondall hoard represented a sum of about £12,000, Aston Rowant about £7000, and Woodham Walter over £2000. Whatever their origin, these were major stores of treasure, and evidence of the wealth of Anglo-Saxon England.

73 Coins from the Crondall hoard, c.645

Gold tremisses, both Merovingian and Anglo-Saxon, totalling one hundred coins, equal to the *wergild* of one hundred gold shillings of a free peasant as set out in the Kentish law-codes.

Electrotype copies in the BM of originals in the Ashmolean Museum, Oxford. Crondall, Hampshire, 1828.

Sutherland 1948, nos 4, 8, 14b, 28a, 29a, 45a, 45b, 60b, 71 and 97b.

74 Coins from the Aston Rowant hoard, c.710

Silver pennies ('sceattas'), some Anglo-Saxon, but mostly from Frisia and north Francia, totalling about 350 coins. This hoard illustrates the wealth being derived directly or indirectly from contacts with continental Europe, including trade.

BM, CM 1971, 12–16–3, 13, 14, 49, 55, 62, 78, 81, 154 and 171. Aston Rowant, Oxfordshire, 1971–4.

Kent 1972; *CH* I (1973), no. 87; Grierson and Blackburn 1986, 167–8; Metcalf 2 1993, *passim*.

75 Coins from the Woodham Walter hoard, c.730 (fig. 101)

Silver pennies ('sceattas'), many slightly base, totalling 118 coins, about two-thirds Anglo-Saxon, the rest mainly Frisian. The varied sources of the coins in this hoard, buried just outside the east coast port of Maldon, is evidence of the lively internal and external trade which was creating the wealth of Anglo-Saxon England, and which was soon to attract Viking raiders.

BM, CM 1994, 4–24–1, 23, 35, 47, 49, 66, 71, 75, 87 and 104. Woodham Walter, Essex, 1992–4.

Archibald forthcoming.

76 Coins from the Middle Harling hoard, c.760

Base silver pennies ('sceattas'), all Anglo-Saxon and totalling sixty-two coins and two blanks. Most are issues of Beonna, king of the East Angles, 749–c.760 or later, probably initiated as a reformed coinage for military purposes.

BM, CM 1982, 4–9–36; 1984, 5–72–1, 4, 6, 10, 11 and 12; 1984, 12–34–4, 6 and 17. Middle Harling, Norfolk, 1980–3.

Archibald 1985; Rogerson 1995.

Fig. 101
The Woodham
Walter hoard
(selection), Anglo-
Saxon, cat. 75.

77 Coins from the Aiskew hoard, 770s or 780s

Silver pennies of Offa, king of Mercia 757–96, totalling eleven coins. The coinage of the Northumbrian kings at this time was of base silver, so the fine-metal coins of Southumbria (and, in other instances, of the Carolingians) were used for purposes where good silver money was required.

BM, CM 1996, 4–3–1, 2, 3 and 4. Aiskew, Bedale, North Yorkshire, 1992–5.

Barclay, NC 1997 (forthcoming).

CHARTERS AS EVIDENCE OF WEALTH AND ITS EXPLOITATION

From their introduction in the 7th century onwards charters developed as a means of controlling and dispensing wealth in the form of property and rights. Through them we witness the Anglo-Saxon kings extending their political and territorial power and supervising trade. Kings were not the only ones to recognise their potential – nobles and clerics also used them to enhance and manipulate their status and resources.

78 Political power and the granting of land

Control of land grants was a powerful political tool, and was one of the chief means by which King Offa curbed the independence of kingdoms conquered by Mercia in the 8th century. Kent temporarily withstood him, but after Offa resumed control he revoked land grants made by King Ecgberht II of Kent, insisting that as overlord it was his right to approve all such grants. Offa's successor, King Coenwulf, later attempted to appease Kent (and the archbishop of Canterbury) and restored the estates seized by Offa. Coenwulf lost out financially in compensating those concerned, this charter recording that he only received 100 mancuses in return for restoring some of the estates, much less than the market price.

BL, Stowe Charter 7. Vellum; 259 × 185 mm. Latin; 799. Canterbury (Christ Church).

Sawyer 1968, no. 155; Webster and Backhouse (eds) 1991, no. 161.

79 Trade and tolls

This 9th-century copy and confirmation of a charter originally issued by King Æthelbald of Mercia in 733 confers upon the bishop of Rochester the right to dock a ship at London without paying toll. This demonstrates both the organised character of trade and urban administration in the busy international port situated around the site of the modern Strand in London, and the increasing royal exploitation of such resources.

BL, Cotton Charter xvii.I. Vellum; 197 × 302 mm. Latin; 844–5. Rochester.

Sawyer 1968, no. 88; Webster and Backhouse (eds) 1991, no. 151.

MAKING MANUSCRIPTS: MATERIALS AND RESOURCES

Producing books was a costly business, in terms of material and spiritual resources. Work in the monastic scriptorium was, for both men and women, an extension of the *opus dei* (the Lord's work). The number and quality of animal skins used as writing materials and the range of pigments, both local and exotic, give some indication of the input of material resources alongside the human resources needed. Often the choice of materials indicated a conscious perception of cultural and political resonance. Records of gifts of books also give some idea of their material value, although their spiritual value to their contemporaries is more difficult for us to evaluate.

80 The Harley Golden Gospels: visible consumption of Antique influences

The ostentatious use of gold and silver and of purple pages in the early Middle Ages was redolent of imperial and Byzantine power, expressed through visible display of resources and colour symbolism (to be 'born of the purple' was to be empire-worthy). In the Court School of the Carolingian emperor Charlemagne these connotations were exploited in the production of sumptuous manuscripts such as this. Here the evangelist Luke is depicted as a scribe in a palatial interior and the Insular device of the historiated initial is adopted for a depiction of the annunciation to Zachariah.

BL, Harley MS 2788, ff. 108v–109. Gospel Book. Vellum; ff. 208; 369 × 252 mm. Latin; c.800. Court School of Charlemagne.

Hubert, Porcher and Volbach 1970; Alexander 1978, pl. 5.

81 The Stockholm Codex Aureus (photograph): ransomed from the Vikings

Chi-rho page, with an Old English inscription recording the volume's redemption from a Viking army, in return for pure gold, by Ealdorman Alfred

of Kent and his wife, Werburh, in the mid-9th century. The ostentatious use of gold in the volume itself may well have made it seem a valuable prize on the part of its heathen kidnappers. Alfred and Werburh gave it to Christ Church, Canterbury, for love of God and the good of their souls – an interesting case of varying perceptions of worth.

Stockholm, Royal Library, MS A.135, ff. 9v–11. Gospel book. Vellum; ff. 193; 935 × 314 mm. Latin, with Old English inscription of the second half of 9th century; mid-8th century. Kent (?Canterbury).

CLA xi, no. 1642; Whitelock 1970, no. 35; Alexander 1978, no. 30; Webster and Backhouse (eds) 1991, no. 154.

82 The Lichfield Gospels (photograph): traded for a fine horse

St. Luke miniature, with a Latin inscription of the early 9th century, recording that the volume was exchanged for his best horse, by the Welshman Gelhi, son of Arihtiud, who offered it to God and on the altar of St. Teilo (Llandeilo-fawr, Carmarthenshire). We do not know where the volume was made, but by the 9th century it had evidently fallen into lay hands and had to be restored to the Church. Horses are mentioned in the Welsh law-codes and were extremely valuable. The spiritual gains of such a redemption were evidently considerable.

Lichfield, Cathedral Library, MS s.n., p. 218. Gospel book. Vellum; pp. 236; 308 × 235 mm. Latin; mid-8th century (with early 9th-century inscription). ?Northumbria (or Iona or Ireland).

CLA ii, no. 159; Alexander 1978, no. 21; Webster and Backhouse (eds) 1991, no. 90.

83 Lindisfarne Gospels (photograph): materials and resources)

The Lindisfarne Gospels represents a remarkable input of manpower and resources. Written and illuminated by one artist/scribe at a time when library books produced at Lindisfarne might occupy a team of five or more, this is one person's *opus dei* – a spiritual endeavour befitting a major cult object. For this is no ordinary service-book, but presumably a tribute to God and St. Cuthbert. At least 129 meticulously selected calf-skins were used and the pigments include exotic items such as ultramarine, made from lapis lazuli, at that time almost exclusively obtained from Persia and indicating the trade network into which such seemingly remote centres were keyed. These lavish resources may have included gifts from both clerical and lay patrons wishing to be associated with the work.

BL, Cotton MS Nero D.iv, f. 94v. Gospel book; carpet page. Vellum; ff. 258; 340 × 240 mm. Latin, with a 10th-century Old English gloss; c.698. Northumbria (Lindisfarne).

CLA ii, no. 187; Alexander 1978, no. 9; Webster and Backhouse (eds) 1991, no. 80; Backhouse 1981; facs. Kendrick *et al.* 1956 and 1960.

SIGNALS OF STATUS, BADGES OF RANK

One of the more revealing aspects of Roman culture that was taken over by the Anglo-Saxons, among other Germanic tribes, was the transferred use of certain symbols of rank and status. For example, the massive late Roman buckled belt which denoted official status (see p. 25), especially that associated with military service, was adopted by most of the Germanic successors, including Anglo-Saxons, as one of the authentic male signifiers of social rank. More recently, it has been suggested that the chip-carved geometric ornament of some Anglo-Saxon female costume may reflect a directly related status, by using motifs derived from the late Roman military federate equipment of their male relatives and forebears.

84 Roman badge of rank: the military buckle

Bronze military buckle with chip-carved scroll decoration.

BM, MLA 1856, 7–1, 1470. Smithfield, London. Roman, late 4th century.

Hawkes and Dunning 1961, 62, pl. IIa.

85 Anglo-Saxon status symbol: glass- and garnet-inlaid gold buckle

Gold buckle, inlaid with blue glass and garnets, and heavily encrusted with filigree, including animal ornament. From the early 7th-century prestige barrow burial at Taplow (after Sutton Hoo, the outstanding burial of an Anglo-Saxon leader), this supreme status-symbol ultimately derives its potency from the late Roman military equivalents.

BM, MLA 1883, 12–14, 1. Gift of the Rev. C. Whately. Taplow, Buckinghamshire. Anglo-Saxon, late 6th century.

Smith 1905, 199–204; Meaney 1964, 59 and refs; Speake 1980, 52ff; East and Webster, forthcoming.

86 Female status signals: saucer brooches

Gilded silver and bronze Saxon women's brooches, decorated with geometric chip-carved ornament of the kind seen on late Roman soldiers' belt-mounts.

BM, MLA 1923, 5–7, 1; given by G. H. Hadfield; 1862, 6–13, 99; 1964, 7–2, 367–8. Merton, Surrey; Long Wittenham, Berkshire, grave 186; Great Chesterford, Essex, grave 120. Anglo-Saxon, 5th and 6th century.

Dickinson 1991.

COPYING BYZANTIUM

Partly through the Christian missions sent to England from Rome after 597, but also as a result of enhanced political and commercial contacts with the Mediterranean world around this same time, many aspects of Anglo-Saxon life began to change in the 7th century. This is particularly true of traditional costume accessories, which were gradually replaced by the equivalent versions used in Byzantine dress. The traditional paired brooches and heavy beaded necklace gave way to pin-suites and pendants, singly, or occasionally in flamboyant multiples.

87 Copying Byzantium: gold and garnet pendant necklace

Necklace of gold *bullae*, beads and cabochon garnet pendants, with central gold cross. This Anglo-Saxon necklace proclaims a new order not only through the Christian cross at its centre, but also through the Byzantine-style nature of its components. The domed gold *bullae* could have come straight out of Italy.

BM, MLA 1876, 5–4, 1. Desborough, Northamptonshire, from the Anglo-Saxon cemetery. Anglo-Saxon, second half of 7th century.

Webster and Backhouse (eds) 1991, no. 13 and refs.

88 Copying Byzantium: garnet cameo pendant

Gold pendant set with a garnet cameo with the head of a bearded oriental in a Phrygian cap. Garnets and classical gems had always been prized by Germanic peoples; more regular long-distance Eastern commercial contacts and the new Mediterranean dress modes refuelled this taste.

BM, MLA 1970, 3–1, 1. Ewell, Epsom, Surrey, probably from the Anglo-Saxon cemetery. Anglo-Saxon, second half of 7th century.

Webster and Backhouse (eds) 1991, no. 35 and refs.

89 New Christians: cross pendant

Gold cross pendant with cloisonné garnet inlay, and set with a *solidus* of the emperor Heraclius and Heraclius Constantine, his son (period 613–32). The imperial Byzantine coin set at the centre of this pendant was prized for the cross of victory, which is on the reverse of the coin, but on the face of the pendant.

BM, MLA 1859, 5–12, 1. Wilton, Norfolk. Anglo-Saxon, second half of the 7th century.

Webster and Backhouse (eds) 1991, no. 12 and refs.

Word and image

Late antique models and conventions

ASSIMILATION AND IMITATION: THE IMPACT OF THE MEDITERRANEAN WORLD ON MANUSCRIPTS

The use of images to accompany texts was thought of in antiquity as somewhat naive, but by the late Roman period illustrations featured in many luxury books. Early Christian manuscripts followed suit and absorbed Christian iconography. Narrative images were introduced to the Insular world, especially in the form of books and panel paintings. Occasionally, as in the products of the scriptoria of Monkwearmouth/Jarrow and Canterbury, their styles of painting, as well as scripts and physical techniques, were consciously emulated as statements of *romanitas*. But the Insular approach was often to assimilate such influences to create innovative and influential expressions of the fusion of indigenous and Mediterranean culture.

90 Manuscript facsimile of the Vatican Virgil: the late antique picture cycle

Laocoon and the Trojan horse, from one of the earliest and most extensive set of images in book form, the *Vergilius Vaticanus*, copied for Cardinal Camilli Maximi in the mid-17th century from an early 5th-century Roman original. With the official recognition of Christianity during the 4th century, the book, which had been favoured by the early Christians for its ease of portability and cross-referencing, supplanted the papyrus roll. Much of the literature of antiquity did not survive this publishing initiative. Likewise, prepared animal skin ('parchment' or 'vellum') gradually replaced the more fragile papyrus. Images from frescoes and rolls were adapted to the new form, and picture cycles accompanying or integrated with text emerged.

BL, Lansdowne MS 834, ff. 23v–24. Virgil, *Aeneid*, Bk II. Vellum; ff. 75; 264 × 215 mm. Latin; copy of 1642 of a Roman early 5th-century original (Vatican, Biblioteca Apostolica Vaticana, cod. lat. 3225). Rome.

Codices e Vaticanis selecti 1930; de Wit 1959; Weitzmann 1977, pls 1–4.

91 The Cotton Genesis: imaging the biblical narrative

These charred fragments, damaged by fire in 1731, are amongst the remains of a cycle of some 330 miniatures illustrating dramatic episodes from the Book of Genesis. During the early Christian period biblical books took their place alongside the classics as vehicles for narrative illustration in a few de luxe volumes. Their style derived from the illusionistic, naturalistic paintings of antiquity or from the more stylized treatment of late Roman and Byzantine art.

BL, Cotton MS Otho B. vi, ff. 27v, 28 Genesis. Vellum; frag.; 144 × 87 mm; 160 × 105 mm; 110 × 94 mm. Greek; late 5th or 6th century. Eastern Mediterranean, perhaps Egypt (Alexandria).

Christian Orient, 1978 no. 1; Buckton (ed.) 1994 nos 66–7; Weitzmann 1977, pls 21–2.

92 The Gospels of St. Augustine (photograph): importing iconography to England

Scenes from the Life of Christ, from a Gospel book made in Italy during the 6th century which is by tradition thought to have accompanied St. Augustine on his mission to England in 596–7. Along with panel paintings and other portable objects, such imported books inspired the development of Christian iconography in Britain, where narrative illustration was to prove less popular, however, than complex symbolic schemes and images.

Cambridge, Corpus Christi College, MS 286, f. 125. Gospel book. Vellum; ff. 265; 245 × 180 mm. Latin; 6th century. Italy.

CLA ii, no. 126; Webster and Backhouse (eds) 1991, no. 1; McGurk 1961, no. 3; Weitzmann 1977, pls 41–2; Wormald 1984, 13–35.

93 The St. Cuthbert Gospel of St. John (Stonyhurst Gospel): an essay in Mediterranean techniques

This book was found in 1104 amongst the relics contained in the coffin of St. Cuthbert (died 687). It was made at the twin monasteries of Monkwearmouth/Jarrow, perhaps as a contribution to the cult of this renowned Northumbrian saint whose relics were translated to the altar at Lindisfarne in 698. Monwearmouth/Jarrow were strongly influenced by contemporary Rome, which their founder, Benedict Biscop, visited on several occasions, bringing back books, paintings and choral personnel. The Gospel's uncial script was modelled on that of the Rome of Gregory the Great. Its parchment is prepared in the antique/continental fashion, rather than that developed independently in the Insular world. Its binding (which is original and is the earliest surviving European binding) adopts a sewing technique favoured in parts of the late Roman Mediterranean (such as early Christian Egypt) sometimes known as 'Coptic sewing'.

The English Province of the Society of Jesus, on loan to the British Library, Loan MS 74. Gospel of St. John, with original binding (and photograph of script, f. 29v). Vellum; ff. 90; 135 × 90 mm (138 × 93 mm, binding). Latin; *c*.698. Northumbria (Monkwearmouth/Jarrow).

CLA ii, no. 206; Webster and Backhouse (eds) 1991, no. 86; facs. Brown 1969.

94 The Codex Amiatinus (photograph): more Roman than the Romans

The scribe Ezra, adopted from an image of Cassiodorus (6th-century Italian politician, author/ educator and founder of the Vivarium monastery). From one of three Bibles made at the romanising twin monasteries of Monkwearmouth/Jarrow for Abbot Ceolfrith before his final journey to Rome in 716. Ceolfrith died en route, and during the Middle Ages this volume, originally intended as a gift for the Pope, was at the monastery of Monte Amiato in central Italy. Ceolfrith's dedication inscription was altered and it was not until 1886 that the volume was recognised as an Anglo-Saxon work, so convincing was its mastery of the Italian repertoire of illumination and script, and so pure its Vulgate text.

Florence, Biblioteca Medicea-Laurenziana, MS Amiatinus 1, f. V. Bible. Vellum; ff. 1030; 505 × 340 mm. Latin; before 716. Northumbria (Monkwearmouth/Jarrow).

CLA iii, no. 299; Alexander 1978, no. 7; Webster and Backhouse (eds) 1991, no. 88.

95 St. Matthew, the Lindisfarne Gospels (photograph): a local response to exotic exemplars

The Lindisfarne scriptorium probably referred to the same Italian model for its image of St. Matthew as Monkwearmouth/Jarrow did for its portrait of Ezra in the Codex Amiatinus (see cat. 94). The difference in stylistic treatment is striking. Whereas Amiatinus attempts to recreate the style and technique of a classicising Italian work, Lindisfarne dispenses with illusionistic painting and conventions such as perspective in order to emphasise the linear, pattern-making aspects of the design. In this it has

been traditionally viewed as departing from the late antique/early Christian stylistic tradition in favour of Celto-Germanic tastes, although Mediterranean art can also exhibit such graphic trends. Lindisfarne is not attempting to recreate Rome, but to assimilate its influence within its own rich traditions, thereby reflecting the admixture of Mediterranean, Germanic and Celtic cultures which constituted the Insular world.

See cat. 83, f. 25v.

ROMAN MODELS IN COINAGE

She-wolf and twins

The 4th century coins with the she-wolf and twins type are among the commonest of Roman coins to be found in England, and examples would have been discovered in Anglo-Saxon times, as now. This motif was used as a religious symbol of Christ nurturing his church, but it has also been interpreted on the coins (cat. 97–8) as a secular punning allusion to the Wuffingas dynasty and to the two regions which made up the kingdom of East Anglia.

Campbell 1982, 67. Webster and Backhouse (eds) 1991, no. 74.

96 Roman coin showing the she-wolf and twins

Bronze coin of the VRBS ROMA issue commemorating the foundation of the city of Rome, struck at Trier *c*.330.

BM, CM 1846, 10-2-7.

RIC VII, Trier no. 553.

97 Anglo-Saxon coin showing the she-wolf and twins

Silver penny ('sceat') struck in Kent or East Anglia *c*.730.

BM, CM 1994, 4–24–96. From the Woodham Walter, Essex, hoard 1993.

Metcalf 3 1994, 570–5.

98 Coin of Æthelbert, king of the East Angles, d. 794

Silver penny showing the she-wolf and twins.

BM, CM acquired in 1803.

BMC 2. Webster and Backhouse (eds) 1991, no. 222(a).

Two emperors with Victory above

The Roman coin-type of two seated emperors with a Victory above (cat. 99) is related to the Byzantine motif of Christ blessing a married couple which is the prototype for the design of cat. 100 showing Sts Peter and Paul. Such two-figure motifs can thus have either a secular or a religious meaning.

Archibald forthcoming.

99 Roman coin showing two emperors with Victory above

Gold solidus of Valentinian II, 375–92, struck at Lyon showing, on the reverse, Valentinian and his co-emperor.

BM, CM 1860, 3–29–131, pres. Count de Salis.

RIC IX, Lyons no. 39(a).

100 Roundel from base of a bowl

Glass roundel with gold image of Sts Peter and Paul, identified by name, with Christ above holding over them the wreaths of martyrdom.

BM, MLA 1863, 7–27, 4. Roman, 4th century. Probably from the catacombs.

Dalton 1901, no. 636.

101 Anglo-Saxon coin-pendant

Gold *solidus* devotional pendant (suspension loop removed) probably showing Sts Peter and Paul *c.* 600.

BM, CM 1935, 11–17–915. Found at Merton, Norfolk.

102 Anglo-Saxon coin copied from the 'two emperors' type

Gold shilling of *c.*670, probably showing two saints and issued by a religious foundation with two patrons. A likely candidate would be the Canterbury

monastery dedicated to Sts Peter and Paul which, under its later name, St. Augustine's, enjoyed the right to strike coins.

BM, CM 1862, 7–8–2. *BMC* 2.

103 Coin of Alfred, king of Wessex, 871–99

Silver penny, struck at London in the mid 870s. The design was possibly chosen to commemorate an alliance between Alfred and Ceolwulf II of Mercia who issued coins of the same type.

BM, CM 1896, 4–4–63.

BMA 476. Webster and Backhouse (eds) 1991, no. 262a.

Reading without texts: Anglo-Saxon animal art

Like other essentially pre-literate societies, the Anglo-Saxons (and other Germanic peoples) in the 5th and 6th centuries were well aware of the power of the written word, and indeed themselves made use of texts in certain contexts (see below). But the reading of images played a much more central part in their culture, as their surviving decorated artefacts show. The decorative artefacts of the early Anglo-Saxons – and indeed the later ones too – are crammed with visual incident which clearly had meaning for them, though it is now mostly impenetrable to us. The teeming jungle of animals which writhe and grapple with one another over the surfaces of belt-buckles and brooches again derives from the vocabulary of late Roman symbolic motif. These are images to be read in a very real sense, and the familiarity with reading visual rather than verbal messages was to continue to play a very important role in the development of Anglo-Saxon Christian iconography.

Fig. 102 *Solidus* of Valentinian II (375–92), with two emperors motif, and Anglo-Saxon copy, cat. 99 and 102.

104 Sub-Roman symbols: the Mucking belt-set

Bronze five-piece belt-set of late Roman military type, inlaid with silver in the 'quoit-brooch style'. The buckle-set was found in a damaged male grave in the Anglo-Saxon cemetery, along with a knife. Its geometric ornament, human masks and crawling animals represent an indigenous version of the geometric patterns, sea-beasts, griffins and representations of sea-deities seen on the late Roman belt equipment, and its scheme of monsters and masks could still be read within this tradition.

BM, MLA 1970, 4–6, 26. Gift of the Trustees of the Estate of F. W. Surridge. Mucking, Essex, Cemetery I, grave 117. Sub-Roman, early 5th century.

Evison 1968, 231ff, pls liii–liv; Haseloff 1974, 5; Hirst and Clark forthcoming.

105 Germanic messages: an Anglo-Saxon belt-set

Gilt-bronze and garnet-inlaid three-piece buckle-set, with Style I animal ornament. This prestige item of male costume reflects the continuing importance of the buckle as a paramount emblem of male status in the Roman tradition; its typically Anglo-Saxon animal ornament also ultimately derives from the same late Roman provincial metalwork fashions which gave rise to the quoit-brooch style (cat. 104), and the highly formulaic animals which process around its borders also held meaning which was to be understood by the viewer.

BM, MLA 1935, 10–29, 1–3. Gift of the Trustees of the Estate of F. W. Surridge. Howletts, Kent, Anglo-Saxon cemetery, grave 20. Anglo-Saxon, first half of 6th century.

Smith 1936, 131–2, pl. xxxix, 9.

106 Germanic messages: the Chessell Down square-headed brooch (pl. 67)

Gilded silver square-headed brooch with niello inlay, the head and foot-plates covered with precisely structured panels of animal ornament including human masks, and geometric motifs. This is the high-status female equivalent to the buckle (cat. 105); its decorative vocabulary is also drawn entirely from late Roman antecedents, but organised in new ways, and on a characteristically Anglo-Saxon object type. What might seem to eyes unaccustomed to reading visual images chaotic and meaningless pattern, is in fact a coherent and carefully articulated programme.

BM, MLA 1867, 7–29, 5. Chessel Down, Isle of Wight, Anglo-Saxon cemetery, grave 22. Anglo-Saxon, early 6th century.

Leeds 1949, 11–16, cat. 8; Arnold 1982, 52–4 and refs; Hines forthcoming.

107 Translating the Roman image: bracteates and related pendants

a Gold pendant with impression of the obverse of a coin of Constantine I (307–37) minted at Trier, set in a filigree frame.
Unprovenanced. Continental Germanic, ?5th century.

b Gold A-bracteate based on both sides of an *Urbs Roma* coin of Constantine I minted at Trier, with a Germanicised version of the head of Roma, and below it, the she-wolf and twins, symbol of the city.
A magical runic inscription around the edge reads GÆ GO GÆ MÆGÆ MEDU (fig. 48).
Undley, Lakenheath, Suffolk. Anglo-Saxon, 5th century.

c Gold D-bracteate with Style I bird-headed animal.
Dover, Kent, Anglo-Saxon cemetery, grave 20. Southern Jutland or North Germany, late 5th or early 6th century.

d Gold bracteate with two Style II interlacing animals.
Dover, Kent, Anglo-Saxon cemetery, grave 1. Anglo-Saxon, later 6th century.

e Gold bracteate with four interlacing Style II animals, within a key-pattern border.
Dover, Kent, Anglo-Saxon cemetery, grave 134. Anglo-Saxon, mid-7th century.

Bracteates, a term used for gold and silver die-impressed disc pendants, began in north Germany and Scandinavia as copies of the late Roman coins and medallions which passed beyond the frontier in considerable quantities, e.g. (a). Many of them seem to have been worn as amulets by women, and the Roman motifs were adapted to Germanic purposes, e.g. (b, c). Later, local versions developed, becoming ever further removed from their late Roman models, but still embodying something of the original idea of the power of the image contained in precious metal, e.g. (d, e).

BM, MLA AF 511, Franks Bequest; 1984, 11–1, 1; 1963, 11–8, 1; 1963, 11–8, 145; 1963, 11–8, 617. Hines and Odenstedt 1987; Hines 1991, 74–5, 83; Evison 1987, 50–5; Axboe and Kromann 1992, and refs.

108 Adapting antiquity: 7th-century pendants

a Gold bracteate with design of three Style II bird-headed beasts.
Dover, Kent, grave 29. Anglo-Saxon, late 6th century.

b Gold and garnet-inlaid pendant with design of a triskele of bird heads.
Faversham, Kent, from the Anglo-Saxon cemetery. Anglo-Saxon, early 7th century.

c Gold and garnet cloisonné pendant set with a gold *solidus* of Valentinian II (375–92), the apparently geometric border composed of a double-headed creature.
Forsbrook, Staffordshire. Anglo-Saxon, first half of 7th century.

d Gold and garnet cloisonné pendant, set with a Provençal copy of a *solidus* of Maurice (582–602), minted at Arles; what appears to be an encircling cloisonné wreath terminates in two long-jawed animal heads.
Foreshore between Bacton and Mundesley, Norfolk. Anglo-Saxon, first half of 7th century.

The latest Anglo-Saxon bracteates have different, more elaborate designs (a), and the Byzantine-influenced pendants which succeeded them express a new version of the classical heritage (c, d); yet these too, like other more explicit versions (b), adapt late antique images and motifs to a native idiom.

BM, MLA 1963, 11–8, 101; 1145'70; 1879, 7–14, 1; 1846, 6–20, 1; gift of Miss A. M. Gurney. Speake 1980, 34, 42, 50, 68, 86, figs. 3a, 11a, b, 13j, pls 3c, 131; Evison 1987, 53–5, fig. 17; Webster and Backhouse (eds) 1991, no. 9 and refs.

109 Coin pendant

Gold *tremissis* struck at Marseille in the name of the Byzantium emperor Maurice, 582–602, with attached loop. Contemporary gold coins which came to Britain in the 6th and 7th centuries were often converted into pendants to show the wealth and status of their owners.

BM, MLA 1884, 12–21, 9. Gift of Sir A. W. Franks. Faversham, Kent; one of a group of similar pendants from the Anglo-Saxon cemetery.

Rigold 1975, 668, no. 51; Grierson and Blackburn 1986, 111–15.

ANIMAL ART IN MANUSCRIPTS

The heirs of Rome were quick to assimilate their own traditions of ornament into the new medium – the book. Such ornament carried with it a long tradition of signalling wealth and status and would have been seen as a fitting accompaniment to the authority and prestige of the written word. The Germanic peoples adapted their repertoire of animal ornament for use as decorated initials and as the interlaced substructure of their display pages. Such animal motifs had a long history of use and meaning in Germanic and Celtic art, whilst others were imbued with a Christian allegorical meaning expounded in commentaries and in works such as the *Physiologus* and the *Marvels of the East* which paved the way for the medieval bestiary.

110 Zoomorphic initial and Pre-Carolingian 'az Minuscule' Script: Germanic ornament in manuscript form

In Frankish manuscripts birds, fish and dogs are often contorted to form letters in a simple, legible fashion.

BL, Additional MS 31031, ff. 55v–56. Gregory the Great, *Moralia in Iob*. Vellum; ff. 145; 262 × 175 mm. Latin; mid-8th century. Northern France (?Laon).

CLA ii, no. 174; Zimmermann 1916, 86–7, 223.

111 The Lindisfarne Gospels (photograph): an Insular menagerie

Insular manuscripts carried the tradition of adapting indigenous ornament for use in the book much further than their continental counterparts. Zoomorphic motifs were subtly combined with other Germanic devices and curvilinear Celtic ornament and were woven into fabulous interlaced designs, as in the initials and display script of the Lindisfarne Gospels. Here the amorphous menagerie of Germanic animal ornament gives way to more characteristic motifs including birds, hounds and cats.

See cat. 83, f. 139.

112 The Tiberius Bede (photograph): Southumbrian animal ornament

During the late 8th and early 9th centuries the Mercian taste for more independent animal motifs, less enmeshed in interlace, acquired an increasingly exotic and often whimsical character. This is reflected in manuscripts, as in other media. The 'Tiberius group' of southern English manuscripts, to which this volume lends its name as a key member, also features black and white designs and zoomorphic ornament reflecting contemporary silver-niello metalwork of the 'Trewhiddle' style. The bow of this initial **b** could almost be a disk-brooch.

See cat. 31, f. 5v.

MESSAGES IN ANIMAL ART: COINAGE

The coins of Northumbria from *c.*700 to 779 (and a late revival in the mid-9th century) have an animal on the reverse. Although its anatomical details vary, it is likely to represent the symbol of the dynasty or kingdom.

113 Coin of Aldfrith, king of Northumbria, 685–704

Silver penny ('sceat') with animal reverse type.

BM, CM 1854, 6–21–28.

BMC 3; Booth 1984; Metcalf 3 1994, 576–93.

114 Coin of Eadberht, king of Northumbria, 737–58

Silver penny ('sceat') with animal reverse type.

BM, CM ex S. Tyssen, 1802.

BMC 5; Booth 1984; Metcalf 3 1994, 576–93.

115 Coin of Alchred, king of Northumbria, 765–74

Silver penny ('sceat') with animal reverse type.

BM, CM 1850, 8–12–1, pres. Revd J. M. Mason. Found in the churchyard at Jarrow, Tyne and Wear.

BMC 13; Booth 1984; Metcalf 3 1994, 576–93.

Fig. 103 Silver pennies of Northumbrian kings, with recurrent animal symbol, cat. 113, 114, 115

Image and text, image as text

NEW WAYS WITH TRADITIONAL THEMES

116 The Franks Casket (pl. 35)

Whale bone box, carved in relief with figurative scenes drawn from classical mythology, Christian and Jewish tradition and Germanic legend. Romulus and Remus, the Adoration of the Magi, the Sack of Jerusalem and the revenge of Weland the Smith are recognisable, together with two other scenes from Germanic legend which cannot be identified with certainty. Each panel, with the exception of the incomplete lid, has an accompanying inscription; these are mostly in runes and in Old English, but on the back panel, move briefly into Latin and the Roman alphabet.

This unique object is modelled in its construction, layout and iconographical programme on a late antique ivory reliquary of a type similar to the Brescia casket. Through contacts with the Roman church, such things were certainly reaching England by the later 7th century, and must have been immensely influential in the subsequent development of narrative and exegetical art in England. In particular, they offered new ways of dealing with, at one level, narrative, and at another, complex iconographical programmes. The mixed, but carefully structured, iconography of the Franks Casket suggests that it was made for a courtly rather than ecclesiastical purpose, but its clearly learned content implies manufacture in a monastic milieu; in particular, the subtle deployment of language and script to suit the context, and the flamboyant manner of the text's execution, seem to treat the text as if it were an integral part of the visual image – in a way very close to that seen in contemporary manuscripts.

BM, MLA 1867, 1–20, 1. Gift of A. W. Franks. Auzon, Haut-Loire, France. Anglo-Saxon (Northumbria), first half of 8th century.

Napier 1901; Page 1973, 66–8, 174–82, 188–9 and refs; Webster and Backhouse (eds) 1991, no. 70 and refs.

117 Late Roman Christian narrative: ivory panels from a casket

Four ivory panels carved in high relief with scenes from the Passion of Christ; they originally formed the side panels of a square box with a lid. As well as manuscripts, sculpture and Roman panel paintings of the kind described by Bede, other late antique models influenced the development of Anglo-Saxon and other

Insular exegetical and narrative art. Ivories such as these certainly entered England (cat. 116), suggesting new ways in which complex messages could be presented.

BM, MLA 1856, 6–23, 4–7. Maskell Collection. Rome, between about 420 and 430.

Dalton 1901, cat. 291; Delbrueck 1929, 95–8; Buckton (ed) 1994, no. 45 and refs.

INTEGRATING ANTIQUE AND INDIGENOUS TRADITIONS

Although the figurative art and comparative naturalism of late antique and early Christian art would appear ill-matched with the exuberant decorative and stylised approach of the Insular artist, these traditions were successfully synthesised to produce a distinctive mode of visual expression redolent of the cultural melting-pot of the early Middle Ages. As 'Caesar' joins Woden in the Anglo-Saxon genealogies, so images derived from Byzantine mosaics could be integrated with decoration influenced by English brooches.

118 The Royal Bible: the fusion of Mediterranean imagery with English ornament (pl. 68)

This once magnificent volume reflects an early introduction into England of Carolingian influence in book production. In its lavish use of gold, silver and purple pages it is redolent of Byzantine culture and of the Court School of Charlemagne (cat. 80). The bust of Christ finds its closest parallel in the mosaics of Ravenna, the former Byzantine power-base in the West, and the naturalistic style of its figural painting is fused with display lettering in contemporary southern English ('Tiberius group') style with 'Trewhiddle style' metalwork influence. Standing at the end of the Insular period, it reflects a renewed rapprochement with antiquity and the Continent, well-integrated with indigenous culture.

BL, Royal MS I.E.vi, ff. 42v–43. Bible (frag.), opening of St. Luke's Gospel. Vellum; ff. ii + 78; 467 × 345 mm. Latin; 9th century (c.820–40). Canterbury (?St. Augustine's).

CLA ii, nos 214, 245, 262 and Suppl. 5; Alexander 1978, no. 32; Webster and Backhouse (eds) 1991, no. 171; Budny 1985.

119 The enduring animal style: the Pentney Hoard

Six silver disc brooches, some with niello inlay and one with a gilded base plate. Buried together for safekeeping in what is today, and was probably then, a parish churchyard, these splendid brooches reflect the continuing interplay of classical and Germanic themes in Anglo-Saxon visual art, here seen in the so-called 'Trewhiddle' style. On most of these, the image of the tree of life, the fruiting vine of classical tradition that also represents Christ in unity with creation, is grafted onto the ever-inventive traditional animal ornament.

BM, MLA 1980, 10–8, 1–6. Pentney, Norfolk. Anglo-Saxon, early 9th century.

Webster and Backhouse (eds) 1991, no. 187 and ref.

INTEGRATED TEXT AND IMAGE

The integration of text, script and image was one of the most important and influential aspects of Insular book production. Germanic and Celtic ornament, with its established connotations of power and wealth, were applied to that new symbol of authority, the book, giving rise to the development of the decorated word as an icon in its own right. Textual openings were articulated by ever more elaborate initials and display script, in which motif and meaning were embedded. Insular artists seem to have invented the historiated initial, a letter which contains an image related to the text, the ultimate expression of such integration and one which was to be of enduring importance in medieval art.

120 The Cathach ('Battler') of Columcille (photograph): introducing decoration as textual articulation

This is amongst the earliest of Insular manuscripts and was traditionally thought to be the Psalter which occasioned St. Columba's voluntary religious exile (*peregrinatio*) from Ireland resulting from a charge of plagiarism. It is now generally dated later, but its association with Columba (Columcille) led to its enshrinement and its later medieval role of preceding armies into battle. The book exerted a powerful role as cult object and talisman in the post-Roman world. The Irish, followed by the English, were quick to introduce their own ornamental repertoires, with their connotations of wealth and prestige, into the new medium of the book. Here the initial grows in stature and the letters following gradually diminish in scale ('diminuendo'). Such devices are not purely decorative, but serve to highlight important breaks in the text, such as lections (to be read in the liturgy). Its script represents one of the earliest surviving examples of the Irish response to the middle-grade handwriting of the clerics of late antiquity by whom they were introduced to Christianity and to full literacy.

Dublin, Royal Irish Academy, MS s.n., f. 19. Psalter (Cathach of Columcille). Vellum; ff. 58; 200 × 130 mm. Latin; ?early 7th century. Ireland.

CLA ii, no. 266; Alexander 1978, no. 4; Brown 1993, 221–41.

121 The Vespasian Psalter (photograph): integrating text, script and image

This romanising work, produced at Canterbury around 725, contains what are probably the earliest historiated (story-telling) initials, in which aspects of the iconography of David are explored. Here, protecting his flocks from the lion, he simultaneously symbolises Christ, the Good Shepherd. In the early medieval West, the potential idolatry inherent in images was overcome by an emphasis upon their didactic qualities (Pope Gregory the Great – 'in them the illiterate read') and by validation through association with text (inscriptions, miniatures in books, etc.). The Insular world was instrumental in achieving this fusion of text, script and image, embodied in the historiated initial.

See cat. 66, f. 53.

122 Historiated initial and Visigothic Minuscule Script: word and image

In Spain and Gaul human figures were also occasionally used in initials, where they assume the form of the letter ('anthropomorphic initials'). Here the archangel Gabriel forms an initial I and announces the coming of Christ to the Virgin.

BL, Additional MS 30844, ff. 40v–41. Offices and Masses of the Mozarabic Liturgy; rite for Saints' Days, from the Annunciation (15 Dec.). Vellum; ff. ii + 179; 393 × 300 mm. Latin; 10th century. Spain (?Silos).

Brown 1990, no. 15; Férotin 1897; Collins 1995.

123 Chi-rho page, the Book of Kells (photograph): the Word made word

From the 7th century onwards the major openings of texts ('incipits') attracted more and more decoration in Insular manuscripts. This trend reached its zenith in the Book of Kells, a veritable encyclopaedia of Insular art and thought. Here the chi-rho ('XP'), 'Christ' in Greek, occupies virtually the whole page

and has become an icon in its own right. It is as much a depiction of Christ as an image of him would be – literally the Word (Christ as *Logos*) made word. Such non-figural representations might even have carried more complex spiritual connotations. Iconographic details (figures and motifs imbued with theological meaning) have also been introduced into the decorated incipits (fish, moths and other symbols of Christianity and resurrection, figures of deacons and biblical characters, etc.).

Dublin, Trinity College Library, MS 58, f. 34. Gospel book. Vellum; ff. 340; 330 × 250 mm. Latin; ?c.800. Ireland, Scotland (possibly Iona) or Northumbria.

CLA ii, no. 274; Alexander 1978, no. 52; facs. Alton and Meyer 1951; facs. Meehan *et al.* 1991; Henry 1974; O'Mahony 1995.

LAYERS OF MEANING: THE MULTIVALENT IMAGE

The Insular mind loved complexity and multivalence – why settle for one meaning when several could be simultaneously conveyed? Ostensibly narrative images could also carry several layers of meaning in Insular art. Exegetical texts expounding theological meaning, and the relationship of images to the liturgical functions of their accompanying texts, can often help in their interpretation. The reading of such complex and literate images would probably always have taken place on a number of levels, from the deliberations and intellectual game-playing of their ecclesiastical authors, through their explanation to the devout, to straightforward veneration by the faithful.

124 St. Luke, the Book of Cerne: a multivalent image (pl. 69)

The evangelist miniatures in this Mercian devotional compilation are indebted to a number of cultural sources (English, Celtic, Roman, Byzantine), as are its texts. They adopt an unusual format; when the human figures of the Gospel-writers and their symbols (Matthew the Man, Mark the Lion, Luke the Ox, John the Eagle) are shown together the symbol usually fulfils a secondary, identifying role. Here the relationship between human and symbolic representations is reversed and the inscriptions give the key that these images should be read in several ways simultaneously: the evangelists as human authors; the evangelists as symbols (e.g. Luke's Gospel emphasising the immolatory aspect of the human Christ – the sacrificial victim denoted by the calf); Christ in his human (incarnate) form; a symbolic aspect of Christ (the sacrificial victim of the

Crucifixion – emphasised here in an allusion to Philippians 2.7 in the inscription); the aspirations of the faithful in partaking of Christ's redemptive role.

Cambridge, University Library, MS Ll.1.10, ff. 21v–22. Prayerbook. Vellum; ff. 98; 230 × 184 mm. Latin and Old English; 9th century (820–40, ?c.818–30). Mercia (?Lichfield).

Alexander 1978, no. 66; Ker 1957, no. 27; Webster and Backhouse (eds) 1991, no. 165; Kuypers 1902; Brown 1996.

125 The Temptation, the Book of Kells (photograph): narrative and metaphor

This image simultaneously represents the Temptation of Christ on the roof of the Temple and a metaphorical depiction of the concept of the Communion of Saints – the Church (here physically the Temple) representing the faithful on earth, with Christ as their head (literally here). The Church Triumphant (the saints in heaven) might be the onlookers, and the Church Expectant (those awaiting salvation in purgatory) those below.

See cat. 123, f. 202v.

Language, alphabets and scripts

LATIN AND THE WRITTEN VERNACULARS

The feat of creating a Christian learned tradition for sophisticated but largely illiterate societies is a tribute both to the abilities of those societies and to those who undertook their initial instruction. Insular schools and manuscripts were to play a strategic role in the transmissions of elements of late antique culture to the Middle Ages and were to add significantly to the learned traditions of the Christian Church. But first the linguistic problems had to be confronted and the mechanics of book production established, sometimes with reference to the Mediterranean world and sometimes as experimental ventures.

126 An Irish epic, the Táin: from oral tradition to written text

The Táin ('The Cattle Raid of Cooley') is a major Irish epic. It deals with the expansion of Connaught at the expense of Ulster through means of a tale of an armed host attempting to abduct a famous Ulster bull, involving the exploits of the hero Cú Chulainn. The epic was first committed to writing in the early Christian period, but linguistic features and details

described in the text indicate that it may already have enjoyed centuries of oral currency, originating during the Iron Age. The Irish love of learning and their interest in language and grammar meant that the process of adopting writing and of learning Latin as a foreign language, as an adjunct to their conversion from the 5th century onwards, rapidly stimulated them to produce writing in their own language (Old Irish). In this they, and the English, were far ahead of the rest of Europe.

BL, Egerton MS 93, ff. 29v–30. The Táin Bó Cuailnge (The Cattle Raid of Cooley). Vellum; ff. 125; 230 × 155 mm. Old Irish; 16th-century additions to a MS of 1477. Ireland.

Flower 1926, ii, 434–7; Kinsella 1979.

127 Beowulf (digitised facsimile): the Old English heroic epic

Christian and pagan imagery are entwined in this epic tale of the hero Beowulf and other of the forebears of the Anglo-Saxons. Opinion varies concerning its date. It survives in a charred single copy of around 1000, but was probably also recited in oral versions. Correspondences in detail to archaeological evidence suggest to some a date for the earliest version around the time of the early Germanic settlements whilst others prefer to see this version as the result of renewed pagan influence by the Vikings at the time that this written copy was made.

BL, Cotton MS Vitellius A.xv (part ii). Vellum; ff. 116; approx. 195 × 120 mm. Old English; c.1000 (composite volume).

Zupitza 1959; Malone 1963; Chase 1981; Kiernan 1981; Webster and Backhouse (eds) 1991, no. 4.

128 The Codex Argenteus (facsimile): Ulfila and the invention of written Gothic (pl. 10)

Ulfila (c.311–83) is known as the 'Apostle of the Goths'. Of Cappadocian ancestry, he was born among the Goths. Trained and consecrated as a bishop in Constantinople, he returned to the Goths of Moesia II, and those beyond the confines of the Empire, as a missionary and, viewing access to Scripture in their own language as an essential element in his mission, translated the Bible into the Gothic language. This was a crucial first step in the process of developing the written vernaculars of the successor states and foreshadows the Insular experience. The adherence of Ulfila and the Goths to the Arian heresy was to prejudice their cultural and political success, alienating them from the Church and minimising their contribution. This splendid copy of the Gospels in Gothic, in silver and gold on purple pages, was made in Ravenna for the Ostrogothic king, Theoderic.

Uppsala, UB, DG I, f. 97. Gospel book ('Codex Argenteus'). Vellum; ff. 180; 244 × 200 mm. Gothic; 500–25. Ravenna.

Facs., University of Uppsala 1927; Olsen and Nordenfalk 1952, no. 6.

129 Latin/Old English glossary: learning Latin as a foreign language

Although the British (Welsh) church and its schools continued to use Latin in the post-Roman period, they eschewed contact with the illiterate pagan Germanic settlers. Nevertheless, within a century and half of St. Augustine's mission to Kent (597) English schools were the most renowned in Europe. Instrumental in this were Theodore of Tarsus and Hadrian, from Africa, who were despatched by the Pope to Canterbury to become archbishop and abbot (respectively). The programme of liberal arts (a christianised version of the education system of late antiquity) and the knowledge of Latin, Greek and even Hebrew which they promoted were to produce scholars of international stature, such as Aldhelm, Bede and Alcuin. Their classroom teaching is reflected in the Latin glossaries in which they explained terms derived from a number of texts, or gave them English translations. As with the missions, the language-learning task confronting both Mediterranean scholar and English pupil must have been formidable and presumably involved, on occasion, translators of some sort.

BL, Cotton MS Cleopatra A.iii, ff. 76v–77. Glossary. Vellum; ff. 117; 165 × 115 mm. Latin with Old English gloss; mid-10th century. Canterbury (St Augustine's).

Wright and Wülcker 1884; Ker 1957, no. 143; Lapidge 1986; Webster and Backhouse (eds) 1991, 71–4.

130 Graeco-Latin glossary: the study of ancient languages

A knowledge of Greek was also transmitted, along with Latin, to post-Roman Europe, via the intermediary of the Church and its schools. Graeco-Latin glossaries such as this would probably have been used in teaching Greek in the monastic schools of Italy and France. Insular scholars were also acquainted with Greek. It is often unclear what levels of proficiency were achieved by either teacher or pupil, however (cat. 143–4).

BL, Harley MS 5792, ff. 112v–113. Pseudo-Cyril, Glossary. Vellum; ff. 278; 293 × 220 mm. Greek and Latin; 8th century. Italy or France (?Laon).

CLA ii, no. 203; Berschin 1980; Bodden 1988.

131 Old English glosses to the Vespasian Psalter (photograph): the earliest extant translation of part of the Bible into English

By the early 8th century, when Bede worked on a translation of St. John's Gospel, the translation of the Bible into English had already begun. The earliest surviving witness to this process is the Vespasian Psalter of c.725, to which an interlinear Old English gloss was added in the mid-9th century. Glosses, either between the lines or in the margins, were an essential stage in the translation and editing process and demonstrate a growing need for vernacular texts, even for use by the Church.

See cat. 66, f. 93v.

132 Carolingian lexicon of Tironian 'notae': a Roman shorthand system transmitted to the Middle Ages

In order to save time and space when writing, abbreviations were introduced in antiquity and grew in use and range during the Middle Ages. One sort of abbreviation is the shorthand symbol, denoting a word or syllable. The most influential shorthand system of antiquity was that devised during the 1st century BC by Tiro, the freedman secretary of Cicero, which was studied and adapted for interpolation in Latin texts, both in Insular and continental writing. This opening shows the thornlike symbol for 'es' and variant symbols for words containing this syllable.

BL, Additional MS 37518, ff. 77v–78. Carolingian lexicon of shorthand symbols originally devised by Cicero's freedman secretary, M. Tullius Tiro. Vellum; ff. iv + 117; 270 × 195 mm. Latin; late 9th century. ?France.

CLA ii, no. 176; Schmitz 1893; New Pal. Soc., pls 132–3.

133 Irish pocket Gospel book: producing books for study

This Gospel book illustrates how the Irish, with the use of an extremely fine quill pen, a tiny Insular cursive minuscule script and judicious use of abbreviations (including Tironian notae) could condense a large amount of text for ease of portability and study.

243

BL, Additional MS 40618, ff. 22v–23. Gospel book. Vellum; ff. 66; 131 × 100 mm. Latin; second half of 8th century. Ireland, ?S.E. (with southern English repainting, of second quarter of 10th century).

CLA ii, no. 179; McGurk 1961, no. 20; Alexander 1978, no. 46.

134 Tools of the monastic trade: writing tablets and styli

a Whale bone writing tablet leaf, with a recess for wax on the inside, and with an interlaced design on the outside; traces of runic text survive on the interior.
Blythburgh, Suffolk.

b Bone and bronze styli.
Whitby, North Yorkshire, from the Anglo-Saxon monastery.

These implements derive directly from the traditions of the classical world, reintroduced into England through the Christian missions.

BM, MLA 1902, 3–15, 1, gift of J. Seymour Lucas; W334, 148, 343, lent by Miss L. Strickland. Anglo-Saxon, 8th century.

Webster and Backhouse (eds) 1991, nos 65 and 107, and refs.

USING ALPHABETS, WHICH, WHERE AND WHY

At the time of the settlement of England, Anglo-Saxons used only the runic alphabet and the vernacular to inscribe short texts on special objects, for example, on a specially made funerary urn (cat. 135), or an amulet (cat. 136b). After Christian Anglo-Saxons adopted the Roman alphabet, the use of runes did not cease; indeed their use was for long preserved in learned ecclesiastical circles, especially for vernacular inscriptions on wood, metalwork, bone and above all, stone, though their use in manuscripts was rare, and confined to very specialised, sometimes cryptic, contexts. On highly sophisticated monuments produced in courtly or ecclesiastical milieux, such as the Franks Casket (cat. 116) and the Ruthwell Cross, careful distinction may be made between the use of runes for the vernacular, and Roman letters for Latin inscriptions.

135 A pagan runic memorial: cremation urn

Hand-made pottery cremation urn with a runic inscription beginning 'siþebæd . . .' The meaning of this particular text (one of the longer ones to survive from the pre-Christian period) is uncertain, but like many early inscriptions, it seems to focus on a personal name.

BM, MLA 1963, 10–1, 14. Loveden Hill, Lincolnshire, from the Anglo-Saxon cemetery, cremation 61.A/11/261. Anglo-Saxon, early 6th century.

Myres 1977, no. 1437, fig. 369; Odenstedt 1980; Hines 1991, 71.

136 Riddles and charms: two runic rings

a Gold ring with magical runic inscription reading 'ærkriufltkriuriþonglæstæpontol'.
Greymoor Hill, near Carlisle, Cumbria. Anglo-Saxon, 9th century.

b Silver ring set with three red glass inlays (two missing) and with a riddling runic inscription in Old English which translates as 'I am called ring'.
Wheatley Hill, Co. Durham. Anglo-Saxon, 8th century.

Although runes continued to have a particular currency in learned circles, they still played a role in popular culture, especially on rings, which often bore amuletic inscriptions.

BM, MLA OA 10262; 1995, 9–2, 1, gift of the British Museum Society.

Wilson 1964, no. 27, 73–5; Webster 1995.

ENGLISH RUNIC COINS

Runic inscriptions are found on some gold Anglo-Saxon coins of the 7th century struck in the south-east and probably in York. Where legible, they are usually simply moneyers' names. From the early 8th century runes are particularly associated with East Anglian and, more rarely, with Northumbrian coins. The occasional runic letter is still found on coins of these areas into the early 9th century.

137 Runic coin-pendant, late 5th–early 6th century

Gold solidus pendant, traces of a suspension loop. It is struck, not cast, and is inscribed in runes 'skanomodu' which has been interpreted as a personal name in runes of Frisian origin.

BM, CM acquired in 1824 from the collection of King George III.

BMC Anglo-Saxon I, 1, no. 1; Page 1973, 186–8, Page 1996.

138 Anglo-Saxon coin, c.675

Base gold shilling (*tremissis*/'thrymsa'), possibly struck at London, inscribed in runes 'pada', the name of the moneyer.

BM, CM acquired before 1838.

BMC Anglo-Saxon I, 23, no. 1; Metcalf 1 1993, 73–9.

139 Coin of Beonna, king of the East Angles, 749–c.760 or later

Base silver penny ('sceat') inscribed in Roman capitals, BEONNA REX.

BM, CM 1992, 11–35–30, pres. British Museum Society. Excavated at Burrow Hill, Suffolk.

Archibald 1985; Archibald and Fenwick 1995; Rogerson 1995.

140 Coin of Beonna, king of the East Angles, 759–c.760 or later

Base silver penny ('sceat') inscribed in mixed Latin capitals and runes, 'bEOnna rEx'.

BM, CM 1982, 4–9–12. From the Middle Harling, Norfolk, hoard, 1980–3.

Archibald 1985; Rogerson 1995.

141 Coin of Beonna, king of the East Angles, 749–c.760 or later

Base silver penny ('sceat') inscribed completely in runes 'beonna rex'.

BM, CM 1982, 4–9–37. From the Middle Harling, Norfolk, hoard, 1980–3.

Archibald 1985; Rogerson 1995.

The three coins (cat. 139–41), which were struck almost contemporaneously, show Roman capitals and runes being used interchangably to set out a Latin inscription.

Fig. 104 Base silver pennies of Beonna, king of the East Angles, showing interchangeable use of runes and Roman letters, cat. 139, 140, 141.

142 A Celtic bilingual memorial: stone monument

Stone commemorative pillar with inscriptions in ogham and Roman characters; both commemorate a man, Maccutrenus Salicidunus. The figurative and other carvings on the stone belong to a later re-use. The Celtic peoples of western and northern Britain continued to write in Latin and Roman characters after the end of Roman rule, which was in places supplemented by the use of ogham script, an alphabetic system based on knowledge of the Roman alphabet, which originated in Ireland, and came to Britain through Irish settlements in Wales and Scotland.

BM, MLA 1878, 11–2, 1. Pentre Poeth farm, Trianglas parish, Trecastle, Breconshire, Wales. Celtic, 5th–6th century.

Macalister 1945, no. 341; Nash-Williams 1950, no. 71.

SCRIPT AS A CULTURAL SIGNIFIER

The use of a certain language or script could carry cultural and even political overtones. Just as runes would be used for Old English inscriptions, so minuscule scripts were favoured for texts in English, especially as the earliest examples of these were written in tiny script between the lines of Latin texts. The introduction of words or characters in Greek were an exotic element; they were obviously thought to display a cosmopolitan knowledge of Mediterranean culture, or were imbued with a talismanic quasi-magical quality.

143 Chi-rho page, Gospels (with added Old English manumission of Eadhelm by King Athelstan): perceptions of the written word

This early 8th-century Northumbrian Gospel book is perhaps closer to the working service-book end of the spectrum of production than cult objects such as the Lindisfarne Gospels. Its decorated incipits are not as grand, but its artist/scribe was out to display a cosmopolitan, erudite knowledge of Greek. Sadly this backfired. He has mistaken the Greek 'P' of the chi-rho ('XP', Christ in Greek) for a Latin **p** and has substituted the Greek letter 'pi', thereby making a nonsense of the word. The use of a different alphabet as a cultural signifier did not necessarily denote understanding (fig. 105).

Another interesting indicator of Insular perceptions of writing lies in the later addition of a document freeing slaves – association of documents with liturgical volumes carried extra bonuses for the

Fig. 105 Detail of chi-rho page from a Northumbrian Gospel book, with misunderstood use of the Greek alphabet, cat. 143.

soul of the donor and also bestowed heightened authority as legal evidence.

The script of the original text is a fine Insular half-uncial – an indigenous response to the high-grade book scripts of antiquity. The addition is in an Anglo-Saxon minuscule – an indigenous lower-grade script, but one that was infinitely more legible than Roman cursive hands (cat. 42).

BL, Royal MS 1.B.vii, ff. 15v–16. Gospel book. Vellum; ff. 155; 275 × 215 mm. Latin (with Old English addition of c.925); first half of 8th century. Northumbria.

CLA ii, no. 213; Alexander 1978, no. 20; Bodden 1988; Webster and Backhouse (eds) 1991, no. 84.

144 The Royal Prayerbook: a passing acquaintance with Greek

This Mercian prayerbook displays an acquaintance with Greek, but seems to include it primarily for its talismanic qualities, in a quasi-magical fashion (like the modern use of 'abracadabra'), in association with prayers and charms of healing.

BL, Royal MS 2.A.xx, ff. 49v–50. Prayerbook. Vellum; ff. 52; 233 × 170 mm. Latin, with added Old English glosses; first quarter of 9th century. Mercia (?Worcester).

CLA ii, no. 215; Alexander 1978, no. 35; Bodden 1988; Webster and Backhouse (eds) 1991, no. 163; Kuypers 1902, 200–25.

COINS WITH MONOGRAMS

Monograms, known in western Europe from Byzantine coins and seals, were used on coins for kings' names (cat. 28), mint names, and moneyers' names. They are not common on coins outside Italy, which had closer ties with Byzantium, until Charlemagne adopted a monogram of his name as a coinage type. Anglo-Saxon monograms on coins were derived at second hand from Francia.

145 Coin of the eastern Roman emperor Marcian, 450–7

Bronze coin with the emperor's monogram.

BM, CM 1930, 7–9–15, pres. L. A. Lawrence.

RIC X, no. 545.

146 Municipal coin of Ravenna, 536–40

Bronze 10 nummi with the monogram of the city name on the reverse.

BM, CM 1844, 4–25–1758.

BMC Vandals etc., 107, no. 36; Grierson and Blackburn 1986, 38.

147 Merovingian coin struck at 'Atunberix' or 'Autuberix', early 7th century

Gold tremissis from a mint in the Rodez area with the monogram of the moneyer's name, Bertulfus(?).

BM, CM 1939, 10–3–19. From the Sutton Hoo Mound I burial, 1939, pres. Mrs E. M. Pretty.

Kent 1975, 644, no. 37.

148 Coin of Nemfidius, patrician of Provence, c.700/710

Base silver denier with the monogram of the principal letters of the patrician's name.

BM, CM pres. Count de Salis, c.1860.

Grierson and Blackburn 1986, 142–4 and 147–9.

149 Coin of Archbishop Wulfred of Canterbury, 805–32

Silver penny with the monogram of the mint name c.810–15; the earliest monogram on an English coin.

BM, CM 1893, 12–4–61, pres. A. W. (later Sir Augustus) Franks.

BMA no. 202.

In the post-Roman world the script system of late antiquity continued in certain areas, notably Italy and Francia in the West, but rather like the romance languages it began to assume a regional and somewhat debased form. Other areas developed their own scripts, with varying degrees of Roman influence. Such was the case in Ireland, which had never formed part of the Roman Empire and which escaped the influence of the less formal business hands of antiquity, taking as its starting point the educated middle-grade hands of the clerics responsible for introducing Christianity. Coupled with increasing influence from Rome following the papal mission to the English, the Insular hierarchy of scripts emerged, from uncials and half-uncials for luxurious liturgical volumes to minuscules for lesser grade works and documents. So successful was this system (as were the scripts of Visigothic Spain and Beneventan Italy) that they resisted the uniformity of Caroline minuscule which was promoted as part of a policy of textual (and quasi-cultural) uniformity by the Carolingian emperor Charlemagne and his circle and which swept throughout the West from around 800. In 10th–11th-century England Anglo-Saxon minuscule script and Caroline minuscule would finally appear side-by-side, the former used for English and the latter for Latin, and the processes of integration and transformation would be completed.

150 Uncial script: the major book script of the Graeco-Roman world

The script of this Italian Gospel book is uncial, the major formal bookhand of antiquity. Manuscripts produced in Rome under Pope Gregory the Great, around 600, are produced in this style and would have accompanied the early missionaries to England, serving to inspire Insular scripts.

BL, Harley MS 1775, ff. 265v–266. Gospel book. Vellum; ff. 469 + 1*; 177 × 120 mm. Latin; 6th century. Italy.

CLA ii, no. 197; Brown 1990, no. 5.

151 Merovingian uncial script: continuity of form

Higher grade books produced in post-Roman Gaul continued to use uncial script, as well as cursives (cat. 43) and minuscules (cat. 110) for less formal items. Certain letter-forms, such as **t**, assumed distinctive forms as the script evolved, giving it a regional character.

BL, Burney MS 340, ff. 27v–28. Origen, *Homiliæ de*

Visionibus Balaam. Vellum; ff. iii + 60; 312 × 225 mm. Latin; 7th century. France (?Corbie).

CLA ii, no. 182; Zimmermann 1916, 72, 201.

152 Leaf from one of the Ceolfrith Bibles (the Greenwell leaf): English uncial script, reinventing antiquity

Leaf from one of three Bibles made for Ceolfrith, Abbot of Monkwearmouth/Jarrow, before he left for Rome in 716. The elegant, restrained layout and the uncial script, modelled on Roman examples of the time of Gregory the Great, are conscious evocations and emulations of the early Christian, and specifically Roman, past. This volume was presented by King Offa to Worcester Cathedral in the late 8th century, by which time it was already thought to have been produced in Rome, rather than Northumbria.

BL, Additional MS 37777. Bible (frag.). Vellum; f. 1; 460 × 320 mm. Latin; before 716. Northumbria (Monkwearmouth/Jarrow).

CLA ii, no. 177; Webster and Backhouse (eds) 1991, no. 87; Bischoff and Brown 1985, 351–2.

153 Caroline minuscule, script and politics: Pisces and Perseus from Cicero, 'Aratea'

From the late 8th century a script known as Caroline minuscule was developed (initially in centres such as Corbie, Tours and the Palace School) and was promoted by the Emperor Charlemagne and his scholarly English adviser, Alcuin of York, as an adjunct of their attempts to establish liturgical, textual and cultural uniformity throughout a disparate and transient empire. By the mid-9th century it was in general use throughout Carolingian territory, only those area which had escaped annexation and which had already evolved acceptable, legible script systems of their own initially avoiding its use – namely Britain, Ireland, Visigothic Spain and the Duchy of Benevento in Italy. Caroline minuscule was to form the base of many later medieval hands and its revival in the Renaissance inspired early type-faces.

Pisces and Perseus, from a late example of a classical astronomical poem written in Caroline minuscule and illuminated by an Anglo-Saxon artist working abroad.

BL, Harley MS 2506, ff. 36v–37. Cicero's Latin translation of the *Phaenomena* of Aratus of Soli. Vellum; ff. 93; 293 × 212 mm. Latin; late 10th century. France (?Fleury).

Temple 1976, no. 42; Backhouse, Turner and Webster (eds) 1984, no. 43.

154 The Book of Nunnaminster: Insular minuscule script

During the post-Roman period Britain and Ireland were left to establish their own system of scripts, rather than perpetuating traditions as on the Continent. This was guided by form and function (the script of a shopping list or letter is not appropriate for high-grade books) and took as its starting point the middle-grade handwriting of the educated of late antiquity – in this case the clergy. Uncial (cat. 152) and an Insular version of half-uncial (cat. 143) were developed upwards from this (under increasing influence from Rome) and a more cursive (rapider lower-case) minuscule evolved for less formal use, as seen in this Mercian prayerbook. Its confrontation of issues of legibility (including word separation, a device introduced by the Irish to clarify sense during silent reading, rather than the oration practised in antiquity) may have contributed to its continued use in England (even after the introduction of Caroline minuscule there in the 10th century) and its use in Ireland into modern times.

BL, Harley MS 2965, ff. 36v–37. Prayerbook. Vellum; ff. 41; 215 × 160 mm. Latin, with Old English glosses; first quarter of 9th century. Mercia.

CLA ii. no. 199; Ker 1957, no. 237; Alexander 1978, no. 41; Webster and Backhouse (eds) 1991, no. 164; Birch 1889.

155 The Easter office (with neumatic musical notation): Visigothic minuscule script

With its fusion of elements of antique scripts, Visigothic minuscule was amongst the more successful national hands and had achieved a developed form by the 8th–9th century. It withstood the incursion of Caroline minuscule (just as parts of Spain avoided Carolingian rule, the Islamic authorities tolerating continued Mozarabic Christian culture to some extent), surviving into the 12th century.

BL, Additional MS 30850, ff. 105v–106. Antiphoner. Vellum; ff. 243; 330 × 250 mm. Latin; 11th century. Spain.

Férotin 1897; Collins 1995.

156 The Monte Cassino Psalter: Beneventan minuscule script

Beneventan minuscule was another independent 'national' hand. Evolved from the mid-8th century onwards in the Duchy of Benevento, in centres such as Monte Cassino, it survived in parts of southern Italy until around 1300, and into the 15th century in some conservative centres.

BL, Additional MS 18859, ff. 31v–32. Psalter. Vellum; ff. 100; 203 × 130 mm. Latin; first quarter of 12th century. Southern Italy, Benevento (Monte Cassino). Lowe 1914, 340; Turner 1966, 25.

157 'The Marvels of the East': a bi-lingual, bi-scriptual book with Caroline minuscule and Anglo-Saxon minuscule scripts

Insular minuscule was bequeathed to the England of Alfred the Great, following the Viking incursions of the 9th century, and formed the basis of Anglo-Saxon minuscule which survived until after the Norman Conquest in 1066. The ecclesiastical reforms of the second half of the 10th century, conducted under strong continental influence, led to the adoption of Caroline minuscule – but only for texts written in Latin. Old English continued to be written in Anglo-Saxon minuscule and the two may be seen side-by-side in bi-lingual manuscripts such as this copy, with English translation, of the late antique *Marvels of the East*. Here the varied cultural experiences of the heirs of Rome were finally acknowledged, integrated and reconciled.

BL, Cotton MS Tiberius, B.v (part i), ff. 80v–81. Scientific Treatises; Ants as large as dogs, camels, an elephant and the bifrons Liconia, from the *Marvels of the East*. Vellum; ff. 88; 260 × 220 mm. Latin and Old English; second quarter of 11th century. Canterbury (Christ Church).

Temple 1976, no. 87; Backhouse, Turner and Webster (eds) 1984, no. 164; facs. McGurk 1983; James 1929.

Bibliography

General bibliography to the essays (pp 8–127)

ALEXANDRE-BIDON, D. and TREFFORT, C., (eds), 1993, *A réveiller les morts. La mort au quotidien dans l'Occident médiéval*, Lyons

ARCE, J., 1982, Los caballos de Symmaco, *Faventia*, 35ff

ARCE, J., 1988 *España entre el mundo antiguo y ei mundo medieval*, Madrid

ARCE, J., 1992, Los villae romanas no son monasterios, *AEspA* 65, 32ff

ARCE, J., 1993, Los mosaicos come documentos para la historia de Hispania tardia, *AEspA* 265ff.

ARCE, J., 1994, *El último siglo de la Hispania romana (284–409)*, Alianza Ed., 2nd edn

ARCHER, S., 1979, Late Roman gold and silver coin hoards in Britain, in P.J. Casey (ed.), *The End of Roman Britain*. British Archaeological Reports, British Series 71, 29–64

BARATTE, F., 1993, *La vaisselle d'argent en Gaule dans l'Antiquité tardive*, Paris

BARRAL I ALTET, X., 1978, *La circulation des monnaies suèves et visigotiques. Contribution à l'histoire économique du royaume visigot*. Supplements to Francia 4

BASSETT, S., (ed.), 1989, *The Origins of Anglo-Saxon Kingdoms*, Leicester

BERSCHIN, W., 1986–91, *Biographie und Epochenstil im lateinischen Mittelalter*, 3 vols, Stuttgart

BLOEMERS, J.H.F., 1969, Ein spätrömischer Goldmünzenfund aus Obbicht, Prov. Limburg, *Berichten van de Rijksdienst voor het Ouheidkundig Bodemonderzoek* 19, 73–80

BÖHNER, K., 1958, *Die fränkischen Altertümer des Trierer landes*, Berlin

BONNET, C., 1977, Les premiers édifices chrétiens de la Madeleine à Genève, *Mémoirs et documents publiées par la Société d'Histoire et d'Archeologie de Genève*, I, VII.

BOLIN, St., 1929, Die römischen und byzantinischen Münzen im freien Germanien, *Bericht der Römisch-Germanischen Kommission*, 19, 86–145

BORGOLTE, M., 1985, Stiftergrab und Eigenkirches: ein Begriffspaar der Mittelalterarchäologie in historischer Kritik, *Zeitschrift für Archäologie des Mittelalters* 13, 27–38

BOST, J.-P., CAMPO, M. and GURT, J.M., 1992, Trouvailles d'aurei et de solidi dans la péninsule ibérique, in C. Brenot and X. Loriot (eds), *L'or monnayé III: Trouvailles de monnaies d'or dan l'occident romain*. Cahiers Ernest Babelon 4, 33–89

BROWN, P., 1971, *The World of Late Antiquity*, London

BROWN, P., 1981, *The Cult of the Saints*, London

BROWN, P., 1996, *The Rise of Western Christendom*, Oxford

BROWN, T.S., 1984, *Gentlemen and Officers, Imperial Administration and Aristocratic Power in Byzantine Italy, AD 554–800*, Rome

BRUCE-MITFORD, R.L.S., 1975–83, *The Sutton Hoo Ship Burial*, 3 vols, London

BULLOUGH, D., 1983, Burial, Community and Belief in the Early Medieval West, in P. Wormald *et al.* (eds), *Ideal and Reality in Frankish and Anglo-Saxon Society, Studies Presented to J.NM. Wallace-Hadrill* Oxford, 177–201

CAHN, H.A. & KAUFMANN-HEINIMANN, A.M., (eds) 1984, *Der spätrömische Silberschatze von Kaiseraugst*. Basler Beiträge zur Ur-und Frühgeschichte 9

CAILLET, J.-P., 1985, *L'Antiquité classique, le haut moyen-âge et Byzance au musée de Cluny*, Paris

CAMERON, A., 1970, *Agathias*, Oxford

CAMERON, A., 1985, *Procopius and the Sixth Century*, London

CAMERON, A., 1991, *Christianity and the Rhetoric of Empire*, Berkeley and Los Angeles

CAMERON, A., 1993, *The Mediterranean World in Late Antiquity, AD 395–600*, London/New York

CAMPBELL, J., (ed.) 1982, *The Anglo-Saxons*, Oxford

CHADWICK, H., 1981, *Boethius: the consolations of music, theology, logic, theology and philosophy*, Oxford

CHRISTLEIN, R., 1978, *Die Alamannen. Archäologie eines lebendigen Volkes*, Stuttgart

CHRYSOS, E., 1972, *To Byzantio kai hoi Gotthoi*, Athens

CHRYSOS, E. & SCHWARCZ, A., (eds) 1989, *Das Reich und die Barbaren*, VIÖG 29, Vienna

CLAUDE, D., 1970, *Geschichte der Westgoten*, Stuttgart

CLAUDE, D., 1973, Beiträge zur Geschichte der frühmittelalterlichen Königsschätze, *Early Medieval Studies* 7. Antikvariskt archiv 54, 5–24

CLAUDE, D., *Der Handel im westlichen Mittelmeer während des Frühmittelalters (Untersuchen zu Handel und Verkehr der vorund frühgeschichtlichen Zeit in Mittel-und Nordeuropa, II)*, Göttingen

COLARDELLE, M., 1983, *Sépultures et traditions funéraires du Ve au VIIIe siècle dans les Alpes française du Nord*, Grenoble

COLLINS, R., 1983, *Early Medieval Spain*, London

CONTAMINE, P., BOMPAIRE, M., LEBECQ, S. and SARRAZIN, J.-L., 1983, *L'economie médiévale*, Paris

COURTOIS, C., 1995, *Les Vandales et l'Afrique*, 2nd edn, Paris

CURLE, A.O., 1923, *The Treasure of Traprain. A Scottish Hoard of Roman Silver Plate*, Glasgow

DEGANI, M., 1959, *Il tesoro romano barbarico di Reggio Emilia*, Florence

DEMANDT, A., 1984, *Der Fall Roms. Die Auflösung des römischen Reiches im Urteil der Nachwelt*, Munich

DEMANDT, A., 1989, *Die Spätantike. Römische Geschichte von Diocletian bis Justinian, 284–565 n. Chr.*, Munich

DIERKENS, A., 1981, Cimetières mérovingiens et histoire du haut Moyen Age. Chronologie-Société-Religion, *Acta Historica Bruxellensia, t.4: Histoire et méthode*, Bruxelles, 15–70

DIERKENS, A., 1991, Interprétation critique des symboles chrétiens sur des objets d'époque mérovingienne, *Actes due colloque tenu au Musée royal de Hongrie et en Wallonie, Actes due colloque tenu au Musée royal de Mariemont du 9 au 11 avril 1979*, Mariemont, 109–24

DOPPELFELD, O., 1960, Das frankische Frauengrab unter dem Chor der Kölner Domes, *Germania*, 89–113

DURAND, M., 1988, *Archéologie du cimetière médiéval au sud-est de l'Oise. Relations avec l'habitat et évolution des rites et des pratiques funéraires du Vie au XVIe siècle*, S.I. 17

DURLIAT, J., 1990, *Les finances publiques de Dioclétien aux Carolingiens*, Signmaringen

DUVAL, N., et al. 1995/96. *Naissance des arts chrétiens. Atlas des monuments paléocrétiens de la France*, Paris

DUVAL, N. et al., 1995/96, *Les premiers monuments chrétiens de la France, t. 1: Sud-est et Corse, t. 2: Sud-Ouest et Centre*, Paris

DUVAL, Y., 1988, *Auprès des saints corps et âme. L'inhumation ad sanctos dans la chrétienité d'Orient et d'Occident du IIIème au VIIème siècle*, Paris

DUVAL, Y. & PICARD, J.-C. (eds), 1986, *L'inhumation privilégiée du IV au VIIIe siècle en Occident*, Actes du colloque tenu IV à Chréteil les 16–18 mars 1984, Paris

DÜWEL, H., JANKUHN, H. SIEMS, H. & TIMPRE, D., (eds) 1985, *Der Handel des frühen Mittelalters (Untersuchungen zu Handel und Verkehr frühgeschichtlichen Zeit in Mittel-und Nordeuropa, III*, Göttingen

DÜWEL, K., JANKUHN, H., SIEMS, H. & TIMPRE, D., (eds) 1987, *Der Handel der Karolinger-und Wikingerzeit (Untersuchungen zu Handel und Verkehr der vor-und frühgeschichtlichen Zeit in Mittel-und Nordeurope, IV*, Göttingen

EFFROS, B., 1994, *From Grave Goods to Christian Epitaphs: Evolution in Burial Tradition and the Expression of Social Status in Merovingian Society* (unpub. diss., University of California)

EFFROS, B., 1997, *De patribus Saxoniae* and the Regulation of Mortuary Custom. A Carolingian Campaign of Christianization or the Suppression of Saxon Identity?, *Revue Belge de Philologie et d'Histoire*, 75 (in press)

ELSNER, J., 1995, *Art and the Roman Viewer*, Cambridge

ERCOLANI COCCHI, E., 1992, Trouvailles de monnaies d'or en Emilie, in C. Brenot and X. Loriot (eds), *L'or monnayé III: Trouvailles de monnaies d'or dans l'occident romain*. Cahiers Ernest-Babelon 4, 129–54

EWIG, E., 1988, *Die Merowinger und das Frankenreich*, Stuttgart

FEHRING, G., 1979, Missions-und Kirchenwesen in archäologischer Sicht, in H. Jankuhn and R. Wenskus (eds), *Geschichtswissenschaft und Archäologie. Untersuchungen zu Siedlungs-, Wirtschafts- und Kirchengeschichte*, Sigmaringen, 547–91

FERNANDEZ CASTRO, M. CRUZ, 1982, *Villas romanas en España*, Madrid

FONTAINE, J., 1959, *Isidore de Séville et la culture classique dans l'Espagne wisigothique*, Paris

FONTAINE, J., 1973, *L'art préroman hispanique*, vol. 1, La Pierre qui-vire

GEARY, P., 1988, *Before France and Germany*, New York

GEISSLINGER, H., 1967, *Horte als Geschichtsquelle dargestellt an den völkerwanderungs-und merowingerzeitlichen Funden des südwestlichen Ostseeraumes*, Offa-Bucher 19

GEISSLINGER, H., 1984, Depotfund, *Reallexikon der Germanischen Altertumskunde*, 2nd edn, vol., 5, 320–38

GEORGE, J. (ed. and transl.), 1995, *Personal and political poems, Venantius Fortunatus*, Liverpool

GIBBON, E., 1981, *The Decline and Fall of the Roman Empire* (abridged version), Harmondsworth

GIBSON, M., 1981, *Boethius, his life, thought and influence*, Oxford

GLOB, P.V., (ed.) 1980, *Danafæ Til Hendes Majestæt Dronning Margrethe II*, Copenhagen

GOFFART, W., 1980, *Barbarians and Romans AD 418–584: The Techniques of Accomodation*, Princeton

GOFFART, W., 1988, *The Narrators of Barbarian History*, Princeton

GORINI, G., 1992, Trouvailles de monnaies d'or de la X Regio: Venetia Histria, in C. Brenot and X. Loriot (eds), *L'or monnayé III: Trouvailles de monnaies d'or dans l'occident romain*. Cahiers Ernest-Babelon 4, 155–214

GRIERSON, P., 1979, *Dark Age Numismatics*, London

GRIERSON, P. & BLACKBURN, M., 1986. *Medieval European Coinage I: The Early Middle Ages (5th–10th centuries), with a catalogue of the coins in the Fitzwilliam Museum, Cambridge*, Cambridge

HAGBERG, U.E., 1984, Opferhorte und Völkerwanderungszeit in Schweden. *Frühmittelalterliche Studien* 18, 73–82

HALSALL, G., 1995, *Early Medieval Cemeteries. An Introduction to Burial Archaeology in the Post-Roman West*, Skelmorlie

HARRISON, D., 1993, *The Early State and the Towns. Forms of Integration in Lombard Italy AD 568–774*, Lund

HAUSER, S.T., 1992, *Spätantike und frühbyzantinische Silberlöffel*, Jahrbuch für Antike und Christentum, suppl. vol. 19

HEATHER, P., 1991, *Goths and Romans, 332–489*, Oxford

HEATHER, P. & MATTHEWS, J.F., 1991, *The Goths in the Fourth Century*, Translated Texts for historians 11, Liverpool

HEDEAGER, 1991, Die danischen Golddepots der Völkerwanderungszeit, *Frühmittelalterliche Studien*, 25, 73–88

HEIDINGA, H.A., 1990, From Kootwijk to Rhenen: in search of the elite in the Central Netherlands in the Early Middle Ages, in J.C. Besteman *et al.* (eds), *Medieval archaeology in the Netherlands. Studies presented to H. H. van Regteren Altena*, 9–40

HEITZ, C., 1980, *L'architecture religieuse carolingienne: les formes et leurs fonctions*, Paris

HENDERSON, G., 1987, *From Durrow to Kells: the insular Gospel Books 650–800*, London

HERRIN, J., 1987, *The Formation of Christendom*, Princeton

HIRSCHFELD, Y., 1992, *The Judean Desert Monasteries in the Byzantine Period*, New Haven

HODGES, R., 1982, *Dark Age Economics. The origin of towns and trade A.D. 600–1000*, London

HODGES, R. & WHITEHOUSE, D., 1983, *Mohammed, Charlemagne and the origins of Europe. Archaeology and the Pirenne thesis*, London

HODGES, R. & HOBLEY, B., (eds) 1985, *The rebirth of town in the West (AD 700–1050)*, London

HÜBENER, W., 1975, Goldblattkreuze auf der Iberischen Halbinsel in W. Hübener (ed.), *Die Goldblattkreuze des frühen Mittelalters*, 85–90

HUBERT, J., PORCHER, J. & VOLBACH, W.F., 1969, *Europe in the Dark Ages*, London

HUNT, E.D., 1981, The traffic in relics: some late Roman evidence, in S. Hackel (ed.), *The Byzantine Saint*, London, 171–80

HUNT, E.D., 1982, *Holy Land Pilgrimage in the Later Roman Empire A.D. 312–460*, Oxford

JARNUT, J., 1982, *Geschichte der Langobarden*, Stuttgart

JOHNS, C., 1994, Romano-British Precious-Metal Hoards: some comments on Martin Millet's paper, in *TRAC 1994. Proceedings of the Fourth Annual Theoretical Roman Archaeology Conference Durham 1994*, 107–17.

JOHNS, C. & BLAND, R., 1993, *The Hoxne Treasure*, London

JOHNS, C. & POTTER, T., 1983, *The Thetford Treasure. Roman Jewellery and Silver*, London

JOHNS, C. & POTTER, T., 1985, The Canterbury Late Roman Treasure, *The Antiquaries Journal* 65, 315–52

JONES, A.H.M., 1964, *The Later Roman Empire*, 3 vols, Oxford

KAISER, R., 1993, *Das römische Erbe und das Merowingerreich*, Munich

KAZANSKI, M., 1991, *Les goths (1er-VIIe siècle aprés J.-C)*, Paris

KENT, J.P.C., 1994, *The Roman Imperial Coinage 10: The divided Empire and the Fall of the Western Parts AD 395–491*, London

KLINGSHIRN, W., 1985, Charity and power: Caesarius of Arles and the ransoming of captives in Sub-Roman Gaul, *Journal of Roman Studies* 75, 183–203

KRAUTHEIMER, R., 1980, *Rome, Profile of a City, 312–1308*

KÜNZL, E., 1993, *Die Alamannenbeute aus dem Rhein bei Neupotz*. Monographien des Römisch-Germanischen Zentralmuseums Mainz, 34

LAFAURIE, J., 1959/60, Le trésor d'Escharen (Pays-Bas), *Revue numismatique*, 6e série, 2, 1959/60, 153–210

LAFAURIE, J., 1991, Imitations d'argentei impériaux du début Ve siècle trouvés dans la sépulture 10, in R. Brulet, *Les fouilles du quartier Saint-Brice à Tournai: L'environnement funéraire de la sépulture de Childéric*, 2, 76–80

DE LASTEYRIE, F., 1860, *Description du trésor de Guarrazar*, Paris

LEBECQ, S., 1983, *Marchands et navigateurs frisons du haut Moyen Age*, 2 vols, Lille

LEBECQ, S., 1990, *Les origines franques, Ve-IXe siècle*, Paris

LENOIR, A., 1867, *Statistique monumentale de Paris*, 2 vols, Paris

LOPOEZ, R.S., 1951, The dollar of the Middle Ages, *Journal of Economic History* XI, 209–34

MacCORMACK, S., 1981, *Art and Ceremony in Late Antiquity*, Berkeley

MacCORMICK, M., 1986, *Eternal Victory. Triumphal Rulership in Late Antiquity, Byzantium and the Early Medieval West*, Cambridge

McGRAIL, S., (ed.) 1990, *Maritime Celts, Frisians and Saxons*, London

McKITTERICK, R., (ed.) 1990, *The Uses of Literacy in Early Medieval Europe*, Cambridge

MARAVAL, P., 1985, *Lieux saints et pèlerinages d'Orient. Histoire et géographie. Des origines à la conquête arabe*, Paris

MATTHEWS, J., 1975, *Western Aristocracies and Imperial Court AD 364–425*, Oxford

MAYEUR, J.-M., PIETRI, C.H. & VAUCHEX, L. & VENARD, M. (eds), 1993, *Histoire du christianisme 4. Évéques, moines et empereurs (610–1054)*, Paris

MERCATI & MERCANTI 1993: *Mercati e Mercanti nell'alto medioevo: l'area euroasiatica e l'area mediterranea* (Settimane di studio del Centro Italiano di studi sull'alto medioevo, XL), Spoleto

MERTENS, J., 1976, *Tombes mérovingiennes et églises chrétiennes*, Bruxelles

MILAN 1990, see Sena-Chiesa 1990

MILAN 1994, *I Goti*, exh. cat., Milan

MOMIGLIANO, A., 1955 Cassiodorus and the Italian Culture of his time, *Proceedings of the British Academy* xli, 207–45

MONETA E SCAMBI 1962, *Moneta e Scambi nell'alto medievo* (Settimane di studio del Centro Italiano di studi sull'alto medioevo, VIII), Spoleto

MOORHEAD, J., 1992, *Theodoric in Italy*, Oxford

MÜLLER-WILLE, M. & SCHNEIDER, R., (eds) 1993 *Ausgewählte Probleme europäischer Landnahme des Früh-und Hochmittelalters*, vol. 1, Vorträge und Forschungen 41, Sigmaringen

MUNKSGAARD, E., 1987, Spätantikes Silber, *Frühmittelalterliche Studien* 21, 82–84

NIELSEN, P.O., RANDSBORG, K. & THRANE, H., (eds) 1994, *The Archaeology of Gudme and Lundeborg*. Papers presented at a conference at Svendborg 1991.

OEXLE, O.G., 1983, Die Gegenwart der Toten, in H. Braet and W Verbeke (eds), *Death in the Middle Ages*, Louvain, 19–77

ONIANS, J., 1988, *Bearers of Meaning: the classical orders in Antiquity, the Middle Ages and the Renaissance*, Princeton

ØRSNES, M., 1988, *Ejsbøl I: Waffenopferfunde des 4.–5. Jahrhunderts nach Chr.*, Nordiske Fortidsminder series B, vol. 11

PAINTER, K.S., 1977, *The Water Newton Early Christian Silver*, London

PAINTER, K.S., 1993, Late Roman Silver Plate: a reply to Alan Cameron, *Journal of Roman Archaeology* 6, 109–15

PARIS 1989, *Trésors d'orfèvrerie gallo-romains*, exh. cat., Paris

PAULI, L., 1983, Eine frühkeltische Prunktrense aus der Donau, *Germania* 61, 459–86

PAXTON, F., 1990, *Christianizing Death. The Creation of a Ritual Process in Early Medieval Europe*, Ithaca/London

PERCIVAL, J., 1976, *The Roman Villa: An Historical Introduction*, London

PÉRIN, P., 1987, Des nécropoles romaines aux nécropoles tardives aux Haut Moyen Age. Remarques sur la topographie funéraire en Gaule mérovingienne et à sa périphérie, *Cahiers Archéologiques* 35, 9–30

PICARD, J.-C., 1992, *Cristianizzazione e pratiche funerarie (tarda Antichità e alto Medioevo IV-VII sec.)*, Turin

PILET, C., 1980, *La Nécropole de Frénouville*, 3 vols, Oxford

PIRENNE, H., 1939, *Mohammed and Charlemagne*, London

PIRENNE, H., LYON, B., GUILLOU, A., ABRIELE, F. & STEUER, H., 1995, *Haut Moyen Age, Byzance, Islam, Occident*, Paris

POHL, W., 1988, *Die Awaren. Ein Steppenvolk in Mitteleuropa, 567–822 n. Chr.*, Munich

POHL, W., 1996 (ed.), *Kingdoms of the Empire. The Construction of Political Identities*, Leiden (in press)

RAMOS FERNANDEZ, R., 1975, *La ciudad romana de Illici. Estudio arqueologico*. Publicaciones del Instituto de Estudios Alicantinos, ser. II, Numéro 7

RANDSBORG, K., 1991, *The First Millennium A.D. in Europe and the Mediterranean*, Cambridge

REECE, R., 1988, Interpreting Roman Hoards, *World Archaeology* 20, 261–9

RIPOLL, G. & VELAZQUEZ, I., 1995, *La Hispania visigoda. Historia de España* 6, Madrid

ROSS, M.C., 1965, *Catalogue of the Byzantine and Early Medieval Antiquities in the Dumbarton Oaks Collection 2: Jewelry, Enamels and Art of the Migration Period*, Washington, D.C.

SAWYER, P. & WOOD, I. (eds), 1977, *Early Medieval Kingship*, Leeds

SCAPULA, J., *Un haut lieu archéologique de la haute vallée de la Seine. La Butte d'Isle-Aumont en Champagne (Aube), 1ere partie: Du Néolithique au Carolingien*, Troyes

SCHARER, A. & SCHEIBELREITER, G. (eds), 1994, *Historiographie im frühen Mittelalter*, VIÖG 32, Vienna

SCHOPPA, H., 1962, Ein spätrömischer Schatzfund aus Wiesbaden-Kastel, *Fundberichte aus Hessen*, 2, 158–67

SCHÜLZE, M., 1984, Diskussionsbeitrag zur Interpretation früh- und hochmittelalterlicher Flussfunde, *Frühmittelalterliche Studien* 18, 222–48

SENA CHIESA, G. et al., 1990, *Milano Capitale dell'impero romano 286–402 d.c.*, Milan

SHELTON, K.J., 1981, *The Esquiline Treasure*, London

SICARD, D., 1978, *La liturgie de la mort dans l'église latine des origines à l'époque carolingienne*, Münster

STEUER, H., 1987, Gewichtsgeldwirtschaften im frühgeschichtenlichen Europa. Feinwaagen und Gewichte als Quellen zur Währungsgeschichte, in K. Düwel, H. Jankuhn, H. Siems and D. Trimpe (eds), *Untersuchungen zu Handel und Verkehr der vor- und frühgeschichtlichen Zeit in Mittel und- Nordeuropa, Der Handel der Karolinger- und Wikingerzeit*, Teil IV, Göttingen, 405–527

THOMPSON, E.A., 1985, *Who was St. Patrick?*, Woodbridge

Cat. TOULOUSE: 1987, *De l'Age du Fer aux Temps barbares. Dix ans de recherches archéologiques en Midi-Pyrénées*, exh. cat., Toulouse

TROMBLEY, F.R., 1993–4, *Hellenic Religion and Christianization, AD 370–529*, 2 vols, Leiden

VAN DAM, R., 1993, *Saints and their Miracles in Late Antique Gaul*, Princeton

VAN DER VIN, J.P.A., 1988, Late fourth century gold hoards in the Netherlands. *Rivista italiana di numismatica e scienze affini*, 90, 263–79

VAN ES, W.A., 1968, *Grafrituteel en kerstening*, Bussum

VERHULST, A., 1992, *Rural and Urban Aspects of Early Medieval Northwest Europe*, Variorum reprints, London

VIKAN, G., 1982, *Byzantine Pilgrimage Art*, Washington, D.C.

VON HESSEN, O., 1968, *I ritrovamenti barbarici nelle collezioni civiche veronesi del Museo di Castelvecchio*, Verona

VON HESSEN, O., KURZE, W. & MASTRELLI, C.A., 1977, *Il tesoro ecclesiastico di Galognano*, Florence

WERNER, J., 1935, *Münzdatierte austrasische Grabsunde*, Berlin

WERNER, J., 1950, Zur Enstehung der Reihengräberzivilisation, *Archaeologia Geographica*, 23–32

WERNER, J., 1954, *Waage und Geld in der Merowingerzeit*, Munich

WHITTAKER, D., 1995, L'importance des invasions du bas-empire: peut-on sert confiance aux historiens?, *Revue du nord-archéologie* 77, 11–20

WICKHAM, C., 1981, *Early Medieval Italy: Central Power and Local Authority, 400–1000*, London

WIGG, D.G., 1991, Münzumlauf in Nordgalilien um die Mitte des 4. Jahrhunderts n. Chr., *Studien zu Fundmünzen der Antike* 8

WILSON, D., 1984, *Anglo-Saxon Art: from the seventh century to the Norman Conquest*, London

WHITBY, M., 1991, John of Ephesus and the pagans: pagan survivals in the sixth century, in M. Salomon (ed.), *Paganism in the Later Roman Empire and Byzantium*, Crakow, 111–31

WOLFRAM, H., 1979, Gotischen Königtum und römisches Kaisertum, *Frühmittelalterliche Studien*, 13, 1ff

WOLFRAM, H., 1988, *Die Goten. Von den Anfängen bis zur Mitte des 6. Jahrhunderts*, Munich (English edn Berkeley-Los Angeles)

WOLFRAM, H., 1990, *Das Reich und die Germanen*, Berlin

WOLFRAM, H., 1995, *Grenzen und Räume. Österreichische Geschichte*, vol. 1, 375–907, Vienna

WOLFRAM, H. & SCHWARCZ, A. (eds), 1980, *Die Völker an der mittleren und unteren Donau im 5. und 6. Jahrhundert*, Vienna

WOLFRAM, H. & SCHWARCZ, A. (eds), 1988, *Anerkennung und Integration. Zu den wirtschaftlichen Grundlagen der Völkerwanderungszeit 400–600*, Vienna

WOLFRAM, H. & POHL, W. (eds), 1990, *Typen der Ethogenese*, vol. 1, Vienna

WOOD, I., 1994, *The Merovingian Kingdoms, 450–751*, London

WOOD, I., 1996, *The Most Holy Abbot Ceolfrid*, Jarrow Lecture 1995, Newcastle upon Tyne

YOUNG, B., 1977, Paganisme, christianisation et rite funéraires mérovingiens, in *Archéologie médiévale* 7, 5–81

YOUNG, B., 1986, Exemple aristocratique et mode funéraire dans le Gaule mérovingienne, *Annales, Economie, Civilisations, Sociétés* 41, 379–407

ZADOKS-JOSEPHUS JITTA, A.N., 1976, Beilen, *Reallexikon der germanischen Altertumskunde*, 2nd edn, vol. 2, 162–3

From the Elysian Fields to the Christian paradise

ABBREVIATIONS

ΑΔ: *Αρχαιολογικόν Δελτίον*

ΑΕΜΘ: *Το Αρχαιολογικό Έργο στη Μακεδονία και Θράκη*

ACIAC: *Atti del Congresso Internazionale di Archeologia Cristiana*

BCH: *Bulletin de Correspondance Hellénique*

CA: *Cahiers Archéologiques*

ΕΙΕ: *Εθνικό Ίδρυμα Ερευνών*

Γ. Γούναρης 1990: Οι τοιχολαφίες του τάφου αρ. 18 της Θεολογικής Σχολής του ΑΠΘ, *Περιοδικό Εγνατία* 2, 245–57.

Κ. Ελευθεριάδου, 1989: Ανασκαφή χριστιανικού χοιμητηρίου στην περιοχή του νοσοκομείου "Άγιος Δημήτριος" στη Θεσσαλονίκη, *ΑΕΜΘ* 3, 271–82.

D. FEISSEL, 1980: Notes d'epigraphie chretiénne (IV), *BCH (104)*, Athenes.

D. FEISSEL, 1983: Recueil des inscriptions Chretiénnes de Macedoine du IIIe au VIe siècle, *BCH CVII, Supplement VIII*, Athenes.

A. GRABAR, 1966: *Le premier art chretien, (200–395)*, Paris.

Κακριδής, Ιω. 1986. *Ελληνική Μυθολογία*, τ. 2 Οι Θεοί, τ. 3 Οι ήρωες, Αθήναι.

Μακροπούλου, Δ. 1990: Ανασκαφή τάφων στο ανατολικό παλαιοχριστιανικό νεκροταφείο της Θεσσαλονίκης, *Μακεδονικά* 27, 190–207.

Μακροπούλου, Δ. *Χρονικά ΑΔ* 45 (1990) in press

Μακροτούλου, Δ. 1994: Ταφικά ευρήματα, νομίσματα και νομισματικοί θησαυροί στα παλαιοχριστιανικά κοιμητήρια της Θεσσαλονίκης.

Μαρκή, Ε. 1990: Η ταφική ζωγραφική των πρώτων χριστιανικών χρόνων στη Θεσσαλονίκη, *Επιστημονικό Συμπόσιο Χριστιανική Θεσσαλονίκη, Από του Αποστόλου Παύλου μέχρι της Κωνσταντινείου εποχής*, Thessaloniki, 171–94.

Μαρκή Ε. 1995: Θέματα κοσμικής ζωγραφικής σε τάφο της Θεσσαλονίκης, *Μουσείο Βυζαντινού Πολιτισμού, Δελτίο* 2/1995, 32–37.

MARROU, H. I., 1977: *Decadense romaine ou antiquité tardive? III–IV siecle*, Paris.

Μαυροτούλου-Τσιούμη, 1983: Παράσταση της Σωσάννας σε παλαιοχριστιανικό τάφο της Θεσσαλονίκης, *Αφιέρωμα στη μνήμη Σ. Πελεκανίδη*, Thessaloniki 1983, 247–259.

Ναλπάντης, Δ. 1987: *ΑΔ* 42, *Χρονικά*, 403–6.

Ναλπάντης, Δ. 1988: *ΑΔ* 43, *Χρονικά*, 381–3.

Ναλπάντης, Δ. 1992: Νεότερα ευρήματα από σωστικές ανασκαφές στη Θεσσαλονίκη, *ΑΕΜΘ*, 6, 311–26.

Παζαράς, Θ. 1981: Δύο παλαιοχριστιανικοί τάφοι από το δυτικό νεκροταφείο της Θεσσαλονίκης, *Μακεδονικά* 21, 373–89.

Παπούλια, Β. 1994: Το τέλος της αρχαιότητας και η του Μεσαίωνα στην Νοτιοανατολική Ευρώπη, *Μνήμη Δ. Α. Ζακυνθηνού, Β, ΕΙΕ Σύμμεικτα*, τ. 9, Athens.

Πελεκανίδου, Ε. 1994: Η ζωγραφική των παλαιοχριστιανικών τάφων της Θεσσαλονίκης, *Ανακοίνωση στο Ἡ Επιστημονικό Συμπόσιο "Χριστιανική – Θεσσαλονίκη Ταφές και κοιμητήρια", Θεσσαλονίκη 6–8 Οκτωβρίου* in press.

PELEKANIDIS, S. 1965: Die malerei der Konstantinischen zeit, *ACIAC VII*, 230–35.

Πέτσας, Φ. 1966: Ανασκαφή Πανεπιστημιουπόλεως Θεσσαλονίκης, *ΑΔ* 21, *Χρονικά*, 334–9.

Τσιλαρίδας, Ε. & Λοβέρδου-Τσιλαρίδα, Α. 1979. Κατάλογος χριστιανικών επιλαφών στα μουσεία της Θεσσαλονίκης, Thessaloniki.

VELMANS, T. 1969: Quelques versions rares due thème de la fontaine de vie dans l' art paléochrétien, Ca XIX.

Death on the Rhine

BOHME, H.W., 1993, Adelsgräber im Frankenreich: Archäologische Zeugnisse zur Herausbildung einer Herrenschicht unter den merowingischen Königen, *Jahrbuch des Römisch-Germanischen Zentralmuseums Mainz* 40. 397–534

GORECKI, J., 197 . Studien zur Sitte der Münzbeigabe in römerzeitlichen Körpergräbern zwischen Rhein, Mosel und Somme. *Bericht der Römisch-Germanischen Kommission* 56, 182–467

KOVACSOVICS, W., 1983, Römische Grabdenkmäler

NIERHAUS, R., 1969, Römerzeitliche Bestattungssitten im nördlichen Gallien: Autochtones und Mittelmeerländisches, *Helinium* 9, 246

REECE, R., 1977, *Burial in the Roman World*

ROTH, H., 1977, Archäologische Beobachtungen zum Grabfrevel im Merowingerreich in: H. Jankuhn, H. Nehlsen & H. Roth, *Zum Grabfrevel in vor- und frühgeschichtlicher Zeit*. Kolloquium, 53ff

STRUCK, M. (ed.), 1993, *Römerzeitliche Gräber als Quellen zu Religion, Bevölkerungsstruktur und Sozialgeschichte*

WALKER, S., 1985, *Memorials to the Roman Dead*

WITTEYER, M. & FASOLD, P., 1995, *Des Lichtes beraubt. Totenehrung · in der römischen Gräberstrasse von Mainz-Weisenau*. Exh. cat., Frankfurt, 1995

V. HESBERG, H. & ZANKER, P., 1987, *Römische Gräberstrassen, Selbstdarstellung, Status, Standart*. Kolloquium München 1985

On Cologne

DECKERS, J. & NOELKE, P., 1985, *Die römischen Grabkammer in Köln-Weiden*, 2nd edn

DOPPELFELD, O. & WEYRES, W., 1980, *Die Ausgrabungen im Dom zu Köln*

FREMERSDORF, F., 1955, *Das fränkische Gräberfeld Köln-Mungersdorf*

FRIEDHOFF, U., 1991, Der römische Friedhof an der Jakobstrasse zu Köln, *Kölner Forschungen* vol. 3

Führer zu vor- und frühgeschichtlichen Denkmälern 37–39, Köln 1–3 (1980)

GABELMANN, H., 1972, Die Typen römischer Grabstelen am Rhein, *Bonner Jahrbuch* 172, 65ff

GALSTERER, B.H., 1975, *Die römischen Steininschriften aus Köln*

GOLLUB, S. 1977, Neue Gräber an der Luxemburgerstrasse in Köln, *Kölner Jahrbuch für Vor- und Frühgeschichte* 17, 92ff

LA BAUME, P., 1967, *Das fränkische Gräberfeld von Junkersdorf bei Köln*

NEU, S., 1994, *Antike Welt* vol. 1

NEU, S., 1989, Romische Reliefs vom Kölner Rheinufer, *Kölner Jahrbuch fur Vor- und Fruhgeschichte* 22, 241ff

NOELKE, P., 1995, *Niedergermanische Grabstelen des 3. Jahrhunderts mit Protomendarstellung*, unpublished manuscript

NOELKE, P., 1984, Reiche Gräber von einem römischen Gutshof in Köln, *Germania* 62, 373–423

NOELKE, P., 1996, Römische Grabaltäre in der Germania Inferior. *Beiheft zu dem Bonner Jahrbuchen*

NOELKE, P., 1995, *Römische Grabreliefs der Rheinzone mit Mahldarstellungen*, unpublished manuscript

PÄFFGEN, B., 1992, Die Ausgrabungen in St. Severin zu Köln. *Kölner Forschunge* vol. 5

RIEDEL, M., 1980, Die Grabung 1974 im römischen Gräberfeld an der Luxemburgerstrasse in Köln, *Kölner Jahrbuch fur Vor- und Frühgeschichte* 17, 92ff

SCHMITZ, W., 1995, *Die spätantiken und frühmittelalterlichen Grabinschriften der Stadt Köln (4.-7. Jahrhundert n. Chr.)*, unpublished manuscript

SPIEGEL, E.M., 1994, Die Römische Westnekropole an der Aachenerstrasse in Köln. Ansätze zu einer Strukturanalyse. *Kölner Jahrbuch* 27, 595ff

SPIEGEL, E.M., 1987, Köln - Graberfelder in: H.G. Horn (ed.), *Die Römer in Nordrhein-Westfalen* 460: 493ff

SPIESS, A., 1988, Studien zu den römischen Reliefsarkophagen aus dem Provinzen Germania Inferior und Superior, Belgica und Raetia, *Kolner Jahrbuch* 21, 253ff

STEUER, H., 1980, *Die Franken in Köln*

Elite lifestyle

Van Friezen, Franken en Saksen, 350–750 (exh. cat. Fries Museum Leeuwarden 1959/Haags Gemeetemuseum 1960)

APPADURAI, A. (ed.), 1986, *The social life of things. Commodities in cultural perspective*, Cambridge

AUSTIN, D. & Alcock, L. (eds), 1990, *From the Baltic to the Black Sea. Studies in medieval archaeology* (One World Archaeology 18), London

COLLINS, R., 1991, *Early Medieval Europe, 300–1000*, Houndmills/Basingstoke/London

DRINKWATER, J. & Elton, J. (eds), 1992, *Fifth-century Gaul: a crisis of identity?*, Cambridge

ENRIGHT, M.J., 1996, *Lady with a mead cup. Ritual, prophecy and lordship in the European warband from La Tène to the Viking Age*, Blackrock

GEARY, P.J., 1994, *Living with the dead in the Middle Ages*, London

GRIERSON, P. & Blackburn, M., 1986, *Medieval European coinage, I; The early Middle Ages, 5th-10th centuries*, Cambridge 81–154

HEIDINGA, H.A., 1900, From Kootwijk to Rhenen; in search of the elite in the Central Netherlands in the Early Middle Ages, in: J.C. Besteman et al. (eds) *Medieval archaeology in the Netherlands. Studies presented to H.H. van Regteren Altena*, Assen/Maastricht, 9–40

HODDER, I., (ed.) 1989, *The meanings of things. Material culture and symbolic expression* (One World Archaeology 6), London

KUPER, A., 1988, *The invention of primitive society. Transformations of an illusion*, London/New York

ROYMANS, N., 1995, Romanisation, cultural identity and the ethnic discussion. The integration of Lower Rhine populations in the Roman Empire, in M. Millett and J. Slofstra (eds) *Romanisation in the early Roman West. The role of culture and ideology* (Publications du Musée de Luxembourg), Luxembourg

THEUWS, F., 1995, De vele lagen van de vroeg-middeleeuwse geschiedenis, *Madoc* 9:3, 133–49

THOMAS, N., 1991, *Entangled objects. Exchange, material culture and colonialism in the Pacific*, Cambridge (Mass.)/London

VAN ES, W.A. & Hessing, W.A.M., 1994, *Romeinen, Friezen en Franken in het hart van Nederland. Van Traiectum tot Dorestad 50vC –900nC*, Utrecht

WIGHTMAN, E., 1978, North-eastern Gaul in Late Antiquity: the testimony of settlement patterns in an age of transition, *Berichten Rijksdienst Oudheidkundig Bodemonderzoek* 28, 241–50

The Firebed of the Serpent

AXBOE, M., 1982, The Scandinavian Gold Bracteates. *Acta Archaeologica* 52: 1–87, Copenhagen

AXBOE, M. & HAUCK, K., 1985, Hohenmemmingen -B, ein Schlüsselstück der Brakteatenikonographie. *Frümittelalterliche*

Studien, vol. 19: 98–130. Walter de Greyter. Berlin, New York

HAUCK, K., 1976p, Bilddenkmäler zur Religion, *Reallexikon der Germanischen Altertumskunde*, begr. von Johannes Hoops. Band 2, Lieferung 4/5: 577–98. Walter de Greyter. New York

WATTS, M., 1990, Sorte Muld. Hvdingesaede og kultcentrum fra Bornholms yngre jernalder. In P. Mortense & B. Rasmussen (eds), *Fra Stamme til Stat I Danmark. 2. Høvdingesamfund og Kongemagt Jysk Arkaeologisk Selskabs Skrifter* XXII:2, 89–107, Aarhus. (With English summaries.)

See also: articles by M. AXBOE, M. WATTS and others in Olsen, O. (ed.), 1990, *Oldtidens Ansigt - The Face of the Past, Festkrift to H.M. Queen Margrethe II, on her fiftieth anniversary 16 April 1990. Det kongelige Nordiske Oldskriftselskab. Jysk Arkeologisk Selskab.* København, 140–56

Heirs of Rome

AGER, B. 1985, The smaller variants of the Anglo-Saxon quoit brooch, *Anglo-Saxon Studies in Archaeology and History* 4, 1–58

ALCOCK, L. & ALCOCK, E. 1992, Reconnaissance excavations on Early Historic fortifications and other royal sites in Scotland, 1974–84: 5. Excavations and other fieldwork at Forteviot, 1981, *Proceedings of the Society of Antiquaries of Scotland*, 120, 94–149

ANDERSON, M.O., 1980, *Kings and Kingship in Early Scotland*, 2nd edn, Edinburgh

ARNOLD, C., 1982, *The Anglo-Saxon Cemeteries of the Isle of Wight*, London

AXBOE, M. & KROMANN, A. 1992, *DN ODINN P F AUC?* Germanic 'imperial portraits' on Scandinavian gold bracteates, *Acta Hyperborea* 4; *Ancient Portraiture, Image and Message*, 271–305

BACKHOUSE, J.M., TURNER, D.H. & WEBSTER, L. (eds), 1984, *The Golden Age of Anglo-Saxon Art 966–1066*, London

BAILEY, R.N., 1979, *The Durham Cassiodorus* (The Jarrow Lecture 1978), Jarrow

BIDDLE, B. & KJØLBYE-BIDDLE, B., 1985, The Repton Stone, *Anglo-Saxon England* 14, 233–92

BRUCE-MITFORD, R.L.S. & contributors, 1975, 1978, 1983, *The Sutton Hoo Ship Burial; I, Excavations, Background, The Ship, Dating and Inventory; II, Arms Armour and Regalia; III A.C. Evans (ed.), Silver, Hanging Bowls, Drinking Vessels, Containers, Musical Instruments, Textiles, Minor Objects*, London

BUCKTON, D. (ed.), 1994, *Byzantium*, London

BULLOUGH, D., 1975, *Imagines Regum* and their significance in the early medieval West, in G.Robertson and G. Henderson (eds), *Studies in Memory of David Talbot Rice*, Edinburgh, 223–76

CAMERON, A. & SCHAUER, D., 1982, The last consul: Basilius and his diptych, *Journal of Roman Studies* 72, 126–45

CAMPBELL, E., 1996, Trade in the Dark Ages: a peripheral activity? in B. Crawford (ed.), *Scotland in Dark Age Britain*, St Andrews, 79–92

DALTON, O.M., 1901, *Catalogue of Early Christian Antiquities and Objects from the Christian East in the Department of British and Medieval Antiquities and Ethnography of the British Museum*, London

DELBRUECK, R., 1929, *Die Consular Diptychen und verwändte Denkmäler*, Berlin

DELBRUECK, R., 1952, *Probleme der Lipsanothek von Brescia*, Bonn

DICKINSON, T., 1991, Material culture as social expression: the case of Saxon saucer brooches with running spiral decoration, *Studien zur Sachsenforschung* 7, 39–70

EAST, K. & WEBSTER, L., forthcoming, *The Anglo-Saxon High-Status Burials at Taplow (Bucks.), Broomfield (Essex) and Caenby (Lincs.)*, London

EDWARDS, N., 1990, *The Archaeology of Early Medieval Ireland*, London

EVANS, A.C., 1986, *The Sutton Hoo Ship Burial*, London

EVANS, A.C., forthcoming, *The pony-bridle from Sutton Hoo Mound 17*, London

EVISON, V.I., 1968, Quoit brooch style buckles, *Antiquaries Journal* XLVIII, 17–102

EVISON, V.I., 1987, *Dover: The Buckland Anglo-Saxon Cemetery* (Historic Buildings and Monuments Commission Archaeological Report 3), London

EVISON, V.I., 1994, *An Anglo-Saxon Cemetery at Great Chesterford,*

Essex (Council for British Archaeology Research Report 91), London

FORSYTH, K., 1995, The inscriptions on the Dupplin cross, in C. Bourke (ed.), *From the Isles of the North: Early Medieval Art in Ireland and Britain*, Belfast, 237–44

FOSTER, S.M., 1996, *Picts, Gaels and Scots: Early Historic Scotland*, London

HARDEN, D.B., 1956, Glass vessels in Britain and Ireland AD 400–100, in D.B. Harden (ed) *Dark Age Britain: Studies presented to E.T. Leeds*, London, 132–67

HASELOFF, G., 1974, Salin's Style I, *Medieval Archaeology* XVIII, 1–15

HAWKES, S.C. & DUNNING, G.C., 1961, Soldiers and settlers in Britain, fourth to fifth century, *Medieval Archaeology* V, 1–70

HENDERSON, I., 1986, The David cycle in Pictish art, in J. Higgitt (ed.), *Early Medieval Sculpture in Britain and Ireland* (British Archaeological Reports 152), Oxford, 87–123

HENDERSON, I., 1994, The insular and continental context of the St Andrews Sarcophagus, in B. Crawford (ed), *Scotland in Dark Age Europe*, St Andrews, 71–102

HINES, J., 1991, Some observations on the runic inscriptions of early Anglo-Saxon England, in A. Bammesberger (ed.), *Old English Runes and their Continental Background (Anglistische Forschungen* 14) Heidelberg, 61–3

HINES, J., forthcoming, *A Corpus of Anglo-Saxon Square-Headed Brooches*, London

HINES, J. & ODENSTEDT, B., 1987, The Undley bracteate and its runic inscription, *Studien zur Sachsenforschung* 6, 73–94

HIRST, S. & CLARK, D., forthcoming, *The Anglo-Saxon Cemeteries* (Excavations at Mucking, Essex, 3; English Heritage Monograph) London

KENT, J.P.C. 1975, Catalogue of the Sutton Hoo coins, blanks and billets, in Bruce-Mitford 1975, 607–47

KENT, J.P.C. & PAINTER, K.S. (eds), 1977, *Wealth of the Roman World: Gold and Silver. AD 300–700*, London

LANE, A., 1994, Fifth to seventh-century trading systems in western Britain and Ireland, in B. Crawford (ed.), *Scotland in Dark Age Europe*, St Andrews, 103–15

LEEDS, E.T., 1949, *A Corpus of Anglo-Saxon Great Square-Headed Brooches*, Oxford

MACALISTER, R.A.S., 1945, *Corpus Inscriptionum Insularum Celticum*, I, Dublin

MEANEY, A., 1964, *A Gazetteer of Early Anglo-Saxon Burial Sites*, London

MYRES, J.N.L., 1977, *A New Corpus of Anglo-Saxon Pottery*, I and II, Cambridge

NAPIER, A.S., 1901, The Franks Casket, in *An English Miscellany presented to Dr Furnivall*, Oxford, 362–81

NASH-WILLIAMS, V.E., 1950, *The Early Christian Monuments of Wales*, Cardiff

NETZER, N., 1983, Redating the consular ivory of Orestes, *Burlington Magazine* 125, 265–71

ODENSTEDT, B., 1980, The Loveden Hill runic inscription, *Ortnamssällskapets I Uppsala Årsskrift*, 24–37

PAGE, R.I., 1973, *An Introduction to English Runes*, London

RIGOLD, S.E., 1975, The Sutton Hoo coins in the light of the contemporary background of coinage in England, in Bruce-Mitford 1975, 653–77

SMITH, R.A., 1905, Anglo-Saxon remains, in *Victoria County History of Buckinghamshire*, I, London, 199–204

SMITH, R.A., 1936, Jutish finds in Kent, *British Museum Quarterly* X, 131–32

SPEAKE, G.H., 1980, *Anglo-Saxon Animal Art and its Germanic Background*, Oxford

THOMAS, G., 1887, An Anglo-Saxon cemetery at Sleaford, Lincolnshire, *Archaeologia* 50, 383–406

VOLBACH, W.F., 1976, *Elfenbeinarbeiten der Spätantike und des Frühen Mittelalters*, 3rd edn, Mainz

WEBSTER, L., 1995, Ring's runic riddle, *British Museum Magazine* 23, 21

WEBSTER, L. & BACKHOUSE, J. (eds), 1991, *The Making of England: Anglo-Saxon Art and Culture AD 600–900*, London

WILLIAMSON, P., 1982, *Medieval Ivory Carvings*, London

WILSON, D.M., 1964, *Anglo-Saxon Ornamental Metalwork 700–*

1100 in the British Museum; Catalogue of Antiquities of the Later Saxon Period, 1, London

Manuscripts

ALEXANDER, J.J.G., 1978, *Insular Manuscripts 6th to 9th century* (A Survey of Manuscripts Illuminated in the British Isles, vol. I), London

ALEXANDER, J.J.G., 1978, *The Decorated Letter*, London

ATTENBOROUGH, F., 1922, *The Laws of the Earliest English Kings*, Cambridge

ALTON, E.H. & MEYER, P., 1951, *Evangeliorum Quattuor Codex Cenannensis*, 3 vols

BACKHOUSE, J., 1981, *The Lindisfarne Gospels*, Oxford

BACKHOUSE, J., TURNER, D.H. & WEBSTER, L.E. (eds), 1984, *The Golden Age of Anglo-Saxon Art 966–1066*, London

BERSCHIN, W., 1980, *Griechisch-lateinisches Mittelalter, von Hieronymus zu Nikolaus von Kues*, Bern

BIRCH, W. DE GRAY, 1889, *An Ancient Manuscript of the Eighth or Ninth Century Formerly Belonging to St Mary's Abbey or Nunnaminster, Winchester*, London

BISCHOFF, B. & BROWN, V., 1985, Addenda to Codices Latini Antiquiores, *Medieval Studies* 47, 317–66

BODDEN, M.C., 1988, Evidence for knowledge of Greek in Anglo-Saxon England, *Anglo-Saxon England* 17, 217–46

BROOKS, N., 1984, *The Early History of the Church of Canterbury: Christ Church from 597 to 1066*, Leicester

BROWN, M.P., 1987, Paris, Bibliothèque Nationale, MS lat. 10861 and the Scriptorium of Christ Church, Canterbury, *Anglo-Saxon England* 15, 119–37

BROWN, M.P., 1990, *A Guide to Western Historical Scripts from Antiquity to 1600*, London and Toronto

BROWN, M.P., 1996, *The Book of Cerne. Prayer, Patronage and Power in Ninth-century England* London and Toronto

BROWN, T.J. (ed.), 1969, *The Stonyhurst Gospel of St John*, Roxburghe Club, London

BROWN, T.J., 1993, *A Palaeographer's View. Selected Writings of Julian Brown*, J. Bately, M.P. Brown and J. Roberts (eds), London

BRUCKNER and MARICHAL, 1981, v. ChLA

BUDNY, M., 1985, London, British Library, MS Royal I.E.VI: the anatomy of an Anglo-Saxon Bible fragment, unpublished Ph.D. thesis, London University

CAMPBELL, J., (ed.) 1982, *The Anglo-Saxons*, Oxford

CHAPLAIS, P., 1965, The Origin and Authenticity of the Royal Anglo-Saxon Diploma, *JSA* 3, 48–61

CHASE, C. (ed.), 1981, *The Dating of Beowulf*, Toronto

ChLA = *Chartae Latinae Antiquiores*, 1963–7, vols III (British Museum) and IV (other British repositories), A. Bruckner and R. Marichal (eds), Olten/Lausanne

CLA = LOWE, E.A., 1934–72, *Codices Latini Antiquiores* (eleven vols and supplement), Oxford

CODICES E VATICANIS SELECTI, I, 1930, *Fragmenta et Picturae Vergiliana Codicis Vaticani Latini 3225*, Rome

COLGRAVE, B. & MYNORS, R.A.B. (eds), 1991, *Historia Ecclesiastica*, Oxford

COLLINS, R., 1995 (2nd edn), *Medieval Spain, Unity in Diversity*, Basingstoke

CRAMER, P., 1989, Ernulf of Rochester and Early Anglo-Norman Canon Law, *Journal of Ecclesiastical History* 40, 483–510

CUBITT, C.R.E., 1995, *Anglo-Saxon Church Councils 650–850*, London

DUMVILLE, D.N., 1976, The Anglian Collection of Royal Genealogies and Regnal Lists, *Anglo-Saxon England* 5, 23–50

DUMVILLE, D.N., 1977, Kingship, genealogies and regnal lists, in P. Sawyer and I.N. Wood (eds), *Early Medieval Kingship*, 72–104

DUMVILLE, D.N. (ed.), 1985, *The Historia Brittonum*, Cambridge

DUMVILLE, D.N., 1985, The West Saxon Genealogical Regnal List and the Chronology of Early Wessex, *Peritia* 4, 21–66

DUMVILLE, D.N., 1985, The West Saxon Genealogical Regnal List: Manuscripts and Texts, *Anglia* 104, 1–32

FARMER, D.H., ed., 1983, *The Age of Bede*, Harmondsworth and New York

FARMER, D.H., ed., 1990, *Bede: Ecclesiastical History of the English People*, Harmondsworth and New York

FÉROTIN, M., 1987, *Histoire de l'Abbaye de Silos*, Paris

FLOWER, R., 1926, *Catalogue of Irish Manuscripts in the British Museum* 3 vols, London

HENRY, F., 1974, *The Book of Kells: Reproductions from the manuscript in Trinity College, Dublin*, London

HIGHAM, N.J., 1994 *The English Conquest, Gildas and Britain in the Fifth Century*, Manchester

HUBERT, J., PORCHER, J. & VOLBACH, W.F., 1970, *Carolingian Art*, London

JAMES, M.R. 1929, *Marvels of the East*, Oxford

KENDRICK, T.D., BROWN, T.J., BRUCE-MITFORD, R.L.S., ROOSEN-RUNGE, H., ROSS, A.S.C., STANLEY, E.G. & WERNER, A.E.A., 1956, 1960, *Evangeliorum Quattuor Codex Lindisfarnensis*, 2 vols, Olten/Lausanne

KER, N.R., 1957, *Catalogue of Manuscripts Containing Anglo-Saxon*, Oxford

KEYNES, S., 1994, *The Councils of Clofesho* University of Leicester, Vaughan Paper no. 38, 11th Brixworth Lecture, 1993

KIERNAN, K.S., 1981, *Beowulf and the Beowulf Manuscript*, New Brunswick

KINSELLA, T., 1979 (1969; reptd), *The Táin*, Oxford and Dublin

KUYPERS, A.B., 1902, *The Prayerbook of Æðeluald the Bishop, commonly called the Book of Cerne*, Cambridge

LAPIDGE, M. & DUMVILLE, D.N. (eds), 1984, *Gildas, New Approaches*, Woodbridge

LAPIDGE, M., 1986, The School of Theodore and Hadrian, *Anglo-Saxon England*, 15, 45–72

LIEBERMANN, F., 1898, *Gesetze der Angelsachsen*, vol. I, Halle

LOWE, E.A., 1914, *The Beneventon Script*, Oxford

McGURK, P., 1961, *Latin Gospel Books from AD 400 to AD 800*, Paris/Brussels

McGURK, P., 1983, *An Eleventh-century Anglo-Saxon Illustrated Miscellany BL Cotton Tiberius B.V. part I*, Copenhagen

MALLON, J., MARICHAL, R. & PERRAT, C., 1939, *L'Écriture Latine*, Paris

MALONE, K. (ed.), 1963, *The Nowell Codex*, Early English Manuscripts in Facsimile 12, Copenhagen

MEEHAN, B. et al., 1990, *The Book of Kells, MS. 58, Trinity College Library Dublin: facsimile*, 2 vols, Luzern

MOISL, H., 1981, Anglo-Saxon Royal Genealogies and Germanic Oral Tradition, *Journal of Medieval History* 7, 215–48

MORGAN, N.J., 1982, *Early Gothic Manuscripts I* (A Survey of Manuscripts Illuminated in the British Isles, vol. 4) London

MORRIS, J. ed. and transl., 1980, *Historia Brittonum*, London

MÜTHERICH, F. & GAEHDE, J. E., 1977, *Carolingian Painting*, London

NELSON, J.L., 1996, *The Frankish World, 750–900*, London

NEW PAL. SOC. 1903–1912: E.M. Thompson et al. (eds), *The New Palaeographical Society. Facsimiles of ancient manuscripts*

O'MAHONEY, F. (ed.), 1994, *The Book of Kells - Proceedings of a conference at Trinity College Dublin, 6 Sept. 1992–9 Sept. 1992*, Aldershot

OLSEN, K. and NORDENFALK, C., 1952, *Gyllene Böcker*, exh. cat., May-Sept. 1952, Nationalmuseum Stockholm, Stockholm

PÄCHT, O. & ALEXANDER, J.J.G., 1966, *Illuminated Manuscripts in the Bodleian Library Oxford*, Oxford

RICHARDSON, H. & SAYLES, G., 1966, *Law and Legislation from Æthelberht to Magna Carta*, Edinburgh

SAWYER, P., 1957–62, *Textus Roffensis*, Early English Manuscripts in Facsimile 7, 11, Copenhagen

SAWYER, P., 1968, *Anglo-Saxon Charters: an annotated list and bibliography*, Royal Historical Society Guides and Handbooks 8, London

SCHARER, A., 1982, *Die Angelsächsische Königsurkunde im 7 und 8 Jahrhundert*, Veröffentlichungen des Instituts für Österreichische Geschichtsforschung 26, Vienna

SCHMITZ, G. (ed.), 1893, *Commentarii notarum Tironianarum*, Leipzig

SEECK, O., 1876, *Notitia Dignitatum*, Rome

SIMPSON, A., 1981, The Laws of Ethelbert, in M. Arnold , T. Green, S. Scully and S. White (eds), *On the Laws and Customs of England: Essays in Honour of Samuel E. Thorne*, 3–15

SISAM, K., 1953, Anglo-Saxon Royal Genealogies, *PBA* 39, 287–348

TEMPLE, E., 1976, *Anglo-Saxon Manuscripts 900–1066* (A Survey

of Manuscripts Illuminated in the British Isles, vol. 2), London
TURNER, D.H., 1966. *Romanesque Illuminated Manuscripts in the British Museum*, London
UNIVERSITY OF UPPSALA, 1927, *Codex Argenteus Upsaliensis*, facsimile, Uppsala
WALLACE-HADRILL, J.M., 1971, *Early Germanic Kingship in England and on the Continent*, Oxford
WATSON, A.G., 1984, *Catalogue of Dated and Datable Manuscripts c. 435–1600 in Oxford Libraries*, Oxford
WEITZMANN, K., 1977, *Late Antique and Early Christian Book Illumination*, London
WHITELOCK, D., revd edn. 1970. *Sweet's Anglo-Saxon Reader*, London
WHITELOCK, D., 1979, *English Historical Documents c. 500–1042*, English Historical Documents 1, 2nd edn, London
WINTERBOTTOM, M. (ed. and transl.), 1978, *De Excidio et Conquestu Britanniae*, London
WIT DE, J., 1959, *Die Miniaturen des Vergilius Vaticanus*, Amsterdam
WORMALD, F., 1984, in J.J.G. Alexander *et al.* (eds), *Francis Wormald: Collected Writings*, I
WORMALD, F., 1984, *Bede and the Conversion of England: the Charter Evidence*, Jarrow Lecture
WRIGHT, T. & WÜLCKER, R.P., 1884, *Anglo-Saxon and Old English Vocabularies*, London
WRIGHT, D.H., 1967, *The Vespasian Psalter*, Early English Manuscripts in Facsimile 14, Copenhagen
YORKE, B., 1985. The Kingdom of the East Saxons, *Anglo-Saxon England* 14, 1–36
ZIMMERMANN, E.H., 1916, *Vorkarolingische Miniaturen Denkmäler Deutscher Kumt, III: Malerei*, Berlin
ZUPITZA, J. (ed.), 1959, *Beowulf*, Early English Text Society 245, London

Coins

ABBREVIATIONS
BAR: British Archaeological Reports, Oxford
BLIA: Bulletin of the London Institute of Archaeology, London
BMA: BMA followed by a number indicates a coin's number in a series of articles by G.C.Brooke, Anglo-Saxon acquisitions of the British Museum, NC 1922, 1–32; 1923, 1–17; 1924, 1–11; 1925, 1–15 and 1926. 1–23
BMC: BMC followed by a number indicates a coin's catalogue number in the British Museum Catalogue of the appropriate series
BNJ: British Numismatic Journal, London
CH: Coin Hoards, Royal Numismatic Society, London
JRA: Journal of Roman Archaeology, Michigan
NC: Numismatic Chronicle, London
PDNHAS: Proceedings of the Dorset Natural History and Archaeology Society
ARCHIBALD, M.M., 1985, The coinage of Beonna in the light of the Middle Harling Hoard, *BNJ* 55, 10–54
ARCHIBALD, M.M. & FENWICK, V., 1995, A sceat of Ethelbert I of East Anglia and recent finds of coins of Beonna, with M.R.Cowell, *BNJ* 65, 1–19.
BARCLAY, C., 1997, A parcel of pennies of Offa from Aiskew, N. Yorkshire, *BNJ* 67 (forthcoming)
BLAND, R. & JOHNS, C., 1993, *The Hoxne Treasure, an Illustrated Introduction*. British Museum, London
BMC ANGLO-SAXON I: Keary, C.F. & Poole, R.S., *A Catalogue of English Coins in the British Museum. Anglo-Saxon Series*, vol. 1, London 1887
BMC BYZANTINE I: Wroth, W., *Catalogue of the Imperial Byzantine Coins in the British Museum*, vol. I, London 1908
BMC VANDALS ETC.: Wroth, W., *Catalogue of the Coins of the Vandals, Ostrogoths and Lombards and of the Empires of Thessalonica, Nicaea and Trebizond in the British Museum*, London 1911
BOOTH, J., 1984, Sceattas in Northumbria, in D. Hill and D.M.Metcalf (eds), *Sceattas in England and on the Continent. The Seventh Oxford Symposium on Coinage and Monetary History*, BAR British Series 128, 71–112, Oxford

CAMPBELL, J., 1982, *The Anglo-Saxons*, Oxford
DALTON, O.M., 1901, *Catalogue of Early Christian Antiquities and Other Objects from the Christian East in the Department of British and Mediaeval Antiquities and Ethnography of the British Museum*, London
FENWICK, V., 1984, Insula de Burgh: Excavations at Burrow Hill, Butley, Suffolk, 1978–81, *Anglo-Saxon Studies in Archaeology and History* 3, 44–53, Oxford
GRIERSON, P. & BLACKBURN, M., 1986, *Medieval European Coinage 1: The Early Middle Ages (5th–10th Centuries)*, Cambridge
JOHNS, C. & BLAND, R., 1993, The great Hoxne treasure: a preliminary report, *JRA* 6, 493–6
KENT, J.P.C., 1961, From Roman Britain to Saxon England, in R.H.M.Dolley (ed.), *Anglo-Saxon Coins*, London
KENT, J.P.C., 1968, Charles the Great or Charles the Bald, NC 7th Series, vol.VIII, 173–6
KENT, J.P.C., 1972, The Aston Rowant treasure trove, *Oxoniensia* 37, 243–4
KENT, J.P.C., 1975, The Coins and the date of the burial, in R. Bruce-Mitford, *The Sutton Hoo Ship-Burial* vol. I, 578–647
METCALF, D.M. 1 1993, *Thrymsas and Sceattas in the Ashmolean Museum Oxford*, vol. 1, London
METCALF, D.M. 2, 1993, *Thrymsas and Sceattas in the Ashmolean Museum Oxford*, vol. 2, London
METCALF, D.M. 3, 1994, *Thrymsas and Sceattas in the Ashmolean Museum Oxford*, vol. 3, London
PAGE, R.I., 1973, *An Introduction to English Runes*, London
PAGE, R.I., 1996, On the baffling nature of Frisian Runes, in T.Looijenga and A.Quak (eds), *Frisian Runes and Neighbouring Traditions*, 131–50, Amsterdamer Beitrage zur Alteren Germanistik, Amsterdam
PROCOPIUS LOEB CLASSICS EDITION VII: *Procopius with an English translation by the late H.B.Dewing, with the collaboration of G.Downey*, vol. VII, London/Cambridge, Mass., 1961 reprint
REECE, R., 1981, The Roman coins from Richborough - a summary, *BLIA*, 49–71
RIC: *Roman Imperial Coinage*, London. Vol. V, pts I and II, P.H. Webb, 1927 and 1933; vol. VI, C.H.V., Sutherland, 1967, *From Diocletian's reform (AD 294) to the death of Maximinus (AD 313)*; vol. VII, P.M. Bruun, 1966, *Constantine and Livinius, AD 313–337*; vol. VIII, J.P.C. Kent, 1981, *The Family of Constantine I, AD 337–364*; vol. IX, J.W.E. Pearce, 1953, *Valentinian I–Theodosius I*; vol. X, J.P.C. Kent, 1994, *The Divided Empire and the Fall of the Western Parts*, AD 395–491.
RICHBOROUGH I-V: Bushe-Fox, J.P., *Excavation of the Roman Fort at Richborough, Kent*, Reports of the Research Committee of the Society of Antiquaries of London nos VI, VII, X, XVI and XXIII, First-Fourth Reports, 1926, 1928, 1932 and 1949; Fifth Report, ed. B.W.Cunliffe, 1968, London
RIGOLD, S.E., 1975, The Sutton Hoo coins in the light of the contemporary background of the coinage in England in R.Bruce-Mitford, *The Sutton Hoo Ship-Burial*, vol. I, 653–77, London
ROBERTSON, A.S., 1936, A find from Shapwick, Somerset, NC Fifth Series, vol. XVI, 245–50
ROGERSON, A., 1995, *A Late Neolithic, Saxon and Medieval Site at Middle Harling, Norfolk*, East Anglian Archaeology, Report No. 74, British Museum and Field Archaeology Division, Norfolk Museums Service, London/Dereham
SALISBURY, F.S., 1929, A hoard of Roman coins from Jordan Hill, Weymouth, *PDNHAS*, 158–82
STAHL, A.M. & ODDY, W.A., 1992, The date of the Sutton Hoo coins in R. Farrell and C. Neuman de Vegvar (eds), *Sutton Hoo: Fifty Years After*, American Medieval Studies 2, 129–47
STEWART, I., 1986, The London mint and the coinage of Offa in M.A.S.Blackburn (ed.) *Anglo-Saxon Monetary History. Essays in Memory of Michael Dolley*, 27–43, Leicester
SUTHERLAND, C.V., 1948, *Anglo-Saxon Gold Coinage in the Light of the Crondall Hoard*, Oxford

Index to essays

(pp. 8–127)

Numbers in *italics* denote figure numbers. The colour plates are referred to by plate number.